PC HARDWARE & COMPONENTS AND PC ARCHITECTURE

According to NIELIT (DOEACC) CHM-'O' Level Revised Syllabus Module–H1 & Module–H2

by

Satish Jain

B.Sc., B.E.(IISc), M.E.(IISc), M.Tech.(IIT Kanpur),
Wing Commander (Retd.)
Ex-Professor of Information Technology,
Institute of Information Technology & Management
GGS Indraprastha University, Delhi.

Shashi Singh

MCA, M.Phil

BPB PUBLICATIONS

20, ANSARI ROAD, DARYA GANJ, NEW DELHI - 110002

FIRST EDITION 2017

ISBN :978-93-8655-145-0

Distributors:

BPB PUBLICATIONS
20, Ansari Road, Darya Ganj
New Delhi-110002
Ph: 23254990/23254991

DECCAN AGENCIES
4-3-329, Bank Street,
Hyderabad-500195
Ph: 24756967/24756400

MICRO MEDIA
Shop No. 5, Mahendra Chambers, 150
DN Rd. Next to Capital Cinema, V.T.
(C.S.T.) Station, MUMBAI-400 001 Ph:
22078296/22078297

BPB BOOK CENTRE 376
Old Lajpat Rai Market,
Delhi-110006
Ph: 23861747

COMPUTER BOOK CENTRE
12, Shrungar Shopping Centre,
M.G.Road, BENGALURU–560001
Ph: 25587923/25584641

Published by Manish Jain for BPB Publications, 20, Ansari Road, Darya Ganj, New Delhi- 110002 and Printed him at Vijeta Offset printers, New Delhi.

Dedicated to

Sri Raja Rajeshwari, Sri Sharda Devi and Sri Sai Baba

Whose blessings will overcome all the hurdles in life

PREFACE

The objective of this book, based on NIELIT (DOEACC) 'O' *Level* CHM–O Module-H1 and Module-H2 syllabus for "PC Hardware & Components and PC Architecture", is to meet the growing needs of students to lay their hands on a text book that explains this highly technical subject in very simple language. The complicated concepts are brought out in an easy-to-understand manner by giving diagrams. It is felt that the books available in the market do not cover the entire syllabus for the course to meet the needs of the students. The 'O' Level CHM course accredited by NIELIT is very comprehensive and needs a thorough understanding of the PC Hardware & components and its Architecture. For this reason, we have pressed into service all our practical experience in PC Hardware technology as well as in academic field in organizing and exploring the topics in this book to meet the specific needs of the Indian students of all streams.

Changes in the field of Hardware are taking place very rapidly and many new terminologies/concepts are being added each day. Accordingly, there is wide coverage of the subjects in the syllabus for 'O' Level CHM Module–H1 and Module–H2 Course. Hence, the scope for the questions set in future examinations will cover more concepts in depth. This has prompted us to bring out this book inserting topics with latest concepts. These topics include: PC Hardware, Primary Memory , Secondary Storage, Power Supply, Cabinet Types. In addition, separate chapters are included on Basics of Microprocessor, ARM Processor and Troubleshooting & General PC Problems.

We have made this book user friendly by adding a very comprehensive glossary of technical terms at the end of the Book. These will be very handy for understanding as well as locating page number of major topics discussed in this Book. We have also added review questions with answers at the end of each chapter along with the exercises.

A special feature throughout this book is that the salient and crucial information has been encapsulated within parallel and horizontal lines with a (☞) mark to draw attention of the reader.

We shall feel obliged to the readers if they send us their critical opinion regarding the presentation, readability and coverage in this book and request them to mail their suggestions if any, to improve the subject matter. The suggestions may be e-mailed to *bpb@vsnl.com*.

Authors

8th June, 2017

USEFUL TIPS FOR THE EXAMINEE

Dear Reader,

Every examination has its peculiarity and the best results are often obtained by identifying that particular feature and working with the help of right strategies, which in turn can be adopted by correctly analyzing the question paper.

The 'O' Level Examination being no exception to this rule, the authors present an effective aid to guide you to analyze the question paper and thus help to chalk out your own effective plan of action.

The instructions given on the first page of the question paper should always be read *very* carefully. As the answer sheets of Part ONE will be evaluated with the help of a computer, you have to be extra cautious.

The answer sheet contains separate boxes for writing answers to each question in this part. You should read the following paragraphs to avoid mistakes and clear the first part without any difficulty. (A specimen copy of the answer sheet for filling Part ONE answers of sample question papers is included at the end of this book).

How to avoid mistakes?

If you are not sure about a particular answer - *do not fill* the box in the first try itself, but make an attempt later. After having given an initial reading to all the questions, first attempt only those questions about which you are very ***sure*** regarding the correct answer. It is while taking a second go at the questions, that you answer the remaining ones, always making sure that you spend only a *limited* amount of time on each one of them. Finally, go through all the answers once decided and fill the boxes with black ink as per the instructions given in the question paper.

How to answer the questions of Part TWO?

Once you have done well in Part ONE, rest assured, passing Part TWO will not pose much of a problem, if you have effectively followed the instructions given below. While answering Part TWO, the time limit should be strictly kept in mind and every effort must be made to complete all the questions, by keeping the answers brief and to the point. Remember you can also resort to making a sketch/diagram in your answer wherever possible, instead of describing it in words, because "a thousand words of description can be effectively expressed by a small diagram." As the number of questions are normally more for an average student, this precious time saved, enables you to have a wider coverage of the paper.

While attempting the descriptive type of questions, keep a check on the length of your answers and keep in mind the time frame available for answering the remaining questions.

The last stage, being the revision stage, you should save at least 5 to 10 minutes to revise all your answers. Try to find the gross errors, like units of measurement, or wrong question number you might have put for a specific answer, etc. This does happen because of the inherent tension of the examination.

How to prepare for the "PC Hardware & Components and PC Architecture" Examination?

Having familiarized with the format of the examination paper, let us turn our attention on the strategy for preparing for it.

This book has covered the complete syllabus in an easy to understand manner. It is advised, however, that in addition to this book, you should also refer to a few books on computer science and IT concepts. This will enable you to broaden the horizon of your knowledge.

Make your own notes, by reading each topic from this book and other standard books. Once you are quite sure about the comprehension of the topic, try to answer the Descriptive Type Questions given at the end of each Chapter of this book.

In the second reading, go through the sample question papers given at the end of the book. Solve these papers without consulting any book. After you have answered them, compare your response with the relevant matter available in the text of this book. Where you find your answers differ, re-study that part again.

Last, but not the least, you should simulate examination conditions by conducting a demo examination, taking any of the sample papers given at the end of the book and attempting to complete the answers within the stipulated time. After a day or two, evaluate your answers and if any doubts still persist, clarify them from a good text book or a computer specialist immediately. This way, you will be sure about the subject and will have confidence while answering the actual question paper.

WISH YOU A GRAND SUCCESS in the 'O' Level Examination, and a very bright future in the field of computer science.

Authors

Contents

Module-H1

PC Hardware & Components

Module-H2

PC ARCHITECTURE

CHM–O Level

MODULE–H1

PC HARDWARE
&
COMPONENTS

CHAPTER 1

PC Hardware

1.1 WHAT IS A COMPUTER?

A term *computer* is derived from the word compute, which means to calculate. A computer is a electronic device that takes data and instructions as an input from the user, processes the data and provides useful information known as output. Figure 1.1 shows parts of computer system. Input such as numbers, text, sound, image, animations, video, etc., are entered by the user in the form of data. *Data* refers to raw facts and figures. On receiving the data and instruction from the user, the computer processes the data and generates some output and displays it to the user. Processed data is known as *information*.

Figure 1.1 Parts of computer system

Data representation refers to the methods used internally to represent information stored in a computer. Computers store lots of different types of information such as numbers, text, sound and graphics.

However, all types of information stored in a computer are stored internally in the simple format: a sequence of 0's and 1's.

☞ *A computer is an electronic device that can perform a variety of operations according to a set of instructions called program. It then displays or prints the result.*

A computer follows the input-process-output model as shown in Figure 1.2. These are:

- **Input:** Data collected and entered into the computer is called input.
- **Process:** A sequence of actions performed on the data to get desired results is called processing.
- **Output:** Processed data received by the user is called output.

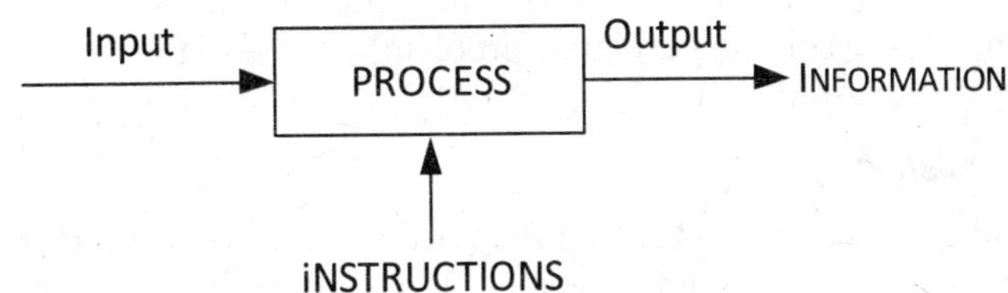

Figure 1.2 Input-Process-Output Model

1.1.1 Types of Computers based on Principles of Operation

Analog Computers

Analog computers handle or process information which is of a physical nature, as for example, temperature, pressure etc. These are based on the measuring of analog or equivalent physical value.

Digital Computers

Digital computers process information which is in a binary or two-state form, namely zero and one. It can give more accurate and faster results. When talking about computers, we mostly refer to the digital type of electronic machines.

Digital computers fall into ranges called microcomputers, minicomputers, mainframes and supercomputers, classified in ascending order of size–small, medium, large and very large.

Hybrid Computers

A hybrid computer combines the desirable features of analog and digital computers. It is mostly used for automatic operations of complicated physical processes and machines. Hybrid computers are used in missiles, space ships and military weapons. An example of a hybrid computer is the computer used in hospitals to measure the heart beat of the patient.

1.1.2 Characteristics of Computers

The five major characteristics of computers which have made them very useful are:

Speed

A computer is a very fast device. It can perform, in a few seconds, the amount of work that a human being can do in an entire year working round the clock. To put it in a different manner, a computer does in one minute what would take a man his entire lifetime. The speed of a computer is usually 2 to 4 GHz. A powerful computer is capable of performing about 10 to 40 million arithmetic calculations in a second.

Accuracy

The *accuracy* of a computer is consistently high and the degree of accuracy of a particular computer depends upon its design. But for a particular computer, each and every calculation is performed with the same accuracy. Error can occur in a computer, but these are mainly due to human action rather than technological weaknesses. That is, due to imprecise thinking by the programmer (a person who writes instructions for a computer to solve a particular problem) or due to the inaccuracy of the input data.

Consistency

Unlike human beings, computers are the machines that are highly consistent. They never get bored. A computer never complains of a monotonous job. Hence, they are ideal machines for carrying out repetitive and voluminous work, 24 hours a day and 365 days in a year.

Storage Capacity

Today's computers can store huge amount of data. Once recorded, a piece of information is never forgotten (unless some problem takes place) and any information can be retrieved almost instantaneously. To give you an idea of storage capacity, a single, Compact Disk Read Only Memory (CD-ROM) can contain the entire *Encyclopedia Britanica*, and more. An entire movie can be stored on a CD and played in a computer any number of times without any failure.

Flexibility

A computer is perhaps the first general purpose machine devised by man. All other machines like televisions, refrigerators, or typewriters, do only one thing for which they are designed. Unlike these, a computer can be used to play music, see movies, type letters, send faxes, diagnose illnesses, fix problems in complex manufacturing operations, design buildings and bridges, etc.

Plug and play

It can automatically configure new hardware and software components.

1.1.3 Limitations of Computer

The computers have the following limitations:

No IQ

Computer does what it is programmed. If the program given is not designed properly, then the results may be wrong. Hence it is not able to ascertain the correctness of the results.

No Heuristics

Computer has no capability to think and find out the results based on its past experience as the human being can do.

No Feelings

Computers have no feelings and no instincts because they are lifeless machines. No computer can possess the equivalent of human heart and soul.

No Manual Job

Human beings can be asked to perform certain types of manual jobs such as digging of a ditch or canal. But it is not possible in case of a machine like computers. However, computers can control the machines such as auto pilot can fly an aeroplane.

1.1.4 Basic Applications of Computer

A computer is a general purpose tool, which can do a variety of jobs. You can use a computer for different application by changing various kind of software packages. Some common uses of a computer are shown in Figure 1.3 which are discussed below.

- **Business:** It is used for budgeting, accounting, billing, reporting, presentations etc. in business.
- **Medicine and Health Care:** It used for diagnosing illnesses, monitoring patients and surgery etc. For example, medical students learning surgery can practice operations on computers through virtual reality.
- **Communications:** It is used for communicating to different parts of the world. For example, you can send E-mail to your friends and relatives who live in different countries.
- **Education and Reference:** Computers are effectively used in classrooms, museums and libraries. For examples, in classrooms, computers are used to develop science projects, prepare reports etc.
- **Scientific Research:** Computers are used in research centers and laboratories. They help in maintaining all the results efficiently which can be quickly accessed or retrieved when required.
- **Banks:** Today banks are the first large organizations to invest heavily on computers. Complete book keeping of the bank accounts is done by the computers. Information about deposit, withdrawal, interest charges, etc., are managed by computers.
- **Government:** Computers are also used by government for various things, such as railway reservation, airways reservation income and tax processing etc.
- **Games:** You can play games for hours on computers. Games can be both entertaining and educational.
- **Electronic Publishing: DTP** or **Desk Top Publishing** is a new field created because of efficient use of computer. Nowadays, newspapers are designed using DTP in different parts of a country and printed at one place and distributed so that we can get them every morning.

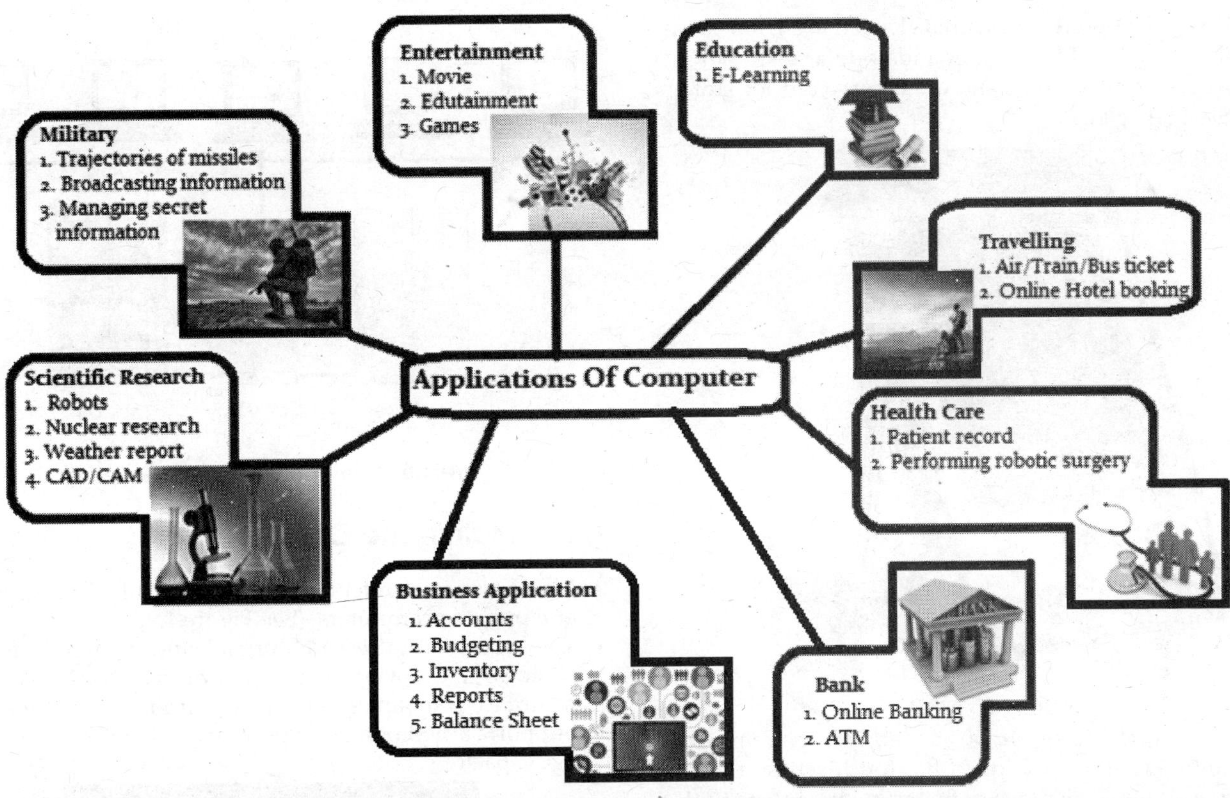

Figure 1.3 Picture showing different jobs where computer can be employed

1.2 CLASSIFICATION OF COMPUTERS

Computers may be classified into following categories according to the size/functions, speed of processing and storage capacity.

1.2 1 Micro Computer

- A microcomputer is a low-cost, small, digital computer.
- It contains a microprocessor unit as its CPU, a memory unit, and is equipped with an input device and an output device.

Figure 1.4 A Desktop computer

- A few examples are: general purpose calculations, industrial control, instrumentation, home appliances, fuel injection control of cars, office automation, etc.
- They are further classified into Desktop, Laptop, Palmtop, PDA etc.

Desktop Computer/Personal Computer: These computers are mainly used in offices, schools, banks, hospitals, and homes. Desktop computers are made up of several components, such as mouse, keyboard, CPU, and monitor. (See Figure 1.4)

Laptops and Notebooks: A laptop PC is a small, compact and portable machine which runs on battery power. You can unfold it and work with it on your lap and hence the name is given to it. It can be carried in your suitcase easily. A Notebook is a smaller and lighter version of the laptop model. Figure 1.5 depicts a laptop model.

Figure 1.5 A laptop

PDAs (Personal Digital Assistants): Personal Digital Assistant (PDA) is a handheld computer and popularly known as a *palmtop*. It has a touch screen and a memory card for storage of data (See Figure 1.6).

Figure 1.6 A PDA

Tablet PC :A *tablet PC* or simply tablet, is a medium-sized mobile computer integrated into a flat touch screen and primarily using stylus, digital pen or fingertip input along with a virtual onscreen keyboard in lieu of a physical keyboard. It is a touch-pad device that combines the features and qualities of a smart phone and a laptop. Figure 1.7 depicts a tablet PC.

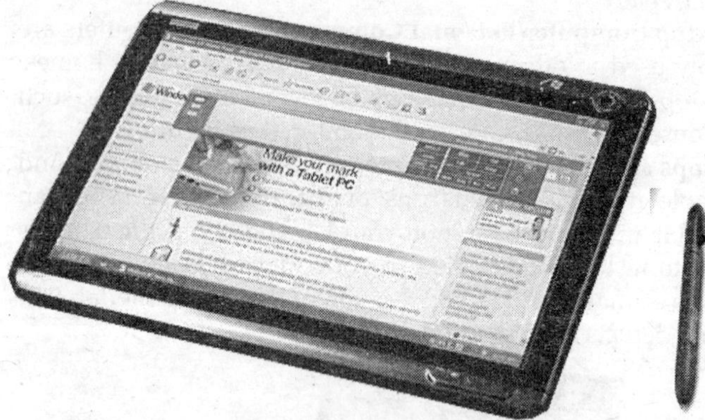

Figure 1.7 A Tablet PC

1.2 2 Mini Computer

- A minicomputer is a small to medium-scale computer used widely for data processing and in industrial applications. See Figure 1.8 showing Mini computer with five terminals.
- Minicomputers are used for payroll preparation, accounting and scientific computation. Minicomputers are also used in universities, industries and research centres.

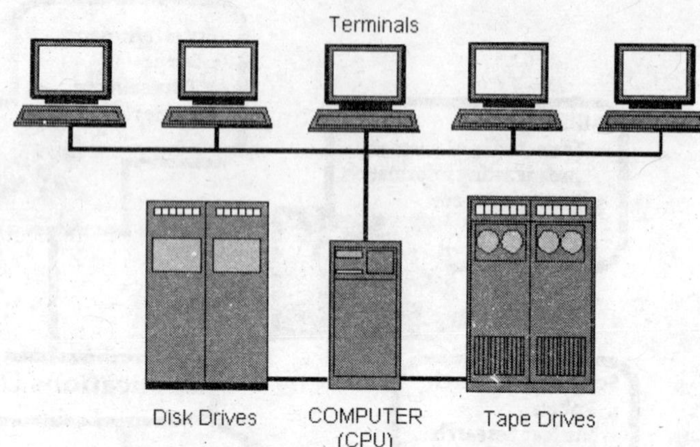

Figure 1.8 Mini computer with five terminals

1.2 3 Mainframe Computer

- Mainframe computers are very powerful, large scale general purpose computers. (See Figure 1.9).
- They are used in research organizations, large industries, business and government organizations, banks, hospitals, insurance companies, railway and airline reservations
- Supports a wide range of peripherals and have large storage capacity.

Figure 1.9 Mainframe computer

1.2.4 Super Computer

- Supercomputers are large, extremely fast and expensive computers. (See Figure 1.10).
- They are being used at some research centres and government agencies involving sophisticated scientific and engineering tasks.
- Based on the concept of parallel processing. Many small computer chips work simultaneously to perform millions of arithmetic operations per second.

☞ *CRAY-I is the first Super Computer. An Indian made super computer is the series of PARAM. Famous supercomputers are Cray X-MP, Cray-2, Cray-3 and ETA-10. These computers can perform 10 to 100 billion calculations per second.*

Figure 1.10 Supercomputer

☞ *Today, computers come in different shapes and sizes, for example smart phones, digital cameras, smartwatch/wristwatches etc. Smartwatch/Wristwatch is computerized wearable computer (See Figure 1.11) which offers full mobile phone features capabilities such as phone calls, send and receive messages, Wi-Fi, GPS (Global Positioning System), monitor heart beat rate etc.*

Figure 1.11 Smartwatch/Wristwatch

1.3 COMPONENTS OF COMPUTER SYSTEM

The five major functional units of a digital computer are:

1. Central Processing Unit (CPU)
2. Visual Display Unit(VDU), Keyboard and Mouse
3. Other Input and Output Devices
4. Computer Memory
5. Concepts of Hardware and Software

All the above computer systems are discussed in the following sections:

1.3.1 Central Processing Unit

The CPU is the brain of a computer. Its primary job is to run program and control the operation of all other components, such as memory, keyboard and printer. A block diagram of the basic computer organization is shown in Figure 1.12.

The Figure shows the basic arrangement of different units of a computer. It depicts the five major building blocks or functional units of a digital computer system. These five units correspond to the five basic operations, namely inputting, storing, processing, outputting and controlling data, carried out by all computer systems. The five units are:

Inputting: Refers to the process of entering data into the computer, by the user using an input device, such as keyboard.

Storing: Refers to the holding of data and instructions in the computer's main memory, for manipulations.

Processing: Refers to performing operations (both arithmetic and logical) or manipulation of data entered into the computer so that useful information may be taken out of the entered data.

Outputting: Refers to the process of showing the information or result to the user either on screen (monitor) or on paper (through printer).

Controlling: Refers to directing all the above processes, in coordination. This controlling is done by the Control Unit (CU) in a CPU.

The CPU of a small computer has a single microprocessor. A microprocessor contains a control unit and an Arithmetic and Logic Unit (ALU). When main memory is added to a microprocessor, it becomes a CPU.

The major sections of a CPU are Primary memory, ALU and Control Unit.

Primary Memory

- Primary memory or the Main memory unit is one of the major parts of a computer.
- It holds data which is currently manipulated by the CPU.
- Since Primary memory is present within the CPU itself, it is also known as *internal memory* or RAM.
- It is directly addressed by the CPU.
- Primary memory stores the necessary programs of system software, which are required to execute user programs.

Arithmetic Logic Unit

- The ALU is like the heart of computer.
- ALU of a computer system is the place where the actual execution of instructions takes place.
- All calculations are performed and all comparisons (decisions) are made in the ALU.
- All ALUs are designed to perform the four basic arithmetic operations–add, subtract, multiply, divide, and logic operations, such as less than, equal to or greater than.
  Intermediate results generated in the ALU are temporarily stored in the memory unit until needed again at a later time. The data and instructions, stored in the main memory prior to processing, are transferred, as and when needed, to the ALU, where processing takes place. No processing is done in the memory unit.

Control Unit (CU)

- This unit is responsible for controlling the entire working of the computer.

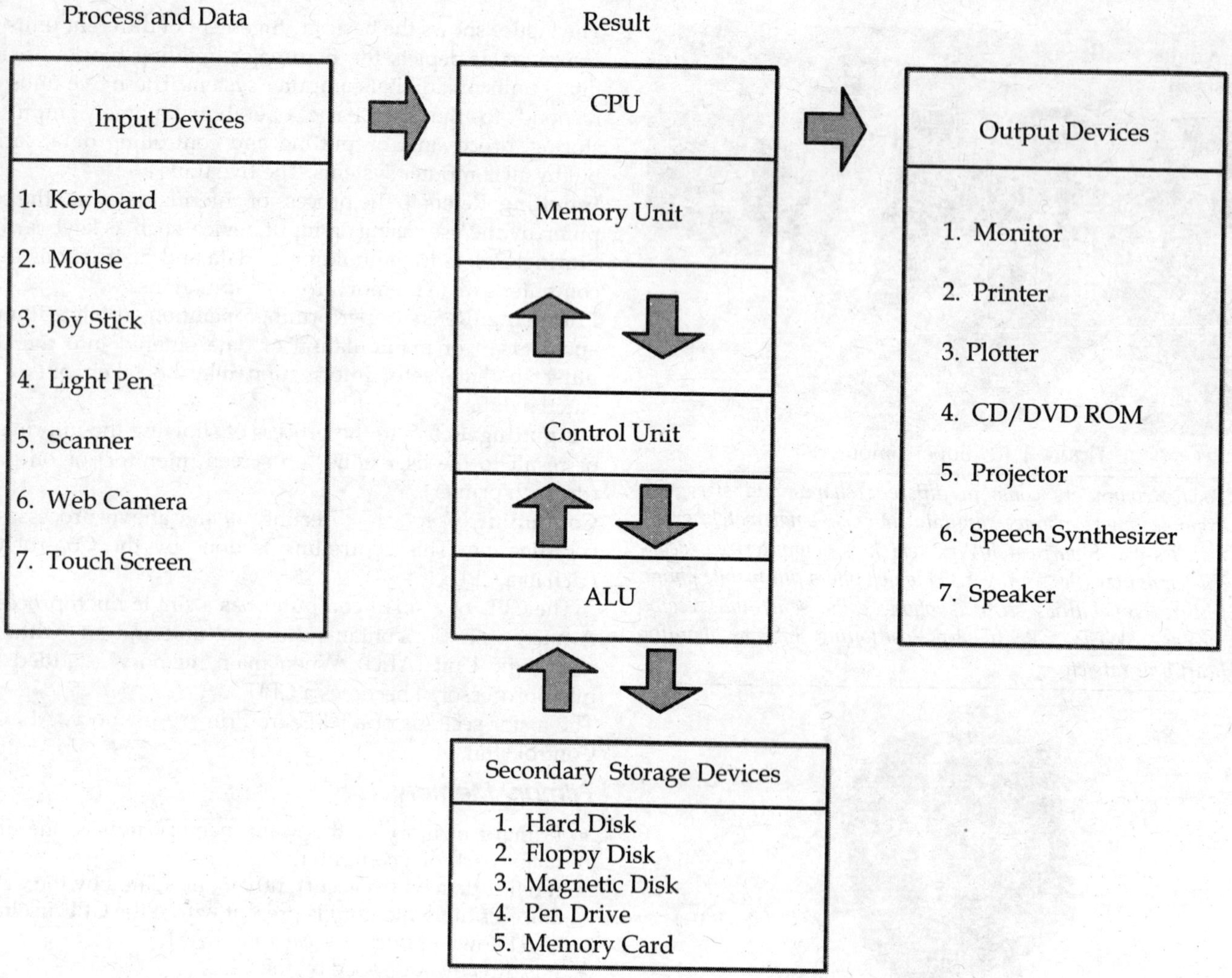

Process and Data

Input Devices

1. Keyboard
2. Mouse
3. Joy Stick
4. Light Pen
5. Scanner
6. Web Camera
7. Touch Screen

Result

CPU

Memory Unit

Control Unit

ALU

Output Devices

1. Monitor
2. Printer
3. Plotter
4. CD/DVD ROM
5. Projector
6. Speech Synthesizer
7. Speaker

Secondary Storage Devices

1. Hard Disk
2. Floppy Disk
3. Magnetic Disk
4. Pen Drive
5. Memory Card

Figure 1.12 Block diagram representation of a computer system

- The timing and control signals are generated by this unit and sent to other units for execution of the program for proper control.
- It also controls the transfer of data between memory and input/output devices.
- It acts like our central nervous system for the other data-manipulating components of the computer.

VDU or Monitor, Keyboard and Mouse

Input/Output (I/O) devices are those devices which are used to enter information into a computer or display results of data processing devices. These devices are discussed below.

Visual Display Unit (VDU) or Monitor Monitors are the most popular output devices for producing soft-copy output. They display the generated output on a television like screen. At present, computer monitors are available in a variety of shapes, designs, and colors. However, based on the technology used to make computer monitors, they can be broadly categorized into following types. (See Figure 1.13).

Figure 1.13 Types of monitor

Cathode Ray Tube (CRT): These monitors employ the CRT technology used most commonly in the manufacturing of television screens. A cathode ray tube is a basically a vacuum tube containing an electron gun at one end and a fluorescent screen at another end. From this electron gun, a process called thermionic emission generates a strong beam of electrons.

Liquid Crystal Display (LCD): Liquid crystal display, also known as liquid crystal diode, is one of the most advanced technologies available at present. Typically, an LCD monitor consists of a layer of color or monochrome pixels arranged schematically between a couple of transparent electrodes and two polarizing filters.

At present, there are two types of LCD technology available. These include the active matrix or TFT and a passive matrix technology. Among these, TFT technology is more secure and reliable, and generates better picture quality.

Some major advantages of using an LCD monitor include:

- These monitors are compact, lightweight, and do not consume much desk space.
- Secondly, these monitors do not consume much electricity and can even be operated by using batteries.

However, LCD monitors have certain disadvantages. These monitors are very expensive. Secondly, image quality is not constant when viewed from different angles. LCD monitor's resolution is always constant.

Light-Emitting Diodes (LED): LED monitors are the latest types of monitors in the market today. Like LCD, it is again a flat panel display making use of light-emitting diodes for back-lightning instead of Cold Cathode Fluorescent (CCFL) back-lightning used in LCDs. Primarily, the display is of LCD only but the back-lightning is done by LEDs. LED monitors use much lesser power than CRT and LCD. Some advantages of LED monitors are:

- They produce images with higher contrast
- Lifespan and durability of LED monitors is more than CRT or LCD monitors
  Because of the technology, the monitor panels can be made very thin.
- Do not produce much heat while running.

Organic Emitting Diodes : These monitors provide higher contrast and better viewing angles.

3-D Monitors: It conveys depth perception to the viewer. It gives an experience of virtual reality and are expensive.

Keyboard Keyboard is most common input device used to enter data. It is similar to the keyboard of a typewriter. It contains alphabets, digits, special characters, function keys and some control keys. (See Figure 1.14).

Mouse A mouse is a pointing device. It is held in one hand and is moved across a flat surface. The mouse can also be used to draw sketches, diagrams, etc., on the monitor screen. It is also used to edit text on the screen, the cursor can be quickly placed close to the desired point of the screen by moving the mouse (See Figure 1.15).

Figure 1.14 A Keyboard

Figure 1.15 A Mouse

1.3.2 Other Input Devices

Input devices are those devices which are used to enter data into a computer or other data processing devices. Some examples of input devices are Keyboard, Mouse, Scanner, Light pen, Voice input and recognition system, Optical mark reader(OMR), Optical Character Reader (OCR), Magnetic Ink Character Reader (MICR), Graphic tablet, touch screen, Web camera and Video camera.

We will discuss here in detail about input devices:

Scanner

Scanners are a kind of input devices. It is a device that scans images, printed text, or an object and converts it into a digital image. Scanners can be used for storing photographs and important documents in their original form (See Figure 1.16).

Scanners are of three types. They are:

Flatbed scanner: A Flatbed scanner is also known as desktop scanner and it works just like a photocopier. This scanner allows the user to place a full piece of paper, book, magazine, photo or any other object onto the glass surface of the scanner. It has the capability to scan that object and convert it into digital form.

Sheetfed scanner: Sheetfed scanner is also known as rollerfed scanner. It works like a fax machine. The image is passed over a roller where it is captured. Sheetfed scanner is very versatile in scanning loose sheets of paper.

Handheld scanner: A handheld or portable scanner is an optical scanner which is designed to be moved by hand across the object or document being scanned. It is for optically reading image or data from a document. It is operated by hand.

Joystick

A joystick is also a pointing device. It is used to move the cursor position on a monitor screen. Its function is similar to that of a mouse and is used for playing games. The joystick can be moved right or left, forward or backward. (See Figure 1.17).

Figure 1.16 Scanner

Figure 1.17 Joystick

Light Pen

A light pen is a pointing device. It is used to select a displayed menu option on the monitor. It is a photosensitive pen-like device. It is capable of sensing a position on the monitor screen when its tip touches the screen (See Figure 1.18).

Voice Input and Recognition System

Voice input and recognition system is an input device, consisting of a microphone or telephone that converts human speech into electrical signals (See Figure 1.19).

Figure 1.18 Light pen

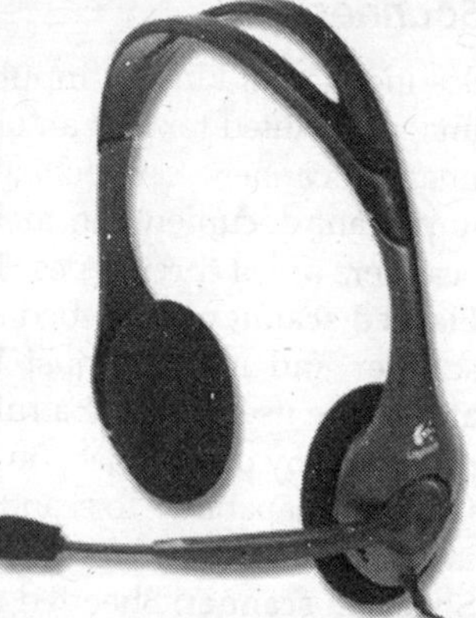

Figure 1.19 Microphone with earphone

Optical Mark Reader

Optical mark readers are special scanners used for recognizing a pre-specified type of mark made by pencil or pen. For example, in the objective test paper of competitive examinations, you mark your answers on a special sheet by darkening a small square or circle, using a pen or pencil (See Figure 1.20).

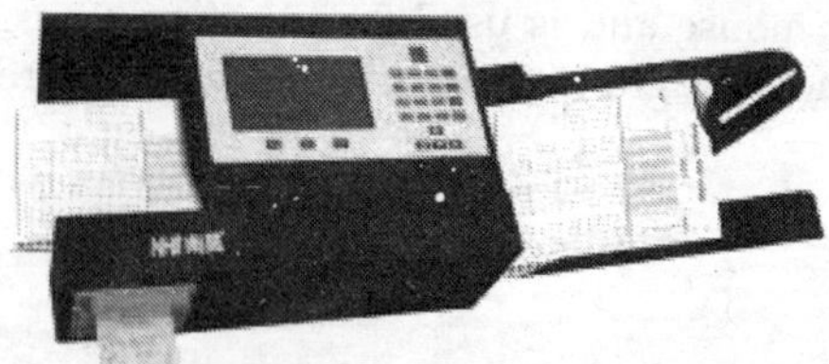

Figure 1.20 Optical marks in an answer sheet

Bar Code Reader

Bar-code readers are special devices used to read bar coded data. Bar code is a specialized code used for fast identification of items. It consists of a series of small lines, known as bars (See Figure 1.21).

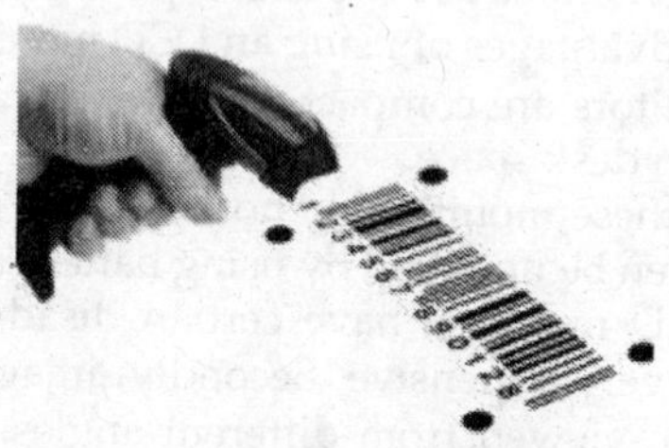

Figure 1.21 Bar code Reader

Smart Card Reader

A *smart card* is a plastic card about the size of a credit card. It has a microchip that can be loaded with data. The data loaded in microchip can not be read visually so they are ideal for storing confidential data. It can be used for electronic cash payments and other applications. A special kind of machine called *smart card reader* is used to read the data loaded in smart cards.

Figure 1.22 Smart Card Reader

Optical Character Reader

Optical character readers is technique for inputting text into a computer by means of a document reader. In other words, an OCR converts images into actual text, which can be edited using word processors. There is also an advanced OCR, which can even read handwritten text. Figure 1.23 shows functioning of OCR. OCR is used, for example, by gas and electricity companies to input data collected on meter-reading cards, and by personal digital assistants to recognize user's handwriting. (See Figure 1.24).

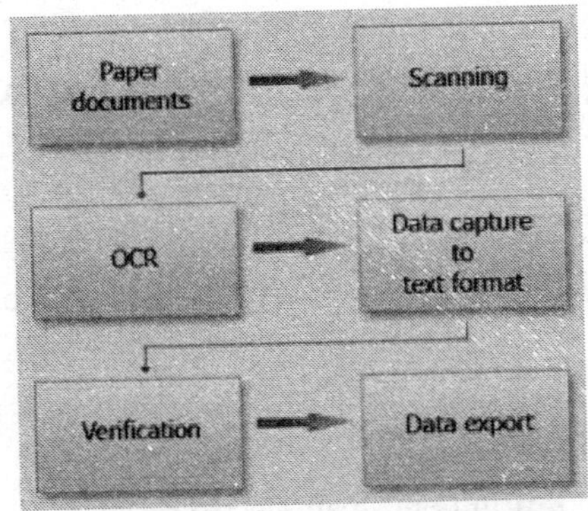

Figure 1.23 Functioning of OCR

Figure 1.24 OCR

Magnetic Ink Character Recognition

MICR detects the special encoded characters on bank cheques and deposit slips. After detecting the encoded characters, the MICR converts them into digital data for the computer (See Figure 1.25 & 1.26).

☞ *MICR uses 10 digits and 4 special characters needed for bank processing. No alphabetic characters are available.*

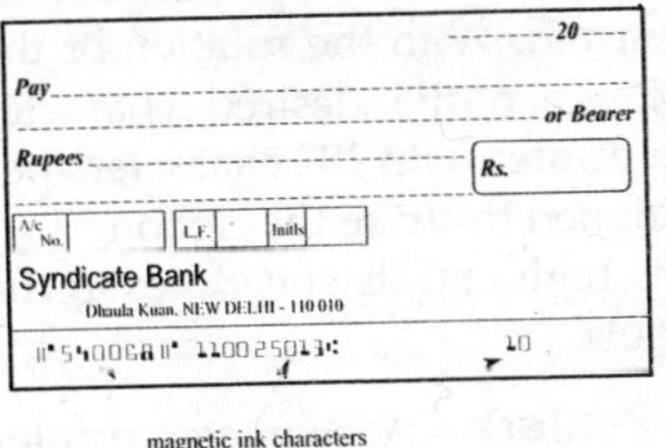

Figure 1.25 A sample bank cheque

Figure 1.26 MICR

Web camera

A Web camera allows a computer to accept input just by focussing on an object. The image of the object can be seen on the monitor of the distant computer connected through a network or through Internet (See Figure 1.27).

Video camera

A video camera is a camera that takes continuous pictures and generates a digital/or analog signal for display on a monitor or for permanent recording (See Figure 1.28). The latter converts analog signals into digital form.

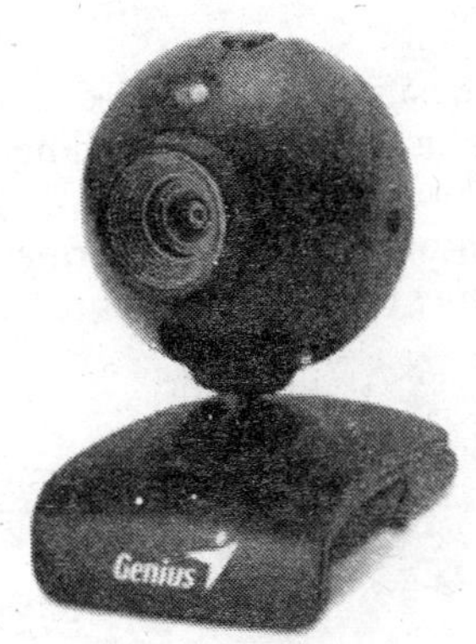

Figure 1.27 Web Camera

Figure 1.28 Video Camera

Digital Camera

A *digital camera* records and stores photographic images in digital form that can be fed into a computer as the impressions are recorded or stored in the camera for later loading into a computer. Currently, Kodak, Canon and several other companies make digital cameras. (See Figure 1.29).

Trackball

A trackball is also a pointing device and contains a ball which can rotate in any direction. The user spins the ball in different directions to move the cursor on the monitor (See Figure 1.30).

Figure 1.29 Digital Camera

Figure 1.30 Trackball

Graphic Tablets/Digitizer

A graphic tablet as digitizer is used for doing fine works of drawing and image manipulation applications. It is an input device used to create graphics. It is commonly used in computer Aided (CAD) terminals. Graphic tablet is also used to enter digital signatures. It is a flat surface which can be kept on a table. A *stylus* (an electronic pen) is provided with the tablet. (See Figure 1.31). Digitizer can convert a signal from the television or camera into a series of numbers that could be stored in a computer. A graphic tablet as digitizer is used for doing fine works of drawing and image manipulation applications.

Touch Screen

It is a computer monitor screen designed or modified to recognize the location of a touch on its surface. By touching the screen, the user can make a selection or move a cursor. Touch screens are very popular in applications such as information kiosks and automatic teller machines (ATM). (See Figure 1.32).

Figure 1.32 Touch Screen

Figure 1.31 Graphic Tablet

Biometric Sensor

Biometric is the science and technology that usually refers to methodology for measuring and analyzing human body characteristics that is unique to an individual. *Biometric Sensor* is the device that is used to identifies fingerprints, DNA identification, eye retinas and irises, voice patterns, facial patterns, hand measurements, face shape and signature verification. (See Figure 1.33).

Fingerprint Scanner

A fingerprint scanner can also take the form of one of four different sensors. An optical sensor uses digital imaging to capture the visual image of the fingerprint. A passive capacitance sensor uses pixels to form the image.
When referring to computer hardware, a fingerprint scanner or fingerprint reader is a hardware device that verifies a user or enters password information by scanning their finger. Computers that do not already include a fingerprint scanner can connect devices such as USB ports (See Figure 1.34).

Figure 1.33 Biometric Sensor

Figure 1.34 Finger print scanner

1.3.3 Other Output Devices

Output devices are those devices of computer system that supplies information or results either in the form of hardcopy (printer) or softcopy (monitor). The example of output devices are VDU/Monitor, Printers, Plotters, Multimedia Projector and Speech Synthesizer. We will discuss here in detail about output devices:

Printer

Printers provide information in a permanent readable form called hardcopy. They produce printed outputs of results and programs. The printers can be classified as Impact printers and non-impact printers.

Impact Printer

These type of printers use an electro-mechanical mechanism, that causes hammers or pins to strike against a ribbon and paper to print the text. Impact printers are slow, noisy, and cheaper. The impact printers are further classified into the following categories: *Line printers* and *Character printers.*

Line Printers A line printer prints one line of the text at a time. Printing speeds may vary from 300–3000 lines per minute. (See Figure 1.35). Different types of line printers are–*Drum printer* and *Chain printer*.

Drum Printer: A drum printer consists of a cylindrical drum on which characters are embossed. One complete set of characters is embossed for each and every print position on a line. The drum is rotated at a high speed. There is a magnetically-driven hammer in each character position of the line. A character is printed by striking a hammer against the embossed character on the surface.

Chain Printer : A chain printer uses a rapidly, rotating chain which is called print chain. Magnetically-driven hammers are located in each print position. To print a line, the characters in the line are transmitted from the memory to printer buffer. The band is rotated at a high speed. With the rotation of the band, a hammer is activated when the desired character comes in front of it. Thus, for a printer with 132 characters per line, 132 hammers will be positioned to strike the ribbon.
The noise level of the printer is high and its speed lies in the range of 400-2400 lines per minute.

Character Printers (Serial Printer): A character printer prints one character of the text at a time. They are low-speed printers. Their printing speed lies in the range of 30-600 characters per second. Different types of character printers are–*Dot matrix printers* and *Letter quality printers.*

Dot matrix Printer : A dot matrix printer is the most popular serial printer. The printhead contains a vertical array of pins. As the printhead moves across the paper, selected pins fire against the ribbon to form a pattern of dots on the paper. A dot matrix printer is faster than a letter quality printer. (See Figure 1.36).

Letter Quality Printer: These printers print full characters, which means that a character is not made up of dots. The most common popular printer of this type is daisy-wheel printer. The daisy wheel printer has a speed up to 90 characters per second.

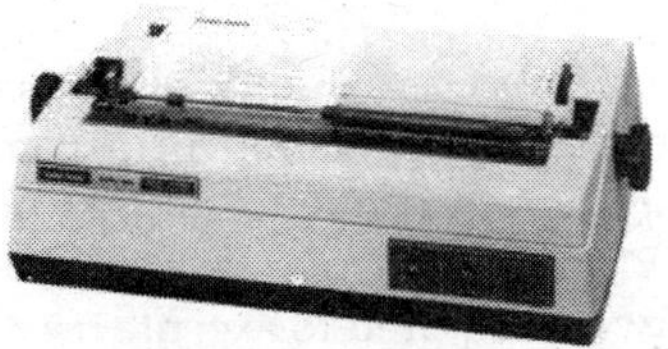

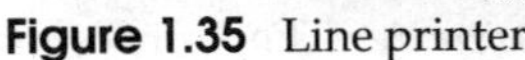

Figure 1.35 Line printer

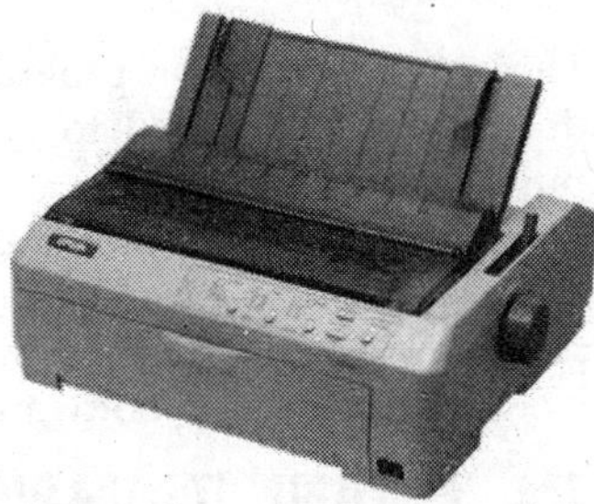

Figure 1.36 Dot matrix printer

Non-impact printer

This type of printer use thermal, chemical, electrostatic, laser beam or inkjet technology for printing the text. Usually, a non-impact printer is faster than an impact type. These printers are categorized as:
Electromagnetic printer, Thermal printer, Inkjet printer, Laser printer.

Electromagnetic Printer This printer uses magnetic recording techniques. By using this technique, the required output is written on a drum surface. Then this surface is passed through magnetic powder which adheres to the charged areas. The powder is then pressed onto the paper.

Thermal printer This type of printer uses a special heat-sensitive paper. These papers have a special heat-sensitive coating. When a spot on the paper is heated, it becomes dark. A character is printed with a matrix of dots.

Ink-Jet Printer Inkjet printers are more efficient than dot matrix printers. The inkjet's printhead has many tiny nozzles that spray ink into the paper. Each nozzle is thinner than human hair. It use a continuous stream of ink drops to print characters on paper. The print quality is good because the character is formed by dozens of tiny ink dots. These printers produce better quality of text and graphics and are faster (See Figure 1.37).

Laser Printer Laser printers are non-impact type printers. They print one page at a time. These printers use laser or other light source to produce an image on a photosensitive drum. The computer controls the laser beam to turn it on and off. An image is produced following the raster scan principle. The laser-exposed areas attract toner (an ink powder). Thereafter the drum transfers the toner to the paper. The paper then moves to a fusing station where the toner is permanently fused on the paper with heat or pressure. After this the drum is discharged and cleaned. Now the drum is ready for processing the next page. Figure 1.38 shows a modern high speed laser printer.

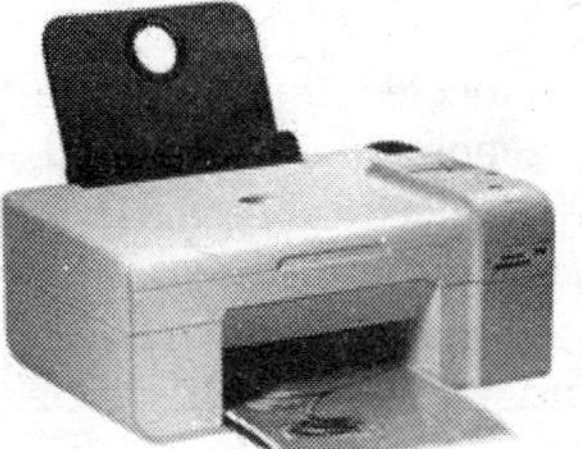

Figure 1.37 Inkjet printer

Figure 1.38 Laser printer

Plotters

Plotters are output devices. They are used to produce precise and good quality graphics and drawings under control of the computer. They use ink pen or inkjet to draw graphics or drawings. Either single colour or multicoloured pens can be employed. Figure 1.39 shows a plotter.

Projector

Multimedia Projector is an output device connected to a PC and used to project information from a computer on to a large screen (a cloth screen or wall). It is widely used for giving presentations. Audio, video, image and animation can be prepared on a PC and using a multimedia projector the presentation can be made more lively and interesting. (See Figure 1.40).

Figure 1.39 Plotter

Figure 1.40 Projector

Speech Synthesizer

Speech Synthesizer is an output device that converts textual data into spoken sentences. Speech Synthesizers find wide application in treating blind or dumb people. Text information can be read out to the blind people using the speech synthesizer. (See Figure 1.41)

Visualizer

Visual presenter is a document camera designed to display any object or material onto a screen. It is a powerful presentation tool as one can place documents, such as A4 size printed handouts, books or 3D objects. Once connected to a projector, it becomes an effective tool in the hands of a presenter. It can be used as a part of Interactive classroom or standalone tool to presenting document to a large or small group of audience. (See Figure 1.42).

Speakers

Speakers are hardware devices connected to a computer's sound card that outputs sounds generated by the card. A speaker makes sound by being fed on electrical signals which is changed or modulated, corresponding to the sound that is to be made. The speaker converts the changes or waves in the electrical signal to matching sound waves, which we hear. (See Figure 1.43).

Figure 1.41 Speech Synthesizer

Figure 1.42 Visualizer

Figure 1.43 Speakers

1.3.4 Computer Memory

A computer needs memory to store data. It also needs memory to perform arithmetical operations and storing programs and pictures. Computer memory is of two types:

(a) Primary Memory
(b) Secondary Memory

Primary Memory

Primary memory is a part of the CPU whereas the secondary memory is external to the CPU. Primary memory is made up of electronic circuits and keeps data as long as voltage supply is on. When power supply to a PC is switched off, the data is lost. As compared to secondary memory, the primary memory is fast.

Secondary Memory

Since a computer's main memory is temporary, the secondary memory is used for bulk storage of programs, data and other information. It has a much larger capacity than the main memory. The secondary memory is non-volatile. The two most common secondary storage devices are the floppy disk, hard disk, compact disk, pen drive and blue-ray disk, etc.

1.3.5 Concept of Hardware and Software

A computer system consists of hardware and software for its proper functioning.

Hardware

The physical components of a computer are called *hardware*. Such items may be electronic, electrical, magnetic, mechanical or optical components. Examples of components are microprocessors, ICs, hard disks, pen drives, optical disks, monitors, keyboard, printer, plotter, etc.

Software

The set of computer programs, procedures and associated documentation related to the effective operation of a computer system are termed as *software*. A sequence of instructions given to a computer to perform a particular task is called a *software* or *a program*. The software required to execute user's programs is known as *system software*. The term software includes both system software and user's programs.

1.4 PC AND ITS VARIOUS PARTS

A PC (Personal Computer) consists of electronic components connected to various peripherals, accessories that let users send data to the computer (input) or receive information from the computer (output). Although PCs vary in shape, size, capacity, speed and price, they all include elements that enable them to perform the following essential task:

(a) Receive data
(b) Save data
(c) Manipulate data in various ways and
(d) generate a result after processing data

Computers receive most data from either the keyboard or a hard disk. Information is usually saved on hard disk. Data is manipulated and changed (processed) by the microprocessor, and the resulting output is either displayed on a monitor or printed on paper. Although many computers may include additional components, such as scanners, modems, magnetic tape drives, sound cards and so on.

The system unit, monitor, keyboard, mouse, etc. are essential components of a computer and its functions are regulated by software and electronic parts. All the parts of a computer are internally built by using electronic circuits. The electronic components and internal connection within the system unit of computer are discussed below:

(a) **Monitor:** The monitor displays both data entered by the user and information processed by the computer.
(b) **Keyboard:** The keyboard is the principal means of communicating with the computer. It enables users to enter data or to type commands that instruct the computer to perform specific operations.
(c) **Mouse:** A mouse lets users communicate with the computer by moving an onscreen arrow to point at graphical objects, and then clicking a button to execute a command or display information.
(d) **Printer:** The printer lets users create a hard copy of information by transferring the results of their work onto paper.
(e) **Motherboard:** The motherboard is the large printed circuit board inside the computer that carries and connects all of the principal electronic components, such as the microprocessor and memory.
(f) **Floppy Disk Drive:** Floppy Disk Drive is obsolete now. Earlier it was used to read and write data on removable magnetic diskettes, thus enabling users to transfer information between computers, make copies of data for backup purposes etc.

(g) **Power Supply:** The power supply transforms the 220 volt alternating current of electrical outlets into the low-voltage direct current that sensitive electronic components and peripherals require.

(h) **Expansion Cards:** Expansion cards, also called interface cards, connect peripherals (such as monitors, disk drives, and so on) to the PC's motherboard. They are essential for transferring and translating data to and from electronic devices.

(i) **Hard Disk:** The hard disk is the main storage area of a PC. It can hold huge amount of programs and information in magnetic form. It retain that data even when the computer's power is turned off.

(j) **CD/DVD Drives:** A CD-ROM (Compact Disk Read Only Memory) is a drive that users disks that store large amount of information. The disk for the CD-ROM drive is known as CD or CD-ROM disk. The data contained on these disks are audio files, software applications and graphics. Combo drives are also fitted that contain DVD(Digital Video Disk) and CD drive.

1.4.1 Front Panel of PC

Various panel components of a personal computer (PC) are described in the following sub-sections.

(a) Front panel (b) Rear panel

Figure 1.44(a) Front Panel

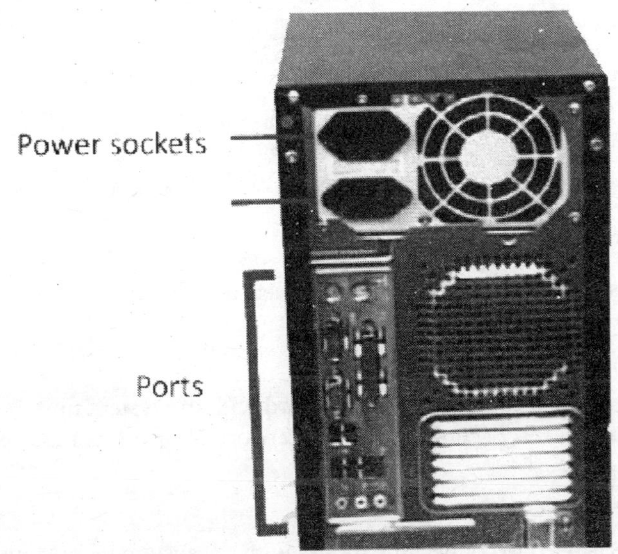

Figure 1.44(b) Rear Panel

Components of the Front Panel

Various components of the front panel of a PC are shown in Figure 1.44.

Power Switch

Depending on the model, this switch is located either in the front or at the rear of the system unit and it is used to switch the system ON or OFF.

Reset Button

This is a press switch which can be used to restart the PC without switching off the mains power supply. Use this switch as a last resort when the PC hangs and does not accept a command from the keyboard. When you restart the PC, it will lose all the information currently stored in its memory.

Power Light

It glows when the PC is ON and remains ON all the time. It is usually green in colour.

Hard Disk Light

It glows when the hard disks is being accessed. It flashes when the hard disk reads or writes. It goes out when there is no disk activity. Hard disk light can be either green or red.

CD-ROM Drive

It accepts CD-ROM disks.

Components of the Rear Panel

If you look at the rear panel of the system unit of your PC, you will see certain holes and slots fitted with different cables. Details of such parts are explained in the following sections. (See Figure 1.45).

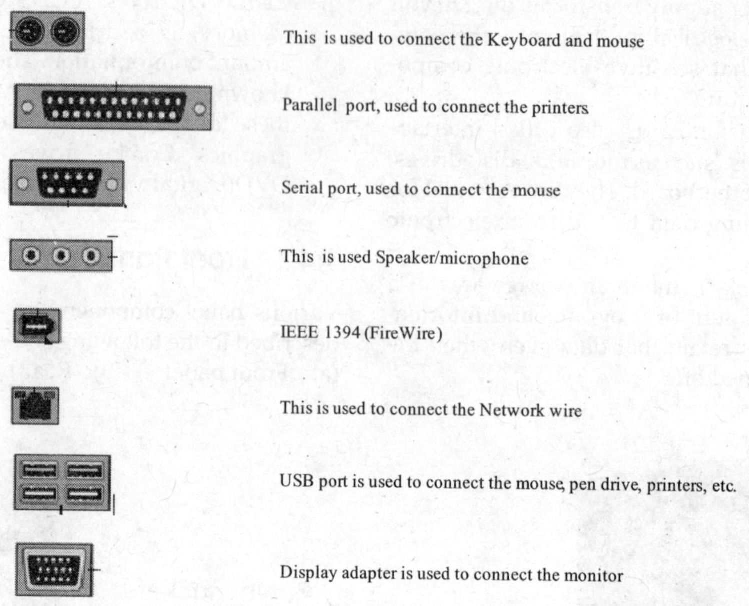

Figure 1.45 Different ports and jacks of computer

Video Port for Monitor

This is a 5–pin socket used to connect a monitor with the system unit.

Keyboard Port

This is used to connect the keyboard with the system unit. It is usually a PS/2 (Personal System/2) port. Now this is replaced be USB port.

Mouse Port

This is used to connect the mouse with the system unit. Mouse can be plugged into either serial port or PS/2 port. Now this is replaced be USB port.

Power Sockets

Cables plugged into these sockets carry electric power supply from the electrical outlet to your system unit and from the system unit to your monitor.

Parallel and Serial Port or Sockets

These ports or sockets are used for expanding the capability of your PC. For example, you can connect a printer, mouse, modem or some other peripheral to your system unit by using these ports. Serial port is used to connect a modem or a mouse. Parallel port is used to connect a printer.

Fan Housing

The power supply fitted inside the system unit has a small fan to take the heat out of the machine. You should make sure that the system unit is placed away from the wall so that the hot air from the fan of the supply unit can be thrown out.

USB Port

Universal Serial Bus (USB) port is a kind of port available in modern computers. Many devices can be connected in series on the same USB. In comparison with serial and parallel ports, a large amount of data can be transferred at a very high speed through USB ports. All peripherals like printer, modem and scanner are now available in versions that can be connected to USB port. Two or more USB ports are normally seen in a motherboard.

Sound Connectors

On some PCs, the sound connectors are built-in but, in some systems they are on a separate in an expansion slot. There are three identical round rings, i.e., output for speakers, input for microphone, and input for other devices.

Joystick Connector

A joystick connector is a 15-pin female D-sub connector with two rows: one with 8 holes and the other one is 7.

Network Interface

It is a (Registered Jack) RJ-45 connector. It is used to connect the network wire in the system.

1.5 MOTHERBOARD

The main component inside the main system unit is the motherboard. This is the biggest electronic circuit board inside the computer system, on which many other boards are attached. The boards that attach to the motherboard are known as daughter board or expansion board.

The motherboard is a circuit board to which all the electronic components of computer are connected (See Figure 1.46. These include both internal parts of the system unit like processor, display card of the monitor, sound card, memory, etc. and external parts like mouse, keyboard etc. The 'ports' and 'slots' which connect these components. The motherboard helps in data transfer among the components.

The main board is called motherboard because all other circuit boards, inside the computer, are attached to this board, i.e., it is the mother of all the boards.

Inside the PC, data is constantly being exchanged between or through the various input/output devices. Most of the data exchange takes place on the motherboard itself, where all the components are connected to each other. In relation to the PC's external devices, the motherboard functions like a central unit.

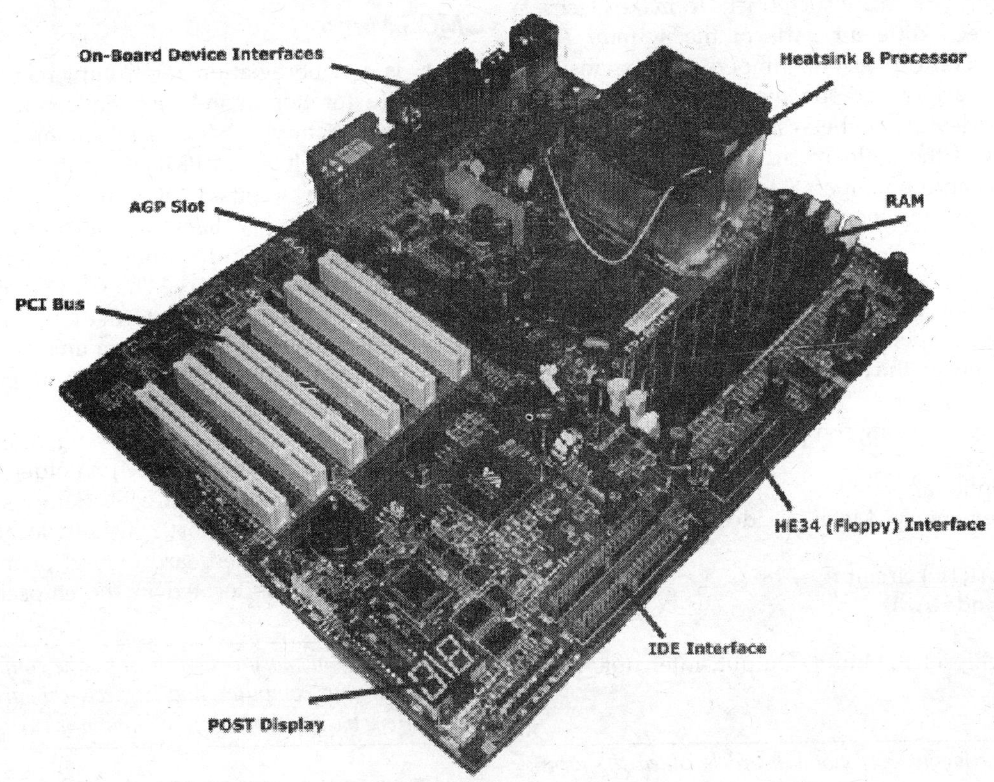

Figure 1.46 A Motherboard

1.5.1 Role of Motherboard

The motherboard plays an important role in the following important aspects of the computer system:

- Organization: In one-way or another, everything is connected to the motherboard. The way that the motherboard is designed and laid out dictates how the entire computer is going to work.
- Control: The motherboard contains the chipset and BIOS (Basic Input Output System) program ROM, and they control most of the data flow within the computer.
- Communication: All communications between PC and its peripherals, goes through the motherboard.
- Processor Support: The motherboard dictates directly your choice of processor for use in the system, will use (ISA or (Industry Standard Architecture), VLB or (Video Electronics Standards Association Local Bus), PCI or Peripheral Component Interconnect) is dependent on what system buses your motherboard uses.
- Performance: The motherboard is a major determining factor in PC's performance for two main reasons. First, the motherboard determines what types of processors, memory, system buses, and hard disk interface speed your system can have, and these components dictate directly PC's performance. Second, the qualities of the motherboard circuitry and chipset have an impact on performance.
- Upgradability: The capabilities of the motherboard dictate to what extent you will be able to upgrade the machine.

1.5.2 Form Factors of Motherboard

Motherboards come in different sizes and shapes. The form factor of a motherboard refers to its physical shape, layout, and the positioning of the components on it. The form factor of the motherboard determines the type of system case it will fit into. Two motherboards can have essentially the same components, but these parts can be arranged differently. Thus, the two motherboards would have different form factors.

☞ *A The shape and layout of a motherboard is called the form factor.*

1.5.3 Motherboard Components

The motherboard is the most important part of a PC, completely determining the computer's internal architecture. On the motherboard Printed Circuit Board (PCB), the components are placed and connected with the help of thin copper tracks. Motherboard PCB contains many such tracks to make electrical connection between different parts of the system. The motherboard has several connectors, jumpers and expansion slots for connecting various components of the system. You can connect various devices of the system to the connectors and expansion slots of the motherboard. You can configure the motherboards using the jumpers (small removable plugs that connect specific pins on the motherboards). Jumpers lets you change the motherboards configuration to match the processor and other

components installed on the system, such as the amount of cache memory, the clock speed and type, and amount of RAM (Random Access Memory), the type of video display card, and so on.

Motherboard contains following components:

- CPU (Microprocessor)
- Co-processor (Optional)
- CMOS (Complementary Metal Oxide Semiconductor) memory
- Real Time Clock (RTC) circuit
- Memory (ROM and RAM)
- BIOS
- Support chips/chipset for Input/Output, interrupts and DMA, etc.
- Expansion slots

☞ *A The shape and layout of a motherboard is called the form factor.*

CPU

The Central Processing Unit (CPU), contains a microprocessor, and it is the heart of a computer. It is located on the motherboard and is an integrated circuit that contains millions and millions of transistors and other electrical components. A PC's performance depends on the capability and speed of the microprocessor. The microprocessor itself consists of a silicon chip on which tiny circuits are etched through a photochemical process. Those circuits are equivalent of millions of transistors. CPU is usually inserted into the socket and is not soldered onto the motherboards, this makes its replacement very easily in case of any problem, or for upgrade.

Co-processor

Co-processor is a special purpose microprocessor which is used to speed up main processor job by taking over some of the main processor's work. Most common type of co-processor are math co-processor and graphic co-processor. A math co-processor helps main processor in performing mathematical calculations. A graphic co-processor help the main processor in carrying out video/graphic related operations.

☞ *An Old system required a co-processor chips to be inserted into special socket on the motherboard, but the current generation of CPU's have math co-processor built inside the main processor itself.*

CMOS Memory

CMOS is an abbreviation for Complementary Metal Oxide Semiconductor. It is an on-board semiconductor chip powered by a CMOS battery. CMOS uses a complimentary arrangement of both NMOS and PMOS, negative and positive Metal Oxide transistor circuits. CMOS memory draws a very little current (nano-amps). Values stored in it can be maintained for a very long period of time while the computer is off with a rechargeable lithium battery. The CMOS memory is used to store system configuration information, such as disk drive parameters, memory configuration, and the date-time, some of which you enter in the CMOS Setup program. It is used by the Basic Input Output System (BIOS), a program permanently stored in the Flash memory on recent motherboards and in Read Only Memory (ROM) on older motherboards, to configure the computer. The CMOS Setup is part of the BIOS program. The CMOS memory is usually located with the real-time clock in the motherboard chipset or in a separate real-time clock chip. It is located in the chipset on most recent motherboards.

☞ *A CMOS memory is used to store the configuration information of your computer, and its electrical current is supplied by battery backup when your computer is turned off.*

Real Time Clock (RTC) Circuit

The real time clock is the calendar and watch of the computer. It lets the PC keep track of the current data and time with the help of a battery and CMOS memory. This circuit maintains correct date and time even when the main AC supply to the computer is switched off.

☞ *The real time clock chip is a battery operated chip that maintains basic settings and the system time.*

Memory (ROM and RAM)

Memories are one of the most important parts of a computer system. The term memory refers to any device that can be used for storage. There are two basic ways to store memory. One way is to store the memory within the actual circuitry of the computer, which allows for it to be quickly accessed by the central processing unit. These memory devices are generally used for temporary storage of data and programs that are currently used by the CPU. The second type of memory storage is to store the memory in external storage devices. They include hard drives (also known as hard disks), floppy disks, and CD-ROMs. Programs and information that you are not currently using can be permanently stored on these devices. The term 'memory' usually pertains to the devices stored within the circuitry of the computer. They are temporary, meaning that when the computer is turned off, they will be deleted. These devices are connected directly to the CPU and are very fast. On the other hand, the external storage devices are not considered part of a computer's memory.

There are basically two types of memory used in the computer:

- RAM (Random Access Memory)
- ROM (Read Only Memory)

RAM RAM is an acronym for random access memory. It is used to temporarily store the programs currently in use by the user and by the main processing unit of the computer, the central processing unit. When you first turn your computer on, the RAM is empty. There will be no data and no information in it until you open or load a program. These programs are originally permanently stored in the external storage devices, like a hard disk, a pen drive, or a CD-ROM. When you open up the program, it is copied from the external device it is located on to the RAM, which is directly connected to the CPU. This is because if the CPU was to directly access this program from the external storage device, it would be extremely slow. However, programs cannot be permanently stored on the RAM because the RAM, unlike hard drives, is not big enough to store all the programs a computer system contains. RAMs are also expensive. The RAM is useful because it can feed information to the central processor at extremely high speeds. However, it does not permanently store information. The RAM is volatile, which means that when you exit out of a program or when the computer is turned off, all the information stored in it will be erased. This is why you need to save all of your work before you close a program. Once the program is closed, it is purged from the RAM, and if the information was not saved to a permanent location like the hard drive, or a pen drive, CD or which are non-volatile (meaning that the information stored on them will not be deleted when the computer is shut off), then it will be lost forever. The RAM is a read-write memory. The information in a read-write memory can be read, and the new information can be written into the memory.

ROM The ROM is a read only memory. This means that you can only read its contents, but you cannot write over it and you cannot change or alter it in any way. A computer needs some sort of instructions when it is first turned on. These instructions are stored in the ROM. The ROM is also used to store certain information not needing to be changed, and it is nonvolatile, meaning that the information it stores is not erased when you turn the computer off. Like the RAM, the ROM also has a spreadsheet layout. However, unlike the RAM, the ROM does not have capacitors in the cells where the columns and rows meet. Instead, it uses a diode. A diode allows an electrical current to flow in one direction. If a diode is present in a certain cell, then an electrical charge will be conducted through the cell to the ground, and the bit in the cell will be a 1. However, if there is no diode, then the cell will store a 0. ROMs are very cheap and reliable, but unfortunately, they are read-only.

BIOS (Basic Input Output System) BIOS is an abbreviation of Basic Input output system. BIOS is an essential set of solutions stored in a chip that provides an interface between the operating system and the hardware of a PC.

☞ *The BIOS is special software that interfaces the major hardware components of your computer with the operating system. It is usually stored on a Flash memory chip on the motherboard, but sometimes the chip is another type of ROM.*

Supporting Chipset The term chipset means a set of chips. It is a group of integrated circuits and microprocessors. The motherboard's bus are regulated by a number of controllers. These are small circuits which have been designed to look after a particular job, like moving data to and from EIDE (Enhanced Integrated Drive Electronics) devices (hard disks, etc.). A number of controllers are needed on a motherboard, as there are many different types of hardware devices which all need to be able to communicate with each other. Most of these controller functions are grouped together into a couple of large chips, which together forms the chipset. The most widespread chipset architecture consists of two chips, usually called north and south bridge. This division applies to the most popular chipset from VIA and Intel. The north bridge and sough bridge are connected by a powerful bus, which sometimes called a link channel. The north bridge and south bridge share the work of managing the data traffic on the motherboard. Modern developments in electronics have made it possible to produce Very Large Scale Integrated Circuits (VLSIC), and now just two or three of these VLSIC chips can do the work which were previously performed by dozens of different chips. These set of VLSIC chips are called chipsets. A typical chipset contains in two or three VLSIC chips all the support logic required by the processor to function as a complete system.

Expansion Slots and Adapter Cards The expansion slots are long thin connectors on the motherboard, which enables you to connect the expansion cards to the motherboard. Different expansion cards are connected to the motherboard through data, address and control lines/buses on these slots. The bus can contain various adapter slots and types. Adapter card slots and types that reside on a motherboard, which are connected to the BUS. As the computer age progresses forward at lightening speed, new slots and types are added and older generation types are removed from motherboards.

1.5.4 Onboard Components of Motherboard

Motherboard has several components that form parts of the onboard components. These components are sockets, ports and jacks that are integral parts of the motherboard. The other ports, sockets and onboard components of the motherboards are as follows:

- **CPU Socket** : The motherboard has sockets for inserting cards, such as video cards or audio cards. It also has a socket for the Central Processor Unit (CPU), and this socket determines what kind of CPU can be used in the motherboard. Motherboards are classified by their CPU socket.
- **North bridge**: The term 'bridge' comes from the north bridge which is one of the most important components on the motherboard. It is a chip that handles the communication between the CPU, main memory AGP port and another very important component known as south bridge controller.
- **South bridge**: It handles all the operations of devices and buses that are not controlled by the north bridge. The south bridge is intended as the place to integrate all the (slower) peripherals like IDE, ISA, USB, etc.
- **DDR DIMM Sockets**: It provides support for memory using DDR (Double Data Rate) DIMMs (Dual In-line Memory Module). This motherboard has four DDR DIMM sockets.
- **Super I/O Controller** : It provides super I/O functionality.
- **Flash ROM**: It contains programmable BIOS. A ROM based BIOS cannot be changed without going through the various lengthy process and requires additional devices to program it. A new type of BIOS chip is gaining popularity with the new systems. This new BIOS is called 'Flash BIOS' is a particular type of EEPROM (Electrically Erasable Programmable Read Only Memory) chip that can be erased and programmed in the PC system itself.
- **Standby Power LED (Light Emitting Diode)** : It indicates if there is standby power on the motherboard.
- **Audio Codec**: It enables audio playback by providing DAC (Digital-to-Analog Converter) channels.
- **LAN Controller** : It supports networking functions.
- **Mouse Port** : It connects to the PS/2 (Personal System/2) mouse. If the system does not contain mouse port then the mouse is plugged into a serial port. The 4-pin USB connector for keyboard is fast replacing the 6 Pin PS/2 port as the most widely used connector for keyboards. A USB connection is faster than other older connectors. Moreover, a USB device does not require special device drivers for it to operate. You simply plug the device in, and it starts working. In recent years, USB has become popular interface for the mouse, keyboard etc.
- **Parallel Port** : It is used for connecting printers and some types of external removable media drives. Parallel ports are 25-pin D-shaped female connection.
- **Registered Jack or RJ-45 port** : It enables connection to LAN through a hub.
- **Line In Jack**: It connects audio devices like a tape player.
- **Microphone Jack**: It connects microphone.
- **USB Port** : USB was developed by INTEL, in 1996, and enabled the connection of portable devices and peripherals to computers without having to open the case to install it. USB uses Hot-Swappable technology, which means devices and peripherals can be connected as needed, externally, via a special USB cable, and not have to reside permanently inside the case. It also enables easy sharing of devices with other computers. However, the device must be installed the first time, if it is not recognized by the OS. Once it is recognized, the OS will auto-open any applications needed as soon as you plug in the device, and without the need to shut down and reboot the computer.
  USB port is used to connect USB devices. USB is not only a connection for printers but also a bus standard that can be used to connect various external hardware devices, such as keyboard, mouse, speakers, and digital camera, etc., to the computer. USB devices can be powered by drawing current directly from the USB cable. If you have old system you can connect a PCI USB adapter card, to get USB facility. If you have a new computer you will find four/six USB ports on motherboard.
  Although there really does not seem to be a logical reason at present, the USB interface allows up to 127 peripherals or devices to plug sequentially into a single external port, using just a single interrupt and port address.
- **Video Port** : It is used to connect VGA (Video Graphics Adapter/Array) monitor or another BFA compatible device. It is a 15-pin D-shaped female connector.
- **Serial Port** : Serial port is used for connecting serial communication devices such as modems, printers, plotters, etc. Serial ports can be either 9- or 25-pin D - Shaped, male connections. Typically you find two serial ports labeled 1 and 2 or A and B.
- **Keyboard Port** : Keyboard is connected here by one of the two types of keyboard connectors. A USB connection is faster than other older connectors. Moreover, a USB device does not require special device drivers for it to operate. You simply plug the device in, and it starts working.

The important parts of a motherboard are:

(a) Processor socket
(b) Interface slots
(c) Memory slots
(d) Ports

Processor Socket

The processor in a modern computer is an Integrated Circuit (IC) chip. A chip consist of millions of transistors and capacitors which can process the data obtained through input devices and transfer the result to the output units. The processor socket is used to fix the processor in a computer. Different kinds of motherboards are available today, depending upon the size and the number of pins in a processor.

☞ *A fan is often fixed on the processor to remove the head generated by continuous activity. This fan is known as processor fan.*

The two main parts of a processor are Arithmetic and Logical Unit (ALU) and Control Unit (CU). The function of the ALU is to do the processing and mathematical calculations of the information obtained through input devices. The control unit sorts of this information and sends it to the different pats of the computer like the manager of an office. The control unit organises and co-ordinates various functions of a computer. The orderly and fast functioning of a computer indicates the efficiency of the control unit.

Interface Slots

Interface cards are the circuit board which connect the equipment outside the system unit with motherboard. These are connected to the slots of motherboard in such a manner that the ports to which the external equipments are to be connected can be seen externally. The TV tuner card used to watch television programmes in a computer, the sound card is used to hear recorded sounds, the network card is used to interconnect several computers are examples of add-on-cards.

☞ *The slots present in a motherboard that are used to connect add-on-cards to it are called interface slots.*

Memory Slots

Information for the functioning of a computer is temporarily stored in a chip called RAM (Random Access Memory). The slot where the RAM board, which has to interact constantly with motherboard, is fixed to the motherboard is called memory slot. RAM is also an integrated circuit. There are several RAM slots in a motherboard.

☞ *All motherboards include a small block of Read Only Memory (ROM) which is different from the main system memory used for loading and running software.*

The ROM contains the PC's Basic Input/Output System (BIOS). BIOS is fixed on the motherboard. BIOS first checks the working condition of each part of the computer. BIOS checks the hard disk and memory during booting. Activation of BIOS is otherwise called POST (Power on Self Test). Being a ROM, the commands in a BIOS are permanent and will be safe even during a sudden power failure.

1.6 PORTS AND INTERFACES

Ports and Interfaces are the rear panel of the system unit of your PC, you will see certain holes found at the back of the computer, using which external devices are connected to the computer motherboard. A port is a means by which data is transferred between an input device to output device or vice versa. The CPU receives or transfers data from main memory and thus uses the memory addresses to send or receive data. Specialized hardware are used to place data from the devices in the memory addresses and to send data from the memory addresses to the devices. All computer systems have ports for connecting peripheral devices, such as printers, keyboard, mouse and modems.

These ports are connected directly to the motherboard or through add-on-cards. The internal communication in a motherboard takes place through the tiny circuit printed on it.

We can connect a computer to another computer to an input/output device to a data storage device. Different kinds of ports are discussed below:

1.6.1 PS/2 PORT

The PS/2 (Personal System/2) standard was introduced by IBM in 1987. It is an electronic plug which connects mouse or keyboard. Most PCs come with two PS/2 ports. It accepts a PS/2 cable with a mini-DIN connector, and is most often used to plug in a keyboard or mouse. The PS/2 port is female while the mini-DIN cable is male. The connector is small with a diameter of about 1/3 inch (9.5mm). The PS/2 port was initially a large DIN plug used for a keyboard, while the mouse was commonly plugged into a serial port.

The PS/2 mouse connector has replaced the older DE-9 RS-232 "serial mouse" connector, while the keyboard connector has replaced the larger 5-pin DIN used in the IBM PC/AT (Personal Computer/Advanced Technology) design. The keyboard and mouse interfaces are electrically similar with the main difference being that open collector outputs are required on both ends of the keyboard interface to allow bidirectional communication. Normal desktop motherboards will not identify the keyboard and mouse if they are placed on each other's sockets. Female pin connection of the PS/2 from the front is shown in Figure 1.47 and the details of these pins are described in Table 1.1.

Table 1.1 Female Connector from the front

Pin 1	+DATA	Data
Pin 2	Not connected	Not connected
Pin 3	GND	Ground
Pin 4	Vcc	+5 V DC at 100 mA
Pin 5	+CLK	Clock
Pin 6	Not connected	Not connected

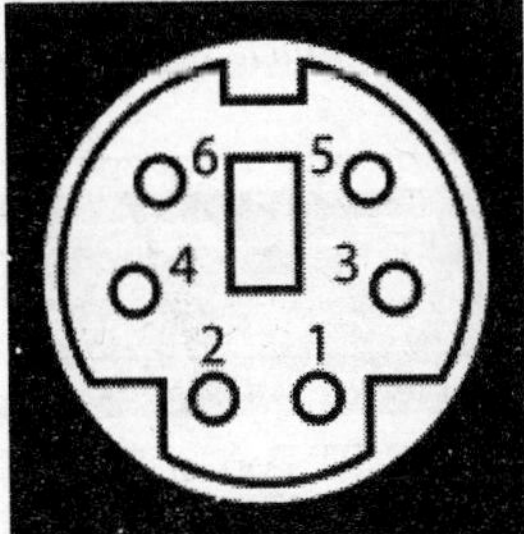

Figure 1.47 PS/2 Port

1.6.2 Serial Port

Serial port is an asynchronous port through which information transfers in or out one bit at a time. Usually referred to as a DB9 or DB25 connection. Where D represents the shape of the connector. The number 9/25 indicating the number of pins found on the connector. DB9 Serial connections are now commonly found on modern PCs and DB9 serial connection is identified first by its 9 pins. The DB9 is shaped like a D (See

Figure 1.48). It will generally be a male connector on the back of the computer whereas DB25 is commonly found on older computers.

Following is the list of component that is used with serial port in computer:

(a) Mouse
(b) Keyboard
(c) Modem
(d) Network

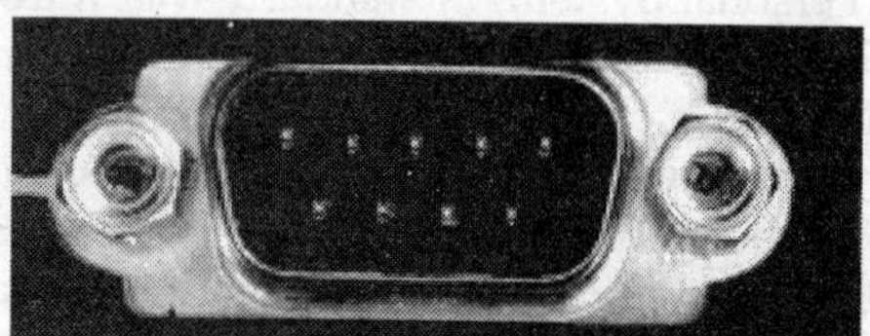

Figure 1.48 COM Port or Serial Port

☞ *In present day PCs, USB interface is used to replace the serial port.*

1.6.3 Parallel Port

LPT (Line Printing Terminal) is the original name of the parallel port interface on IBM PC compatible computers. It was designed to operate a text printer that used IBM's 8-bit extended ASCII (American Standard Code for Information Interchange) character set. A parallel port is a type of socket found on personal computers for interfacing with various peripherals. It is also known as a printer port. LPT port which you might have seen on the back of the PC is shown in Figure 1.49.

Usually, a PC will have 2 LPT ports. You may also find some PCs with 3 LPT ports. These ports are each with their own name LPT1, LPT2 and LPT3. They were designed primarily for printers. However, there is a variety of peripherals that can be connected to these ports.

☞ *Modern printers are connected through USB connection. On many high-end PCs, the parallel port is omitted for cost savings. Printers print at much higher speed when connected with USB port.*

Figure 1.49 LPT Port or Parallel Port

1.6.4 USB Port

Universal Serial Bus (USB) is standardized by the USB Implementers Forum (USB-IF), an industry standards body incorporating leading companies from the computer and electronics industries. USB is a serial bus standard which was designed to allow peripherals to be connected using a single standardized interface socket, to improve plug-and-play capabilities by allowing devices to be connected and disconnected without rebooting the computer (See Figure 1.50). Other convenient features include powering low-consumption devices without the need for an external power supply and allowing some devices to be used without requiring individual device drivers to be installed.

☞ *The Universal Serial Bus (USB) is a single, standardized, easy-to-use way to connect up to 127 devices to a computer.*

Figure 1.50 Commonly used USB Plug

A sample list of USB devices that you can buy today includes:

(a) Printers
(b) Scanners
(c) Mice
(d) Joysticks
(e) Flight yokes
(f) Digital cameras
(g) Webcams
(h) Modems
(i) Speakers
(j) Network connections

1.6.5 SCSI Port

SCSI (pronounced as "scuzzy"), stands for Small Computer System Interface. It is a set of ANSI (American National Standard Institure) standard electronic interfaces that allow personal computers to communicate with peripheral hardware, such as disk drives, tape drives, CD-ROM drives, printers, and scanners faster and more flexibly than previous interfaces. The present set of SCSIs are parallel interfaces in many personal computers today and are supported by all major operating systems.

In addition to faster data rates, SCSI is more flexible than earlier parallel data transfer interfaces. The latest SCSI standard, Ultra-2 SCSI for a 16-bit bus can transfer data at up to 80 megabytes per second (Mbps). SCSI allows up to 7 or 15 devices (depending on the bus width) to be connected to a single SCSI port in daisy-chain fashion. This allows one circuit board or card to accommodate all the peripherals, rather than having a separate card for each device, making it an ideal interface for use with portable and notebook computers.

The latest SCSI standard is Ultra-3 (sometimes spelled "Ultra3") which increases the maximum burst rate from 80 Mbps to 160 Mbps by being able to operate at the full clock rate rather than the half-clock rate of Ultra-2. The standard is also sometimes referred to as Ultra160/m. New disk drives supporting Ultra160/m will offer much faster data transfer rates. Ultra160/m also includes Cyclical Redundancy Checking (CRC) for ensuring the integrity of transferred data and domain validation for testing the SCSI network.

1.7 EXPANSION CARDS

The expansion card also known as expansion board or adapter card in circuit board that can provides additional capabilities to the computer system. The cards are plugged into the expansion sockets present on the computer's motherboard to provide the computer an added functionality. However, now-a-days most of the adapters come in-built on the motherboard and no expansion card is required, unless the need for high performance is required.

- **Sound Card:** Sound card is applied to external audio interfaces that use software to generate sound. The use of sound cards include providing the audio component for multimedia applications, such as music composition, editing video or audio, presentation, education and entertainment (games) and video projection. Most sounds cards use a Digital-to-Analog Converter (DAC), which converts digital data into an analog format. The output signal is connected to an amplifier or headphones.
- **Video Card:** A video card also called a video adapter, display card, graphics card. It is an expansion card which generates a feed of output images to a display (such as a computer monitor).
- **Network Interface Card:** A Network Interface Card (NIC) is a circuit board or card that is installed in a computer so that it can be connected to a network. A network interface card provides the computer with a dedicated, full-time connection to a network. Personal computers and workstations on a local area network typically contain a network interface card specifically designed for the LAN (Local Area Network) transmission technology.
- **Modem:** Modem is an expansion card that allows two computers to communicate over ordinary phone lines. It converts digital data into analog data, transmits over the telephone lines and also converts incoming analog signals back to digital signals for the receiving computer.
- **PC Card:** A PC Card (known as a PCMCIA or Personal Computer Memory Card International Association card) is a credit card-size memory or I/O device that fits into a personal computer. The most common use of a PC Card is the telecommunications modem for notebook computers. There are 16-binary digit and 32-bit (CardBus). The PC Card is based on standards published by the PCMCIA, an industry group organized in 1989 to promote standards for both memory and I/O integrated circuit card.

1.8 CONNECTORS

The part of a cable that plugs into a port or interface to connect one device to another. Most connectors are either male (containing one or more pins) or female (containing holes in which the male connector can be inserted).

1.8.1 DIN Connector

DIN is short for Deutsches Institute for Normung. A DIN connector is an electrical connector that was originally standardized by German national standards organization. DIN connectors are used in personal computers. For example, the keyboard connector is a DIN connector (See Figure 1.51).
A DIN (or DIN5) connectors is a plug with 5 pins, formerly used to connect keyboards to computers.

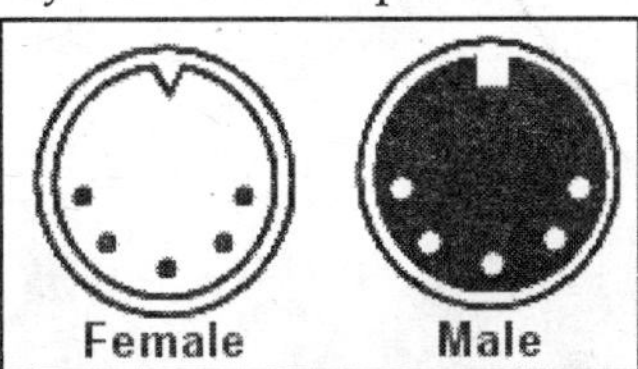

Figure 1.51 DIN connector

The DIN 5 connector has been made by PS/2 and USB connectors.

Pin number	Function
1	Reset (_RST)
2	+ 5 V (power)
3	Data
4	Ground
5	Clock

Mini-DIN connector

Mini-DIN connectors are cylindrical in shape and feature between three and nine pins, each compatible with various audio and/or visual devices. Four-pin mini-DIN connectors are used to carry a separate video (commonly called S-video) signal.
Some examples of standard mini-DIN connectors include:

- Mini-DIN-3 connectors were used in early implementations of Apple LocalTalk.
- Mini-DIN-4 connectors are used for S-video, and were used for Apple Desktop Bus.
- Mini-DIN-6 connectors were used for IBM PC compatible PS/2 keyboard and mouse ports.
- Mini-DIN-8 connectors were used for Apple and Sun Microsystems keyboard and mouse ports, as well as for serial printer, modem, and Apple LocalTalk connections.
- Mini-DIN-7 and Mini-DIN-9 connectors have been used for a variety of audio and video applications.
- Mini-DIN-6 and Mini-DIN-8 connectors are frequently used in ham radio applications to interface with computers for data packet communications and radio programming.

1.8.2 RCA Connector

An RCA (Radio Corporation of America) connector, sometimes called a phono connector or cinch connector, is a type of electrical connector commonly used to carry audio and video signals. The RCA plug is used to send video and audio signals (in mono or stereo) through a two-wire cable, with either an analog or digital transmission method.

The connector's colour indicates how it is meant to be used. For stereo analog audio transmissions, the connectors are red and white as shown in Figure 1.52.

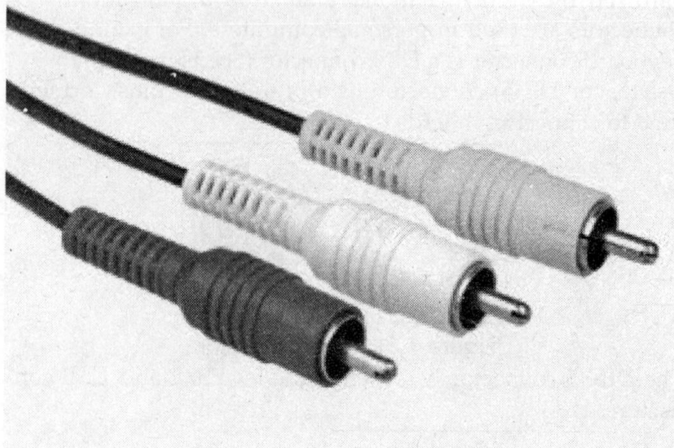

Figure 1.52 RCA connector

For a composite video signal, the connector is yellow (See Figure 1.53).

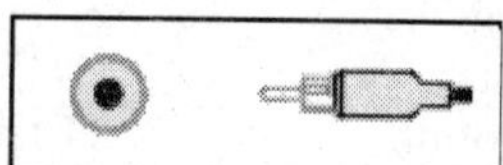

Figure 1.53 RCA cable in yellow colour

The RCA connector is also used for sending component video, also called YUV or YCrCb, is a color representation model in which Y represents luminance (black and white), and U and V represent the chrominance (information regarding the color). In YUV representation, U is sometimes written as Cr and V is sometimes written as Cb therefore YCrCb notation is also used in color representation. For such a video signal, 3 connectors, colored red, green, and blue, are used (See Figure 1.54).

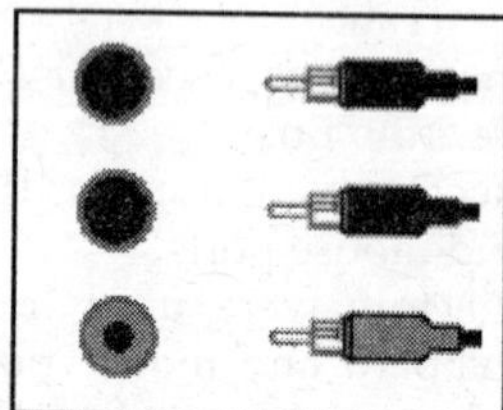

Figure 1.54 Three RCA cables: 1 green, 1 blue and 1 red

1.8.3 AV (Audio Video) Connector

Audio connectors and video connectors are electrical connectors (or optical connectors) for carrying audio signal and video signal. Either analog or digital format. Analog A/V connectors often use shielded cables to inhibit Radio Frequency Interference (RFI) and noise. The most common types of connectors used between your new A/V receiver, video display (with an emphasis on HDTV), DVD/CD player, loudspeakers, and subwoofer.

Audio connectors are electrical connectors designed and used for audio frequencies. They can be analog or digital. Common audio connectors include:

- **Banana Connector:** A banana connector (commonly banana plug for the male, banana socket or banana jack for the female) is a single-wire (one conductor) electrical connector used for joining wires to equipment. The term 4 mm connector is also used in Europe. Although not all banana connectors will mate with 4 mm parts. The plug is a four-leafed spring tip that snaps into the jack. The plugs are frequently used to terminate patch cords for electronic test equipment. They are also often used as the plugs on the cables connecting the amplifier to the loudspeakers in hi-fi (high fidelity) sound systems (See Figure 1.55).

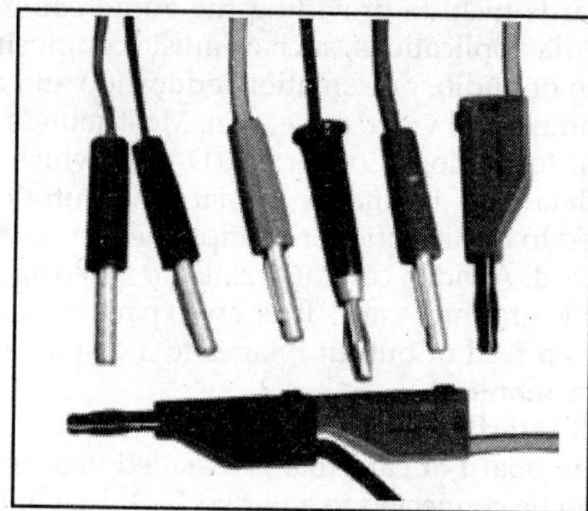

Figure 1.55 Various banana plugs

- **Five-way Binding Posts:** A type of speaker cable input and receiver/amplifier output connector that accepts bare speaker wire when you unscrew the top and push the wire through the hole. It is also used for high-level connections for amplified audio signals from an A/V receiver's speaker outputs to the speakers. Stereo systems with amplifiers or preamps lacking a subwoofer output would also use the amplifier's high-level outputs and the subwoofers hi-level inputs. Signals may be routed through the subwoofer and then to the main speakers, or separately from the amplifier to the main speakers with a second set to the subwoofer (See Figure 1.56).

Video connectors carry only video signals. Common video-only connectors include:

Figure 1.56 Five-way binding posts

- **Component Video:** The most common type of connector used for both standard-quality video and HD video, it uses three coaxial RCA cables and plugs color-coded red, green and blue (the three cables may be wrapped together for convenience) to carry analog standard or high definition video between a set top satellite or cable-TV box to the A/V receiver and TV display or projector (See Figure 1.57).

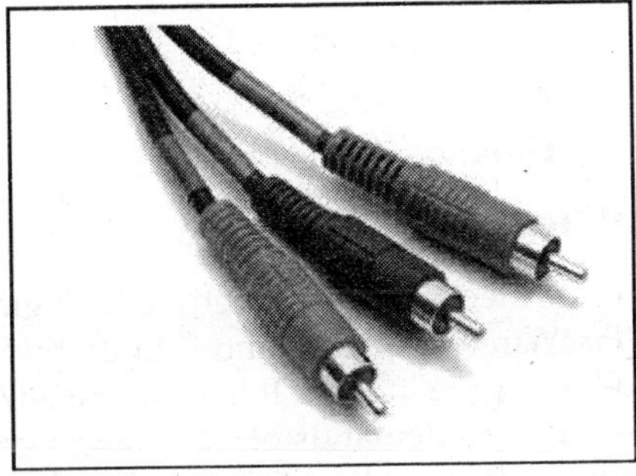

Figure 1.57 Component video cable

- **Composite Video:** A single video connector that combines all the color, brightness, and sync signals into one cable using a single RCA connector. It is the most common type of analog video connection between older VCRs and TVs (except for RF (Radio Frequency) connectors). Use composite video only if your TV, VCR or DVD player lacks S-video or component-video connectors. Composite video will not carry High Def or progressive-scan video signals (See Figure 1.58).

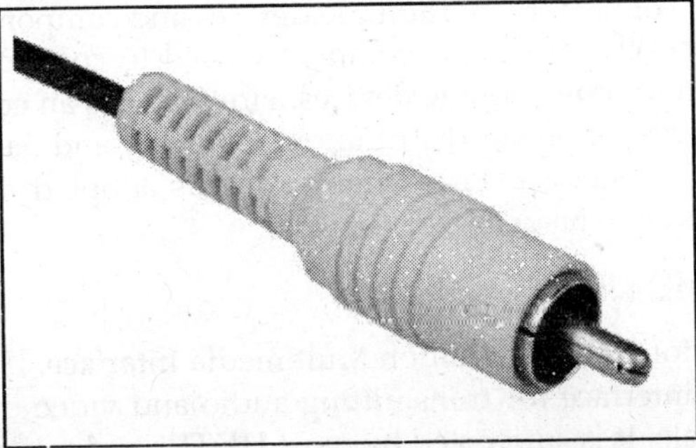

Figure 1.58 Composite video cable

1.8.4 USB Connectors

Most computer users are familiar with USB, which has become the most commonly used way to connect peripheral devices to a computer. For example, mouse, printer, digital camera, scanner, and other devices probably all connect to your computer via a USB port. Many memory storage devices, such as portable hard drives, flash drives, and memory card readers, also connect to a computer via USB.

USB connectors make it possible to connect a device to your computer using USB. A long cable is used to connect the device to your computer. Usually, the connectors on each end of the cable are quite different, making it necessary to know which of them goes to your computer and which gets plugged into the device.

Different types of USB Connectors

There are many types of UBS connector cards you may use depending on the device you are connecting.

Type-A These types of USB connectors are identified by their rectangular shaped plug. The plug is always found in the cable and the receptacle is found in the device. They are commonly used with keyboard, mouse, data cards etc. The image of a type A connector and the pin position are shown in Figures 1.59 and 1.60, respectively.

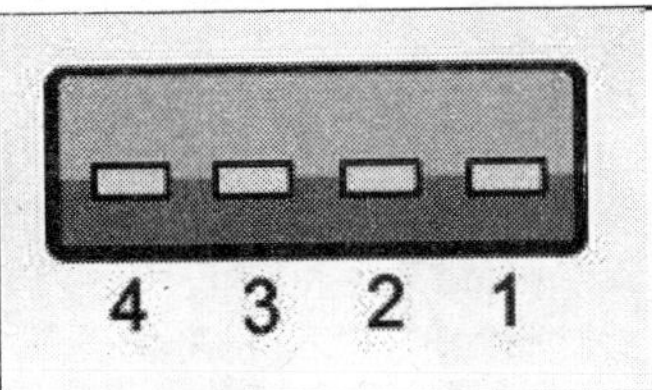

Figure 1.59 The pin-position of Type A USB connector

Figure 1.60 The image of Type A male and female USB connector

The pin-out of the Type A USB Connector.

Pin 1	VBus
Pin 2	D-
Pin 3	D+
Pin 4	Ground

Type-B The Type-B connectors are designed to be used with devices which are meant to be connected with the device having Type-A receptacle. These connectors are square shaped with beveled exterior corners. They are found in USB devices like printers, USB to serial converters, simple USB powered devices like battery chargers, etc. The image of a type B connector and the pin position are shown in Figures 1.61 and 1.62, respectively.

Figure 1.61 Female Type B connector

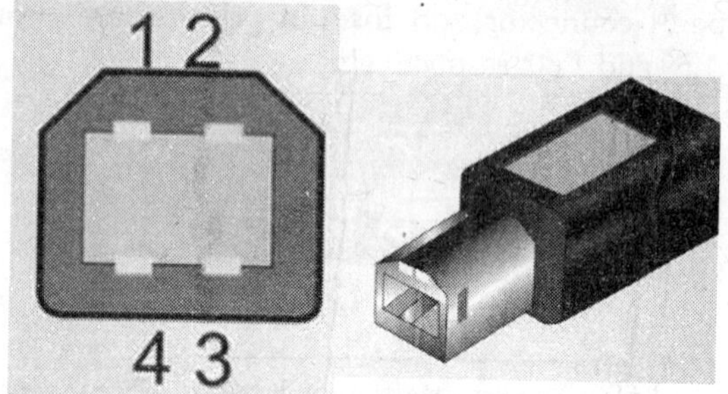

Figure 1.62 Male Type B connector and pin position

Figure 1.63 The image of Mini A and B male USB connector and Pin position

Micro-A and Micro-B The Micro-A and B connectors are introduced to replace the Mini-A and Mini-AB connectors. They are smaller in size than the Mini connectors. They have up to 10, 000 mating cycles. The Micro connectors are used with small devices like mobiles, smart phones, PDAs (Personal Digital Assistants), etc. (See Figure 1.63).

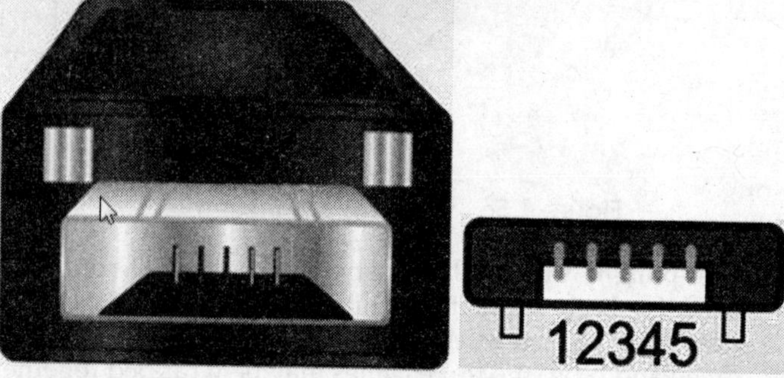

Figure 1.64 The image of Micro B and A male connector and pin position

The pin-out of the Micro USB connector

Pin 1	VBus
Pin 2	D-
Pin 3	D+
Pin 4	ID
Pin 5	Ground

1.8.5 FireWire (IEEE 1394)

IEEE (Institute of Electrical and Electronics Engineers) 1394, also named "FireWire" by Apple, and "i.Link" by Sony, and it was developed by Apple in 1986. It is a standard I/O interface designed to service the demands of the emerging multimedia bus requirements. It includes a plug-and-socket connection with a serial bus interface. Up to 63 devices may be connected at the same time with (relatively) high data transfer speeds.

The IEEE 1394 standard has proved very popular for communication between computers and peripheral devices. IEEE 1394 interface has the following features:

- Real-time data transferring for multimedia applications
- 100-800 Mb/s data transfer rate
- Hot plugging is allowed (at a minimum ratio)
- Line terminators are not required
- Plug-and-play
- Auto-configuration for many peripheral devices
- Same connectors for multiple devices and components

The FireWire system is commonly used to connect digital cameras and other storage devices. FireWire has an edge over USB in terms of power distribution, reliability and data transfer speed. Moreover, FireWire system has adopted the functionalities and characteristics of SCSI.

1.8.6 HDMI

It stands for "High-Definition Multimedia Interface." HDMI is a digital interface for transmitting audio and video data in a single cable. It is supported by most HDTVs and related components, such as DVD and Blu-ray players, cable boxes, and video game systems.

While other types of A/V connections require separate cables for audio and video data, HDMI carries the audio and video streams together, greatly eliminating cable clutter. For example, a component cable connection requires three cables for video and two for audio, totaling five cables in all. The same information can be transmitted using one HDMI cable.

Because HDMI is a digital connection, HDMI cables are less prone to interference and signal noise than analog cables. Also, since most components, such as DVD players and digital cable boxes process information digitally, using HDMI eliminates the analog to digital conversion other interfaces require. Therefore, HDMI often produces the best quality picture and sound compared to other types of connections.

1.9 UPS (UNINTERRUPTED POWER SUPPLY)

UPS provides backup power for a computer system when the electrical power fails. Different models offer different levels of protection. The amount of time the battery can provide power varies with the model of the UPS. Small UPS units are equipped with a battery and a sensor (which detects the loss of power). If the sensor detects a loss of power, it immediately switches over to battery so that the user has enough time to save his or her work and shut off the computer. But, high-end UPS models offers longer battery time.

There are five types of UPS. These are the following:

(a) Standby
(b) Line Interactive
(c) Standby-Ferro
(d) Double Conversion On-Line
(e) Delta Conversion On-Line

1.9.1 Standby UPS

It is the most common type of UPS used for Personal Computers. In the block diagram shown in Figure 1.65, the transfer switch is set to choose the filtered AC input as the primary power source (solid line path), and switches to the battery/inverter as the backup source should the primary power source fails. When that happens, the transfer switch must operate to switch the load over to the battery/inverter backup power source.

☞ *The inverter starts when the power fails, hence the name "Standby." High efficiency, small size, and low cost are the main advantages of Standby UPS.*

1.9.2 Line Interactive UPS

The Line Interactive UPS connection is shown in Figure 1.66. It is the most common design used for PCs. In this design, the battery-to-AC power converter (inverter) is always connected to the output of the UPS.

Operating the inverter in reverse during times when the input AC power is normally provides battery charging. When the input power fails, the transfer switch opens and the power flows from the battery to the UPS output.

The Line Interactive design incorporates a tap-changing transformer. This adds voltage regulation by adjusting transformer taps as the input voltage varies. Voltage regulation is an important feature when low voltage conditions exist. High efficiency, small size, low cost and high reliability coupled with the ability to correct low or high line voltage conditions make this as the dominant type of UPS in the 0.5-5 kVA power range.

1.9.3 Standby Ferro UPS

Standby Ferro UPS has three windings (power connections). The primary power path is from AC input, through a transfer switch, through the transformer, and to the output. In the case of a power failure, the transfer switch is opened, and the inverter picks up the output load. In the Standby-Ferro design, the inverter is in the standby mode, and is energized when the input power fails and the transfer switch is opened. The transformer has a special "Ferro-resonant" capability, which provides limited voltage regulation and output waveform "shaping". The isolation from AC power transients provided by the Ferro transformer is as good as or better than any filter available. But the Ferro transformer itself creates severe output voltage distortion and transients, which can be worse than a poor AC connection.

Standby Ferro UPS are quite large and heavy. Figure 1.67 illustrates this Standby Ferro topology. High reliability and excellent line filtering are this design's strengths.

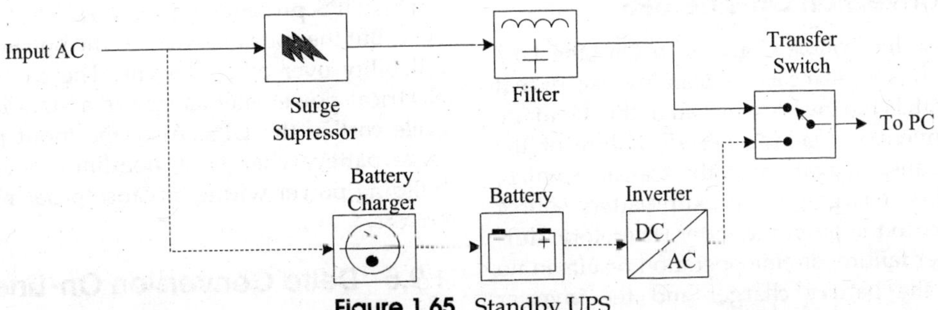

Figure 1.65 Standby UPS

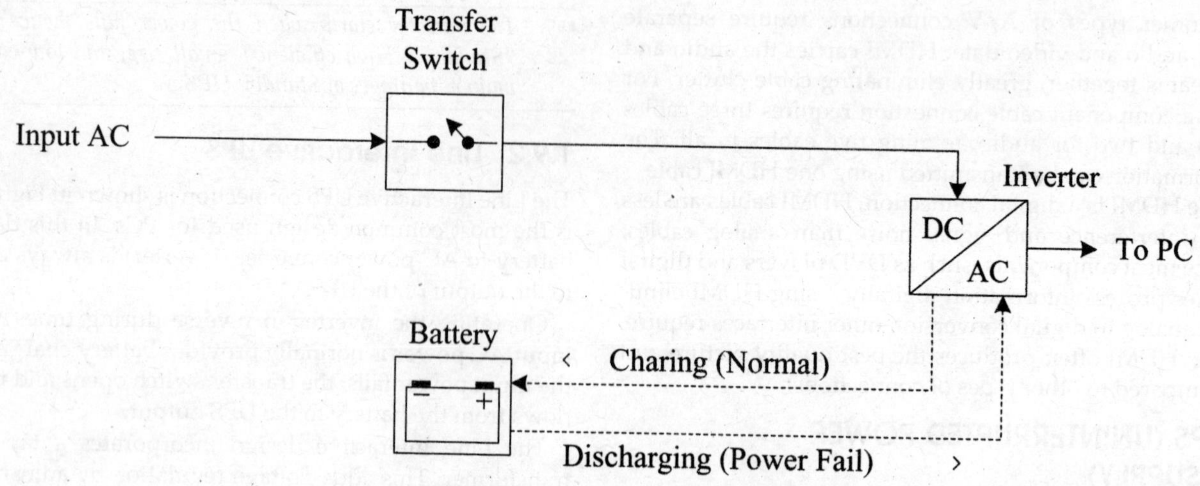

Figure 1.66 Line Interactive UPS

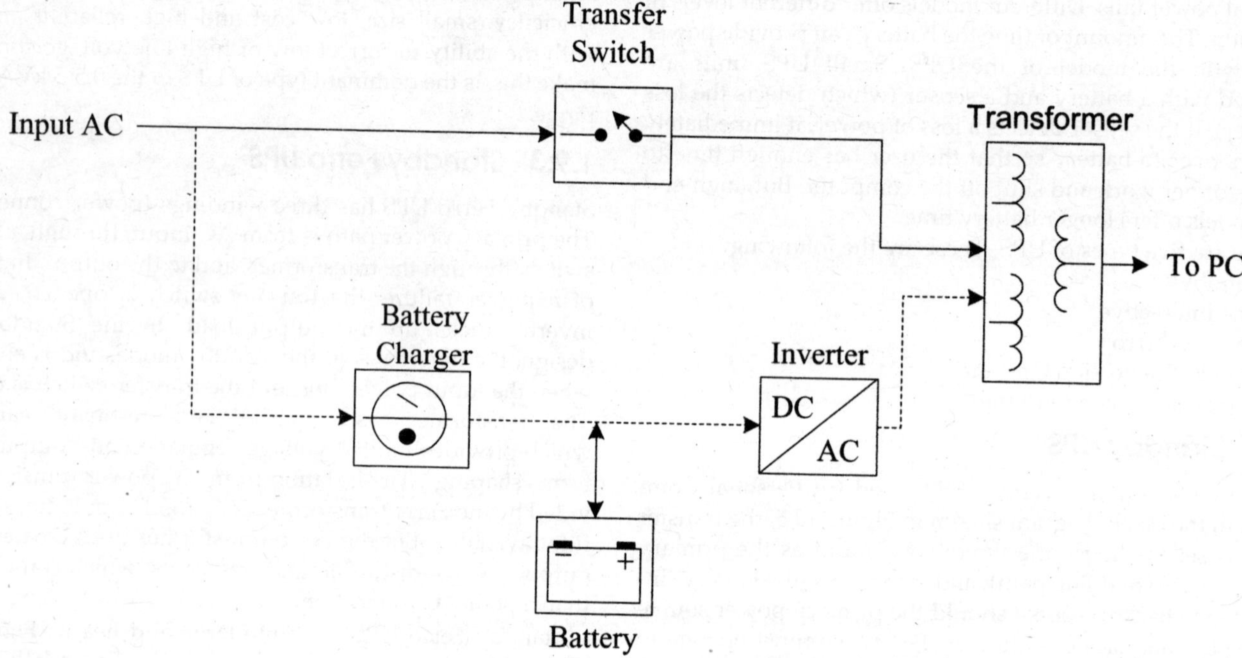

Figure 1.67 Standby-Ferro UPS

1.9.4 Double Conversion On-Line UPS

The block diagram of the Double Conversion On-Line UPS shown in Figure 1.68. It is the same as the Standby, except that the primary power path is the inverter instead of the AC main.

In the Double Conversion On-Line design, failure of the input AC does not cause activation of the transfer switch, because the input AC is charging the backup battery source which provides power to the output inverter. Therefore, during an input AC power failure, on-line operation results in no transfer time. Both the battery charger and the inverter convert the entire load power flow in this design, resulting in reduced efficiency with its associated increased heat generation.

This UPS provides nearly ideal electrical output performance. But the constant wear on the power components reduces reliability over other designs. The energy consumed by the electrical power inefficiency is a significant part of the life-cycle cost of the UPS. Also, the input power drawn by the large battery charger is non-linear and can interfere with building power wiring or cause problems with standby generators.

1.9.5 Delta Conversion On-Line UPS

Delta Conversion On-Line UPS shown in Figure 1.69 is a newer technology introduced to eliminate the drawbacks of the Double Conversion On-Line design. It is available in sizes

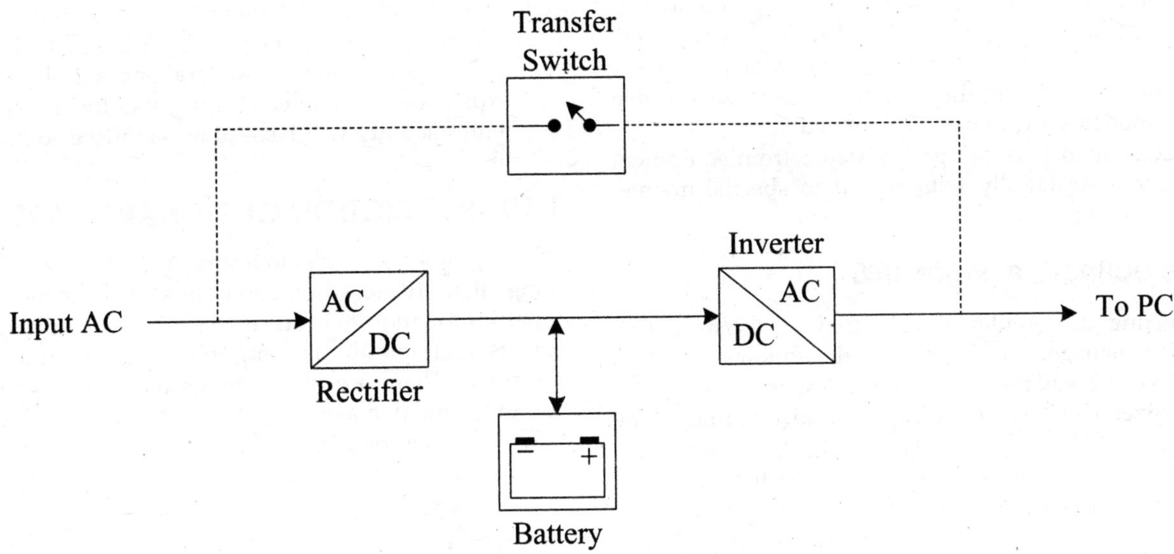

Figure 1.68 Double Conversion On-Line UPS

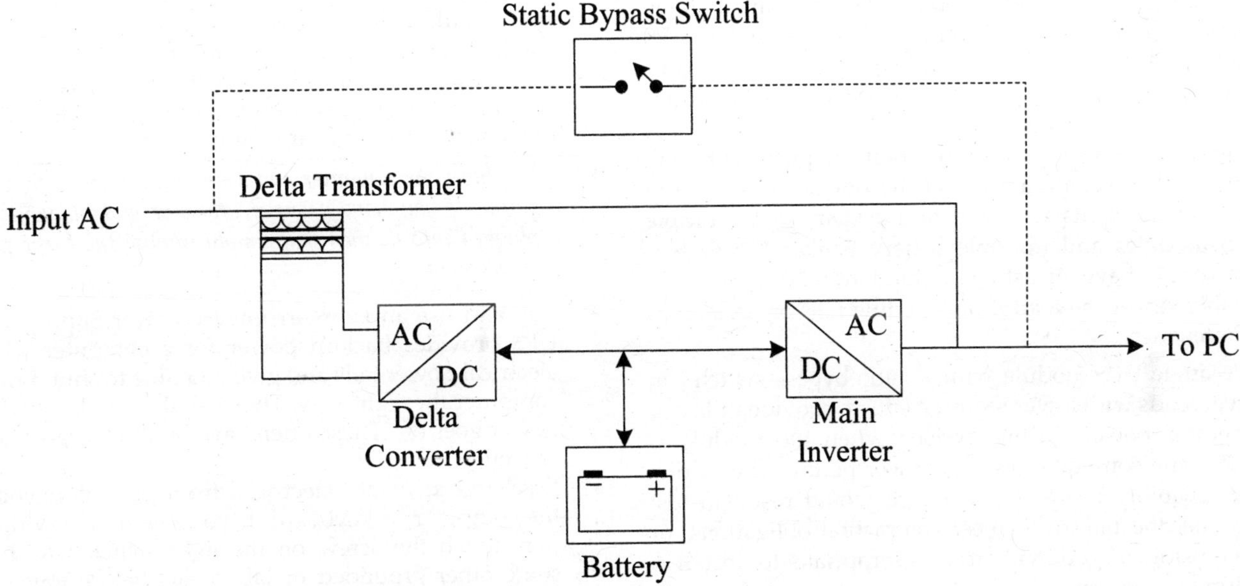

Figure 1.69 Delta Conversion On-Line UPS

ranging from 5 kVA to 1.6 MW. The Delta Conversion On-Line UPS always has the inverter supplying the load voltage. The additional Delta Converter contributes power to the inverter output. Under conditions of AC failure or disturbances, this design exhibits behaviour identical to the Double Conversion On-Line.

1.9.6 Maintenance of UPS

UPS modules are designed to provide maximum power in minimum footprint. UPS design varies considerably among manufacturers, and specialized knowledge is necessary to identify inspection and maintenance points within the unit.

Routine UPS maintenance consists of a variety of inspections, measurements, calibrations and preventive actions. The technician shuts down the affected module for these procedures and remaining modules – or, in non-redundant systems, a standby generator or the local electric utility – provides power to the load until the module returns to service.

You should inspect the interior of the unit for corrosion and heat damage, records and adjusts the battery-charger float voltage, calibrates metering and protection functions, tighten power connections, clean the module and perform other unit-specific maintenance activities as recommended by the manufacturer.

During the battery run-down test, technicians should perform thermal scans on internal power connections and components to identify poor or marginal connections. Scanning should be repeated during the recharge cycle to ensure that rectifier components are adequately scanned.

Maintenance managers can get assistance from equipment manufacturers – especially with regard to specific maintenance requirements.

1.9.7 Selecting the 'Right' UPS

When selecting an uninterruptable power system (UPS), maintenance manager must consider the following factors that can make or break the success of the system:

(a) **Load Size:** The size of the critical load determines the capacity of the initial installation. The UPS must have adequate capacity to reliably serve the critical load and additional loads, without immediate expansion. The excess capacity of a UPS will depend on the facility's plans for expansion of the supported load.
In general, capacity should be 150 percent of the initial installed load. For small critical loads involving a single computer a single-phase desktop or rack-mounted UPS might be the optimal solution. For larger critical loads, such as data centers, freestanding three-phase modules generally are installed.

(b) **System Reliability:** System-reliability requirements will determine the configuration of the power system. Very high requirements will lead to a system with multiple UPS modules and multiple battery banks. The system also should have atleast one redundant module so it can reliably server the load if one module fails or undergoes maintenance.

A single UPS module with a static bypass switch can server loads with lower requirements to provide utility or generator power during periods when the module is down. The consequences of a power failure tend to dictate reliability needs. If an outage would result in lost revenue, the failure to meet contractual obligations, or lost customer goodwill, it is appropriate to install a redundant system.

(c) **Battery Run Time:** The battery run time of a UPS is the length of time the UPS can reliably supply power to the critical load after input power has failed. Run time usually is defined as the length of time required for connected data-processing equipment to save data files and shut down in an orderly fashion, along with a margin of safety.

(d) **Future Expansion:** Requirements for future expansion affect UPS configuration and determine space requirements for future modules and battery banks. Depending on the timing of the expansion, it might be more economical to install a single module and add modules as needed, rather than installing a single, larger module.

(e) **Budget Constraints:** Budgetary constraints play a key role in determining the final UPS design. Often, a system that satisfies other considerations simply will be too expensive to implement, and some functionality or system reliability will have to be sacrificed to keep costs in line.

1.10 PROTECTION OF PC HARDWARE

Our computer is a big investment. Not only that, but the things that are stored on computers, from financial and personal information to work or schoolwork to photographs of friends and family, are important to you and should be protected. There are many things that can happen to your computer and damage it but if you are careful, you can protect your computer for years.

- Computers or computer media are the most temperamental objects. A power surge or spike due to any external reason may either corrupt the data on computer disk or spoil some hardware component. Power surges can come during lightening, stroms or even simple activity like plugging a heavy duty device or motor on the same electricity outlet where the computer is connected. A power stablizer/spike guard is recommended for surge protection. Make sure all things that are plugged into your computer are plugged into the surge protector. Even use one when charging your laptop battery.

☞ *Unplug your computer and accessories during any electrical storm. If you have a surge protector and all your stuff is plugged into it, then you simply unplug the surge protector power strip.*

- Buy and use an Uninterruptedly Power Supply, or UPS. UPS provides backup power for a computer when the electrical power fails and give you time to shut down your computer the right way. They usually will beep when the power goes off. These often have built in surge protection as well.
- Discharge any static electricity from you before you touch the computer or keyboard. If you live in a very dry location, touch the screw on the light switch wall plate or some other grounded metal contact before touching the computer. They used to make these power strips that had a static discharge touch point, that you set your monitor on.
- Store your CDs and DVDs VERTICALLY (not flat or horizontally) once you put data on them. Keep them in a cool, dry place, away from excessive heat or sunlight.
- Wipe the area on your desk that your mouse runs over (if you don't have a mouse pad) once a week. Turn off your computer, and wipe the keyboard. Turn the keyboard upside down and shake to get those crumbs out.
- Keep food, and especially DRINKS, away from your laptop or desktop box. Not eating or drinking while using your computer can prevent you from the damage that can be caused by spilling food or beverages on your keyboard or other components.

- Operate the computer away from extreme hot and cold weather. Humidity or water vapor in the air that penetrates your computer can damage internal components such as the motherboard. This water vapor is moisture that collects in the air which can lead to the growth of dust mites. These dust mites can penetrate a computer and cause it to over heat. To protect the computer from humidity you will need to control the moisture levels in your home. During the summer months when the humidity levels are high, you can easily control the moisture level in your home with an air conditioner.
- Do not place two monitors close to one another. The magnetic fields may cause either or both to suffer from shaking images. Likewise, do not place a monitor next to a TV, if possible.
- Place loudspeakers and other sources of storing magnetic fields away from the monitor. This reduces the possibility of colour purity or geometry problems. The exception is with respect to good quality shielded multimedia which are designed to avoid magnetic interference problems.
- Keep other devices away from the monitor, which may cause interference, such as problem with power transformers including audio equipment, AC or DC wall adapters and laptop power supplies, fluorescent lamps with magnetic ballast and motorized or heavy duty appliances.
- Some data is also confidential; not only do you not want to lose it, you don't want others to even view it without authorization. The single most important step in protecting your data from loss is to back it up regularly.
- Use file-level and share-level security. To keep others out of your data, the first step is to set permissions on the data files and folders. If you have data in network shares, you can set share permissions to control what user accounts can and cannot access the files across the network.
- Keep your data password protected. Make sure that you have to enter a password to log in to your computer
- Use disk encryption to protect your data. Encryption allow you to encrypt an entire disk. Whole disk encryption locks down the entire contents of a disk drive/partition and is transparent to the user. Data is automatically encrypted when it's written to the hard disk and automatically decrypted before being loaded into memory. Some of these programs can create invisible containers inside a partition that act like a hidden disk within a disk. Other users see only the data in the "outer" disk. Disk encryption products can be used to encrypt removable USB drives, flash drives, etc. Some allow creation of a master password along with secondary passwords with lower rights you can give to other users.
- Data that you send over a wireless network is even more subject to interception than that sent over an Ethernet network. Hackers don't need physical access to the network or its devices; anyone with a wireless-enabled portable computer and a high gain antenna can capture data and/or get into the network and access data stored there if the wireless access point isn't configured securely. You should send or store data only on wireless networks that use encryption, preferably Wi-Fi Protected Access (WPA), which is stronger than Wired Equivalent Protocol (WEP).
- Use rights management to retain control. If you need to send data to others but are worried about protecting it once it leaves your own system, you can use Windows Rights Management Services (RMS) to control what the recipients are able to do with it. For instance, you can set rights so that the recipient can read the Word document you sent but can't change, copy, or save it. You can prevent recipients from forwarding e-mail messages you send them and you can even set documents or messages to expire on a certain date/time.
- Use a firewall. Firewalls prevent infiltration of hackers and other malicious threats. You should keep a well maintained firewall between your computers and the Internet, and between your computers and your in-house users. If you are a home user, you should have firewall software implemented on your home computer and/or on your home router.

1.11 PROTECTING PORTABLES

Laptop computers are more sensitive and more easily damaged physically than desktop computers. With that in mind, take extra precautions with your laptop computer.

- Always travel or transport it in a special case that has padding to keep it safe from bumping around. In addition, be careful when balancing your laptop on your knees, so it doesn't go crashing to the floor. Use your laptop on a table or counter when possible. Get the extended warranty.
- Keep liquids away from your laptop a. As tempting as it might be to drink coffee, water or any other liquid near your laptop, accidents can happen all too easily. Alternatively, use a cup with a cover on it, so even if it does spill, the liquid doesn't go anywhere. Spilled liquids may damage the internal micro electronic components or cause electrical injury to the laptop. Short circuits can corrupt data or even permanently destroy some parts. The solution is very simple: Keep your drinks away from your computer.
- Keep food away from your laptop. a. Don't eat over your laptop, the crumbs can go down between the keys in the keyboard and provide an invitation to small bugs. The crumbs can also damage the circuitry.
- Always have clean hands when using your laptop a. Clean hands make it easier to use your laptop touchpad and there will be less risk of leaving dirt and other stains on the computer.
- When you shut your laptop, make sure there are no small items, such as a pencil or small earphones, on the keyboard. These can damage the display screen when shut; the screen will scratch if the item is rough. Close the lid gently and holding from the middle. Closing the lid using only one side causes pressure on that hinge, and over time can cause it to bend and snap.

- Don't pull on the power cord. Tugging your power cord out from the power socket rather than putting your hand directly on the plug in the socket and pulling can break off the plug or damage the power socket. Also, if you have the power point near your feet, avoid constantly bumping into the plug or you could loosen it and eventually break it.
- Avoid placing heavy materials, such as books, on top of your laptop and keyboard a. This can push the LCD screen into the keyboard, and will eventually damage it.
- When traveling by plane or rail, do not ever place a portable computing device (or other valuables) in checked baggage. If your aircraft departure is delayed and you are directed or invited to deplane and wait in the terminal, take your laptop and other valuables with you. Don't leave them unattended at your seat or in the overhead.
- Avoid insecure networks if at all possible, but if you cannot, then be sure that all sensitive data is encrypted.
- Cover up your portable devices to the extent possible. Carry your laptop in a briefcase or other preferably grungy-looking case, and keep smaller devices such as a PDA in your pocket. The distinctive size and shape of a laptop computer make it an easily spotted target for thieves.
- Make adequate backups. Test your backups by doing restoration of the data to a test system. Store your data in two different locations. Keep virus protection up to date.

1.12 BASIC COMPUTER MAINTENANCE

a. **Backup:** Backing up your data means saving your files to a separate location (like a CD ROM, floppy, pen drive, or zip disk) so that in the event of disaster, you can easily copy your files back onto your computer.

b. **Invest in an UPS (uninterruptible power source):** A UPS works as a surge protector and a battery backup. Not only does it keep your computer safe from electrical spikes, it also gives you time to save your work and properly power down your computer in the event of a power failure.

c. **Never turn the computer off with the power switch:** The one exception to this rule is when your computer locks up and your hard drive is not running (the hard drive light is not blinking). In this situation, you can turn the power off.

e. **Scan disk and defrag once a month:** These utilities help to keep your hard drive in optimal shape and free from error.

f. **Do not unplug peripheral devices while the power supply is on:** Unplugging devices such as your mouse, keyboard, printer, etc. with the power on can short out the connector socket or even the motherboard itself.

g. **Remove programs from your startup:** Often, when you install a program, it will ask you whether it should load up as soon as Windows loads (or just decide to do so on its own). The more programs you have trying to start up at the same time, the slower your computer will start. Also, all those programs running in the background while you try to work can slow your computer's response time.

h. **Run virus checks and adware/spyware scans regularly (at least once a week):** Regular scans with your virus scanner and adware scanners can ensure your computer remains healthy.

i. **Keep disks handy:** If the worst thing happens, and you need to format your system for one reason or another, then it is a good idea to have all your driver disks, operating system disks, backup disks, etc. in a readily available place.

j. **Keep your software updated:** Software developers are always writing and releasing patches that update the software you have already bought from them. A lot of these patches fix problems you may be experiencing with a particular program.

k. **Develop a schedule of maintenance practices:** Write yourself up a maintenance schedule, with a list of what tasks should be performed daily, weekly, and monthly.

If you develop a routine and stick to it, then you should avoid the larger problems by always being on top of the smaller ones.

1.12.1 Why Proper Computer Maintenance is Important?

Proper computer maintenance is important because of the following reasons:

1. Because it will increases the speed of your PC.
2. Prevent errors, which will save money.
3. Secure your data and information.
4. Save time.

By maintaining your PC in good condition and operating it in dust free air condition environment you will notice that you will work for more number of hours without its failure. In this way you will save your data as well as damaged to the machine you will not require any hardware engineer for repair and spend money on the repair of the machine.

1.13 CLEANING THE MONITOR, KEYBOARD AND CPU

Cleaning your computer, components, and peripherals helps to keep everything in good working condition and helps to prevent germs from spreading. While you cleaning with a Computer there is a risk of static electricity passing an electronic component inside of the computer or by cleaning accessories attached to the computer while they are still plugged into the computer, such as a Keyboard, Mouse or Monitor. Once the Power Cord is unplugged there is no Electricity running through the computer, there are some parts in the Power Supply that hold an Electrical charge. Before you touch anything inside the computer case touch the Metal Frame to discharge any static electricity supply.

Cleaning the Monitor

While cleaning monitors you must take some precautions. Normally, there is a special coating on monitor screens that will permanently streak if you use an ammonia-based cleaning product to bathe the screen. If you wipe the screen while it is on and warm, a static electricity is generated which is harmful to your system. The best way to clean your monitor's screen is, to dry-dust with a lint-free cloth or by spraying some window cleaner with a soft cloth.

☞ *Never spray cleaning solution directly on the screen.*

Precautions to take while cleaning the monitor:

- Do not use glass cleaner to clean a monitor. Many screens have anti-glare coatings that can be damaged by glass cleaner.
- Turn off the computer.
- Unplug the monitor from the power. If you are using a laptop, unplug the laptop.
- Use a soft clean cloth moistened with water to wipe the screen.
- Do not spray any liquids directly onto the screen. The liquid could leak into the monitor and damage the internal components.

Cleaning the Keyboard

Shutdown your PC and remove the main plug. Unplug the keyboard and hold it upside down to release any debris present in between the keys (pressing the key is a good way to clean it).

A dirty keyboard does not look nice and may not work properly. Dust, food, liquid, and other particles can get stuck underneath the keys, which can prevent them from working properly. The following steps are basic cleaning tips that can help to keep your keyboard clean.

- Unplug the keyboard from the USB or PS/2 port. If the keyboard is plugged into the PS/2 port, you will need to shut down the computer before unplugging it.
- Turn the keyboard upside down, and gently shake it to remove dirt and dust.
- Use a can of compressed air to clean between the keys.
- Moisten a cotton cloth or paper towel with rubbing alcohol, and use it to clean the tops of the keys. Do not pour alcohol or any other liquid directly onto the keys.
- Reconnect the keyboard to the computer once it is dry. If you are connecting it to a PS/2 port, you will need to connect it before turning on the computer.

Cleaning the CPU

Dust inside your computer can slow down your computer and cause some computer components to fail. The steps for cleaning the CPU from inside are:

1. **Gather the tools**: You need compressed air and a screwdriver (only needed if you use a screwdriver to open the computer case). A small vacuum might clean up the mess you make around the computer, but should never be used inside it. A dust mask is suggested because it can save you a bit of sneezing if you need to clean a computer quickly.
2. Shut down and unplug your computer.
3. Disconnect the LAN cable and all peripherals, such as monitors, scanners, printers, keyboards, mice and speakers.
4. **Open your computer:** Once you have a suitable work area, open your computer. Most machines have screws holding a side panel down. After removing these, you can then slip the side off your machine.

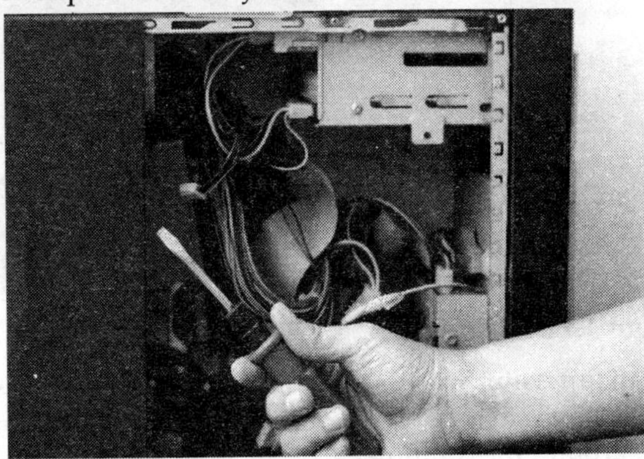

Figure 1.70

5. **Prepare to Clean:** After opening the computer cabinet, use compressed air to remove a dust mask. Never touch the inside of your computer unless it is necessary.
6. **Begin dusting:** Use compressed air to blow out the dust inside the machine. In this manner you can sweep out all the dust that settles on lower components. Keep your air source a moderate distance from the component you are working on.
   - Make sure to hold your can of compressed air upright. If inverted, it can let out liquid which can cause severe damage to your computer.
   - Compressed air is freezing cold when it leaves. Don't let frost to form on your chips.
   - A lot of dust can be raised; try not to breathe it. If the PC is very dusty, take it out of doors before using the compressed air.
7. **Clean the CPU cooling fan and heatsink:** The heatsink/fan area accumulates dust easily because the fan moves a lot of dust-laden air through the closely spaced heatsink fans. As dust accumulates, it covers the blades of the heatsink, insulating them and thereby reducing their ability to radiate the heat produced by the processor. The CPU cooling fan spins faster (and makes more noise) as it tries to draw enough air through the heatsink to cool the processor. Eventually, the air channels in the heatsink become completely clogged and the heatsink loses its ability to cool the processor.

   To avoid such problems, it is important to keep the CPU cooler clean. To begin cleaning the CPU cooler, use a brush or vacuum cleaner to remove the muck from the top of the cooling fan.
8. **Look inside and outside the CPU for any dust you may have missed.**

Figure 1.71 Clean the CPU cooling fan and heatsink

9. **Clean up your work space:** Depending on your workspace, you may need to get a small vacuum and clean the area around the computer.
10. **Close your computer:** Once the machine is tightly shut reattach the power cord and other cables. A clean computer will run significantly cooler and last much longer.

EXERCISE

1. What is a computer? What are the advantages and disadvantages of a computer?
2. What are the main components of a PC system? Explain each component.
3. What is the role of input and output devices in a computer system?
4. What is scanner? Explain different types of scanners.
5. Name some of the input and output devices used with computers.
6. What are the five basic operations performed by any computer system? Explain each one of them.
7. How many types of memory does a computer have? Justify the need for each type.
8. Write short note on super computer.
9. What are advantages of Mainframe computers?

REVIEW QUESTIONS WITH ANSWERS

1. Multiple Choice

1.1 Which one of the following is not an input device?
a. Microphone b. Mouse
c. Scanner d. Plotter

Ans (d)

1.2 Information retrieval is fastest from
a. Floppy disk b. Magnetic tape
c. Hard disk d. CD-ROM

Ans (c)

1.3 In a video camera, CCD stands for
a. Charge Coupled Device b. Carbon Crystal Digitizer
c. Colour Coding Data d. None of the above

Ans (a)

1.4 During data processing, the actual execution of the instructions takes place in the
a. Output unit b. Control unit
c. Hard disk d. Arithmetic logic unit

Ans (d)

1.5 The term LPT is related to
a. Serial port b. Centronics port
c. Parallel port d. None of the above

Ans (c)

1.6 Indicate which, of the following best describes the term 'software'
a. Operating system programs
b. Application programs
c. Both (a) and (b)
d. None of the above

Ans (c)

1.7 The input device that is most appropriate for playing games on a playstation is
a. Joystick c. Keyboard
b. Touch Panel d. Track Ball

Ans (a)

2. State whether the following statements are True or False

2.1 A scanner's resolution is measured in megapixels.
Ans False

2.2 A parallel port allows the transfer of all the bits of a word simultaneously.
Ans True

2.3 SCSI cards are used to attach devices such as scanners and external disk drives to your PC.
Ans True

2.4 Plug and Play is a combination of hardware and software feature.
Ans True

2.5 PnP feature enables the system to automatically search for new hardware connected to the system.
Ans True

2.6 Scanner copies or reproduces text as well as image using special software.
Ans True

2.7 Computers cannot help in decision-making processes.
Ans False

2.8 ALU is a part of CPU.
Ans True

2.9 A floppy disk containing program in it, is not a magnetic storage device.

Ans False

2.10 The main advantage of computer graphics is that it substantially increases productivity.

Ans True

2.11 Computers cannot help in decision-making processes.

Ans False

2.12 Hybrid computer is a mixture of both digital and analog computers.

Ans True

2.13 VDUs can be used both as input and output devices.

Ans False

2.14 OCR is a device that scans written or typed text and transforms it into computer readable form.

Ans True

2.15 Access to data stored on magnetic tape is random.

Ans False

2.16 Computer software is normally classified as system software and application software.

Ans True

2.17 All modern computer use the Binary number System.

Ans True

2.18 Peripheral is an external device connected to the computer, such as input and output devices and external storage devices.

Ans True

2.19 A speech synthesizer converts text information into spoken sentences.

Ans True

3. Match the following:

3.1	Graphics that allow each pixel to be shown on a computer as black, white or a shade of gray	a.	Plug and Play
3.2	PnP	b.	Gray-Scale
3.3	Flatbed	c.	Charge Coupled Device
3.4	Handheld	d.	Scanner
3.5	CCD	e.	Portable
3.6	Analog computers	f.	Storage unit
3.7	Parallel port	g.	Pressure, temperature measures analogus
3.8	Serial port	h.	Printer
3.9	Holds data to be processed and instructions to be executed	i.	Mouse
3.10	CPU	j.	Brain of computer

Ans 3.1 b 3.2 a 3.3 d 3.4 e 3.5 c
3.6 g 3.7 h 3.8 i 3.9 f 3.10 j

4. Fill in the blanks

4.1 Final results of processing, before releasing, to output unit are held in __________ unit.

Ans Memory

4.2 A printer is an __________ device.

Ans Output

4.3 A control unit acts as __________ for all components of a computer.

Ans central nervous system

4.4 The __________ feature is available on newer PC systems and enables the system to automatically search for new hardware connected to the PC.

Ans PnP

4.5 USB stands for __________.

Ans Universal Serial Bus

4.6 __________ is the measuring of unique attributes of a human such as DNA machine finger prints etc.

Ans biometric sensors

4.7 A __________ contains a small processor that holds certain information.

Ans Smart card

4.8 Mouse is a __________ input device.

Ans Pointing

4.9 __________ is an important component of multimedia.

Ans Animation

4.10 __________ is most commonly used to output graphics in hard copy form.

Ans Laser printer

Q.5 (a) Explain the use of the following hardware components in multimedia.

(i) Scanner

(ii) Motherboard

Ans 5(a)(i)

A scanner is a hardware device used to scan text or images into the computer. Sometimes, the information, picture or text that is available on paper is needed on the computer disk. For that we use scanner to convert a document into a digital format. Scanners are basically desktop analog-to-digital converter. They take analog visual things, documents, magazine papers, photos, business cards, etc and turn them into digitized bitmaps that a specialize software package can understand and translate into PC readable file.

Besides text scanning, scanners can also be used in image processing to capture pictures for printed publications, Internet web sites, and electronic presentations. A scanner can digitize a picture by converting dark and light areas of a graphic to dots, or pixels. A file is then saved in computer format for future use.

Ans 5(a)(ii)

Motherboard is the Printed Circuit Board (PCB) which is assembled in computers to hold CPU and memory. Other components, such as sound and video card, hard drives, network drives, Universal Serial Bus (USB) or FireWire slots, etc., are applied to it for better and fast data processing.

Q.6 What is microprocessor?

Ans 6

Microprocessor is a multipurpose and programmable device which accepts data and information as input, processes them according to given instructions, and displays results as output. It operates on numbers and symbols which are arranged in the binary form. Arithmetic Logic Unit (ALU) and control logic are the two prime components of a microprocessor. The function of ALU is to perform arithmetic operations, such as addition, subtraction, and logical (AND, OR, NOT) operations. The function of control unit is to generate control signals which controls the flow of data between the processor, and memory and peripherals

Q.7 Write a short note on IDE port and Power Port.

Ans 7

Integrated Device Electronics (IDE) port is used to connect a hard disk, CDROM drive, CD writer or DVD drive to a motherboard. There are two such ports in a motherboard. These are primary and secondary. Two devices can be connected to each port.

The electrical supply for the working of the computer can be provided through the power port. Power port is located at SMPS (Switched Mode Power Supply), the power monitoring unit of the system of a computer. Each port of a computer requires electric current in different quantities. The power unit of the computer namely the SMPS converts the current obtained from a line into small units required for each of the component like motherboard, hard disk, floppy disk, CD drive, etc., For heat radiation a small fan is also attached in an SMPS.

Q.8 Differentiate between serial and parallel ports.

Ans 8

Serial and parallel ports are two different types of connecting devices. They can be used to connect all types of peripherals like *modem*, *mouse*, and *printer*. The major difference between serial and parallel ports is that serial ports transfer data one bit at a time, while parallel ports can transfer data 8 bits or more at a time. Serial ports have to take apart the 8 bits in a byte, and transfer them one by one. On the other hand, the newer parallel ports line up the 8 bits and can transfer them all at once.

Because serial ports can only transfer data one bit at a time, they are much slower than the parallel ports. However, serial ports require fewer wires. This is because parallel ports need eight wires to be able to transfer all eight bits at one time. Also, serial ports are much cheaper than parallel ports.

Q.9 Explain the working of a scanner.

Ans 9

Scanner takes the basic approach to capturing visual information. A light source is aligned horizontally across the face of the scanner and is used to illuminate the target document. Reflected light passes through a lens, where it is detected by a row of Charge Coupled Device (CCDs). The CCDs convert the reflected light into electrical impulses that vary in voltage according to the intensity of the reflected light. There is one CCD per pixel of resolution, so a 600 dpi scanner would have 600 CCDs array across the scanner's sensor head. Finally one or more analog-to-digital converters turn the analog electrical signals into 1's and 0's that a PC can understand.

Q.10 Define computer architecture.

Ans 10

Computer architecture is defined as the functional operation of the individual hardware unit in a computer system and the flow of information among the control of units.

Q.11 Write short note on USB port.

Ans 11

Universal Serial Bus port are included on most computers sold today. USB makes it easier to connect peripherals to computers and eliminates the need to configure interrupt request (IRQ) settings or dual inline package (DIP) switches. USB can be used to connect various peripherals includes keyboard, mouse, joysticks, scanners, printers, monitors, modems and digital camera. USB is very fast and becoming a popular replacement for serial and parallel ports. This is because USB is highly advanced, fast, and simple to use. USB devices are pluggable, i.e you can add devices to your computer easily without having to shut down the computer. External devices can be connected any time, even when the computer is running.

Q.12 What is the difference between web camera and video camera?

Ans 12

A *web camera* allows a computer to accept input just by focussing on an object. The camera is focussed on the input object to take a picture of the object. Picture so taken can be transferred over network to a distant place.
A *video camera* is a camera that takes continuous pictures and generates a signal for display on a monitor or for permanent recording. Signals generated by video cameras are traditionally analog, but nowadays digital video cameras are available.

Q.13 Differentiate between firmware and liveware.

Ans 13
Firmware are the programmes stored in read-only memory (ROM) chip. Unlike Random Access Memory (RAM), read-only memory programs stay intact even in the absence of electrical power. Startup (bootstrap programmes) and low-level Input/Output instructions are stored in the firmware.
Liveware is the human being employed to handle hardware and software. The programmers, engineers, operators who use the resources of computer system are known as liveware.
Q.14 Write the uses of Mini Computer.

Ans 14
- A minicomputer is a small to medium-scale computer used widely for data processing and in industrial applications.
- Minicomputers are used for payroll preparation, accounting and scientific computation. Minicomputers are also used in universities, industries and research centres.

CHAPTER 2

Primary Memory

2.1 MEMORY AND STORAGE

All computers require storage space and memory to run programs and store files. There are different types of memory and storage, and each has its own purpose.

2.1.1 Memory Organization

The *memory* is an essential part of a computer system. It is required by the computer system to store instructions and data. In the most general sense, secondary memory refers to external systems, such as disk drives or tape drives. But actually, main memory refers only to the fast semiconductor storage (RAM) directly connected to the CPU. Memory can be divided into the following two types:

(a) *Primary Memory:* These are the memory chips which are directly connected to CPU or they are parts of CPU in PCs.
(b) *Secondary Memory:* These are the memory units which are external to CPU.

☞ *Memory is an electronic circuitry that allows data to be stored and retrieved in 0 and 1 form. The secondary memory stores data and keep it even when the electricity to the PC goes off whereas the primary memory looses its contents on switching off power supply.*

Primary memory and Its Properties

Primary memory is one of the most important parts of the computer, as it determines the size and the number of programs that can be simultaneously held within the computer as well as the amount of data that can be processed quickly. Primary memory stores the necessary programs of system software, which are required to execute user programs. The main memory is directly addressed by the CPU. Primary memory is volatile in nature. It is costly than a secondary memory or storage. Different properties of primary memory are discussed below:

1. **Storage capacity** : It is the amount of data that can be stored in the storage unit. Primary storage units have less storage capacity as compared to secondary storage.
2. **Access time:** Access time is required to locate and retrieve stored data from the storage unit in response to a program instruction. Primary storage units have faster access time as compared to secondary storage units.
3. **Cost per bit of storage:** This refers to the cost of a storage unit for a given storage capacity. As compared to secondary storage units, primary storage units have higher cost per bit of storage.
4. **Volatile:** If the data stored are lost when the power is turned off or interrupted, it is called volatile storage. The Primary storage units are volatile and the secondary storage units are non-volatile.
5. **Random Access:** If the time taken to access a piece of data from the storage unit is independent of the location of data in the storage unit, it is called a random access storage or random access memory (RAM). Each separate location of a RAM is as easy to access any other location, and it takes the same amount of time.

2.1.2 Memory Hierarchy

The total memory of a computer system is organised as the hierarchy of memories. Table 2.1 gives the summary of the different levels of memories.

Table 2.1 Memory hierarchy

Memory	Size	Access Time [Nano (10^{-9}) sec]	Managed by	Backed by
Cache Memory	Less than or equal to 4MB	3-10	Hardware	Main Memory
Main Memory	Greater than or equal to 1GB	80-400	Operating System	Disk
Disk Storage	Greater than 1GB	5,000,000	Operating System /User	Magnetic Tape

Figure 2.1 show a block diagram of hierarchy of memory organization in a computer. In this Figure, observe that there is *Main Memory* that communicates directly with the CPU. There is *Auxiliary Memory* or *Secondary Memory* which indirectly communicates with the main memory through Input/Output processor. Also note that *Cache Memory* is present in between the CPU and main memory.

Now you may ask, what is the need of such a hierarchy of memories, when the same purpose can be met with a single large sized memory system. Economics and performance are the basis for such an hierarchy for memory organization. Secondary memory devices namely, zip disks, floppy disks, hard disks, as well as CD-ROMs (Compact Disk Read Only Memory) are the cheapest and have large storage capacity, but they are slow in accessing or storing data.

☞ *Access time is the average time required to locate and fetch an instruction or data from the memory.*

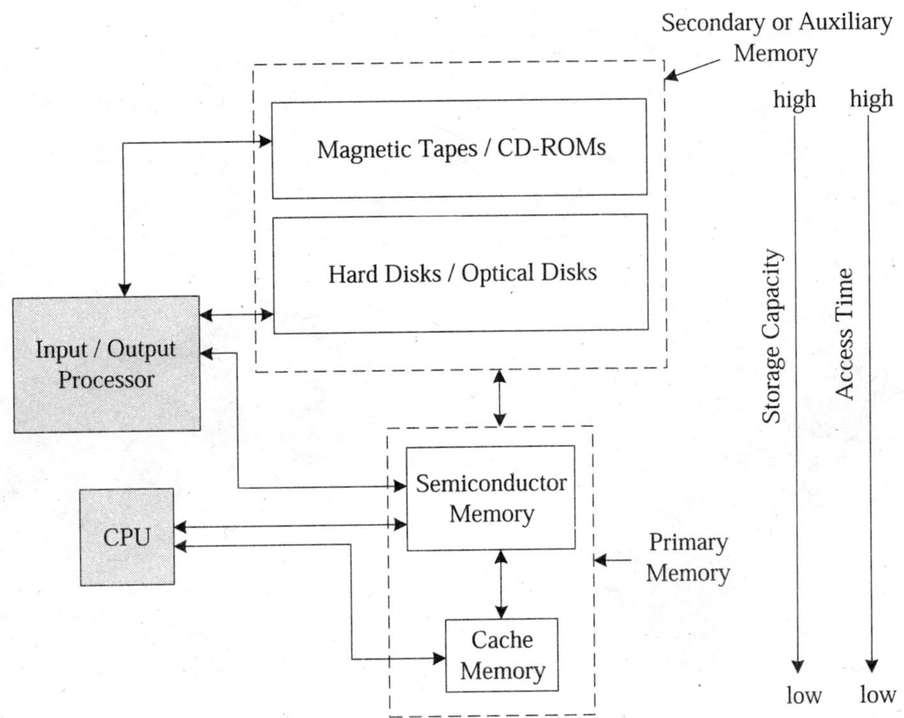

Figure 2.1 Hierarchy of memory organisation

Comparison of Different Types of Memories

Main memory has less storage capacity and are made up of *electronic integrated circuits*. These are more expensive as compared to auxiliary memory but are much faster. That is, the access time required to fetch data or instruction is in the range of nano (10^{-9}) second.

The cache memory is the most expensive, smallest and fastest memory with least access time. It holds only those program parts and data which is currently and frequently used by the processor. This enhances CPU's performance. The cache memory is expensive because it has complicated circuits associated with it for faster access. You would have observed in Figure 2.1 that access time is directly proportional to the storage capacity of a memory. Therefore, you cannot expect to get a faster performance by installing a large sized main memory. The access time of large sized memories is very large. Hence, such a step would decrease the speed instead of increasing it.

Why Hierarchical Memory System?

Had we used a single large sized memory system, the CPU would have taken considerable amount of time to locate an instruction or data. That is, the access time would have been too large. However, using an hierarchical memory system, the currently used program and data can be loaded into the main memory and thus processed very fast. The programs which are not manipulated currently, can be kept in the slow auxiliary memory. As and when these are needed, they can be loaded into the main memory. The cache memory holds even more frequently used programs, such as subroutines and data. Thus, it will further enhance processing speed of the CPU.

2.2 MAIN MEMORY OR PRIMARY MEMORY

Primary Memory, also known as *Main Memory*, is one of the important parts of the computer, because memory's size determines the length and number of programs that can be stored at a time. Its size also indicates the amount of data that can be processed quickly.

Primary memory is a fast RAM made up of ICs (Integrated Circuits) called *cells*. The main memory is directly addressed by the CPU.

☞ *Main Memory is a small and relatively fast storage unit that stores data and instructions which are being currently used by the CPU.*

Main memory is divided into the following two types.

(a) RAM (Random Access Memory)

(b) ROM (Read Only Memory)

2.2.1 RAM (Read/Write)

RAM stands for Random Access Memory and it is a read/write memory. Information can be written to as well read from RAM (See Figure 2.2). The storage locations can be accessed in any order, i.e., Random Access is possible. Term *Random Access Memory* is not appropriate since ROM is also a random access device. Hence we can better call it a *read/write* memory.

Table 2.2 Types of RAM

Static RAM/SRAM	Dynamic RAM/DRAM	Enhanced version of RAM
Requires constant power flow to hold information	It stores its information in cell called capacitor and transistor	EDORAM Extended data output random access memory.
Expensive and faster	Less expensive and slower	SDRAM: Synchronous dynamic random access memory.
More power is required	Less power is required	DDR SDRAM: Double data rate synchronous dynamic random access memory.

Figure 2.2 RAM chip

RAM is a volatile memory. It retains the data as long as it is supplied with power. When power supply is switched off or interrupted, the stored data in the RAM is lost. RAMs of various capacities are available, for example, 256 MB, 512 MB, 4 GB, 8 GB and so on. Types of RAM is shown in Table 2.2.

Static and Dynamic RAM

There are two important types of RAMs: static RAM and dynamic RAM. Static RAMs can retain stored information as long as the power supply is on. But a dynamic RAM loses its stored information in a very short time (a few milliseconds) even though the power supply is on. Therefore, dynamic RAMs have to be refreshed periodically, generally every 2 milliseconds. Dynamic RAMs are cheaper and have high packing densities but moderate speed. They consume less power. They are used where a large capacity of memory is needed. Static RAMs are costlier and consume more power. They do not need refreshing circuitry. They have higher speed or shorter access time as compared to dynamic RAMs. Static RAM and dynamic RAM are also written as SRAM and DRAM, respectively. (See Figure 2.3 and Figure 2.4)

Figure 2.3 SRAM chip

☞ *Robert H. Dennard invented DRAM in 1968.*

Figure 2.4 DRAM chip

SDRAM (Synchronous Dynamic RAM)

DRAM (synchronous DRAM) is a generic name for various types of Dynamic Random Access Memory (DRAM) that are synchronized with the clock speed that the microprocessor is operating. This tends to increase the number of instructions that the processor can perform in a given time. The speed of SDRAM is rated in MHz rather than in nanoseconds (ns). This makes it easier to compare the bus speed and the RAM chip speed. Since SDRAM was introduced, it has been developed to make it faster and more effective. As a result there are a number of different types of SDRAM that are available.

- **SDR SDRAM (Single Data Rate SDRAM)**: This is the basic type of SDRAM that was first introduced. It is referred to as single data rate SDRAM, or just SDRAM. SDRAM can stand for SDR SDRAM, where the I/O, internal clock and bus clock are the same. For example, the I/O, internal clock and bus clock of PC133 are all 133 Mhz. Single Data Rate means that SDR SDRAM can only read/write one time in a clock cycle. SDRAM have to wait for the completion of the previous command to be able to do another read/write operation.
- **DDR SDRAM (Double Data Rate SDRAM)**: The next generation of SDRAM is DDR, which achieves greater bandwidth than the preceding single data rate SDRAM by transferring data on the rising and falling edges of the clock signal (double pumped). This type of SDRAM provides data transfer at twice the speed of the traditional type of SDRAM memory. This is achieved by transferring data twice per cycle.
- **DDR2 SDRAM (Double Data Rate Two SDRAM)**: DDR2 SDRAM can operate the external bus twice as fast as its predecessor and it was first introduced in 2003. Its primary benefit is the ability to operate the external data

bus twice as fast as DDR SDRAM. This is achieved by improved bus signal. The prefetch buffer of DDR2 is 4 bit(double of DDR SDRAM).

- **DDR3 SDRAM (Double Data Rate Three SDRAM)**: DDR3 SDRAM is a further development of the double data rate type of SDRAM. It provides further improvements in overall performance and speed. As a result its use is becoming more widespread. DDR3 memory reduces 40% power consumption compared to current DDR2 modules, allowing for lower operating currents and voltages. DDR3 also adds two functions, such as ASR (Automatic Self-Refresh) and SRT (Self-Refresh Temperature). They can make the memory control the refresh rate according to the temperature variation.
- **DDR4 SDRAM (Double Data Rate Fourth SDRAM)**: This is a further type of SDRAM being developed and anticipated. DDR4 SDRAM provides the lower operating voltage (1.2V) and higher transfer rate. DDR4 can process 4 data within a clock cycle, so DDR4's efficiency is better than DDR3. DDR4 also adds some functions, such as DBI (Data Bus Inversion), CRC (Cyclic Redundancy Check) and CA parity. They can enhance DDR4 memory's signal integrity, and improve the stability of data transmission/access.

  The various types of SDRAM are now widely used and have taken over from some other types of memory.

☞ *SDRAM, or Synchronous Dynamic Random Access Memory is a form of semiconductor memory can run at faster speeds than conventional DRAM and is therefore the use of SDRAM is becoming more widespread.*

RDRAM (Rambus Dynamic Random Access Memory)

RDRAM (Rambus Dynamic Random Access Memory) is a memory subsystem that can transfer up to 1.6 billion bytes per second. The subsystem consists of the RAM, the RAM con troller, and the bus (path) connecting RAM to the microprocessor and devices in the computer that use it. Direct Rambus (DRDRAM), a technology developed and licensed by the Rambus Corporation, is the latest version and is expected to help accelerate the growth of visually intensive interfaces, such as 3-D, interactive games, and streaming multimedia.

Rambus is intended to replace the current main memory technology of Dynamic Random Access Memory (DRAM). Much faster data transfer rates from attached devices, such as video games using FireWire and the Accelerated Graphics Port (AGP) make it important to reduce the bottleneck in getting data into the computer. Direct Rambus (DRDRAM) provides a two-byte (16 bits) bus rather than DRAM's 8-bit bus. At a RAM speed of 800 MHz (800 million cycles per second), the peak data transfer rate is 1.6 billion bytes per second. Direct Rambus uses pipelining to move data from RAM to cache memory levels that are closer to the microprocessor or display unit. Up to eight operations may be underway at the same time. Rambus is expected to fit into existing motherboard standards. The components that are inserted into motherboard connections are called Rambus In-line Memory Modules (RIMMs). Such components can replace conventional dual in-line memory module.

DDR RAM

Double-Data-Rate Synchronous Dynamic Random Access Memory, also known as DDR SDRAM or DDR RAM for short, is a type of very fast computer memory. DDR RAM is based on the same architecture as SDRAM, but utilizes the clock signal differently to transfer twice the data in the same amount of time. In a computer system, the clock signal is an oscillating frequency used to coordinate interaction between digital circuits. Digital circuits designed to operate on the clock signal may respond at the rising or falling edge of the signal. SDRAM memory chips utilize only the rising edge of the signal to transfer data, while DDR RAM transfers data on both the rising and falling edges of the clock signal. Therefore, it attains the higher speed.

☞ *A DDR RAM is essentially twice as fast as SDRAM.*

EDO RAM

EDO (Extended Data Output) RAM is a type of RAM chip that improves the time to read from memory on faster microprocessors, such as the Intel Pentium. EDO RAM was initially optimized for the 66 MHz Pentium. For faster computers, different types of SDRAM are recommended.

SIMM (Single In-Line Memory Module)

SIMM is a type of memory module used for random access memory in personal computers. It differs from a DIMM (the most predominant form of memory module today) in that the contacts on a SIMM are redundant on both sides of the module. In SIMMs, a slender circuit board is dedicated to store memory chips. Each chip is capable of holding 8 to 9 chips per board, the ninth chip usually an error checking chip. The typical bus from the chip to the motherboard is 32-bits wide.

☞ *One should be very careful about the orientation of the SIMM when inserting them into the socket. Many sockets have key tab to prevent the module from inserting in reverse.*

DIMM (Double In-Line Memory Module)

DIMM includes a series of random access memory integrated circuits. These modules are mounted on a printed circuit board and designed for use in personal computers. DIMMs began to replace SIMMs as the predominant type of memory module as Intel's Pentium processors began to control the market.

Table 2.3 Types of ROM

Static RAM/SRAM	Dynamic RAM/DRAM	Enhanced version of RAM
Programmable read only memory	Erasable programmable read only memory	Electrically erasable programmable read only memory
Information cannot be altered once written	Information can be changed by exposing to ultraviolet light	Information can be erased and reprogrammed by using electric charge.

2.2.2 ROM (Read Only Memory)

ROM is a permanent type memory. Its contents are not lost when power supply is switched off (See Figure 2.5). The user cannot write into a ROM. Its contents are written into at manufacturing time. ROMs store permanent programs and other types of data which are needed by the computer to execute user programs. ROMs store functions, such as sine, cosine, logarithm, square root, exponential and code conversion tables, etc. An example of a ROM is Toshiba Mask ROM, TCS 534000, 512 K × 8 bits. Types of ROM is shown in Table 2.3.

Figure 2.5 ROM chip

☞ *ROM is a semiconductor-based memory that contains instructions or data which can be read but not modified. To create a ROM chip, the designer supplies a semiconductor manufacturer with the instructions or data to be stored.*

ROMs are further classified as:

(a) PROMs (Programmable ROMs)
(b) EPROM (Erasable PROM)
(c) EEPROM (Electrically Erasable PROM)

PROMs (Programmable Read Only Memories)

Figure 2.6 PROM chip

The contents of PROMs are decided by the user. User can store permanent programs, data or other information in a PROM. The instrument known as *PROM programmer* is an electronic equipment used for programming the ROM. The PROMs are programmable once only, i.e., user cannot write information again and again in them. IC745287 is a type of PROM available commercially. (See Figure 2.6)

EPROM (Erasable PROM)

An EPROM is an erasable PROM. The stored data in EPROMs can be erased by exposing them to high intensity short wave ultraviolet light for about 12 minutes. When an EPROM is exposed to ultraviolet light the entire data is erased. EPROMs are cheap, reliable, and hence they are widely used. EPROMs are used to store programs which are permanent but need updating. The permanent programs which are at the research and development stage also need to be stored in EPROMs because they are modified several times. Where updating or changes in programs at the development stages are required, EPROMs are far more economical than PROMs because they can be reused. An example of EPROMs is Intel's 87C257. (See Figure 2.7).

Figure 2.7 EPROM chip

EEPROM (E^2PROM)

This is an electrically erasable PROM. The chip can be erased and reprogrammed on the PC's motherboard on a byte-to-byte basis. It requires much shorter time, a few seconds as compared to 10-20 minutes for EPROM. Intel 2816A is a 16K (2K x 8) EEPROM available commercially.

☞ *E^2PROM requires 21 Volts pulses for writing or erasing and 5V for read operation.*

EEPROM Programming Suppose we want to store the following data at the addresses given in Table 2.4.

Table 2.4 Storing of Data in Memory Addresses

Address	Data (nibble)
0	0111
1	1000
2	1011
3	1100
4	0110
5	1001
6	0011
7	1110

For achieving this we can use diodes and connect them as shown in Figure 2.8.

As we know, diode is an electronic device that allows the passage of current in one direction. The conduction takes place when voltage is 1 and does not take place when voltage is at a level 0 at the anode. This fact is used in Diode ROMs.

If we connect diodes as shown in Figure 2.8, then we shall be able to achieve the truth table for data in the memory addresses shown in Table 2.4.

When the electric switch S is in position zero, (or address 0), the first row of diodes is switched on. So, the output at Y_3, Y_2, Y_1, Y_0 is available. The values are 3 because the diodes Y_2 and Y_1 have the value 1 and so it conducts and the diodes Y_3 and Y_0 have value 0 and hence do not conduct. Thus, the sum values of $Y_3Y_2Y_1Y_0 = 0110 = 3$ in decimal.

When the switch S is moved to position 3, the third row of diodes is activated and the output at Y_3, Y_2, Y_1, Y_0 is given as 1011, respectively. Hence, such a diode connection will implement the truth table for addresses of memory location 0,1,2,3,4,...7.

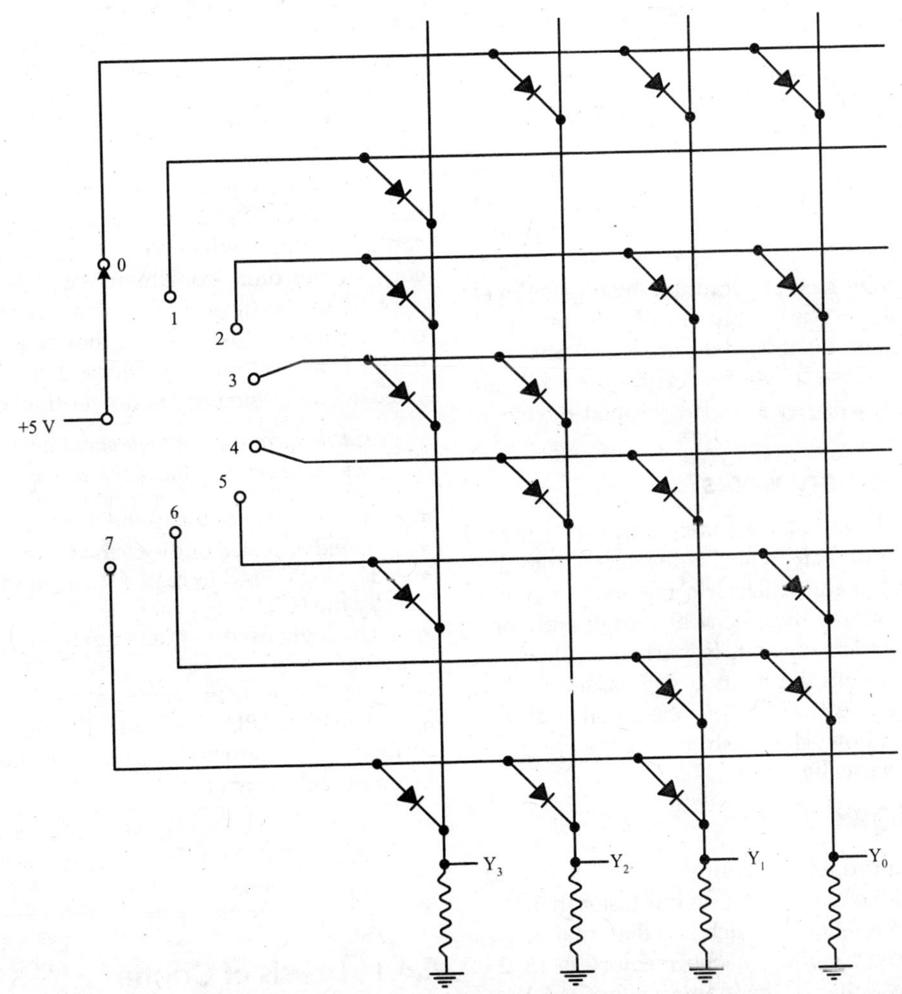

Figure 2.8 Connection of Diodes as ROM for attaining Table 2.4

Volatility of Memory

Volatility of memory refers to the retention of information when power to a computer is switched off. Volatile memory is memory whose contents are lost when power is switched off. A computer's main memory, made up of dynamic RAM or static RAM chips, loses its contents immediately upon interruption of power. RAM is volatile but magnetic core memory containing magnetic elements is not volatile. Magnetic core memory was used in second generation computers.

2.3 FLASH MEMORY

Flash memory is a type of nonvolatile memory that erases data in units called blocks. A block stored on a flash memory chip must be erased before data can be written, or programmed, to the microchip. The term "flash" was chosen because a large chunk of memory could be erased at one time. The name, therefore, distinguishes flash devices from EEPROMs, where each byte is erased individually.

☞ *Dr. Fujio Masuoka invented Flash memory.*

Flash memory evolved from erasable programmable read-only memory (EPROM) and electrically erasable programmable read-only memory (EEPROM). Flash is technically a variant of EEPROM, but the industry reserves the term EEPROM for byte-level erasable memory and applies the term flash memory to larger block-level erasable memory. Devices using flash memory erase data at the block level and rewrite data at the byte level (NOR flash) or multiple-byte page level (NAND flash). Flash memory is widely used for storage and data transfer in consumer devices, enterprise systems and industrial applications. Flash memory retains data for an extended period of time whether a flash-equipped device is powered on or off.

2.3.1 How flash memory works?

A basic flash memory cell consists of a storage transistor with a control gate and a floating gate, which is insulated from the rest of the transistor by a thin dielectric material or oxide layer. The floating gate stores the electrical charge and controls the flow of the electrical current. In particular, the gate oxide between the silicon and the floating gate is thinner for flash technology. Source and drain diffusions are also different. These differences allow the flash device to be programmed and erased electrically.

2.4 CACHE MEMORY

Cache memory (pronounced as the "cash memory") is placed in between the CPU and the main memory. It is faster than the main memory. Hence access time is much less than that of the main memory. The access time of a cache memory is 15-25 nanoseconds (ns) whereas that of the main memory is 80 ns. One nanosecond = 10^{-9} second. The cache memory stores instructions and data which are to be immediately executed. It is used to reduce the average access time for address, instructions or data which are normally stored in the main memory. Thus, it increases the operating speed of the system. Cache memory is much costlier than the main memory. From economical considerations, the size of cache memory is usually smaller than that of the main memory. Sometimes cache is used to store only instructions. One such type of cache is used in 68020 processor. It has 256-byte instruction cache, which allows it to pre-fetch instructions from the main memory and store them in the cache during the period when the system bus would otherwise be idle. The microprocessor 68030 has both 256-byte instruction cache and 256-bit data cache.

The high-speed memory used for the Cache purpose is very costly, the reason why is not used as the main memory. The information frequently required by the processor is kept in the cache memory by the Cache controller. This Cache controller ensures that the data required by the processor in the next memory access is available in the cache memory. This improves the speed of the computer very much because if the required data is in the cache memory it is made available to the CPU without any wait state. When the required data is available in the cache it is called a hit. In case of a cache hit the processor immediately reads or writes the data in the data cache line. The proportion of accesses that result in a cache hit is known as the hit rate, and is a measure of the effectiveness of the cache.

When the required data is not available in the cache memory it is called a miss. In case of a miss, most caches allocate new entry, which comprises the tag just missed and a copy of the data from memory. The reference can then be applied to the new entry just as in case of a hit. Misses are comparatively slow because they require the data to be transferred from the main memory. This transfer incurs a delay, since the main memory is slower than cache memory.

☞ *Cache memory is a high-speed memory built-in the processor and used between the main memory and the processor.*

The performance of the cache depends on the following:

- Speed and size of the cache memory.
- The logic used to read data around the memory area read by the CPU.
- The logic used to guess next required data by the processor.

Most of the new microprocessors have cache memory added in the CPU chip itself to speed up the process even further. Even on these CPUs with built-in cache, you can add external cache memory.

☞ *A multi-ported cache, allows the working of superscalar processors through different cache, can work with more than one request at a time.*

2.4.1 Levels of Cache

In standard PCs, we find processors with Level 1 (L1) and Level 2 (L2) cache. Some processors like the Intel Itanium have three levels of built-in cache, but these are used only for very special server applications.

Table 2.5 L2 cache

CPU Type	L2 cache
Pentium, K5, K6	External, on the motherboard
Pentium Pro	Internal, in the CPU
Pentium II, Athlon	External, in a module close to the CPU
Celeron (Ist generation)	None
Celeron (later gen.), Pentium III, Athlon XP, Duron, Pentium 4	Internal, in the CPU

Level 1 (L1) Cache

Level 1 cache is built into the actual processor core. It is a piece of RAM, typically 64 or 128 KB size, which operates at the same clock frequency as the rest of the CPU. Thus, we could say the L1 cache is part of the processor.

☞ *The L1 cache is also known as internal cache or primary cache, because it is a part of same chip as the microprocessor.*

L1 cache is normally divided into two sections, one for data and another for instructions. For example, an Athlon processor may have a 32 KB data cache and a 32 KB instruction cache. If the cache is common for both data and instructions, it is called a unified cache.

☞ *The main limitation of the L1 cache is its size, as this cache is designed as the internal part of the processor.*

Level 2 (L2) Cache

The Level 2 cache is normally much larger (and unified), such as 256, 512 or 1024 KB. The purpose of an L2 cache is to constantly read in slightly larger quantities of data from the RAM, so that these are available to the L1 cache.

Traditionally, the L2 cache is connected to the front side bus (See Figure 2.9).

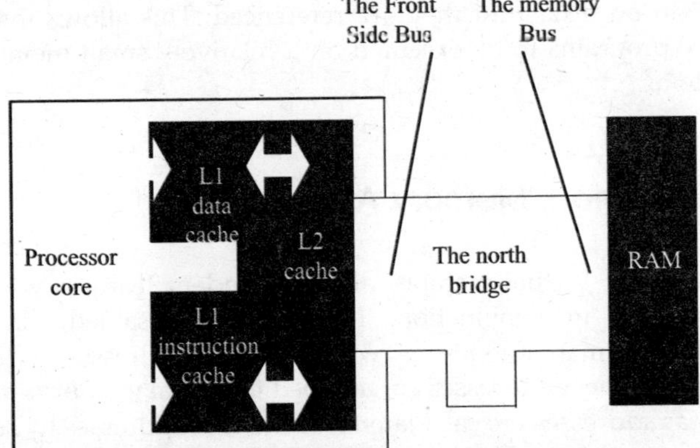

Figure 2.9 Levels of Cache and the North Bridge

How Cache memory is different from Primary memory?

Cache memory is different from main memory in the following ways:

(a) Cache memory is much faster than the main memory.
(b) Access time is much less than that of the main memory. The access time of a cache memory is 15–25 nanoseconds (ns) whereas that of the main memory is 80 ns.
(c) The cache memory stores instructions and data which are to be immediately executed. It is used to reduce the average access time for address, instructions or data which are normally stored in the main memory. Thus, the cache memory increases the operating speed of the system.
(d) Cache memory is much costlier than the main memory. From economical considerations the size of cache memory is usually smaller than that of main memory. The high-speed memory used for the Cache purpose is very costly that is the reason it is not used as the main memory of the computer.

2.5 INSTALLING MEMORY MODULE

Most motherboard today come with between 2 and 8 sockets for the insertion of RAM memory. These are usually either SIMMs (Single Inline Memory Modules) or DIMMs (Dual Inline Memory Modules). These sockets can be of different sizes.

The motherboard usually labels these sockets "SIMM0" through "SIMM7" or "DIMM1" through "DIMM3", etc. The sockets are almost always filled starting with the lowest numbered socket first. Most Pentium class or higher motherboards require SIMMs to be inserted in pairs, but DIMMs may be inserted individually.

- Make sure that you are working in a static-safe environment. Remove any plastic bags or papers from your work space.
- Shut down your system and make sure the power is completely off before unplugging the power cable from your computer.
- Discharge residual power by pressing the power button.
- Remove your computer's cover.
- To protect your new memory modules and your system's components from static damage during the installation process, touch any of the unpainted metal surfaces on your computer's frame before handling and installing memory.
- Locate your computer's memory expansion slots. Most main boards will have two or three black banks for the memory slots. Do not use any tools in the removal or installation of memory modules.

Table 2.6 Comparison Logical Address and Physical Address

Basic	It is the virtual address generated by CPU.	The physical address is a location in a memory unit.
Address Space	Set of all logical addresses generated by CPU in reference to a program is referred as Logical Address Space.	Set of all physical addresses mapped to the corresponding logical addresses is referred as Physical Address.
Visibility	The user can view the logical address of a program.	The user can not directly access physical address.
Access	The user uses the logical address to access the physical address.	The user can not directly access physical address.
Generation	The Logical Address is generated by the CPU.	Physical Address is Computed by Memory-Management Unit (MMU).

- Check the notches of the RAM module. Insert your new memory module(s). Make sure the memory module is correctly oriented. Align the notch(es) on the module with the notch(es) in the slot, and then press the module down until the clips on the slot snap into place.
- Once the module(s) have been installed, replace the cover on your computer and reconnect the power cord or battery. Installation is now complete.

☞ *If your system does not boot and you receive an error message or hear a series of beeps, your system may not be recognizing the new memory. Remove and reinstall the modules to ensure they are securely fixed in the sockets.*

2.6 MEMORY ADDRESSES

A memory address is an exact assigned location in RAM used to track where information is stored. On a single computer memory IC, there can be 1 million, 2 million, or more memory addresses that can be accessed randomly. A number that is assigned to each byte in a computer's memory that the CPU uses to track where data and instructions are stored in RAM. Each byte is assigned a memory address whether or not it is being used to store data. The computer's CPU uses the address bus to communicate which memory address it wants to access, and the memory controller reads the address and then puts the data stored in that memory address back onto the address bus for the CPU to use. Memory addressing is done for different purposes as per the categories listed below:

2.6.1 Logical Memory Address

Address generated by CPU while a program is running is referred as Logical Address. The logical address is a virtual address and can be viewed by the user. The user can't view the physical address directly. This address is used as a reference to access the physical memory location.

2.6.2 Physical Memory Address

The logical address is used like a reference, to access the physical address. The fundamental difference between logical and physical address is that logical address is generated by CPU during a program execution whereas, the physical address refers to a location in the memory unit.

2.6.3 Segmented Memory Address

Segmented memory is a system of addressing computer memory, which may be physical or virtual and may be operating in real-or protected mode. The segmented memory system was used to expand the 64KB limit on first-generation flat address space. Computers made prior to segmented memory used a flat addressing system based on a four-digit hexadecimal code. With hexadecimal, the highest 4-digit number you can create is FFFF (or 65535), which equals 64KB.

2.6.4 Virtual Memory Address

In a virtual memory system, the program memory is divided into fixed sized pages and allocated in fixed sized physical memory frames. The pages do not have to be contiguous in memory. A page table keeps track of where each page is located in physical memory. This allows the operating system to load a program of any size into any available frames. Only the currently used pages need to be loaded. Unused pages can remain on disk until they are referenced. This allows many large programs to be executed on a relatively small memory system.

2.6.5 Linear Memory Address

Linear and Virtual memory are independent features which can work in conjunction. If paging is disabled, linear addresses map one-to-one with physical addresses. When enabled, linear addresses are mapped to virtual memory.
Linear addresses are calculated from virtual addresses by segment translation. The base of the segment referred to by the selector is added to the virtual offset, giving a 32-bit linear address. Physical addresses are calculated from linear addresses through paging. The linear address is used as an index into the Page Table where the CPU locates the corresponding physical address. If paging is not enabled, linear addresses are always equal to physical addresses.

2.7 OTHER FORMS OF MEMORY

2.7.1 Disk Controller Card Memory

Disk controller is the controller circuit which enables the CPU to communicate with a hard disk, floppy disk or other kind of disk drive. Also it provides an interface between the disk drive and the bus connecting it to the rest of the system.

Early disk controllers were identified by their storage methods and data encoding. They were typically implemented on a separate controller card. Modified Frequency Modulation (MFM) controllers were the most common type in small computers, used for both floppy disk and hard disk drives. Run length limited (RLL) controllers used data compression to increase storage capacity by about 50% Priam created a proprietary storage algorithm that could double the disk storage. Shugart Associates Systems Interface (SASI) was a predecessor to SCSI.

Modern disk controllers are integrated into the disk drive. For example, disks called "SCSI disks" have built-in SCSI controllers. In the past, before most SCSI controller functionality was implemented in a single chip, separate SCSI controllers interfaced disks to the SCSI bus.

The most common types of interfaces provided nowadays by disk controllers are PATA (IDE) and Serial ATA for home use. High-end disks use SCSI, Fibre Channel or Serial Attached SCSI. Disk controllers can also control the timing of access to flash memory which is not mechanical in nature (i.e. no physical disk).

2.7.2 Printer Memory

Printer memory is memory (RAM) built in to the printer. Printer memory is separate from computer memory. All printers come with a certain amount of printer memory installed, but most are upgradeable to handle more or larger print jobs. If you are printing more complex documents such as graphics, photographs, charts, or specialized fonts, the printer may require additional memory. In general, the more memory the printer has, the better it can handle larger more complex documents. Printer memory does not affect print speed; adding memory will not make the printer print faster. Additional memory lets the printer print complex jobs, collate large jobs, and operate more efficiently. You can also download fonts and macros to printer memory. However, this type of memory is temporary storage. Anything stored in printer memory is lost when the printer power is turned off.

2.7.3 Video Memory

Video memory is a term generally used in computers for the purpose of holding the information necessary for a graphics card to drive a display device. But, in modern 3D graphics cards, the video memory may also hold the following information:

- 3D vector data
- Textures
- Backbuffers
- Overlays and GPU (Graphics Processing Unit) programs

The video memory is an important component of the video card and indirectly the entire PC, which improves the system performance as high as the video system tries to do more and more. If the video card is integrated in the motherboard, it will use the computer RAM memory. If it is not integrated, the video card will have its own video memory which is called Video RAM or VRAM. The VRAM capacity of most modern video cards range from 128 to 1024 MB. It is based on DDR (Double Data Rate) technology. The memory clock rate is between 400 MHz and 1.6 GHz. A very important element of the video memory is the Z-buffer, which manages the depth coordinates in 3D graphics from the eye's perspective.

Uses of Video Memory

The main use of the video memory is that it is working as the frame buffer. This is the place where the information is stored about the video image itself. Each pixel on the screen has associated with it typically 4 to 32 bits of data that represent its colour and intensity. The video processor manipulates this data to change the screen image and the RAMDAC (Random Access Memory Digital-Analog Converter) reads it and sends it to the monitor.

Higher end video cards also use the video memory for computation work. In particular, cards that support 3D functions, such as filtering need to use video memory for this work. Different video cards use different methods to decide how to allocate memory for these functions. Some will use whatever memory is "left over" after the necessary space for the frame buffer has been set aside, while others will pre-allocate the calculation memory and then limit the size of the frame buffer accordingly.

Since some cards use their video memory for both the frame buffer and additional calculations. They may have more than one type of video memory. The dual porting advantages of VRAM are of course very helpful for the frame buffer, but of no value in memory being used internally for calculations. So, since VRAM costs more than single-ported memory technologies, manufacturers put some VRAM on the card for the frame buffer, and some 'regular' memory on it for other purposes.

2.7.4 Secondary Memory or Auxiliary Memory

Secondary memory or secondary storage devices are permanent storage units used for storing programs and data. They use the principle of magnetization for storing 1 and 0. Therefore, they are also known as *magnetic memory*. They are non-volatile i.e, the memory retains its contents even when power is switched off.

Examples of secondary storage devices include magnetic tapes, magnetic disks, compact disks, magnetic bubble memory, magnetic drums, zip disks etc. The relatively slow magnetic tapes are used for storing very old files. Magnetic disks are used for storing data for backup purposes.

A disk that is permanently attached to the computer unit and cannot be easily removed by user is called the *Hard Disk*.

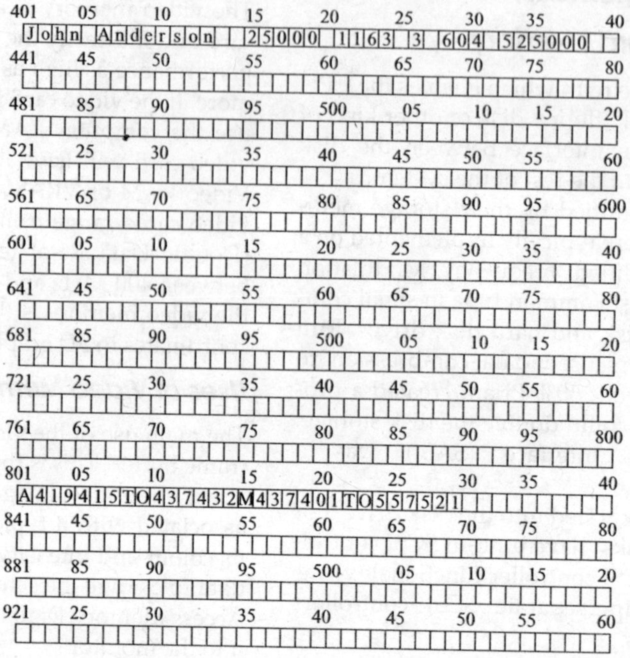

Figure 2.10 Representation of main memory of a computer containing data and a small program

2.8 MEMORY ADDRESSING CAPABILITY OF A CPU

The memory addressing capability of a CPU depends on the number of lines available in an address bus, that is, width of the address bus. With a *n*-bit wide address bus, a CPU can directly address up to 2^n memory locations. For example, a CPU with a 20-bit wide address bus can address 2^{20} memory locations. (2^{20} = 1 million). One memory location stores 1 byte of information and hence a CPU with a 20-bit address bus can directly address up to 1 MB memory. Similarly, a 16-bit address bus can address upto 64 KB memory, a 24-bit address bus upto 16 MB memory and a 32-bit address bus, 2 GB memory. The storing of data and a small program in the memory is shown in Figure 2.10.

2.9 WORD LENGTH OF A COMPUTER

The number of bits that a computer can manipulate or process *at a time* is called its *word length*. The commonly used word lengths are: 8, 16, 32 or 64 bits. It is a measure of the computing power of a computer. Computers with longer word lengths are more powerful. When we talk of a 32-bit computer, it means that its word length is 32 bits.

Bit A microprocessor works on binary digits 0 and 1. These digits are popularly known as *bits*. An 8-bit microprocessor can handle a data of combination of 8-bits formed by 0s and 1s, for example 10011000, 01110001, etc. The number of combinations depends on the number of bits and is given by the formula 2^n, where *n* is the number of bits. Hence, for an 8-bit microprocessor the possible combinations will be 2^8 = 256.

2.10 MEMORY UNITS

All information in the computer is stored using electrical components like the integrated circuits. Two symbols used to represent these two states are 0 and 1, and are known as BITS (an abbreviation for BInary DigiTS). 0 represents the absence of a signal, 1 represents the presence of a signal. A BIT is, therefore, the smallest unit of data in a computer and can either store a 0 or 1. Some memory units are as follows:

(a) **Byte** : A byte is a unit of data that is eight binary digits (0 and 1) long. A byte is the unit most computer used to represent a character, such as a letter, number or typographic symbol. For example, g, 5, #. A byte can also hold a string of bits that need to be used in some larger unit for application purposes.

☞ *A group formed by 8 bits is called a byte and a group formed by 4 bits is called a nibble.*

(b) **Kilobyte** : A kilobyte (KB) is actually 2^{10} = 1024 bytes. Or 1 KB = 1,024 bytes (Apprx. 1,000 bytes)

(c) **Megabyte** : A megabyte (MB) is 2^{20} byte or 1,048,576 bytes in decimal notation. Or 1 MB = 1,024 KB (Approx. 1,000 KB)

(d) **Gigabyte** : A gigabyte (GB) is 2^{30} byte or 1,073,741,824 bytes in decimal notation. Or 1 GB = 1,024 MB (Apprx. 1,000 MB)

(e) **Terabyte** : A terabyte is a measure of computer storage capacity and it is equal to the 2^{40} bytes. Or 1 TB = 1,024 GB (Apprx. 1,000 GB)

(f) **Petabyte** : A petabyte is 2^{50} byte or approx. 1,125,899,900,000,000 bytes in decimal notation. 1 PB = 1,024 TB (Apprx. 1,000 TB)

(g) **Exabyte** : A exabyte is 2^{60} byte. or 1 EB = 1,024 PB (Approx. 1,000 PB)

(h) **Zettabyte** : A Zettabyte is 2^{70} byte. Or 1 ZB = 1,024 EB (Approx. 1,000 EB)

(i) **Yottabyte** : A Yottabyte is 2^{80} byte. Or 1 YB = 1,024 ZB (Approx. 1,000 ZB)

EXERCISE

1. State reasons for the hierarchy of memory.
2. What is the need for secondary storage device?
3. Why do not do with large sized RAMs and ROMs?
4. What is ROM? What types of ROMs are available?
5. Explain the working of a RAM containing diodes.
6. What is ROM? Differentiate between EPROM and EEPROM.
7. The ROM contains the essential information and the hard disk contains all relevant programs. What purpose does the RAM serve?
8. Explain primary memory and its properties and types?
9. What is virtual memory?

REVIEW QUESTIONS WITH ANSWERS

1. Multiple Choice

1.1 The difference between main memory and storage is that main or primary memory is _______ and secondary memory or storage is _______.

a. temporary, permanent b. permanent, temporary
c. Slow, fast d. None of the above

Ans (a)

1.2 Identify the wrong statement?

a. SIMM is a type of memory modules used for random access memory in personal computers.
b. SIMM will come in 30, 72 and 186 pins.
c. SIMM modules are commonly used on the Intel Pentium 4 motherboards.
d. differs from DIMM in that the contact on a SIMM are redundant on both sides of the module.

Ans (c)

1.3 Which one of the following is volatile?

a. Bubble Memory b. RAM
c. ROM d. Magnetic Disk

Ans (b)

1.4 A Nibble consists of _____ Bits.

a. 2 b. 4
c. 8 d. 16

Ans (b)

1.5 Which of the following is a non-volatile memory?

a. Random Access Memory b. Read Only memory
c. Virtual Memory d. Cache Memory

Ans (b)

1.6 Virtual memory is

a. Part of main memory only used for swapping
b. A technique to allow a program, of size more than the size of main memory, to run.
c. Part of secondary storage used in program execution
d. None of the above

Ans (b)

1.7 Which of the following is fastest memory?

a. Secondary Memory b. Auxiliary Memory
c. Cache Memory d. Virtual Memory

Ans (c)

1.8 EEPROM stands for

a. Electrically Erasable Programmable Read Of Memory
b. Erasable Electrically Programmable Read Only Memory
c. Easily Erasable Programmable Read Only Memory
d. Electrically Erasable Programmable Read Only Memory

Ans (d)

1.9 RAM means:

a. Random access memory b. Read also memory
c. Read access memory d. Random also memory

Ans (a)

1.10 Which of the following is the largest memory size?

a. Terabyte b. Gigabyte
c. Kilobyte d. Megabyte

Ans (a)

1.11 _______ Memory is used to store BIOS on Motherboard.

a. ROM b. RAM
c. CACHE d. None of the Above

Ans (a)

1.12 What characteristic of RAM memory makes it not suitable for permanent storage?

a. too slow b. it is volatile
c. unreliable d. too bulky

Ans (b)

2. State whether the following statements are True or False

2.1 A byte is the smallest unit of storage.

Ans False

2.2 A byte is bigger than nibble.

Ans True

2.3 Cache memory is faster than main memory.

Ans True

2.4 The cache is a smaller, faster memory which stores copies of the data from the most frequently used main memory locations.

Ans True

2.5 EPROM is Electronically Programmable Read Only Memory.

Ans False

2.6 EEPROM stands for Electrically Erasable Programmable Read Of Memory

Ans True

2.7 CD-ROM is an example of Volatile memory.

Ans False

2.8 Firmware program resides in the ROM portion of a computer.

Ans True

2.9 Volatile memory is directly accessible by the CPU.

Ans True

2.10 Cache is an area on disk for temporary storage of information.

Ans True

2.11 CMOS memory is used to execute programs.

Ans False

3. Match the following:

3.1	EEPROM	a.	External to CPU
3.2	DRAM	b.	Flash memory
3.3	Secondary Memory	c.	retains data for a few milliseconds
3.4	Primary Memory	d.	Store instructions and data
3.5	Memory	e.	Directly connected to the microprocessor
3.6	A binary digit, either a 0 or 1	f.	Register
3.7	Special memory unit within cpu	g.	Bit
3.8	1 GB	h.	Write Through technique is used in which memory for updating the data
3.9	Cache	i.	used in all major commercial operating systems
3.10	Virtual memory is	j.	1024 MB

Ans 3.1 b 3.2 c 3.3 a 3.4 e 3.5 d
3.6 g 3.7 f 3.8 j 3.9 h 3.10 i

4. Fill in the blanks

4.1 1 KB equals ______ bytes.

Ans 1024

4.2 ______ is known as a primary memory.

Ans RAM

4.3 The function of the ______ is to store information.

Ans Memory

4.4 To store a printable character ______ byte is used.

Ans One

4.5 ______ is placed in between the CPU and the main memory.

Ans Cache Memory

4.6 The difference between main memory and storage is that main or primary memory is ______ and secondary memory or storage is ______.

Ans Temporary, permanent

4.7 ______ is a type of computer memory.

Ans DDR

4.8 Cache Memory is ______ in speed than secondary storage device.

Ans Faster

4.9 ______ memory refers to a small memory on PC motherboards that is used to store BIOS setting.

Ans Nonvolatile BIOS

4.10 Cache memory acts between CPU and ______.

Ans RAM

4.11 ______ in Programmable Read Only Memory.

Ans PROM

4.12 ______ memory is faster than RAM.

Ans Cache

Q.5 (a) Write short notes on the following:

(i) Volatility of Memory

(ii) RIMM

Ans 5(a)(i)

Volatile memory is the memory whose contents are lost when power is switched off. A computer's main memory, made up of dynamic RAM or static RAM chips, loses its contents immediately upon interruption of power supply. A random access memory is volatile but secondary memory containing magnetic elements is non-volatile, because they retain stored data when power supply is switched off.

Ans 5(a)(ii)

RIMM is a trademark of Rambus incorporated for the Direct Rambus or DRAM modules. RIMM is a type of computer memory that resembles DIMMs. However, it is 184-pin and is available with built in ECC (Error Correcting Code) support and Non-ECC at speeds up to 800MHz. RIMM modules are commonly used on the *Intel Pentium 4* motherboards.
Unlike most other types of computer memory, computers that support RIMM require a continuous signal. If a memory socket is left empty, the computer will not work properly. Therefore, users must utilize C-RIMM modules in any slots that do not have RIMM modules.

Q.6 Why memory unit is important?

Ans 6
Memory unit is an essential component of digital electronic systems and PCs (Personal Computers) because it is needed for storing binary information. The typical memory consists of an array of memory cells. The basic memory cell is a transistor flip-flop circuit which is capable of storing binary data in the form of 0 and 1.

Q.7 Explain working of Traditional Memory Hierarchy with a diagram.

Ans 7
Memory hierarchy works because of the locality property of memory references due to the sequentially fetched program instructions. In a hierarchical memory system there are many levels of memory hierarchies. A small amount of very fast memory is allocated and brought right next to the central processing unit to help match up the speed of the CPU and memory. As the distance becomes greater between the CPU and memory, the performance requirement for the memory is relaxed. At the same time, the size of the memory grows larger to accommodate the overall memory size requirement. Some of the memory hierarchies are registers, cache, main memory, and disk.

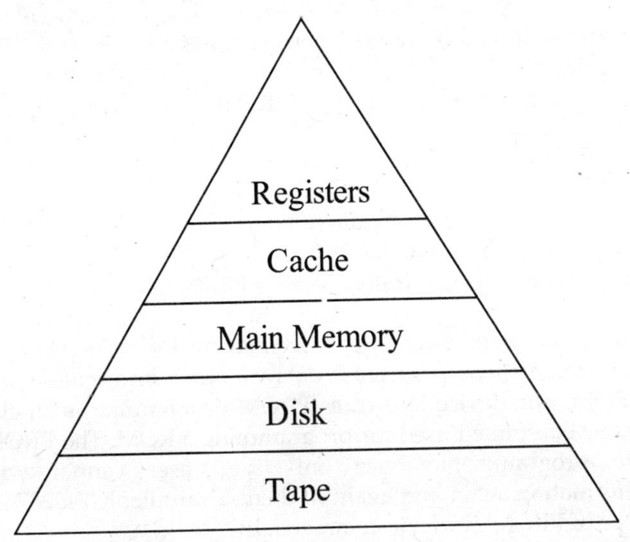

Figure 2.11 Traditional Memory Hierarchy

Figure 2.11 illustrates the general memory hierarchy employed in a traditional system. When a memory reference is made, the processor accesses the memory at the top of the hierarchy. If the desired data is in the higher hierarchy, a "bit" is encountered and information is obtained quickly. Otherwise a miss is encountered. The requested information must be brought up from a lower level in the hierarchy.

Memory is divided into blocks so that it can be transferred between levels in groups. At the cache level a chunk is called a *cache block*. At the main memory level a chunk is referred to as a *memory page*. A miss in the cache is called a *cache miss* and a miss in the main memory is called a *page fault*. When a miss occurs, the whole block of memory containing the requested missing information is brought in from the lower hierarchy. If the current memory hierarchy level is full when a miss occurs, some existing blocks or pages must be removed and sometimes written back to a lower level to allow the new one(s) to be brought in.

Q.8 Explain working of Modern Memory Hierarchy with a diagram.

Ans 8

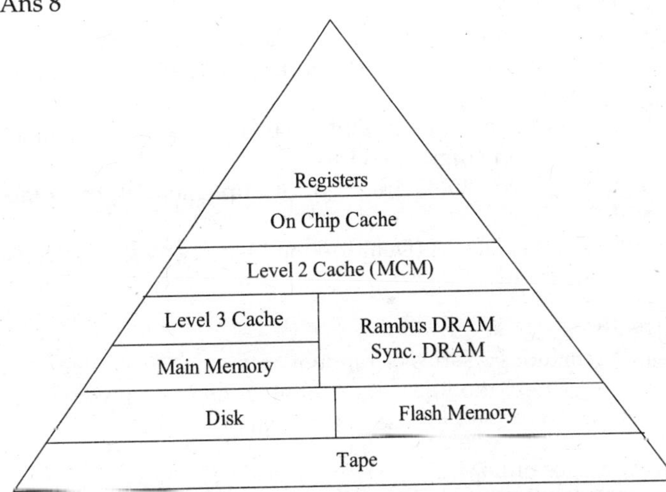

Figure 2.12 Modern Memory Hierarchy

In modern computing systems, there may be several sub-levels of cache within the hierarchy of cache. For example, the Intel Pentium Pro system has on chip cache (on the CPU chip), which is called Level-1 (LI) cache. There is another level of cache, which resides in the same package with the CPU chip, which is called level-2 cache. There could also be level-3 cache on the mother board between the CPU chip(s) and main memory chips. Moreover, there are also newer memory devices such as synchronous RAM (Random Access Memory) which provides enough speed to be interfaced with a processor directly through pipelining. Figure 2.12 shows a possible memory hierarchy that employs these newer devices. The general principle of memory hierarchy is that the farther away from the CPU it is, the larger its size, slower its speed, and the cheaper its price per memory unit becomes. Because the memory space addressable by the CPU is normally larger than necessary for a particular software program at a given time, disks are used to provide an economical supplement to main memory. This technique is called *virtual memory*. Besides disks there are tapes, optical drives, and other backup devices, which we normally call backup storage. They are used mainly to store information that is no longer in use.

☞ *A cache memory is larger than the registers but smaller than the main memory.*

Q.9 What is ROM? What can ROMs do?

Ans 9

ROM stands for read only memory. It is a non-volatile memory which means, the information stored in it is not lost even if the power supply goes off. The device retains data all the time.

ROMs can do the following:

(a) The stored information in ROM can only be read at the time of operation.

(b) Information can not be written into a ROM by user/programmer as in the case of Random Access Memory (RAM)

(c) The contents of ROMs are decided by the manufacturers and they are permanently stored in a ROM at the time of manufacture.

(d) ROMs store function tables, such as square root table, etc., in many digital devices.

(e) Small sized ROMs are used for implementing truth tables.

Q.10 What is DIMM (Dual In-Line Memory Module)? What are its advantages?

Ans 10

DIMM includes a series of random access memory integrated circuits. These modules are mounted on a printed circuit board and designed for use in personal computers.

Advantages of DIMM

(a) DIMMs have separate contacts on each side of the board, thereby providing twice as much data as a single SIMM.

(b) DIMMs have a 64-bit data path as compared to SIMMs which have a 32-bit data path.

(c) The command address and control signals are buffered on the DIMMs. With heavy memory requirements this will reduce the loading effort of the memory.

Q.11 What do you mean by memory *hierarchy*?

Ans 11

The speed of memory devices has been lagging behind the speed of processors. As processors become faster and more capable, larger memory capacities are required to keep up with every increasing software complexity written for these machines. Although CPUs'(Central Processing Units) speed continues to grow with the advancement of technology and design techniques, due to the nature of increasing memory size, more time is needed to decode wider and wider addresses. The speed gap between CPU and memory devices will continue to grow wider. The strategy used to remedy this problem is called memory *hierarchy*.

Q.12 Discuss Classification of Memories.

Ans 12

Memories are classified in the following categories:

(a) Bipolar

(b) Metal-Oxide Semiconductor (MOS) or Complementary Metal Oxide Semiconductor (CMOS)

The construction of memory cell depends on the type of transistor being used. The total capacity of memory can be calculated by knowing total number of memory cells. For example, if a memory chip can store 1024 bits that means it consists of 1024 memory cells. Because a single cell can only store one bit. This cell is constructed using flip-flop and each flip-flop is made up of several transistors.

If we compare the two categories of memories, the faster operation can be obtained using bipolar memory cells. High package density can be obtained using CMOS memory chips. The CMOS memory chip also dissipates low power and costs less.

☞ *Memories can also be classified according to their mode of operations, i.e., random access, read only and read-write memories.*

The write operation is just storing binary information to memory cells. This can be accomplished by a logic circuitry associated with random access memory. The read operation is detecting whether 1 or 0 is stored in the memory cells. The random access means that any bit can be written to or read from memory cell. Two control signals are always available to the memory unit, i.e., read and write, which define the mode of operation whether data is to be read or to be written in the memory.

Memories can also be classified with one more property, i.e., volatile and non-volatile. If data is permanently stored, even when powers is off then memory is called non-volatile. Whereas, if data is erased when power is off, then it is called volatile.

Q.13 Explain different types of ROMs.

Ans 13

ROMs are further classified as:

(a) PROMs (Programmable ROMs)

(b) EPROM (Erasable PROM)

(c) EEPROM (Electrically Erasable PROM)

PROMs

The contents of PROMs are decided by the user. User can store permanent programs, data or other information in a PROM. The device known as PROM programmer is an electronic equipment used for programming a ROM. The PROMs are programmable once only, i.e., user cannot write information again and again in them. Example: IC745287 is a type of PROM available commercially.

EPROM (Erasable PROM)

The stored data in EPROM can be erased by exposing it to high intensity short-wave ultra-violet light for about 12 minutes. EPROMs are used to store programs that are updated frequently and in development stages of a system, where programs may be changed.

EEPROM (E^2 PROM)

This is an electrically erasable PROM. The chip can be erased and reprogrammed on the board on a byte to byte basis. It requires much shorter time, a few seconds as compared to 10-20 minutes for EPROM. Intel 2816A is a 16K (2K x 8) EEPROM available commercially.

☞ *E^2 PROM requires 21 Volts pulses for writing or erasing and 5V for read operation.*

Q.14 Differentiate between Static RAMs and Dynamic RAMs.

Ans 14

Static RAM or SRAM is a form of semiconductor memory. Static RAM storage is based on the logic circuit known as a flip-flop, which retains the information stored in it as long as there is enough power to run the device.

Dynamic RAM or DRAM is a form of semiconductor random access memory. Dynamic RAMs store information in integrated circuits that contain capacitors. Because capacitors lose their charge over time, dynamic RAM boards must include logic to refresh (recharge) the RAM chips continuously. While a dynamic RAM is being refreshed, it cannot be read by the processor. If the processor attempts to read the RAM while it is being refreshed, it is forced to wait. Because their internal circuitry is simple, dynamic RAMs are more commonly used than static RAMs, even though they are slower. A dynamic RAM can hold approximately four times as much data as a static RAM chip of the same complexity.

☞ *A static RAM chip can store only about one-fourth as much data as a dynamic RAM chip of the same complexity, but static RAM does not require refreshing and is usually much faster than dynamic RAM. It is also more expensive. Static RAMs are usually reserved for use a cache memory in microprocessors.*

Q.15 Describe the organization of Random Access Memory using a block diagram.

Ans 15

Figure below shows the block diagram of a RAM chip. Read and Write control signals are provided to read data from the chip or write data into a chip, respectively. When the Read input is set to 1, data is read from the RAM chip. And when the Write input is set to 1, data is written into the RAM chip.

In addition, two control inputs CS1 and CS2 (Chip Selection inputs 1 and 2) are used to select the needed chip to store data. When a chip 1 is given the inputs CS1 = 1 and CS2 = 0, then this chip is selected. The RAM chip shown in Figure above is of capacity 128 words. To address a word out of 128 words, a 7-bit address ($2^7 = 128$) is required. Hence, an input to AD, that specifies the address of the required word, must be of 7 bits. A

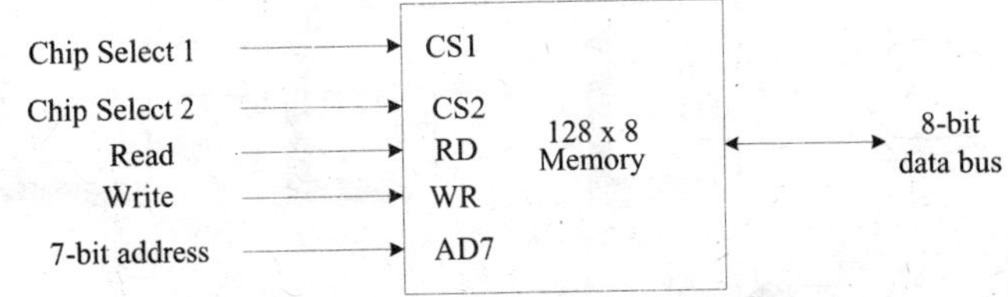

Figure 2.13 Block diagram of RAM Chip

bidirectional bus is needed to transfer data out of (read operation) and into (write operation) a RAM chip. The double head arrow for the bus indicates the bidirectional bus in the Figure 2.13 shown above.

Q.16 Explain working of Cache memory with diagram.

Ans 16

Cache memory, pronounced *'cash memory'*, is a reserved section of main memory that is used to enhance performance of a CPU. It is located between the main memory and the CPU. Cache memory is used to hold data and instructions that are transferred to and from main memory (See Figure 2.14). When a disk is read, a large block of data is transferred into the cache. Subsequently, the same data can be read from the cache. Thus, disk access which is very slow is avoided again and again by using cache memory.

Some operating systems attempt to anticipate future requests of data and transfer data from main memory into cache memory to improve speed. Cache is a special memory subsystem that temporarily stores frequently used instructions and data for quicker processing by the processor of a computer. The high-speed memory used for the cache purpose is very costly that is the reason it is not used as the main memory of the computer. The information frequently required by the processor is kept in the cache memory by the cache controller. This cache controller always tries to make sure that the data required by the processor in the next memory access is available in the cache memory. This improves the speed of the computer very much because if the required data is in the cache memory it is made available to the CPU without any wait state. When the required data is available in the cache it is called a hit. In case of a cache hit the processor immediately reads or writes the data in the data cache line. The proportion of accesses that result in a cache hit is known as the hit rate, and is a measure of the effectiveness of the cache. When the required data is not available in the cache memory it is called a *miss*. In case of cache miss, most caches allocate new entry, which comprises the tag just missed and a copy of the data from memory. The reference can then be applied to the new entry just as in case of a hit. Misses are comparatively slow because they require the data to be transferred from main memory. This transfer incurs a delay since main memory is much slower than cache memory.

Q.17 What do you mean by computer memory? Name the two types of memory.

Ans 17

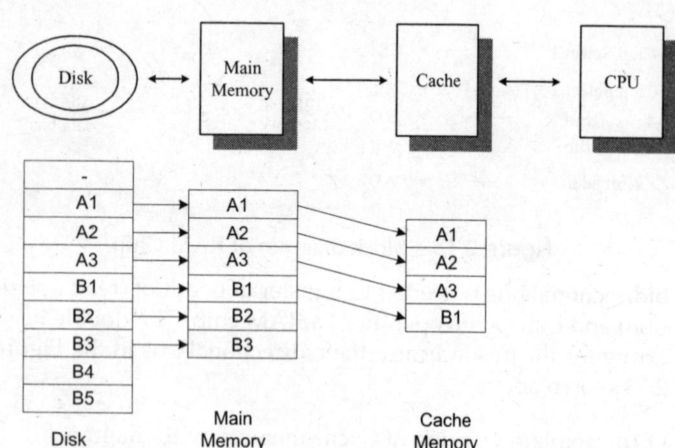

Figure 2.14 Diagram showing transfer of data from disk memory to cache memory via main memory

The *Memory* is an essential component of a computer system. It is required by the computer system to store instructions and data. Memory can be divided into the following two types:

Primary Memory: Memory which is directly connected to the microprocessor forming a CPU in PCs.

Secondary Memory: Memory which is external to CPU and is a permanent nature.

Q.18 What are the differences between RAM and ROM?

Ans 18

RAM: RAM is a read/write memory. Information can be written into and read from a RAM. It is a volatile memory. It retains the stored information as long as it is supplied with power supply. When power supply is switched off or interrupted, the stored information in the RAM is lost.

ROM: ROM is a permanent type memory. Its contents are not lost when power supply is switched off. The user cannot write into a ROM. Its contents are written into at manufacturing time. ROMs store permanent programs and other types of data which are needed by the computer to execute user programs. ROMs store functions such as sine, cosine, logarithm, square root, exponential and code conversion tables, etc.

Q.19 Define the term Byte. What is the difference between bit and a byte?

Ans 19

A binary digit either 0 or 1 is called *bit*. A combination of 8 bits is called a *byte* and is a unit of computer storage.

Information in a computer is stored in the form of strings of 0's and 1's. The symbol 0 and 1, known as binary digits , are called bits.

The memory of a computer can be thought of as cells. Each of these cells contains one bit of information, i.e. each cell will have its state as 0 or 1. The combination of 8 bits form one byte. Each byte represents one character such as A, B, C, etc. Combination of bits is also used to store instructions and data in the computer memory.

Q.20 Can a Read Only Memory (ROM) be also a Random Access Memory (RAM)? Justify your answer.

Ans 20

RAM and ROM are integrated circuits chips that make the main memory of a computer. RAM is the memory unit in which any location can be accessed for a read or write operation in some fixed amount of time independent to the location's address, but ROM is used for permanent storage of information and it also possesses random access property.

Q.21 What is virtual memory?

Ans 21

Virtual memory is nothing but the auxiliary or secondary memory of the computer system seen as main memory by application programs.

Virtual memory scheme gives users an *illusion* of working with a large block of contiguous memory space (perhaps even larger than real memory), when in actuality most of their work is done in a small primary memory. In a computer system that implements virtual memory system, the user has the option to use part of or entire auxiliary memory which behaves as if it is the main memory.

Q.22 What are the reasons for using the virtual memory?

Ans 22

Reasons for using the virtual memory are as follows:

- It gives the users an *illusion* of working with a large block of contiguous memory space (perhaps even larger than real main memory), when in actuality most of their work is done in a small primary memory.
- Virtual memory efficiently utilize the main memory because the larger size program is divided into blocks and partially each block is load in the main memory when it is required.
- Efficient CPU utilization and thus improved throughput.

Q.23 Define volatile and non-volatile memory.

Ans 23

Volatile memory is the memory whose contents are lost when power is switched off. Whereas *non-volatile memory* is the memory whose contents are permanently stored, even when powers is off.

A random access memory (RAM) is made up of dynamic RAM or static RAM chips is volatile because it loses its contents immediately upon interruption of power supply. But secondary memory containing magnetic elements is non-volatile, because they retain stored data when power supply is switched off.

Q.24 What is "Dumb" Memory?

Ans 24

When the contents of section of your computer's memory is written to your disk in an unaltered form, it is called a *dump memory*.

Q.25 Write short note on Tera byte.

Ans 25

A terabyte is a measure of computer storage capacity and it is equal to the 2^{40} bytes. Or

1 TB = 1,024 GB (Apprx. 1,000 GB)

Q.26 Classify memory system in a digital computer according to their use.

Ans 26

Memory is an essential component of a computer system. It is required by the computer system to store instructions and data. Memory system consists all storage devices and can be divided into the following types:

- ***Primary Memory:*** Primary Memory, also known as *Main Memory*, is one of the important parts of the computer, because memory's size determines the length and number of programs that can be stored at a time. Its size also indicates the amount of data that can be processed quickly. Primary memory is a fast Random Access Memory (RAM) made up of ICs called *SIMS*. The main memory is directly addressed by the CPU. Examples of main memory are RAM and ROM.
- ***Secondary Memory:*** Auxiliary memory, also called secondary memory, is used for storing such programs and data which are not needed immediately by the CPU. It uses principle of magnetization for storing 1 and 0. Therefore, it is also known as magnetic memory. It is non-volatile, i.e the memory retains its contents even when power is switched off. Auxiliary memory includes magnetic tapes, magnetic disks, optical disks, magnetic bubble memory, magnetic drums, zip disks, etc. The relatively slow magnetic tapes are used for storing very old files. Magnetic disks are used for storing data for backup purposes.
- ***Associative Memory:*** Associative memory is a type of memory, which does not keep track of addresses of its contents. The data are accessed by its contents. Using specially designed circuits, the requested word is matched against all the words available in the memory. This memory is accessed on the basis of the data contents rather than by specific address or location.
- ***Cache Memory:*** Cache Memory, pronounced *'cash memory'*, is a reserved section of main memory (RAM) that is used to enhance performance of a CPU. It is located between the main memory and the CPU. Cache Memory is used to hold data and instructions that are transferred to and from main memory. When a disk is read, a large block of data is transferred into the cache. Subsequently, the same data can be read from the cache. Thus, a slow disk access is avoided again and again by using cache memory.

Q.27 Distinguish between SRAM and DRAM.

Ans 27

Difference between SRAM and DRAM are as under:

Static Ram (SRAM)	Dynamic RAM (DRAM)
Static RAMs retain stored information only as long as the power supply is on.	Dynamic RAM loses its stored information in a very short time (a few milliseconds) even though the power supply is on.
Static RAMs are costlier.	Dynamic RAMs are cheaper.
Static RAMS consume more power.	They consume less power.
Static RAMs have higher speed than dynamic RAMs.	Dynamic RAMs have high packing density and moderate speed.
Static RAMs do not need refreshing circuitry.	Dynamic RAMs have to be refreshed periodically,
Static RAM storage is based on the logic circuit known as a flip-flop.	Dynamic RAMs store information in integrated circuits that contain capacitors.
Static RAMs are also written as SRAM.	Dynamic RAMs are also written as DRAM.

Q.28 Why is virtual memory called virtual?

Ans 28

Virtual memory is called a virtual because this is a technique not a physical memory which is managed by the operating system.

Q.29 How does cache memory increase the performance of a computer?

Ans 29

The cache memory is placed in between the CPU and the main memory. It is much faster than the main memory. Its access time is much less compared to that of the main memory. The access time of a cache memory is 15–25 nanoseconds (ns) whereas that of the main memory is 80 ns. (One nano second is = 10^{-9} second.) It stores instructions and data which are to be immediately executed. It is used to reduce the average access time for address, instructions or data which are normally stored in the main memory. Thus the cache memory increases the performance of the computer. Cache memory is much costlier than main memory.

Q.30 Differentiate between virtual and cache memory.

Ans 30

The difference between Virtual and Cache memory is as follows:

	Virtual Memory	Cache Memory
Definition	It is an abstraction of the main memory. It extends the available memory of the computer by storing the inactive parts of the content of RAM on a disk. It fetches it back to the RAM when the content is required.	It is used to store frequently accessed data in order to quickly access the data whenever it is required.
Purpose	It extends the memory capacity of a computer beyond the one that is installed.	It reduces the amount of time needed to access the data.
Speed	It operates in the millisecond range.	It operates in the nanosecond range.
Control mechanism	Control mechanism Managed by the operating system.	Managed automatically by the hardware.
Component	It is a part of the hard drive (secondary storage).	Located on the processor itself.

Q.31 Explain primary memory and its characteristics.

Ans 31

Primary memory is one of the most important part of the computer, as it determines the size and the number of programs that can be simultaneously held within the computer as well as the amount of data that can be processed quickly. Primary memory stores the necessary programs of system software, which are required to execute user programs. The main memory is directly addressed by the CPU. Primary memory is volatile in nature. It is costly than a secondary memory or storage.

Characteristics of primary memory

- **Storage capacity** : It is the amount of data that can be stored in the storage unit. Primary storage units have less storage capacity as compared to secondary storage.
- **Access time:** Access time is required to locate and retrieve stored data from the storage unit in response to a program instruction. Primary storage units have faster access time as compared to secondary storage units.
- **Cost per bit of storage:** This refers to the cost of a storage unit for a given storage capacity. As compared to secondary storage units, primary storage units have higher cost per bit of storage.
- **Volatile:** If the data stored are lost when the power is turned off or interrupted, it is called volatile storage. The Primary storage units are volatile and the secondary storage units are non volatile.
- **Random Access:** If the time taken to access a piece of data from the storage unit is independent of the location of data in the storage unit, it is called a random access storage or random access memory (RAM). Each separate location of a RAM is as easy to access any other location, and it takes the same amount of time.

Q.32 Define RAM, ROM and Cache Memory.

Ans 32

RAM: RAM is a read/write memory. Information can be written into and read from a RAM. It is a volatile memory. It retains the stored information as long as it is supplied with power supply. When power supply is switched off or interrupted, the stored information in the RAM is lost.

ROM: ROM is a permanent type memory. Its contents are not lost when power supply is switched off. The user cannot write into a ROM. Its contents are written into at manufacturing time. ROMs store permanent programs and other types of data which are needed by the computer to execute user programs. ROMs store functions such as sine, cosine, logarithm, square root, exponential and code conversion tables, etc.

Cache memory : Cache memory (pronounced as the "cash memory") is placed in between the CPU and the main memory. It is faster than the main memory. Hence access time is much less than that of the main memory. The access time of a cache memory is 15–25 nanoseconds (ns) whereas that of the main memory is 80 ns. One nanosecond = $\mathbf{10^{-9}}$ second. The cache memory stores instructions and data which are to be immediately executed. It is used to reduce the average access time for address, instructions or data which are normally stored in the main memory. Thus, it increases the operating speed of the system. Cache memory is much costlier than the main memory. From economical considerations, the size of cache memory is usually smaller than that of the main memory.

CHAPTER 3

Secondary Storage

3.1 SECONDARY MEMORY

You cannot store data in the main memory of a PC permanently. Firstly because it is very expensive and secondly its contents are erased when the computer is turned off. In order to preserve or save the work which you have done on your computer (permanently for future use) before you shut it off, you need storage media, such as compact disks (CDs) and hard disks, DVD (Digital Versatile/Video Disk), ZIP disk, Pen drive, Blue-Ray Disk, etc.

3.1.1 Characteristics of Secondary Storage Devices

(a) Large capacity
(b) Portability
(c) Durability
(d) Cost
(e) Non-volatility

The primary storage also known as main memory, is used to hold pieces of program instructions and data, intermediate result of processing and recently produced results of processing of the jobs which the computer system is currently working on. These pieces of information are represented electronically in the main memory chips circuitry and while it remains in the main memory, the CPU can access it directly at a very fast speed. However, the primary storage can hold information only while the computer system is on. As soon as the computer system is switched off, the information held in the primary storage disappears. Moreover, the primary storage normally has limited storage capacity, because it is very expensive. The primary storage of modern computer systems is made up of semiconductor devices.

The secondary storage also known as auxiliary storage, is used to take care of the limitations of the primary storage. That is, it is used to supplement the limited storage capacity and the volatile characteristic of primary storage. This is because secondary storage is much cheaper than primary storage and it can retain information even when the computer system is switched off. The secondary storage is normally used to hold the program instructions, data and information of those jobs on which the computer system is not working on currently, but needs to hold them for processing later. The most commonly used storage medium is the magnetic disk.

3.2 DATA STORAGE

Data now a days are stored in hard disk, CD-ROM (Compact Disk Read Only Memory), Digital Video/Versatile Disk (DVD), pendrive and portable hard drive.

Data stored on hard disk and CD-ROM, etc., can be accessed directly. Thus, these storage devices are faster, and can also be used to transfer data from one computer to another or between a computer and a smartphone.

The specific functions of the storage unit are to store the following:

(a) All data and instructions to be processed,
(b) Intermediate results of processing, and
(c) Final results before sending them to output devices.

Storage media can be classified as volatile or non-volatile storage media.

3.2.1 Volatile Storage Media

Data stored in volatile storage media gets deleted when power is switched off. Volatile storage media includes main memory and cache memory. These are made up of IC chips and, hence, data access is very fast. Data stored in volatile storage media is lost when system crashes. However, power failure is normally backed by UPS.

3.2.2 Non-volatile Storage Media

Data stored in non-volatile storage media can survive system crashes. It includes disks and magnetic tapes. Disks are used for online storage and tapes are used for archive storage. These are magnetic devices; hence, data access is slow. Non-volatile storage devices are subject to failures when head crashes or power supply is fluctuating.

3.2.3 Stable Storage Device

Data stored in a stable storage device is never lost. Such a storage media is impossible to obtain, but techniques can be used to implement such a system where data loss is practically nil. Replicating the needed information in several non-volatile storage media, with independent failure mechanisms, is one such technique. The information stored must be updated regularly to ensure that failure at one site does not affect the overall functioning of the system.

Causes of Failures

All electronic devices are subject to failures in one form or the other. A computer system is also an electronic device and is subject to failures of various forms. Since DBMS forms part of the computer system, it is also prone to failures and errors.

Following are the likely reasons for a transaction to fail in the middle of execution.

(a) *System crash:* A hardware, software or network error can occur in the computer system during transaction execution. Hardware crash may also occur due to main memory failure.

(b) *Transaction error:* Some erroneous operations, such as integer overflow or division by zero, etc., in the transaction may cause a failure in between.

(c) Transaction might be terminated before completion due to the detection of a deadlock condition.

(d) *Disk failure:* Some disk blocks may lose their data because of a read/write malfunction or disk read/write head error.

(e) *Natural catastrophes:* This refers to a number of problems including power failure, fire, theft, overwriting tapes or disks by mistake.

Failures due to reasons given in sub-para (a) to (c) are more common than failures given in sub para (d) and (e), above.

3.3 HARD DISK

The hard disk drive is the main, and the largest, date storage device in a PC. The operating system, application software and many other files are stored in the hard disk drive. A hard disk is a device used for mass storage of data. The data stored on a hard disk can be retrieved at a very fast speed, it being a direct address device. Unlike CDs, zip disks, Pen drives etc., you cannot easily remove a hard disk from a PC.

☞ *Hard Disk Drive is also known as hard drive, hard disk, fixed disk, fixed drive or fixed disk drive.*

Advantages

(a) Large storage capacity
(b) Stores and retrieves data much faster than a CDROM
(c) Resuable
(d) Ability to store large number of files in one unit

Disadvantages

(a) Costlier than Tapes
(b) Fixes disks are not portable

3.3.1 Structure of a Hard Disk Drive

A hard disk drive is made up of a group of disks or disk platters, piled on top of one another in an airtight, dust proof case.

Each platter is a thin, circular metal plate coated on both sides with a magnetic material. Most of today's disk platters have a 3.5" diameter (See Figure 3.1). Bigger hard disks are used in Mainframe computers, and the smaller ones in PCs and microcomputers. A PC uses 80 GB or more capacity of hard disk. Seven or more of these disks are mounted on a central shaft which rotates at speeds of 2,400 or more revolutions per minute (rpm). These platters are placed half-an-inch apart from each other and each has an upper and lower surface. Further, each surface has a corresponding read/write head attached to a moveable arm. The arms between the two platters carry two read/write heads. Therefore, a 6-platter disk is referred to as a twelve-head disk.

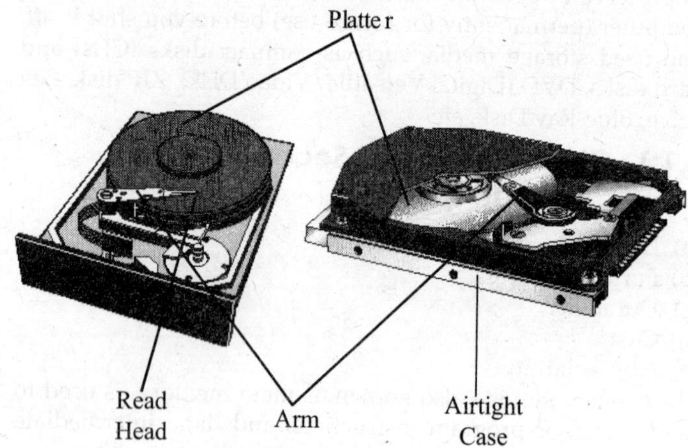

Figure 3.1 Hard disk

All the disks of a hard disk drive, therefore move simultaneously, as the central shaft rotates, in the same direction and at equal speed. In a disk pack, information is stored on both the surfaces of each disk plate, except the upper surface of the top plate and the lower surface of the bottom plate which are not used. Each disk also consists of a number of invisible concentric circles called *tracks*. Tracks are numbered from outside, starting with 0.

The group of tracks having the same track number on different platters form a *cylinder*. Thus a disk pack having 10 disk plates will have 18 recording surfaces and 18 tracks per cylinder.

Each track is further subdivided into sectors. Note that sectors vary in size. Sectors near the centre of the platter are smaller than the ones near the outer edge.

☞ *Although sectors vary in size, the amount of data stored in each of them is the same. This is because sectors towards the centre of the platter are denser than the sectors at the edge.*

The time taken to reach the particular track of a disk is known as the *latency time*. The time taken to read a record on the track is called the *seek time*. The total time, i.e., the sum of latency time and seek time is called the *access time* of a disk pack.

Storage of Information

In a disk pack, information is stored on both the surfaces of each disk plate except the upper surface of the top plate and the lower surface of the bottom plate which are not used. Each disk consists of a number of invisible concentric circles called *tracks*. A set of corresponding tracks in all the surfaces is called a cylinder See Figure 3.2). Thus, a disk pack having 10 disk plates will have 18 recording surfaces and hence it will have 18 tracks per cylinder. Each track is further subdivided into sectors (See Figure 3.3).

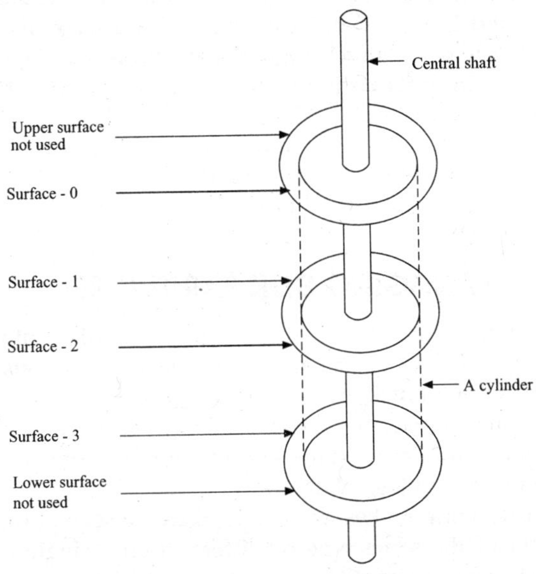

Figure 3.2 A disk having 3 disk platters

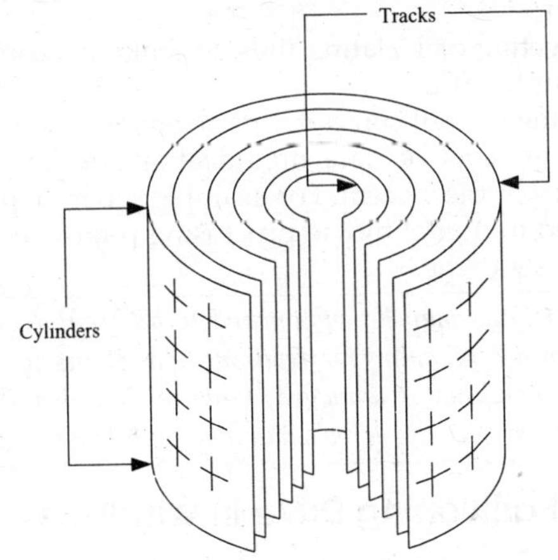

Figure 3.3 Sectors of a disk

3.3.2 Storage Capacity

The more disk surfaces a particular disk pack has, the greater will be its storage capacity. But the storage capacity of a disk drive also depends on the tracks per inch of surface and the bits per inch of track. The total number of bytes that can be stored on a disk pack is:

Number of cylinders × Tracks per cylinder × Sectors per track × Bytes per sector.

The total number of bytes that can be stored is calculated as:

Bytes per sector × Sectors per cylinder × Number of cylinders × Number of heads.

For example, a hard disk drive having 14 heads, 723 cylinders and 51 sectors each sector can store 0.5 KB has a storage capacity of 258 MB.

$$14 \times 723 \times 51 \times 0.5 = 258{,}111.00\ KB = 258\ MB.$$

Example 1

A disk pack has a movable head for each of the 12 recording surfaces. Each surface has 400 tracks. Each track has 16 blocks and each block has 128 words of 32 bits. Calculate the total storage capacity of the disk pack.

Answer

No. of recording surfaces	= 12
No. of tracks on each surface	= 400
No. of blocks on each track	= 16
No. of words in each block	= 128
No. of bits in each word	= 32

∴ Storage capacity in bits

= (No. of recording surfaces) × (No. of tracks on each surface) × (No. of blocks on each track) × (No. of words in each block) × (No. of bits in each word)

$$= 12 \times 400 \times 16 \times 128 \times 32 \text{ bits}$$

$$= \frac{12 \times 400 \times 16 \times 128 \times 32}{8} \text{ bytes}$$

$$= \mathbf{37.5 \times 2^{20}} \textbf{ bytes}$$

3.3.3 Accessing Data

Data are recorded on the tracks of a spinning disk surface and read from the surface by one or more read/write heads. There are two basic types of disk systems—moving-head and fixed-head (See Figures 3.4 and 3.5). The moving-head-system has one read/write head for each disk surface, each mounted on an access arm which can be moved in and out. So in this system, each read/write head moves horizontally across the surface of the disk and is able to access each track individually. Each usable surface of the disk pack has its own head and all the heads move together. In the fixed-head system, the access arm is stationary. A large number of read/write heads are distributed over the disk surfaces, one head for each track (See Figure 3.5).

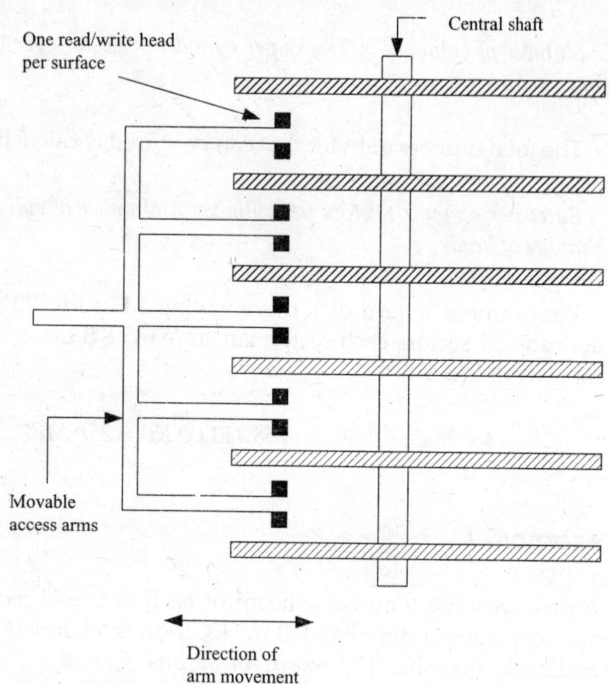

Figure 3.4 Vertical Cross section of a moving head disk system

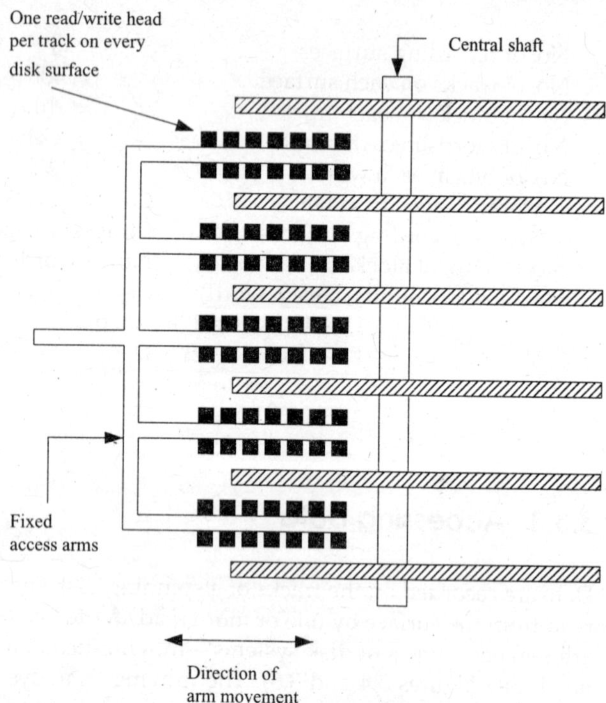

Figure 3.5 Vertical cross section of afixed-head disk system

As a result, no head movement is required and therefore information is accessed more quickly. However, because of the space required for the additional read/write heads, fixed-head disks have less capacity and cost more per byte of data stored than moving-head disks. The disk pack on some disk storage devices is permanently fixed in position, while on others, the pack can be removed and replaced by another one in a matter of seconds. So the storage capacity of a removable disk pack system is virtually unlimited because the storage space can be increased without the heavy expense of buying another complete device. As a hard disk is more stable being rigid and contained in a dust-free environment, its track and bit densities are much higher than those of floppy disks. It stores more information which can be accessed at rate faster. The access time is about 20 ms. The hard disks come in different sizes, such as 3.5 inch and 8 inch. The bigger hard disks are used in Mainframe computers and the smaller ones in PCs and microcomputers. A PC uses 40 GB to 1 TB capacity of hard disk.

3.4 MANAGING DISK PARTITIONS

Partitioning is used to divide the hard disk into sections known as drives. Each partition on the hard disk acts as one or more different disk drives (called logical drives), and can hold a different operating system, such as Windows on the first partition and Linux on the second. Moreover one partition can contain several logical drives.

Partitioning makes it possible to create several file systems (either of the same type or different) on a single hard disk. This has many benefits. These are:

- The use of multiple booting setups, which allows users to have more than one operating system on a single computer.
- Protecting or isolating files, to make it easier to recover a corrupted file.
- Raising overall computer performance.
- Higher level of data organization, raising the user efficiency of the system. For example separate partitions dedicated to digital movie processing photos, e-mail boxes or browser cache.

☞ *Partitions may be customized to different requirements. For example, allowing for read-only partitions to protect data. If one partition is damaged, none of the other file systems are affected, and the drive's data may still be salvaged.*

3.4.1 Partitioning Drive in Windows

To partition and format a new hard disk in a Windows 7, right-click on 'My Computer' and select 'Manage'. Now select 'Disk Management'. (See Figure 3.6).

A screen showing your existing drives, including the new one, will appear. At this point Windows will open a wizard to help you partition and format the new disk drive. If it does not, right-click the new drive in the lower pane and select 'initialize drive'.

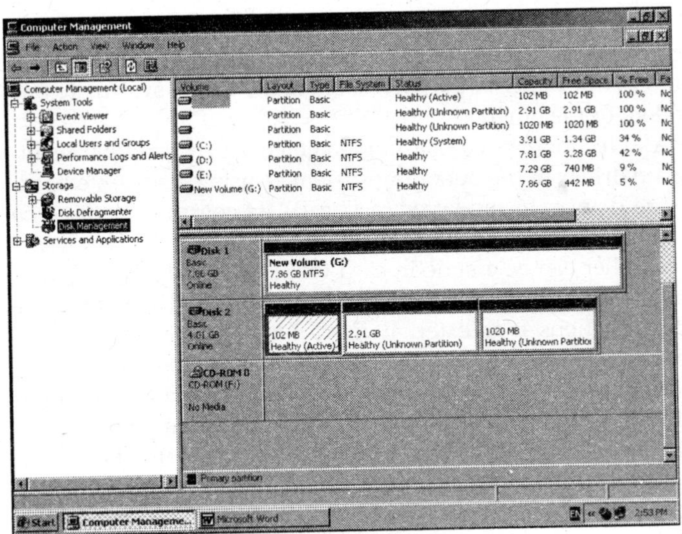

Figure 3.6 Computer Management screen

Now, to partition the drive right-click on the new drive and select 'new partition' to launch the partition wizard. It will for the amount of drive space you wish to be allocated to the new partition. If you opt not to use the full amount of space for the first partition, you can create additional ones in the same way up to a maximum of four partitions per disk. You will then be asked for a drive letter which Windows will use to represent the partition you just created.

Once you have chosen a drive letter or directory, you will be prompted to format the drive. Once the formatting is complete, your drive is ready for storing data.

3.4.2 File System

Data is stored in a computer system as files. The file management module of the operating system manages files contained in various storage devices as well as transfer of files from one storage device to another. This system takes care of organization, storage, retrievals, naming, sharing and protection of different files. It also allows files to be read and modified by using text editors or some other file manipulation software packages.

A file is placed in a directory (folder in Windows) or subdirectory at the desired location in the tree structure. File systems specify conventions for naming files. These conventions include the maximum number of characters in a name. A file system also includes a format for specifying the path to a file through the structure of directories.

3.4.3 Maintenance of Hard Disk Drive

Hard disk drives need little or no preventive maintenance. If it is a fixed hard disk drive, it does not need preventive maintenance because it is a sealed unit that you must not open for any reason.

If it is a cartridge disk drive, the manufacturer will have a special cleaning disk with instructions for doing the preventive maintenance. The technical manual for the disk drive will guide you through this type of preventive maintenance.

Disk Defragmenter

Disk Defragmenter consolidates fragmented files and folders on your computer's hard disk, so that each file occupies a single, contiguous space on the volume. As a result, your system can gain access to your files and folders and save new ones more efficiently. By consolidating your files and folders, *Disk Defragmenter* also consolidates the volume's free space, making it less likely for new files to be fragmented.

After some use, if you feel that your drive has started getting slow, DOS or Windows programs and data files take much more time to load, then most probably this could be due to a fragmentation problem.

Let us first understand this term. On a disk drive, any information is stored in clusters. When all the clusters of a file are stored in consecutive sectors, then it is not fragmented but when the clusters which make a file are scattered across the disk, the file or the disk is said to be fragmented.

As it takes the read/write head longer to read the file scattered across the disk surface, a fragmented file takes longer to load compared to an unfragmented file.

This can be compared with a real life situation: If your room is not in order, it takes you longer to find something compared to a room where everything is arranged properly.

The fragmentation occurs because whenever the operating system wants to write some information on the disk drive, it consults the FAT (File Allocation Table) to find an empty cluster. The FAT keeps a record of used, available and bad (unusable) areas on the disk surface.

After finding an empty cluster, the operating system writes to that area and updates the FAT. If the complete file could not be written in one contiguous empty area, then the operating system looks for other areas where the rest of the file can be written. The FAT keeps record of this chain of clusters taken up by the file. When a file is removed from the disk, the FAT is again updated to show the cluster taken up by the file as an empty area.

After some time, this removing of file and writing of new information produce a lot of holes, i.e., empty areas in between the data area, thus the files scattering across the disk surface. This is known as disk fragmentation.

File fragmentation increases disk access time and decreases the chances of salvaging a file when there is a problem. The disk defragmenter utility reads and rewrites the files on the disk to reorder them so that each file is once again stored contiguously on the disk surface and can be read much more efficiently by the hard disk drive.

☞ *Disk defragmenter moves the pieces of each file or folder to one location on the volume, so that each occupies a single, contiguous space on the disk drive.*

Because the defragmentation software moves the information stored on the disk surface, it is always better to take a backup of the information on the disk surface before using these software. These software are fully tested and the chances of data corruption are very remote, but a power loss during defragmentation or some other unexpected event may corrupt the data, so it is always better to have a current backup of all important information on the drive before using these programs.

Depending on the frequency of creating/editing/deleting of the files on the hard disk drive, you can defragment the drive once a week or once a month to keep the files in one place.

Defragmenting a drive also increases the drive's life as the read/write head will require to move less to get to the data on a properly defragmented drive. Another advantage is if the files are stored contiguously, it is easier to restore them in case of any accidental deletion. Files that are scattered makes it impossible to restore them.

Let us now learn to use the Disk Defragmenter. But first, undertake the following steps to open the Disk Defragmenter window.

Disk CleanUp

You can use Disk Cleanup to free up space on your hard disk by removing temporary Internet files, removing installed components and programs that you no longer use, and emptying the Recycle Bin.

☞ *Disk Cleanup helps to free up space on your hard drive. Disk Cleanup searches your drive, and then shows you temporary files, cache files, and unnecessary program files that you can safely delete. You can direct Disk Cleanup to delete some or all of those files.*

3.5 RAID SYSTEMS

Raid stands for Redundant Array of Independent Disks, a technology for implementing fault tolerance on a disk subsystem by using data redundancy, either with software or with a separate hardware RAID storage unit.

There are many applications, particularly in a business environment, where there are needs beyond what can be fulfilled by a single hard disk, regardless of its size, performance or quality level. Many businesses cannot afford to have their systems go down for even an hour in the event of a disk failure. They also need large storage subsystems with capacities in the terabytes and they want to be able to insulate themselves from hardware failures to any extent possible. Some people working with multimedia files need faster data transfer, exceeding what current drives can deliver, without spending a fortune on specialty drives. These situations require that the traditional "one hard disk per system" model be set aside and a new system employed. This technique is called RAID.

3.5.1 How RAID Works?

The fundamental principle behind RAID is the use of multiple hard disk drives in an array that behaves in most respects like a single large, fast one. There are a number of ways that this can be done, depending on the needs of the application, but in every case, the use of multiple drives allows the resulting storage subsystem to exceed the capacity, data security, and performance of the drives that make up the system, to one extent or the other.

RAID technology can be implemented either through a software driver in the operating system or using a separate hardware device. In the latter case, a RAID controller is used to control and manage two or more disk drives. The RAID controller can be a slide-in card that is inserted into the computer, or it can be embedded into a separate drive enclosure that functions as an external disk drive.

Either way, the RAID controller functions independently from the computer system to which it is attached and is configured through the controller's panel or configuration software. As far as the computer is concerned, the controller and its array of multiple disks looks like one ordinary disk drive.

In the case of software-based RAID, a software module (a "driver") is incorporated into the operating system to create a new device node which looks to the rest of the system as an ordinary disk drive but which actually corresponds to an array of two or more physical disks which are usually housed within the computer cabinet. Under this scenario, the RAID is configured and monitored using operating system commands and utilities.

RAID is a category of disk drives that employs two or more drives in combination for fault tolerance and performance. RAID disk drives are used frequently on servers but aren't generally necessary for personal computers.

3.5.2 What are RAID Levels?

In Redundant Arrays of Independent Disks (RAID) system, multiple disks operate in parallel to store the same information. It improves storage reliability. It eliminates the risk of data loss when one of the disk fails. Also, a large file is stored in several disk units by breaking the file up into a number of smaller pieces and storing these pieces on different disks. This is called data stripping

RAID level 0

Striped Disk Array RAID 0, also known as striping, which combines the sizes of multiple disks to form a single, large volume. Since no data redundancy is provided with this configuration, it is best used for read-only data sets where the highest level of performance is desired and where data survivability is not an issue. (See Figure 3.7).

RAID 0!is used to boost a server's performance. With RAID 0, data is written across multiple disks. This means the work that the computer is doing is handled by multiple disks rather than just one, increasing performance because multiple drives are reading and writing data, improving disk I/O. A minimum of two disks is required. Both software and hardware RAID support RAID 0, as do most controllers. The downside is that there is no fault tolerance. If one disk fails, then that affects the entire array and the chances for data loss or corruption increases.

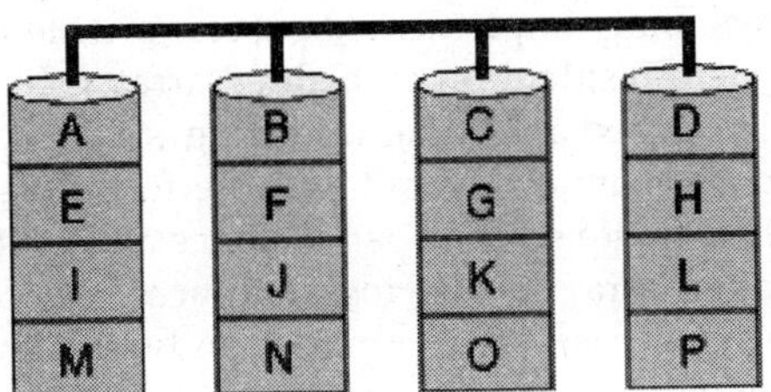

Figure 3.7 RAID level 0 - striped disk array without fault tolerance

RAID Level 1

RAID Level 1 -- Mirroring and Duplexing: Provides disk mirroring. Level 1 provides twice the read transaction rate of single disks and the same write transaction rate as single disks. (See Figure 3.8).

RAID 1!is a fault-tolerance configuration known as "disk mirroring." With RAID 1, two disk drives of equal capacity are used as a twinned pair, and any transaction saved to the array is written to both disks, thus maintaining a pair of mirror images. Similarly, whenever the system requests data from storage, it can come from one disk or the other, at the controller's choice. If the data occupies more than one disk block, the controller will usually fetch different parts of the file from the two drives in parallel, resulting in much faster throughput.

If one disk crashes, the system keeps humming along as if nothing had happened since all read and write operations continue to take place on the remaining healthy disk.

RAID 1, also known as disk mirroring, is best used on smaller system where large disk capacities are not required but where I/O throughput and data survivability are most critical.

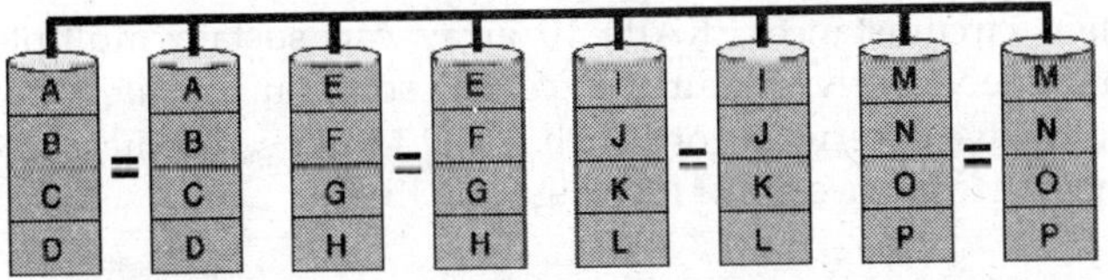

Figure 3.8 RAID level 1 - mirroring and duplexing

RAID Level 2

RAID Level 2 -- Error-Correcting Coding: Not a typical implementation and rarely used, Level 2 stripes data at the bit level rather than at the block level.

RAID 2!stripes data like RAID 0, but at even smaller level (bits instead of blocks) and uses additional hard drives and what's called Hamming code for error protection and parity which allows it to recover corrupt data. (See Figure 3.9).

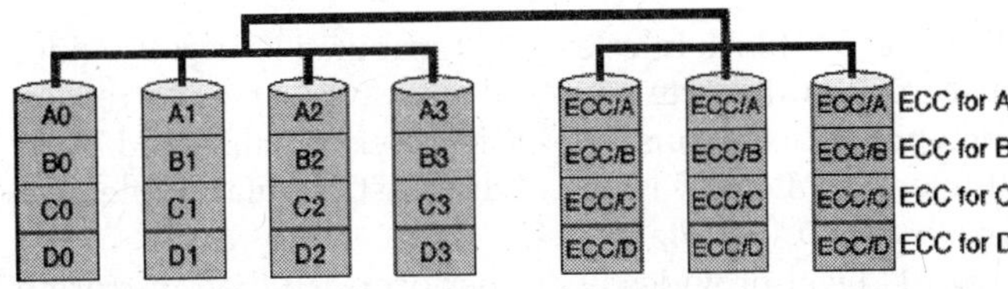

Figure 3.9 RAID level 2 - bit-level striping with Hamming Code ECC

RAID Level 3

RAID Level 3 -- Bit-Interleaved Parity: Provides byte-level striping with a dedicated parity disk. Level 3, which cannot service simultaneous multiple requests, is rarely used. (See Figure 3.10).

RAID 3!stripes data across multiple drives as well, but at the byte level, and it has a single disk dedicated to data parity and error correction. Because of the byte level split, all the drives work together simultaneously as one unit, which means it can only do one one read or write operation at a time.

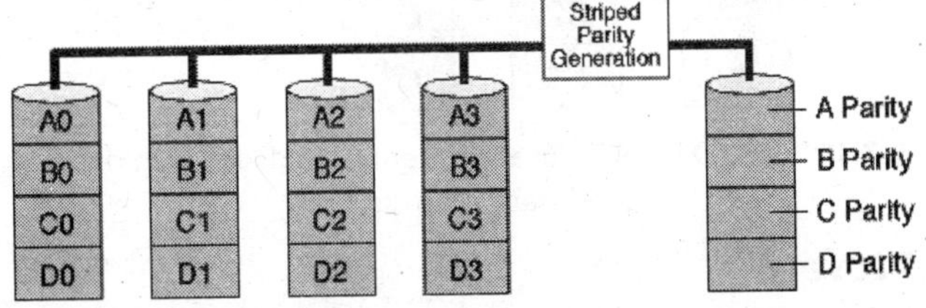

Figure 3.10 RAID level 3 - parallel transfer with parity

RAID Level 4

RAID Level 4 -- Dedicated Parity Drive: A commonly used implementation of RAID, Level 4 provides block-level striping (like Level 0) with a parity disk. If a data disk fails, the parity data is used to create a replacement disk. A disadvantage to Level 4 is that the parity disk can create write bottlenecks.

RAID 4!is a striping+parity disk setup too, but at the larger block level, so disks can be more independent, and you can have multiple read operations in different places going on. Since you're only using a single disk for parity, which has to be written to every time you write data, you can still only have one write operation going on at a time. (See Figure 3.11).

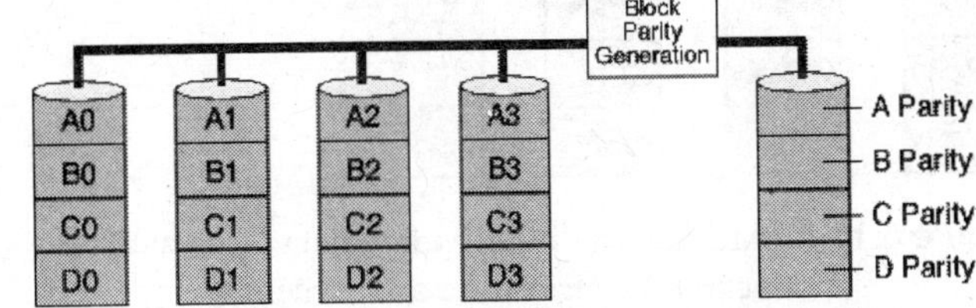

Figure 3.11 RAID level 4 - independent data disks with shared parity disk

RAID Level 5

RAID Level 5 -- Block Interleaved Distributed Parity: Provides data striping at the byte level and also stripe error correction information. This results in excellent performance and good fault tolerance. Level 5 is one of the most popular implementations of RAID. (See Figure 3.12).

This RAID level provides better performance than mirroring as well as fault tolerance. With RAID 5, data and parity (which is additional data used for recovery) are striped across three or more disks. If a disk gets an error or starts to fail, data is recreated from this distributed data and parity block seamlessly and automatically. Low ratio of ECC (Parity) disks to data disks means high efficiency Good aggregate transfer rate. Highest Read data transaction rate and medium Write data transaction rate.

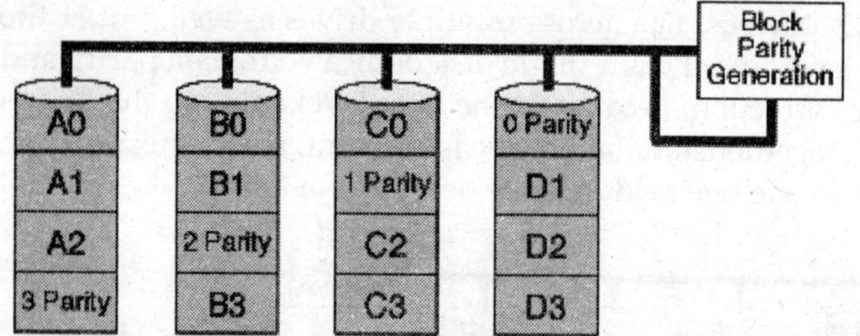

Figure 3.12 RAID level 5 - independent data disks with distributed parity blocks

RAID Level 6

RAID Level 6 -- RAID 6 is essentially an extension of RAID level 5 which allows for additional fault tolerance by using a second independent distributed parity scheme (two-dimensional parity) Data is striped on a block level across a set of drives, just like in RAID 5, and a second set of parity is calculated and written across all the drives; RAID 6 provides for an extremely high data fault tolerance and can sustain multiple simultaneous drive failures Perfect solution for mission critical applications. (See Figure 3.13).

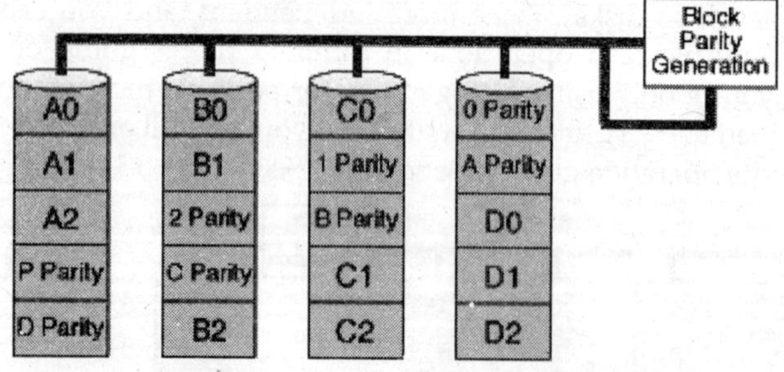

Figure 3.13 RAID level 6 - independent data disks with two independent distributed parity schemes

RAID Level 7

RAID Level 7: Optimized Asynchrony for High I/O Rates as well as High Data Transfer Rates. All I/O transfers are asynchronous, independently controlled and cached including host interface transfers. All reads and write are centrally cached via the high speed x-bus. Dedicated parity drive can be on any channel. Fully implemented process oriented real time operating system resident on embedded array control microprocessor. Embedded real time operating system controlled communications channel. Overall write performance is 25% to 90% better than single spindle performance and 1.5 to 6 times better than other array levels Host interfaces are scalable for connectivity or increased host transfer bandwidth Small reads in multi user environment have very high cache hit rate resulting in near zero access times Write performance improves with an increase in the number of drives in the array Access times decrease with each increase in the number of actuators in the array No extra data transfers required for parity manipulation.

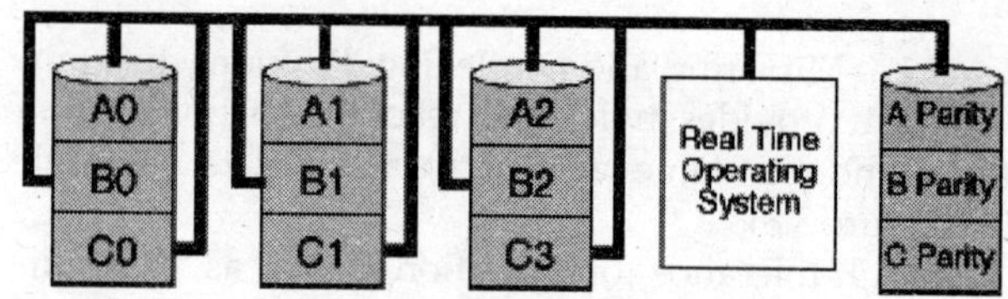

Figure 3.14 RAID level 7 - asynchronous cached striping with dedicated parity

RAID level 10

RAID Level 10 -- RAID 10!is a combination of RAID 1 and 0 and is often denoted as RAID 1+0. It combines the mirroring of RAID 1 with the striping of RAID 0. It's the RAID level that gives the best performance, but it is also costly, requiring twice as many disks as other RAID levels, for a minimum of four. This is the RAID level ideal for highly utilized database servers or any server that's performing many write operations. RAID 10 can be implemented as hardware or software, but the general consensus is that many of the performance advantages are lost when you use software RAID 10. Under certain circumstances, RAID 10 array can sustain multiple simultaneous drive failures Excellent solution for sites that would have otherwise gone with RAID 1 but need some additional performance boost (See Figure 3.15).

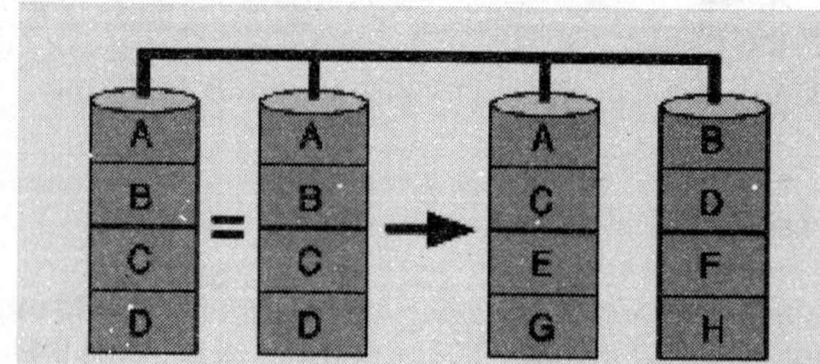

Figure 3.15 RAID level 10 - very high reliability combined with high performance

RAID level 53

RAID Level 53 requires a minimum of 5 drives to implement. RAID 53 should really be called "RAID 03" because it is implemented as a striped (RAID level 0) array whose segments are RAID 3 arrays RAID 53 has the same fault tolerance as RAID 3 as well as the same fault tolerance overhead High data transfer rates are achieved thanks to its RAID 3 array segments High I/O rates for small requests are achieved thanks to its RAID 0 striping Maybe a good solution for sites who would have otherwise gone with RAID 3 but need some additional performance boost. Its disadvantage is that it is Very expensive to implement. All disk spindles must be synchronized, which limits the choice of drives. Byte striping results in poor utilization of formatted capacity

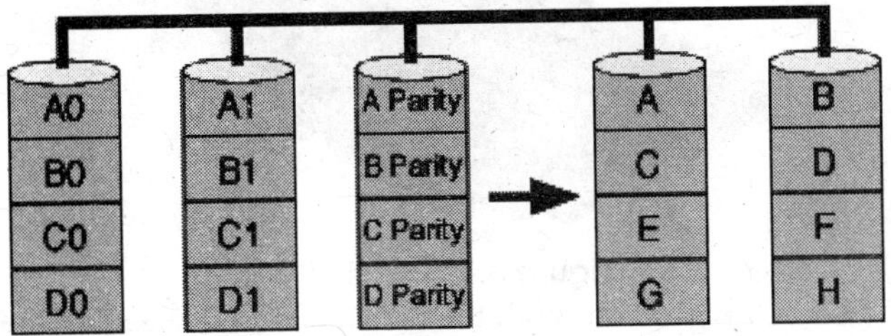

Figure 3.16 RAID level 53 - high I/O rates and data transfer performance

3.6 MINIATURE HARD DISK

Miniature mobile storage media are rewriteable media usually in the forms of flash memory card, usb flash drive or smart card. Miniature mobile storage media allows mobile users to transport digital images, music or documents easily to and from computer and other devices. Used for both internal and external storage. Have form factors of 1.8 inch, 1 inch, and 0.85 inch. Used in some devices such as portable media players, digital cameras, and smart phones.

3.7 HARD DISK CONTROLLER

The disk controller is a device used to manage the physical characteristics of a HDD: availability status, moving read/write heads, waiting for sectors to rotate under the heads, and reading and writing data on a bit level. There are different types of controller based on the harddisk type, I/O speed and relevant data bus or wires which enables the data operations to happen between CPU and storage media. Some of the commonly known types include, Parallel ATA (PATA, also called IDE or EIDE) is very old and widely used controller for older versions of PCs. IDE was enhanced by introduction of Serial ATA (SATA). Other faster controllers are SCSI, Serial Attached SCSI (SAS) and external hard disk interfaces like USB and FireWire, connecting external hard disks to the PC.

3.7.1 AT Attachment (ATA)

AT Attachment (ATA), was the most common hard disk interface used in PCs from early 1990s through 2003. ATA is also called Parallel ATA or PATA, to differentiate it from the newer serial ATA (SATA) interface. ATA is still used in new systems, although it is being superceded by SATA. ATA is also called IDEC (Integrated Drive Electronics).

3.7.2 Serial ATA (SATA)

SATA stands for Serial Advanced Technology Attachment. A SATA controller (Serial ATA controller) is a hardware interface that connects a hard drive to a computer's motherboard and manages or directs the flow of data. Serial ATA is a newer technology that is replacing ATA. This SATA technology has several advantages over ATA, including smaller cables and connectors, higher bandwidth, and greater reliability. Although SATA and ATA are incompatible at the physical and electrical levels, adapters are readily available that allows SATA drives to be connected to ATA interfaces and vice versa. SATA is generally compatible with ATA at the software level, which means that the operating system ATA drivers work with either SATA or ATA interfaces and hard drives. There are three Serial Advanced Technology Attachment controller modes:

- Integrated Drive Electronics (IDE) mode sets the hard drive to run as an IDE or Parallel Advanced Technology Attachment (PATA) hard drive. For older hardware, this mode may offer better compatibility; however, a hard drive in IDE mode usually performs more slowly.
- Advanced Host Controller Interface (AHCI) enables the use of advanced features, such as hot swapping, on SATA drives. Hard drives operating in AHCI mode can operate at higher speeds than those in IDE mode.
- Redundant Array of Independent Disks (RAID) mode enables both AHCI features and RAID functions.

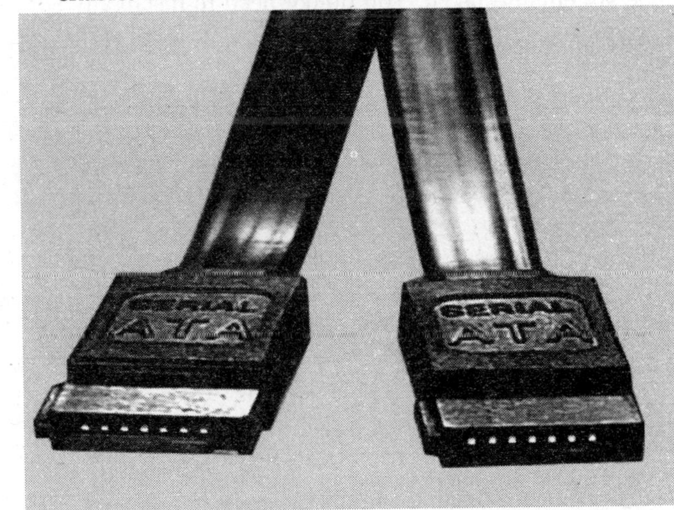

Figure 3.17 SATA cable

☞ *Each interface connector is keyed with an L-shaped body, which prevent the SATA cable from being connected backward.*

3.7.3 IDE (Integrated Drive Electronics)

IDE is a standard electronic interface used between a computer motherboard's data paths or bus and the computer's disk storage devices. The IDE interface is based on the IBM PC Industry Standard Architecture (ISA) 16-bit bus standard. It is also used in computers that use other bus standards. Most computers sold today use an enhanced version of IDE called Enhanced Integrated Drive Electronics (EIDE). In today's computers, the IDE controller is built into the motherboard.

Most drives today are IDE. These drives have the controller built on the motherboard. They plug into a bus connector on the motherboard or an adapter card. Such drives are easy to install and require a minimum number of cables. This is due to the fact that the controller is on the drive itself. Fewer parts are needed and the signal pathways can be much shorter. These short signal pathways improve reliability of the drive. Integrating the controller is easier by the manufacturer because they do not have to worry about complying with another manufacturer's controller. Each drive is an independent entity.

- IDE interface ensures that the data communication between the hard disk and the controller is fast.
- The IDE interface also provides for a high data transfer rate between the hard disk and the system.

3.7.4 EIDE (Enhanced Integrated Device Electronics)

Most computers sold today use an enhanced version of IDE called Enhanced Integrated Drive Electronics (EIDE).

The EIDE interface supports a maximum of four hard disk drives on a system. The EIDE hard disk is a plug and play device. To use this device you must just plug the devices to the system and use it. You do not need to install any special drives to use the hard disk.

Figure 3.18 EIDE data cable

3.7.5 SCSI

SCSI stands for Small Computer Systems Interface. SCSI is an universal parallel I/O interface for microcomputers to link multiple peripheral devices of different types on a single I/O bus. The SCSI interface enables the hard disk to communicate with the system at very fast speed. This interface is used on the network servers that perform a lot of processing. There are three different SCSI Standards: SCSI (or SCSI 1), SCSI-2, and SCSI-3.

The SCSI standard defines the physical and electrical parameters of a parallel I/O bus used to connect computers and peripheral devices in daisy-chain fashion. The standard supports devices such as disk drives, tape drives, and CD-ROM drives. The original SCSI standard (American National Standards Institute or ANSI X3.131-1986) was approved in 1986, SCSI-2 was approved in January 1994.

Figure 3.19 SCSI cable

SCSI-1 : One problem with the original SCSI-1 was that many of the commands and features were optional. This problem caused the industry as a whole to define a set of 18 basic SCSI commands called the Common Command Set (CCS), which would become the minimum set of commands supported by all peripherals. CCS became the basis for what is now the SCSI-2 specification.

SCSI-2 : In addition to formal support for CCS, SCSI-2 provides additional definitions for commands to access CD-ROM drives (and their sound capabilities), tape drives, removable drives, optical drives, and several other peripherals. In addition, an optional higher speed called Fast SCSI-2 and a 16-bit version called Wide SCSI-2 were defined. Another feature of SCSI-2 is command queuing, which enables a device to accept multiple commands and execute them in the order that the device deems to be most efficient. This feature is most beneficial when you are using a multitasking operating system that could be sending several requests on the SCSI bus at the same time.

SCSI-3 : The latest version of SCSI is known as SCSI-3 which can connect up to 15 devices at a time. These devices can be hard disk drive, printer, mouse, graphics tablet, image scanner, etc. Each device connected to SCSI bus is assigned with an identification number. The host adapter uses the highest identification number. The data transfer rate of SCSI-3 is 80 MB/s. But, the high data transfer rate of SCSI-3 is up to 100 MB/s which can generally be done through six-conductor coaxial cable. SCSI-3 works on the basis of SCSI-3 architecture which is defined by a document known as SCSI-3 Architecture Model (SAM). This model is approved by ANSI Standard X3.270-1996. The prime function of this model is to organize and categorize the other Standards which work under SCSI-3. Let us discuss these Standards in brief.

- **Commands**: A set of commands used by SCSI devices.
- **Protocols**: A set of rules used by various devices to communicate and share information. These rules are used to describe the transport layer of interface.

- **Interconnects**: Specific details which are used to describe physical layer interface. These details include electrical interface details and data transfer modes.

Commands, Protocols and Interconnects are closely related by the Common Access Method (CAM). The prime objective of CAM is to define software services for computers (host) to interface with SCSI devices. The SCSI-3 supports more than eight devices and the transfer speed is 20 Mbps. Its main objective is to support optical fiber and long distance.

3.7.6 Serial Attached SCSI (SAS)

SAS stands for Serial Attached SCSI (SCSI Stands for Small Computer System Interface, Abbreviated as SAS, an evolution of parallel SCSI into a point-to-point serial peripheral interface in which controllers are linked directly to disk drives. SAS is a performance improvement over traditional SCSI because SAS enables multiple devices (up to 128) of different sizes and types to be connected simultaneously with thinner and longer cables; its full-duplex signal transmission supports 3.0Gb/s. In addition, SAS drives can be hot-plugged.

Figure 3.20 SAS cable

3.7.7 Managing Data in Hard Disk

Most of the harddisk manufacturers guarantee their hard disks to last approximately three to five years. Many last much longer with proper care. To prevent lass of data stored on harddisk, you should regularly perform preventive maintenance such as defragmenting or scanning the disk for errors.

3.8 INTRODUCTION DAS, NAS ,AND SAN

Data is one of the important asset of a company. If anything goes wrong with data, company will get into trouble. Hence, the data must be stored efficiently and securely. Different techniques are as follows:

(a) DAS (Direct Attached Storage)
(b) NAS (Network Attached Storage)
(c) SAN (Storage Area Network)

3.8.1 DAS

DAS or Direct Attached Storage comprises storage devices such as hard disks or tape drives connected directly to a network server. It could be inside the same box as the server, or reside outside and it may be connected through a cable. This is the most basic and widely used method of storage. It is simple and does not require too much time to set up. A DAS setup can have a single hard disk, multiple independent hard disks called JBOD (Just a Bunch of Disks), or an array of hard disks configured for fault tolerance, known as RAID (Redundant Array of Independent Disks). The most common types of media and protocols used in DAS are SCSI (Small Computer System Interface), fiber channel and SSA (Serial Storage Architecture).

Advantages of DAS

(a) DAS is easy to implement. It gives a reasonably good performance.

(b) It also has relatively lower acquisition and administrative costs.

Disadvantage of DAS

(a) Its capabilities are limited to the server it is connected to. So if the server is down, users can not access their data.

(b) It can not be connected over long distances and the storage capacity is also limited compared to NAS and SAN.

(c) DAS devices also pose management problems, as you have to manage the data on a server-by-server basis.

3.8.2 NAS (Network Attached Storage)

An attempt to overcome problems associated with DAS led to the development of NAS (Network Attached Storage). Unlike DAS devices, which connect to a particular server, NAS devices connect directly to your existing Ethernet network and they are independent of the server. So, if the server fails due to some reason, data is still available to users on the network.

Network Attached Storage (NAS) is the name given to dedicated data storage technology which can be connected directly to a computer network to provide centralized data access and storage to heterogeneous network clients (See Figure 3.21).

NAS differs from the traditional file serving and direct attached storage. They are server appliances.

The Operating System (OS) and other software on the NAS unit provide only the functionality of data storage, data access and the management of these functionalities and usually with Web interface. NAS unit does not limit clients to only one file transfer protocol. NAS systems usually contain one or more hard disks, arranged into logical, redundant storage containers or RAIDs (redundant arrays of independent disks).

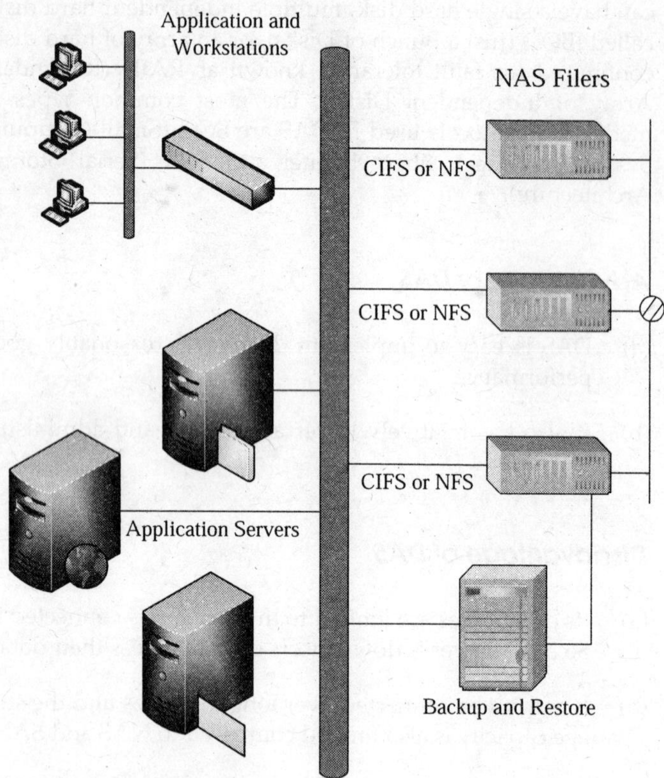

NFS: Network File System
CIFS: Common Internet File System

Figure 3.21 Network Attached Storage

☞ *NAS removes the responsibility of file serving from other servers on the network and can be deployed via commercial embedded units or via standard computers running NAS software.*

NAS is shared storage on a local area network. A NAS server is a storage appliance that consists of a high performance file server that plugs into a LAN. Unlike a general-purpose server, such as a UNIX or NT server, an NAS server is a specialized appliance optimized for file serving, i.e., storing, retrieving, and serving files. NAS server has software only for file serving.

NAS servers use small, specialized, and proprietary operating systems instead of general-purpose operating systems (OSs), such as the UNIX and Windows NT operating systems.

NAS devices can be placed anywhere on your network and can be accessed by any user. Its function is similar to that of a network printer, which can be accessed by anyone when required. NAS devices support most network protocols, such as NFS for UNIX, CIFS (Common Internet File System) for Microsoft, FTP (File Transfer Protocol), and HTTP (Hyper Text Transfer Protocol). This makes them useful for heterogeneous networking environments.

NAS devices comprise a number of hard-disk drives and come with their own OS and management software. They can be used for a variety of applications including Web caching for proxy servers, backup, databases, print spoolers, or simply as file servers.

☞ *Storage capacities for NAS devices can range from 2 GB to over 2 TB (terabytes).*

NAS allows organizations to set up a storage solution using their existing Ethernet backbone, without investing in a separate network.

Since NAS operates on networks that were primarily designed for data transfers and not storage, performance issues, such as network congestion arise. If you exceed storage capacity, then you must add another NAS device.

Advantages of NAS

Advantages of NAS are as follows:

(a) Users running different types of machines (PC, Apple iMac, etc.) and running different types of operating systems (Windows, UNIX, Mac OS, etc.) can share files.
(b) NAS appliances are "plug-and-play" meaning that very little installation and configuration is required beyond connecting them to the LAN.
(c) Less administration overhead than that required for a UNIX or NT file server.
(d) Centralized storage, which makes it easier and cheaper to maintain, backup, and administer (comparable to DAS). Centralized storage is more expensive than local disks on byte cost basis, but users have to do tasks, such as backups and restores on their own.
(e) Fast response times for users, since NAS are on LANs, close to the users, as opposed to being on a backbone SAN, marginally faster than DAS, but slower than a local disk.

Disadvantages of NAS

NAS has the following disadvantages:

(a) Heavy use of NAS will clog up the shared LAN negatively affecting the users on the LAN. Therefore, NAS is not suitable for data transfer of intensive applications.
(b) Somewhat inefficient since data transfer rides on top of standard TCP/IP (Transmission Control Protocol / Internet Protocol) protocol.
(c) Cannot offer any storage service guarantees for mission critical operations since NAS operates in a shared environment.
(d) NAS is shared storage. As with other shared storage, system administrators must enforce quotas.

3.8.3 SAN (Storage Area Network)

A Storage Area Network (SAN) is a high-speed special-purpose network (or subnetwork) that interconnects different kinds of data storage devices with associated data servers. A storage area network is part of the overall network of computing resources for an enterprise.

A storage area network can use existing communication technology, such as IBM's (International Business Machines) optical fiber ESCON (Enterprise System Connection) or it may use the newer Fibre Channel technology. Some SAN system integrators liken it to the common storage bus (flow of data) in a personal computer that is shared by different kinds of storage devices such as a hard disk or a CD-ROM player.

SANs support disk mirroring, backup and restore, archival and retrieval of archived data, data migration from one storage device to another, and the sharing of data among different servers in a network. SANs can incorporate subnetworks with network-attached storage (NAS) systems.

☞ *SAN is a separate network linked to your company's main network via a high-speed interface like a fiber channel or SCSI. This sort of a solution is useful for companies having high transaction volumes like banks and customer-service oriented organizations who need quick access to data at any point of time.*

A SAN consists of multiple storage systems and servers and is much faster than a NAS system. That is because the various storage devices in a SAN are connected through a high-speed interface. Fiber channel typically has a data transfer rate of 1 GB/sec. SCSI transfer rates are lower than fiber-channel, about 80 MB/sec. However, in future these devices are likely to communicate over Gigabit Ethernet using iSCSI or Fiber Channel over TCP/IP (FCIP).

The various storage devices in a SAN interface with the company's main network via switches and hubs, and can be simultaneously accessed by multiple servers and computers. All SAN components are controlled using SAN management software, which allows users and system administrators to remotely control its functioning.

Fiber-channel SANs can be deployed in following two topologies:

(a) Arbitrated loop
(b) Fabric or switched fabric

It can be compared to the token ring topology and enables you to connect up to 127 fiber-channel enabled devices. However, instead of sending a token, devices in this topology, it send a signal that tells other devices that they want to gain control of the transmission medium. When one device gains control, other devices have to wait until that device's I/O cycle is complete. The main disadvantage of this topology is that servers connected in this topology have to share the available bandwidth.

Switched-fabric Topology

Here, servers share the bandwidth only when other servers need to access the same storage device. However, if each server needs to use a separate device, it can make use of the entire bandwidth. This topology provides a virtual dedicated connection between the network servers and the SAN. It lets you interconnect up to 64,000 devices. The switched-fabric topology offers better SAN performance than the arbitrated-loop topology.

Different SAN solutions are available from different vendors. Some offer complete solutions with all necessary products, such as hubs and switches. Others, however, provide SANs that include only the hard disk drive enclosure with the specialized OS. You need to add other SAN components such as bridges, hubs, and switches later on.

Comparison of NAS Vs SAN

At a high level, Storage Area Networks (SANs) serve the same purpose as a NAS system. A SAN supplies data storage capability to other network devices. Traditional SANs differ from traditional NAS in several ways. Specifically, SANs often utilized Fibre Channel rather than Ethernet, and a SAN often incorporated multiple network devices or "endpoints" on a self-contained or "private" LAN, whereas NAS relied on individual devices connected directly to the existing public LAN.

☞ *The traditional NAS system is a simpler network storage solution, effectively a subset of a full SAN implementation.*

Today's SANs use Ethernet, but NAS systems sometimes use Fibre Channel, and NAS systems sometimes incorporate private networks with multiple endpoints. The primary difference between NAS and SAN is the choice of network protocol. SAN systems transfer data over the network in the form of disk blocks (fixed-sized file chunks, using low-level storage protocols like SCSI) whereas NAS systems operate at a higher level with the file itself.

3.9 CLOUD STORAGE

Cloud storage is a cloud computing model in which data is stored on remote servers accessed from the Internet, or "cloud." It is maintained, operated and managed by a cloud storage service provider on a storage servers that are built on virtualization techniques. Cloud storage can provide the benefits of greater accessibility and reliability; rapid deployment; strong protection for data backup, archival and disaster recovery purposes. (See Figure 3.22).

Cloud computing or on-demand computing is an Internet-based computing service which involves the use of the network of remote servers rather than local server or personal computer, which host on the Internet for storing, managing, and processing the data (See Figure 3.23).

In cloud computing, Cloud is a large group of interconnected computers, which may be personal or public.

Consider an example: If you have a Gmail or Yahoo account, then you are already using Cloud Computing. As you donot know where exactly your e-mail and contacts are stored, and you can access your account via Internet.

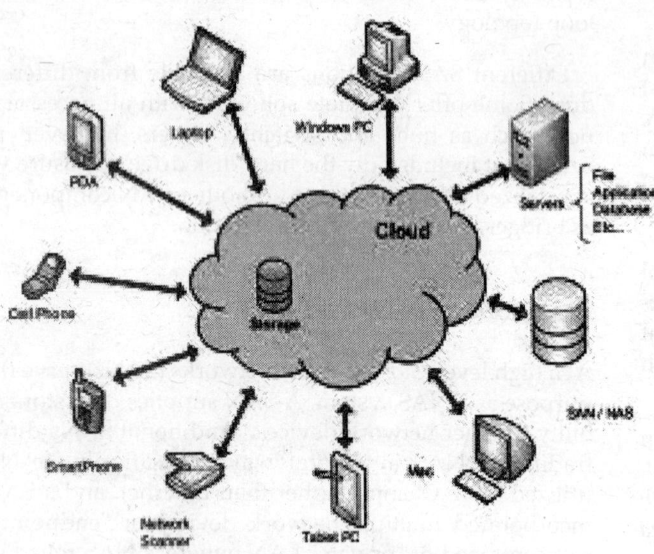

Figure 3.22 Cloud storage

Figure 3.23 Cloud Computing

Cloud computing allows

- Companies to focus on only projects which differentiate their businesses instead of on infrastructure and to avoid upfront infrastructure costs.
- Enterprises to get their applications up and run faster, with less maintenance.
- To rapidly adjust the resources, to meet fluctuating and unpredictable business demand.

Cloud computing is highly demanded service or utility because of its:

- High computing power and performance
- Cheap cost of services
- Scalability, accessibility and availability.

3.9.1 Properties

The key properties of Cloud computing are:

- **User-centric:** Once the user gets connected to cloud, any data which is present there, such as images, videos, applications, becomes his/her property.
- **Task Centric:** In this, documents are given more priority than applications from which they are created.
- **Powerful:** Due to its computing power and mass data storage capability.
- **Self-Healing:** Backups of every document is created automatically in the cloud.
- **Multi-tenancy & Intelligence:** Multi-tenancy means sh ing of data among a large number of users, by using d mining and analysis for accessing information in intelligent manner.
- **Programmable:** Programming is associated with clo computing, as processes such as backing up of data done automatically, which requires programming.
- **Flexible:** It matches with the needs of user.

3.9.2 Characteristics

Key characteristics of cloud computing are:

- **Agility:** It improves with users' ability to re-provis technological infrastructure resources.
- **Cost reductions claimed by cloud providers:** The cap investment in the data centre is assumed by the clo provider and operation costs are passed onto the clo data centre user.
- **Device and location independence:** It enables the users access systems through web browser irrespective of th location or the device they are using.
- **Maintenance:** cloud computing applications maintena is easier, as it does not need to be installed on each us computer and can be accessed from many places, p vided that there must be an internet connection.
- **Multitenancy:** It enables the sharing of resources a costs across a large number of users.
- **Productivity:** It is increased as multiple users work on same data simultaneously than waiting for it to be sa and emailed.
- **Time:** Time is saved as information does not need to re-entered again and again when fields are matched, the users need to install an application software upgra to their computer.
- **Reliability:** It enables the use of multiple redundant si which makes well-designed cloud computing suitable business continuity.
- **Security:** It is improved due to centralization of d security-focused resources, etc.

3.10 OTHER STORAGE DEVICES

3.11 FLASH MEMORY STORAGE

Flash memory is a type of nonvolatile memory that era data in units called blocks. A block stored on a flash mem chip must be erased before data can be written, or p grammed, to the microchip. Flash memory retains data for extended period of time whether a flash-equipped devic powered on or off. Flash memory evolved from erasable p grammable read-only memory (EPROM) and electric erasable programmable read-only memory (EEPROM). Fl is technically a variant of EEPROM, but the industry reser the term EEPROM for byte-level erasable memory and app the term flash memory to larger block-level erasable mem Devices using flash memory erase data at the block level rewrite data at the byte level (NOR flash) or multiple-b page level (NAND flash). Flash memory is widely used for storage and data transfer in consumer devices, enterprise systems and industrial applications.

3.11.1 How flash memory works?

A basic flash memory cell consists of a storage transistor with a control gate and a floating gate, which is insulated from the rest of the transistor by a thin dielectric material or oxide layer. The floating gate stores the electrical charge and controls the flow of the electrical current.

Flash memory technology is a mix of EPROM and EEPROM technologies. The term "flash" was chosen because a large chunk of memory could be erased at one time. The name, therefore, distinguishes flash devices from EEPROMs, where each byte is erased individually. Flash memory technology is today a mature technology. It is a strong competitor to other nonvolatile memories such as EPROMs and EEPROMs, and to some DRAM applications.

3.11.2 Solid State Drives

SSD mass storage devices (solid state drives) were designed to replace hard disk drives that are based on rotating magnetic disks. SSDs do not have mechanical components, and are more silent and often faster than HDDs (at least in reading data), but repeated writing to them may, in some cases, decrease their lifespan. (See Figure 3.24).

A traditional hard disk drive (HDD) consists of a spinning disk with a read/write head on a mechanical arm called an actuator. An SSD, on the other hand, has an array of semiconductor memory organized as a disk drive, using integrated circuits (ICs) rather than magnetic or optical storage media. Like a memory stick, there are no moving parts to an SSD. Rather, information is stored in microchips. Conversely, a hard disk drive uses a mechanical arm with a read/write head to move around and read information from the right location on a storage platter. This difference is what makes SSD so much faster.

A typical SSD uses what is called NAND-based flash memory. This is a non-volatile type of memory. A solid-state drive uses a type of memory called 'flash memory', which is similar to RAM. However, unlike RAM, which clears whenever the computer powers down, SSD memory remains even when it loses power.

Figure 3.24 Solid state drive

3.11.3 Memory Stick

Memory Stick technology is developed by Sony. It is used in CyberShot digital cameras and other Sony electronic devices. Memory Stick uses a serial interface to transfer data between the host device and card. But the Sony Memory Stick has a 128 MB limitation (See Figure 3.25).

Figure 3.25 Memory Stick

Memory stick comes in following varieties:

(a) *PRO:* Sony Memory Stick PRO is the new Standard to eliminate the 128 MB limitation. Currently, Memory Stick PRO is available up to 1 GB. The Memory Stick PRO format has a transfer rates upto 480 MB/s. It is commonly used in high megapixel digital cameras and digital camcorders. Memory Stick PRO will not work in devices that only support the standard Memory Stick. But Memory Stick PRO devices are compatible with the original Memory Stick. Today, all 128 MB, and under, cards are Memory Stick, while all larger cards are Memory Stick PRO.

(b) *DUO:* Memory Stick Duo and Memory Stick Pro Duo are basically smaller version of the Memory Stick Pro. The Duo has pin-to-pin compatibility with its older and larger Memory Stick sibling.

(c) *MagicGate:* MagicGate is Sony's name for Digital Rights Management (DRM), a copy-protection technology. It encrypts the data stored on the card and enforces control over how the files on the card are copied.

Advantages

(a) Transfer rates are very fast.
(b) Best for high megapixel camera.

Disadvantages

It is compatible with Sony products only.

3.11.4 Memory Cards

A memory card is a device offering an easy, fast and reliable way for storing and transferring digital files. It works like a portable hard disk drive but comes with some superior advantages, since almost every memory card is based on flash memory technology, of having much smaller form factor and being non-volatile and solid state. Making flash memory cards much more durable and reliable than hard disk drives. Memory cards are made by a variety of manufacturers and can be found in different storage capacities and transfer speeds.

Memory cards are used, for example, in digital cameras and mobile phones. Newer (laptop) computers often have built-in memory card readers. Memory card formats include, among others, Compact Flash (CF), Secure Digital (SD), Multi Media Card (MMC) and Memory Stick.

3.11.5 MicroSD Memory Card

The microSD card is even smaller than the miniSD card. The microSD card is designed for use in cellular phones and small mobile devices. The microSD card can accessed in a SD card slot via an adapter (See Figure 3.26).

Figure 3.26 SD card

3.11.6 USB Flash Drives

USB flash drives, or pen drives, are NAND-type flash memory data storage devices integrated with a USB (Universal Serial Bus) interface. They are typically small, light-weight, removable and rewritable. It is a flash memory card that plugs into the computer's USB port. It emulates a small disk drive and allows data to be easily transferred from one machine to another. A USB drive is also known as a flash drive, pen drive, keychain drive, key drive, USB key and memory key (See Figure 3.27).

Figure 3.27 Pen drive

Advantages of USB Drive

Pen drives offer potential advantages over other portable storage devices. The advantages are as follows:

(a) It is more compact, faster, holds more data, and is more reliable

(b) It uses the USB mass storage standard, supported natively by modern operating systems, such as Windows, Linux and UNIX.

To access the data stored in a pen drive, the drive must be connected to a computer through a USB host controller. Pen drives are active only when plugged into a USB connection and draw all necessary power from the supply provided by that connection.

Various memory cards and memory sticks (flash memory/USB flash drives) are non-volatile memory, meaning that the information stored in them is retained even if the device is powered off. Non-volatile memory is not designed for long-term preservation, although it is not as vulnerable to problems caused by external factors as optical media. Due to their small size, non-volatile memory devices are fit for transferring working copies from one computer to another. There is a drawback to the small size, though: memory sticks, in particular, tend to get lost surprisingly often.

Memory stick (USB flash drive) is a device with small external dimensions that can be connected to a USB port on a computer. A flash drive is displayed as a removable disk in 'My Computer' and data can be stored on it similarly to a hard disk drive. Commonly, USB flash drives have a capacity of 4-64 GB.

3.11.7 Express Card Modules

Express Card, initially called NEWCARD, is an interface to connect peripheral devices to a computer, usually a laptop computer. The Express Card technical standard specifies the design of slots built into the computer and of expansion cards to insert in the slots. Express Card also has a direct link to the USB bus meaning many USB technologies can be converted to this new technology without needing a bridge. It's actually cheaper for manufacturers to use the Express Card slot than the PCMCIA slot, so reduces the overall cost of a notebook. (See Figure 3.28).

Figure 3.28 Express card module

3.12 MAGNETIC MEDIA

Magnetic storage media have been used for a long time. Digital information can be written magnetically on tapes or hard disks, both of whose storage capacities are larger than, say, those of optical media. Floppy disks (or diskettes) are storage devices that are rapidly becoming obsolete, and modern computers do not have drives to read or write them.
Hard disk drives (hard drives, HDDs) are used as mass storage devices for computers. Data is written to the magnetic surface(s) of the rotating metal or glass disk(s) inside the case. In addition to conventional use as mass storage devices, there are nowadays "external" hard drives (with USB connection) that offer significant portable storage capacity (from 450 GB to 6 TB). External hard drives are considerably slower at writing than "internal" ones. A hard disk drive is an excellent medium for processing a working copy of data, but unreliable for long-term preservation.
Digital magnetic tape systems are designed mainly for backing up extensive data systems long term. They are not very well suited for storing working copies, because retrieving data is slow and the tapes wear out if they are read often. Using and maintaining tape systems require specific skills and a tape system is expensive to use for single research projects.

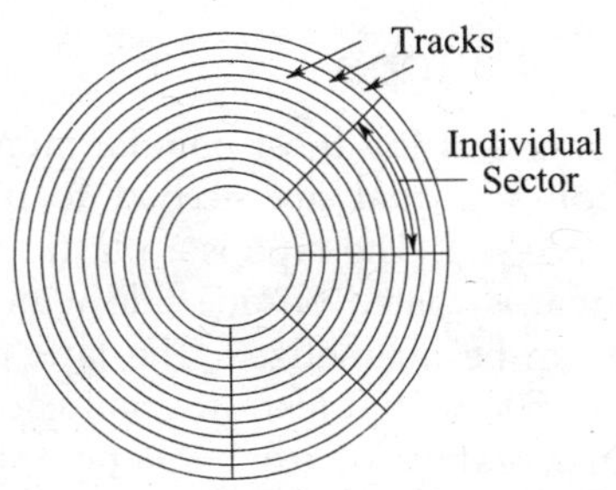

Figure 3.29 Sectors on a disk

☞ *Seek Time is the time taken to position the read/write head over the required track.*

3.12.1 Magnetic Disk

Magnetic disks are direct or random access storage devices, and are the primary storage medium used with computers for fast access to programs and data.

A magnetic disk storage is one in which data are stored as a series of magnetized spots on the flat surfaces of disks. A common spindle rotates the disk spinning at speeds of 60 or more revolutions per second. Disks are analogous to turntables. The flat sides of the disk platter are the recording surfaces, the tone arm is the access arm, and the stylus (needle) is the read/write head.

Tracks and Sectors

The disk surface comprises several tracks arranged in concentric circles. The greater the number of tracks, the more is the storage capacity of the disk. The smaller the spots, the more the bits per inch and hence greater the storage capacity. Most disks hold the same number of bits on each track, even though the outer tracks are physically longer than the inner ones. The circular tracks are further divided into segments, called sectors, which determine the least amount of data that can be read or written back to the disk. A sector can contain several records, or one record can span several sectors (See Figures 3.29 and 3.30).

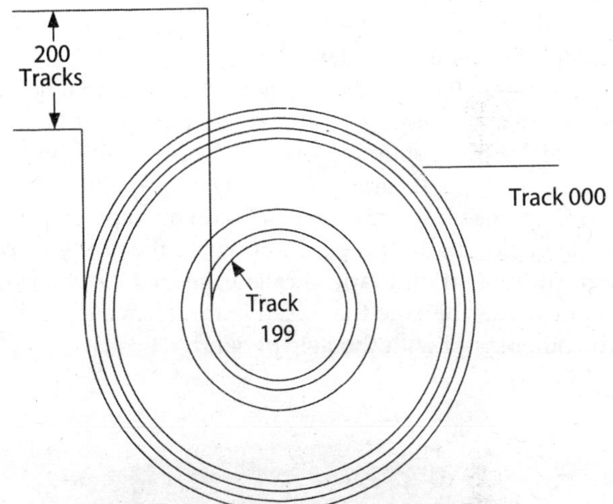

Figure 3.30 Tracks on a disk

Advantages of Magnetic Disks

- Magnetic disks follow direct access mode for reading and writing the data files, thereby making an ideal device for accessing frequently accessed data.
- Magnetic disks are used for both online and offline storage of data.
- Magnetic disks are easily moveable from one place to another because of their small size.
- The data transfer rate of disks is much higher than magnetic tapes.

Disadvantages of Magnetic Disks

- Magnetic disks must be stored in a dust-free environment in order to protect them from crashing.
- Magnetic disks are not ideal devices to use in scenarios where the file access required is of sequential nature rather than direct or random nature.
- Magnetic disks are more expensive than the magnetic tapes.

3.12.2 Magnetic Tape

Magnetic tape is one of the most popular storage media for large volumes of data that are needed to be sequentially accessed and processed. The tape is a plastic ribbon usually 1/2 inch wide that is coated on one side with an iron-oxide material which can be magnetized. The tape ribbon itself is stored in reels of 50 to 2400 feet, in small cartridges or cassettes. It is similar to the tape used on a tape-recorder except that it is of higher quality and more durable. Like the recorder tape, the computer tape can also be erased and reused again and again.

Bits are recorded as magnetic spots on the tape. Seven or nine bits are recorded to form a character along with a parity bit. The tape consists of concentric circles called *Tracks*. Read/Write heads are mounted one in each track to write and read data (See Figure 3.31).

These tapes can be started, stopped, moved forward or backward or can be re-wound. But it cannot directly read any data, located in between other data.

Figure 3.31 shows how a data is recorded on a magnetic tape. A label is a small block of information used in tape processing that makes the beginning or end of a file or the beginning or end of the tape. It can contain other information, such as the number of records in the file or files on the tape. A label that is at the beginning of a tape is known as the *header label* and the one at the end of a tape is called the *trailer label*. The *leader* is a portion of the tape that is left blank for winding the tape on the other spool with the help of hand.

Figure 3.31 Data Recorded on a magnetic tape

Advantages of Magnetic Tapes

The advantages of magnetic tape are given below.

Economical A 0.5 inch wide reel of tape costs much less than other data storage devices. A typical 0.5 inch wide reel of magnetic tape is 2,400 feet long and is able to hold 800, 1600, or 6250 characters per inch of this length. Thus, if 6250 characters are held per inch and if the tape is 28,800 inches long (2400 feet times 12 inches), then the maximum capacity of the tape is 180 million characters.

Fast Input/Output As already discussed, data transfer rate for a magnetic tape can be in excess of 1 million bytes per second.

Long Term Storage Since the reel is compact and weighs less than one kilogram, it obviously occupies much less storage space and is much easier to handle. Large computer centres make use of extensive tape libraries, which contain thousands and thousands of reels of stored information and may occupy an entire room in an organization. The data stored on magnetic reels kept in cool environment and away from dust can be retained for years and retrieved as and when desired.

Reusable An additional cost benefit is that tapes can be erased and reused many times.

Disadvantages of Magnetic Tapes

Only Sequential Recording and Access Magnetic tape is a sequential access device and hence data recorded on tape cannot be addressed directly. Data can only be retrieved serially. So if a required data item is at the end of a tape, all the earlier parts have to be read before accessing this item. If random access is frequently required, then magnetic tape is not a suitable storage medium for such a requirement. Too much operator time would be required to load and unload tapes and too much machine time would be wasted in fetching the exact data that is needed.

Inconvenient for Storing Large Number of Small Records To isolate one record from another stored on a tape, an inter-record gap is provided between two adjacent records. Also, some portion of the tape at one end is left unrecorded for threading purposes. A tape is used for such a requirement.

Non-standarization of Drives makes Compatibility Difficult Variability of tape densities can be a problem since some drives cannot read tapes recorded at very high or very low densities.

3.12.3 Portable Hard Drive

Portable hard disk drive that is plugged into an external port on a computer, such as USB or FireWire are used for backup. For laptops, the PC Card slot may be used to connect a cable to a full-size drive, or the hard disk that may be contained entirely inside the PC Card (See Figure 3.32). The portable size available in the market are 320 GB, 500 GB and 1 and 2 Tetra GB.

It allows the user to back up or store important information separate from the main internal hard drive, which could become compromised by online or offline activities. Documents such as music files, DVD images, movies, disk images, and even a backup of the contents of your main internal hard drive, can all be kept securely and safely on an external hard drive.

Figure 3.32 Portable hard drive

3.12.4 Winchester disk

The Winchester disk is a medium sized non-interchangeable metal disk permanently housed in a sealed, contamination free container. The read/write heads are built-in with the disk. These disks are used with mini computers only.

3.12.5 Zip drive

A zip disk needs a special drive. A Zip drive is a small, portable disk drive used primarily for backing up and archiving personal computer files. The zip drive is a magnetic storage device. Its principle of operation is similar to the floppy disk. It size is 4 inch square, and holds 100 MB, 250 MB or 750 MB of data depending on the model. The 100 MB size actually holds 100, 431, 872 MB of data or the equivalent of 70 floppy disk. The trademarked Zip drive was developed and is sold by Iomega Corporation. The Iomega Zip drive comes with a software utility that lets you copy the entire contents of your hard drive to one or more Zip disks. In addition to data backup, Zip drive has the following additional uses:

- Archiving old e-mail or other files you do not use any more but may want to access someday.
- Storing unusually large files, such as graphic images that you need rarely.
- Exchanging large files with someone.
- Putting your system on another computer, perhaps a portable computer.
- Keeping certain files separate from files on your hard disk (for example, personal finance files).

Disadvantages

- Not all computers come fitted with a Zip drive.
- The disks are expensive.

The Zip drive can be either mounted as an internal drive in a PC or used as an external drive. The Zip drive can be purchased in either a parallel or a Small Computer System Interface (SCSI) version. The SCSI model is the fastest. The fast SCSI version is popularly used in desktop PC and the slower parallel port version in the portables.

The parallel port option increases unit's flexibility, because you can quickly connect to different computers and it is perfect for use with notebook computers. But the parallel port becomes a performance bottleneck for data transfer and can noticeably slow drive access.

3.13 OPTICAL MEDIA

Optical disks are direct access media. They hold very high volumes of data. Especially useful for multimedia (pictures, sound, animation, motion video) which requires a huge volume of storage space.

Characteristics

- Data stored in binary form and read by a laser beam
- Stores audio, video, text, graphics and animation
- Needs a special CD-ROM / DVD drive
- Access to data is slower than hard disk
- Direct Access medium
- Durable, small and portable

3.13.1 Compact Disks (CD)

A CD (Compact Disk) is a round disk with a hole in the center that stores data.

A CD is a very high capacity disk which can store about 600 million characters or roughly 300,000 pages of text (See Figure 3.33).

Figure 3.33 CD

The original CDs were read only media, i.e., they can be used only for reading purpose, no changes can be made on the stored data, but now many different technologies have come up to make CD-R (Compact Disk-Recordable) and CD-RW (CD-Rewritable) media and device, using which one can write the data as well as read data from these optical storage devices.

☞ *A CD is mainly used to store permanent information that does not require any change, such as encyclopedia, dictionary, etc.*

The CD is made out of a clear piece of polycarbonate plastic. The CD has different layers that enable the CD drive to read data from the CD. The layers that make up the CD depend on the type, and the number of times that you can write data on the CD.

The basic layers of the CD are:

- Polycarbonate plastic–layer of the disk.
- Aluminium–Reflects the laser beam from the CD-drive like a mirror that reflects light.
- A crylic–Protects the CD layers.
- Label–Enables you to name the CD for identification.

Compact Disk-Recordable (CD-R)

In CD-R (Compact Disk Recordable) text once written cannot be erased. The CD-R is useful to backup data. The CD-R is also used to create music CDs that can played on music systems.

Most common CD-Rs now-a-days store 700 MB information and 800 MB CD-Rs are also widely available. Maximum capacity of a CD-R nowadays is 860 MB. Actually, maximum capacity of a CD is not strictly defined, depending of production technology and the quality of the disk the maximum capacity could be pushed up to about 875 MB.

☞ *CD-R disks are useful for backing up data that must not be modified.*

CD-Rewritable (CD-RW)

The CD-RW disk enables you to rewrite data, to the disk. The data when not required can be erased from the disk.

☞ *The CD-RW disk are useful for transferring data from one system to another, or for storing files that are to be updated regularly.*

CD-ROM Drive

The CD-ROM drive can read data from the CD-ROM disk or the Audio CD. If one has a CD drive in his/her computer system, then that drive can be used to play music by putting normal Audio CDs in them and also one can watch movies by putting video CDs in the same CD drive.

The CD-ROM drives have a variety of controls on their front panel. The most common are listed as follows:

- Head phone jack – used to connect a set of head phones to the CD-ROM and listen to audio output.
- Value control button – used to control head set volume.
- Start/Stop button – used to start or stop CD playing.
- Eject button– used to manually eject a CD or CD tray.

CD-ROMs drive comes in a variety of types classified by the X factor for example 1 x (Single speed) 2 x (double speed), 3x (triple speed), 4x (quad speed), 6x, 8x, 10x, 12x, 16x, 32 x and higher. There are driver being advertised as 100 x. These drives use hard drive space to cache the CD contents and provide faster speeds (1.5 Mbps).

The mechanism of a CD-ROM drive has ben discussed. It has one motor for rotating the disk and another for moving the laser head, which is guided by slides. A third motor drives the disk insertion and ejection mechanism. The disk can be placed in a protective case called caddy. A button on the front of the disk drive activates the motorized ejection of the disk.

A head phone jack and a volume control knob can also be found on the front of most units. Special software enables almost all CD-ROM drives to play audio disks.

CD-R Drive

The CD-R drive can read data from the CD-ROM, Audio CD, and the CD-R disk. The CD-R drive can also write data to the CD-R disk. This drive is useful for backing up data that must not be modified on a CD-R disk.

The CD-R drive can write to the CD-R disk in a single session or using multiple sessions. In the single session, the data is written to the CD-R disk and the connection is closed such that the CD-R is finalized and no data can be further added to the CD-R disk. Using multiple sessions you can continue adding data to the CD-R disk until the disk is full.

CD-RW Drive

The CD-RW drive enables you to read, write and also rewrite data to the CD-RW disk. This is useful for transferring data from one system to another, especially data files that are large in size such as video movies files.

Characteristics of CD-ROMs

Large Capacity Compared to magnetic tape, CD-ROM provides random access data retrieval and data indexing and the disks have a shelf life of more than 40 years. But it is more expensive than tape. CD-ROM is limited to 680 MB of data, making it impractical for large volume applications and, to-date, recordable disks are not erasable and reusable.

Not Reusable They are written once and can be read again and again. Thus they cannot be reused for storing new data.

High Cost Since the technology is still new, therefore the cost of these storage devices is still high compared to magnetic tapes.

Important Aspects of CD-ROM Drives Following are the important aspects of CD-ROM:

(a) Speed rating (double, quadruple, or hexa), that is, the maximum speed at which it is capable of transferring data. While the first single-speed drives transferred data at 150 Kbps, the double-speed drives have a transfer rate of 300 Kbps, and quad-speed drives 600 Kbps. The hexa or 6-speed drives offer up to 900 Kbps, but they have not been in the market long enough. The best buy, thus, will be a quad-speed drive (transfer rate 600 Kbps) except for those who use CD-based database and graphics files.

(b) Another important aspect of the CD-ROM drive is that it should be able to cope with the 15 frame per second (fps) speed and 320 × 200 resolution required by video-intensive applications.

While single and double-speed CD-ROM drives do not handle video well, the quad-speed drives offer smooth and continuous video playback.

(c) Another important factor is the drive's controller interface. From the perspective of performance, there is not much difference between an enhanced IDE and an SCSI (Small Computer System Interface) CD-ROM drive. But if you have an eye on future expansion, an SCSI drive will be a good choice, which is capable of linking seven devices from a single controller card. If you want to use the same CD-ROM drive on more than one system, select an external CD-ROM drive, which is slightly costlier than the internal one. Internal drives should be equipped with a Red Book-compliant analog audio connector, and a cable to connect the connector to the sound card. Similarly, an external drive should provide analog line-out RCA (Radio Corporation of America) connector. Both configurations permit the user to play compact disks on the CD-ROM drives.

(d) What makes a CD-ROM the most preferred storage device is not just its data storage capacity but also its durability, portability, low replication price and long life. Once the data is imprinted on the disk, it cannot be infected by viruses when it is passed among users. It is also not affected by dust, fingerprints, scratches or magnetic fields. Since CD-ROMs are read only disks, one cannot erase data or overwrite on it accidentally.

3.13.2 Important Aspects of CD-ROM Drives

One of the most important aspect of a CD-ROM drive is its speed rating, (double, quadruple, or hexa), or the maximum speed at which it is capable of transferring data. While the first single-speed drives transferred data at 150 Kbps, the double-speed drives have a transfer rate of 300 Kbps and quad-speed drives 600 Kbps. The more fancied hexa or 6-speed drives offer up to 900 Kbps throughput. Another important aspect of the CD-ROM drive is that it should be able to cope with the 15 frame per second (fps) speed and 320 × 200 resolution needed by video-intensive applications. While single and double-speed CD-ROM drives do not handle video well, the quad-speed and higher drives offer smooth and continuous video playback. Finally, another important factor is the drive's controller interface. From the perspective of performance, there is not much difference between an enhanced IDE and an SCSI (Small Computer System Interface) CD-ROM drive. But if you have an eye on future expansion, your obvious choice should be a SCSI drive which is capable of linking seven devices from a single controller card. In case you plan to use the same CD-ROM drive on more than one system, select an external drive, which is slightly costlier than the internal one. Internal drives should be equipped with a Red Book-compliant analog audio connector and a cable to connect to the Red Book audio connector on the sound card. Similarly, an external drive should provide analog line-out RCA (Radio Corporation of America) connector. Both configurations permit the user to play compact disks on the CD-ROM drives. What makes a CD-ROM the most demanded storage device today is not just its data storage capacity but also its durability, portability, low replication price and long life. Once the data is imprinted on the disk, it cannot be infected by viruses when it is passed among users. It is not adversely affected by dust, fingerprints, scratches or magnetic fields. Since CD-ROMs are only readable disks, one cannot therefore erase data or over write on it accidently.

3.13.3 Maintenance of CD-ROM drive

The CD-ROM drive has its read/write head exposed to the outside air. A significant difference between the two devices is the way they read information from their respective media. The floppy disk drive has the heads contact the disk, which makes it more susceptible both to dirt accumulation and to reliability problems due to dirt. The CD-ROM uses light to read the compact disk, so it is much less sensitive to cleanliness issues. The read lens of most drives can tolerate the normal buildup of dust without any problems.

The tray of CD drive is the main source from where dust reaches into the assembly of the CD drive. The accumulation of dust results into data reading error. However, you can avoid such problem with few precautions. These are:

- Never leave tray open. After using the CD drive, immediately, put the button to put back tray into the CD drive.
- Avoid touching the surface to tray with oily and dirty hands.
- Use CD cleaning kit on regular basis to clean the CD drive. You can purchase one such kit from market. It comes with a special CD. This CD contains small brushes on its surface. When CD is inserted into the CD drive, the brushes on its surface clean dirt in the CD drive.

3.13.4 Combo Drive/DVD Drive

A Combo drive is a type of optical drive that combines CD-R/CD-RW recording capability with the ability to read DVD media. The device was created as a mid-range option between a CD burner and a DVD burner. Combo drives are becoming less and less common on new systems, though they do occasionally appear in lieu of CD-only drives on low-end computers to lower production and sale costs (See Figure 3.34).

Figure 3.34 DVD Drive

3.13.5 WORM disks

WORM stands for Write Once Read Many. WORM disks allow users to create their own CDs by using a CD-R (CD-Recordable) drive. WORM disks are CDs that are purchased blank and written onto using the CD-R drive. The information recorded on a WORM disk can be read by any ordinary CD-ROM drive. But data can be written only once. Data once written cannot be overwritten. Because of their large capacity and non-alterable property, WORM disks are the preferred choice for archival storage.

3.13.6 DVD

DVD stands for digital video disk, or digital versatile disk. DVD disks provide more storage capacity than a CD-ROM disk. The disk used with DVD drives are of the same diameter and thickness as traditional CDs. Like CDs, the DVD disk can tolerate dust, dirt and finger prints. The data on the DVD disk has pits that are smaller and more closely spaced than CD-ROM disks. Hence, DVDs cannot be read by CD drives. DVD disks provide high video resolution and high quality sound.

DVDs are used for storing audio and video entertainment such as movies, videogames and intreactive TV, as well as Internet access and software application that currently require more than one CD space. DVD-ROMs of capacity ranging from 4.7 GB to 50 GB are now available.

Comparison between CD and DVD

Storage Device	CD	DVD
Storage Capacity	700 MB	4700 MB

By comparing the storage capacity of CD and DVD, one can say that 1 DVD can store data of approximately of 7 CD and 1 CD can store data of approximately 466 Floppy disk.

i.e. 1 DVD = 7CD

1 CD = 486 Floppy Disk

Each use for the DVD has its own name. These are

(a) **DVD-Video** for video applications such as the recording and distribution of pictures and movies.

(b) **DVD-Audio**, as a high quality audio disc containing large number of songs.

(c) **DVD-ROM** for the distribution of computer software packages.

(d) **DVD-RAM**, the recordable DVD similar to CD-ROMs.

DVD medium looks just like an ordinary CD. But, unlike the CD, the DVD is made from two platters, each 0.6 mm thick, bound together.

Compared to CD, the DVD tracks are more closely spaced to achieve its higher capacity.

DVD stands for Digital Versatile/Video Disk, is the next generation of optical disk storage technology. It is a faster CD that can hold cinema like video, better than CD audio.

There are various variations of DVD. DVD-ROM or DVD-R are physical formats and DVD-video or DVD-audio are application formats. DVD-ROM is the base format that holds data.

DVDs are of same diameter and thickness as CDs, and they are made using some of the same materials and manufacturing methods. Like a CD, the data on a DVD is encoded in the form of small bits and bumps in the track of the disk.

There are five recordable versions of DVD-ROM. DVD-R for general, DVD-R for authoring, DVD-RAM, DVD-RW and DVD+RW. All recordable drives can read DVD Rom disks, but each uses a different type of disk for recording. DVD-R can record data once (sequentially only), while DVD-RAM, DVD-RW and DVD+RW can be rewritten thousands of times. Various capacities of DVD are given below:

(a) The most common type of DVD is DVD-5 (1 side, 1 layer) having 4.7GB of storage. Double-sided DVDs are rarely used.

(b) DVD-9 8.54GB Single sided, Dual layer.

(c) DVD-10 9.40GB Double sided, Single layer.

(d) DVD-14 13.24GB Double sided, One side single layer, one side dual layer.

(e) DVD-18 17.08GB Double sided, Dual layer.

DVD-Video

DVD-Video goes far beyond today's VHS (Video Home System) and CD-Video systems. It allows both conventional style 4:3 aspect radio image as well as those with the 16:9 ratio used by high definition television systems. The MPEG-2 (Moving Picture Expert Group) encoding delivers a high quality display with 480 lines of 720 pixel each.

DVD Video also introduces the concept of subpictures. These are additional images of limited color depth. These pictures are with the main audio and video data.

DVD-Audio

DVD-Audio takes advantages of the vast storage space of the DVD medium to store either higher quality audio songs or more channels. These CDs are built around a 44.1 KHz sampling rate.

DVD supports this 44.1 KHz rate as well as 48 KHz used by professional audio systems. DVD also supports a super high quality 96 KHz sampling rate.

In addition to today's 16-bit digital audio, DVD will also support 24-bit audio.

DVD-ROM

DVD-ROM storage system allows the storage of files up to a maximum size of 1 GB in the standard format. You can put a MPEG-1 video files on a DVD, enough to play for six hours on a single DVD-5 disk.

☞ *The vast storage area available with the DVD can be put for storing large databases in a very compact form without the fear of damage for many years.*

3.13.7 Blu-Ray Disk

A Blu-ray disk is a high density optical disk storage medium, which is used for the storage of all high-definition digital formats like audio, video, and play-station games and so on. They have the same physical appearance as a DVD. The name Blu-ray is actually a combination of the colour blue and ray. Here blue refers to the blue colour of the laser that is used for its reading and ray refers to the optical ray (See Figure 3.35). Blu-ray was developed by the Blu-ray disk Association with more than 180 members. The data capacity of blu-ray disk is very large because Blu-ray uses a blue laser (405 nanometers) instead of a red laser (650 nanometers). This allows the data tracks on the disk to be very compact. This allows for more than twice as small pits as on a DVD (See Figure 3.36). Because of the greatly compact data Blu-ray can hold almost 5 times

Figure 3.35 Blu-ray disk

ore data than a single layer DVD i.e. 25 GB. Just like a DVD lu-ray can also be recorded in Dual-Layer format. This llows the disk to hold up to 50 GB.

ypes of Blu-Ray Disk

imilar to a DVD, BD also has different versions according to ts application. The common types are:

a) **Blu-Ray Disk Read Only Memory (BD-ROM):** This type of BD can only be read but cannot be written over. The content will be pre-recorded.

b) **Blu-Ray Disk Recordable (BD-R):** This BD is mainly used for storage of PC data.

c) **Blu-Ray Disk Re-writable (BD-RW):** This BD is mainly used for storage of PC data. The contents in this disk can be written over and over.

(d) **Blu-Ray Disk Re-writable (BD-RE):** This BD is mainly used for recording of data to be used in HDTV. This disk can also be written over again and again.

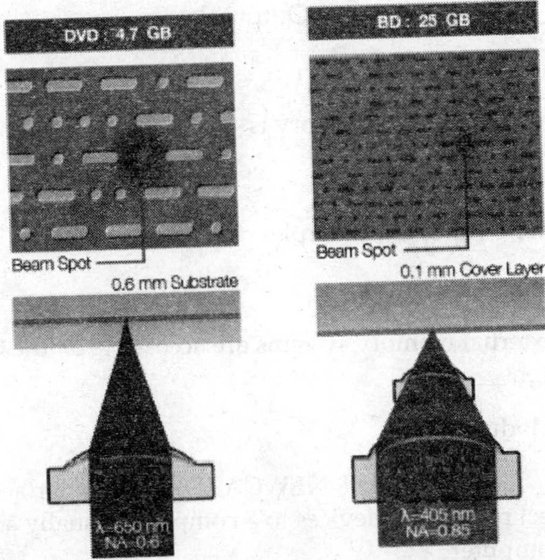

Figure 3.36 Comparison of DVD and Blu-ray Disk (BD)

Advantages of Blu-Ray Disk

Advantages of Blu-Ray disk are as under:

(a) The *sleek design* of blu-ray helps in skipping from any part of the disk to the other.
(b) *Multiple programs* like using the same disk for watching a video as well as recording can be done at the same time.
(c) Watch *HD in its maximum quality* with very little loss.
(d) You can *make your own playlists.*
(e) The programs present on the disk can be *re-ordered in any way* you like.

EXERCISE

1. Write short note on Blu-ray Disc.
2. What is solid state memory?
3. Name any *four* secondary storage devices.
4. What is the function of memory? What are its measuring units?
5. Write differences between volatile memory and non-volatile memory.
6. Why do we require memory hierarchy?
7. What is Cloud computing? Write characteristics of Cloud computing.
8. How Blu-ray disk is different from DVD?
9. Write advantages of Magnetic Disks.

REVIEW QUESTIONS WITH ANSWERS

1. Multiple Choice

1.1 RAID means

a. Redundant Arrays of Inexpensive Disks
b. Redundant Area of Inexpensive Disks
c. Replace Arrays of Inexpensive Disks
d. None of these

Ans (a)

1.2 CD-ROM is a

a. Semiconductor memory
b. Memory register
c. Magnetic memory
d. Storage device

Ans (d)

1.3 Information retrieval is fastest from

a. Floppy disk
b. Magnetic tape
c. Hard disk
d. CD-ROM

Ans (c)

1.4 CD-ROM drive uses

a. Magnetic storage technique
b. Optical storage technique
c. Solid state storage technique
d. Electronic storage technique

Ans (b)

1.5 The RAID _______ uses disk mirroring.

a. level 0
b. level 4
c. level 1
d. level 5

Ans (c)

1.6 ________ is volatile memory.
a. ROM b. RAM
c. PROM d. All of the above

Ans (b)

1.7 SRAM (Static Random Access Memory)
a. stores data till the power is switched off
b. uses a set of transistors for each memory cell
c. more expensive than DRAM
d. All of the above

Ans (d)

1.8 Secondary Memory is
a. RAM b. ROM
c. Cache Memory d. None of the above

Ans (d)

1.9 The cost of storing a bit is minimum in:
a. Cache b. Register
c. RAM d. Magnetic Disk

Ans (d)

2. State whether the following statements are True or False

2.1 RAID 0+1 has the same fault tolerance as RAID level 5.

Ans True

2.2 RAID 0+1: High Data Transfer Performance.

Ans True

2.3 Byte striping results in poor utilization of formatted capacity.

Ans True

2.4 RAID Level 0 is used to combine three hard disk as a single unit.

Ans True

2.5 The concentric rings on the hard disk platter are known as sectors.

Ans False

2.6 RAID level 7 - asynchronous cached striping with dedicated parity.

Ans True

2.7 Clock-speed is a measurement of how fast a memory operates.

Ans False

2.8 Volatile memory is directly accessible by the CPU.

Ans True

2.9 Control unit and Arithmetic logic unit are managed by Memory.

Ans False

2.10 WORM stands for Write Once Read Many.

Ans True

3. Match the following:

3.1	RAID Level 4	a.	Independent Data disks with distributed parity blocks
3.2	RAID 5	b.	Requires a minimum of 3 drives to implement
3.3	RAID 1	c.	Hamming Code ECC
3.4	RAID 2	d.	Mirroring and Duplexing
3.5	RAID 0+1 is implemented as	e.	High I/O Rates and Data Transfer Performance
3.6	RAID 53	f.	a mirrored array whose segments are RAID 0 arrays
3.7	Flash memory	g.	Laser beam
3.8	Magnetic memory	h.	Firmware
3.9	Semiconductor memory	i.	Non volatile
3.10	Optical disk	j.	RAMs, ROMs, Flash memory

Ans 3.1 b 3.2 a 3.3 d 3.4 c 3.5 f
3.6 e 3.7 h 3.8 i 3.9 j 3.10 g

4. Fill in the blanks

4.1 ________ striped disk array without fault tolerance.

Ans RAID level 0

4.2 ________ bit-level striping with Hamming Code ECC.

Ans RAID level 2

4.3 The ________ is the example of Secondary memory.

Ans Harddisk

4.4 ________ is both an Input-Output device.

Ans Hard Disk Drive

4.5 The function of the memory is ________ information.

Ans To store

4.6 Magnetic Tapes are examples of ________ memory.

Ans External

4.7 The external memory systems are accessible by the CPU through ________.

Ans I/O Module

4.8 ______ initially called NEWCARD, is an interface to connect peripheral devices to a computer, usually a laptop computer.

Ans Express Card

4.9 ______ is a cloud computing model in which data is stored on remote servers accessed from the Internet.

Ans Cloud storage

4.10 ______ is a sequential access device.

Ans Magnetic tape

Q.5 (a) Write short notes on

(i) USB and Firewire.

(ii) Digital Audio Tape (DAT)

Ans 5(a)(i)

Universal Serial Bus (USB) and IEEE 1394 (Firewire) are groups of standards for interconnecting peripheral devices. USB 2.0 supports data transfer rates up to 480 Mbps, with as many as 127 devices connected to a single host controller through special hub devices in a tree-like manner. Firewire is similar to USB but has traditionally been faster, up to 800 Mbps. A key advantage of Firewire is isochronous data transfer, in which a continuous, guaranteed data transfer is supported at a predetermined rate. This makes Firewire attractive for digital video and digital audio. (left) USB hub; (middle) USB cable; (right) Firewire cable.

Ans 5(a)(ii)

Digital audio tape (DAT) formatting supports high densities, on the order of 72 GB for a small 73 mm x 54 mm profile. The read / write head is placed at an angle to the tape allowing data to be criss-crossed over the same area, using opposite polarities which maintains separation of the bits.

Q.6 Write advantages and disadvantages of RAID Level 3.?

Ans 6

RAID Level 3 requires a minimum of 3 drives to implement. The data block is subdivided ("striped") and written on the data disks. Stripe parity is generated on Writes, recorded on the parity disk and checked on Reads.

Advantages

- Very high Read data transfer rate
- Very high Write data transfer rate
- Disk failure has an insignificant impact on throughput
- Low ratio of ECC (Parity) disks to data disks means high efficiency
- It is used for Video Production and live streaming, Image and video Editing, and any application requiring high throughput

Disadvantages

- Transaction rate equal to that of a single disk drive at best (if spindles are synchronized)
- Controller design is fairly complex
- Very difficult and resource intensive to do as a "software" RAID

Q.7 Explain RAID 4.

Ans 7

RAID 4: Independent Data disks with shared Parity disk. Each entire block is written onto a data disk. Parity for same rank blocks is generated on Writes, recorded on the parity disk and checked on Reads. RAID Level 4 requires a minimum of 3 drives to implement.

Advantages

- Very high Read data transaction rate
- Low ratio of ECC (Parity) disks to data disks means high efficiency
- High aggregate Read transfer rate

Disadvantages

- Quite complex controller design
- Worst Write transaction rate and Write aggregate transfer rate
- Difficult and inefficient data rebuild in the event of disk failure
- Block Read transfer rate equal to that of a single disk

Q.8 Explain RAID 0+1 with diagram. Also write its advantages and disadvantages.

Ans 8

RAID 0+1: High Data Transfer Performance. RAID Level 0+1 requires a minimum of 4 drives to implement. (See Figure 3.37).

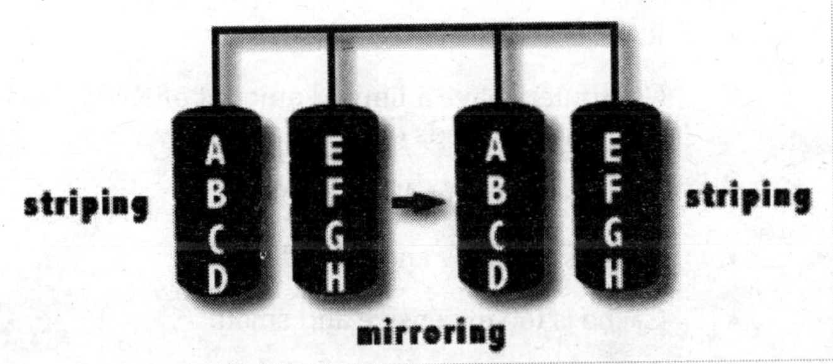

Figure 3.37 RAID Level 0+1

Advantages

- RAID 0+1 is implemented as a mirrored array whose segments are RAID 0 arrays.
- RAID 0+1 has the same fault tolerance as RAID level 5
- RAID 0+1 has the same overhead for fault-tolerance as mirroring alone
- High I/O rates are achieved thanks to multiple stripe segments
- Excellent solution for sites that need high performance but are not concerned with achieving maximum reliability

Disadvantages

- RAID 0+1 is NOT to be confused with RAID 10. A single drive failure will cause the whole array to become, in essence, a RAID Level 0 array
- Very expensive / High overhead
- All drives must move in parallel to proper track lowering sustained performance
- Very limited scalability at a very high inherent cost

Q.9 Explain Spiral Format for Compact Disk.

Ans 9
Unlike a magnetic disk in which all of the sectors on concentric tracks are lined up like a sliced pie (where the disk rotation uses constant angular velocity), a CD is arranged in a spiral format (using constant linear velocity). The speed of rotation is adjusted so that the disk moves more slowly when the head is at the edge than when it is at the center.

Q.10 What is use of RS-232 standard.

Ans 10
The RS-232 standard commonly uses 9-pin and 25-pin connectors, but uses others as well. RS-232 is used for slow-bit-rate devices such as mice, keyboards, and non-graphics terminals.

Q.11 What is secondary storage? Why we need it?

Ans 11
Any storage which is NOT part of Main Memory is called Secondary Storage or just Storage.! Another name which is used is Auxiliary Storage. The media used to store data so that it can be retrieved later for reading, editing, printing etc. Secondary storage devices are part of the hardware of the computer. We need secondary storage because of the following reasons:

- RAM is volatile and expensive.
- Computers have a limited amount of RAM usually measured in hundreds of Mbyte.
- RAM is not normally portable.
- ROM is too slow and is read only.
- Cache is too expensive and small.

Q.12 Explain Secondary storage media types.

Ans 12
Secondary storage media are of following types:

- **Magnetic** : Magnetic media is coated with a magnetic sensitive layer and this layer is magnetized, which then are interpreted as binary 1s and 0s at reading. Examples of magnetic storage media are *hard disk, floppy disk* and *magnetic tapes.*
- **Optical** : On optical storage media information is stored and read using a laser beam. The high intensity laser beam forms a tiny pit along a trace to represent '1' and the surface without a pit, known as 'land', represents '0'. Examples of optical media is *CDs, DVDs, Blue Ray Disks.*
- **Solid State**: The term solid state means no moving parts. Solid state storage devices store data using a special memory called Flash memory. Flash memory is used mainly in *digital cameras, pen drives and USB flash drives.*

Q.13 Explain two types of memories from technology point of view.

Ans 13

There are two types of memories from technology poin view:

- **Analog Memory or Magnetic core Memory:** This ty of memory was used in computers built during 19 The basic storage device in this type of memory cons of a small toroidal (ring shaped) piece of magnetic m rial called a magnetic core. Each magnetic core i memory is capable of storing one binary digit of dig information. Depending on the direction of the curr through the input winding, the core will become mag tized in either clockwise or counter-clockwise direct The retentivity of the core material is such that when magnetizing force is removed, the core remains mag tized, retaining a large part of its flux. These mem devices are now obsolete and have been taken over digital memory devices which consume very l power.
- **Semiconductor Memory or IC Memory:** Semiconduc memories are static, lighter, cheaper than magnetic c analog memories. However, these are volatile and d stored in them is lost when power supply to the mach is switched off. Semiconductor memories can be divi into the following two types:
  RAM (Random Access Memory) and ROM (Read O Memory).

Q.14 What is a secondary storage? How does it differ fro primary storage?

Ans 14
Secondary memory is a computer memory that is not dire accessible to the central processing unit of a computer. I non-volatile memory and has low cost per bit stored, but g erally has an operating speed far slower than that of a prim storage. Secondary memory is used to store large volum data on permanent basis.

You cannot store data in the main memory of a PC per nently. Firstly because it is very expensive and secondly contents are erased when the computer is switched off. T is, main memory stores data and instructions only tem rarily. In order to preserve or save the work which you h done on your computer (permanently for future use) bef you shut it off, you have to use storage media such as drives, compact disks (CDs) and hard disks drives, etc.

Q.15 Give examples of non-destructive read out mem and destructive read out memory.

Ans 15
In some memories the process of reading the mem destroys the stored information. This property is ca *destructive readout (DRO).* Example of a memory having D characteristic is a dynamic RAM. In other memories the p cess of reading information does not destroy the stored in mation. This characteristic of the memory is ca

nondestructive read-out (NDRO). Examples of memories having NDRO features are static RAM, hard disks, magnetic tapes, etc.

Q.16 Compare DVD with BD (Blu-Ray Disk).

Ans 16

Comparison of DVD and BD (Blu-Ray Disk) is shown below.

DVD (Digital Versatile Disk)	BD (Blu-Ray Disk)
1. Physical appearance i.e. thickness of DVD is 1.2 mm	Physical appearance i.e. thickness of BD is 1.2 mm
2. A single layer DVD can hold only 4.7 GB of data.	A single layer Blu-ray disk can store up to 27 GB data.
3. A DVD needs two substrates (semiconductor cystral for integrated circuit or transistor) and they should be bonded.	A Blu-ray disk requires only one substrate.
4. The production cost of DVD is greater than that of a BD because there is a need for bonding of substrates. This causes a more production time than that for a BD.	The production cost of Blu-ray is lesser than that of a DVD because there is no need for bonding of substrates. Thus the production materials are lessened. This causes a lesser production time than that for a DVD.
5. DVD uses red laser.	The Blu-Ray disk uses violet-blu laser with improved lens specifications. This causes the focus to increase, thus helping in the recording of both small and high density pits on the BD.
6. DVD has a wavelength of 650 nanometers.	The wavelength used for BD is 400 nanometers. This allows the data tracks on the disc to be very compact.
7. The layer in a DVD is very far to the laser lens on its player. Thus the precision of the data displayed will be lesser with high distortion than a BD.	The layer in a blu-Ray disk is very close to the laser lens on its player. Thus the precision of the data displayed will be higher with less distortion than a DVD.

Q.17 Define: (a) rotational latency (b) seek time

Ans 17

Rotational latency: It is the time taken for the required sector to come under the head.

Seek Time: Seek time is the time required fo a read/write head to move to the track where the record to be read or written is stored. Maximum seek time equals the time taken for the head to move from the outermost track to the innermost track.

The seek and search time differ for each read or write operation. It will depend on the previous position of the head and the average speed of transfer of data.

Q.18 What do you mean by disk mirroring, disk duplexing, data striping and error correction in respect of RAID?

Ans 18

Disk mirroring : Storing data in more than one disk drive.

Disk duplexing : Access to a hard disk drive via two disk controller.

Data striping : Writing data alternatively across multiple disks.

Error correction : Storing redundant data to enable error detection and correction.

Q.19 Compare IDE and SCSI Hard disks.

Ans 19

IDE stands for Integrated Drive Electronics and SCSI stands for Small Computer System Interface. IDE is currently the more popular and widely used of the two disk types, primarily because IDE devices are cheaper to manufacture than SCSI devices.

IDE drives are slightly faster than SCSI drives. SCSI drives put far less strain on your CPU than IDE drives, which can result in over all higher levels of system performance and reliability.

SCSI drives perform better in 32-bit multitasking operating systems, such as Windows 2003 because SCSI controllers and drives can perform disk reading and writing tasks while other operations and programs are running.

We can attach up to seven SCSI drives or devices to a single SCSI controller; IDE drives and devices are limited to two devices per controller.

A slower SCSI device, such as a CD-ROM drive does not degrade the performance of a faster device such as hard disk. If both are connected to the same controller. On older IDE controllers, a CD-ROM drive degrades the performance of a hard disk if both are on the same controller, that is why most PCs in the past were shipped with two IDE controllers on the motherboard - one for the hard disk drives and one for your CD-ROM drive. On newer systems with EIDE (Enhanced IDE drives), each device can operate at its optimal level of performance.

A SCSI cable can be up to 10 feet long, enabling you to install multiple external SCSI devices; IDE cable can usually be no longer than about 15 inches, which limits most IDE devices to being installed inside PC, cabinet.

Q.20 Explain the need for partitioning a hard disk.

Ans 20

Partitioning is the process of dividing the harddisk into logical sections known as drives. Each partition on the hard disk acts as one or more different disk drives called logical drives. Each partition can hold a different operating systems on different partitions. Partitioning makes our system start faster.

Q.21 What is the function of memory? What are its measuring units?

Ans 21

Memory is an essential component of a computer system. It is required by the computer system to store instructions and data. In the most general sense, secondary memory refers to external systems such as disk drives or tape drives. But actually, main memory refers only to the fast semiconductor storage (RAM) directly connected to the CPU. Memory can be divided into the following two types:

(a) *Primary Memory* : Memory which is directly connected to CPU or part of CPU in PCs.

(b) *Secondary Memory* : Memory which is external to CPU.

Memory Units

All information in the computer is stored using electrical components like the integrated circuits. Two symbols used to represent these two states are 0 and 1, and are known as BITS (an abbreviation for BInary DigiTS). 0 represents the absence of a signal, 1 represents the presence of a signal. A BIT is, therefore, the smallest unit of data in a computer and can either store a 0 or 1. Some memory measuring units are byte, kilobyte, megabyte, gigabyte, terabyte etc.

Q.22 How the Disk Partitions organised?

Ans 22

Partitioning creates a logical file structures on your hard disk so as to divide various potions of a hard disk to be used for different purposes such as a dual operating systems, storage or organizational purposes.

Partitioning your hard disk helps to categorize your files into logical groupings so that you can search for files and make changes more effectively. Folders are made for the same reason too. But partitioning provides better security. Most default primary partition is the C drive. This is the drive which your operating system and most other software applications are installed in. A useful way of protecting your data is to store your personal information into a separate disk partition. For example, if you are using a 250 GB hard disk, you might want to partition it into two drives - drive C & drive D. Drive C will contain your operating system files and software applications such as your Microsoft Office Suite, Adobe Acrobat, Antivirus, Photoshop etc. While drive D can be configured as a storage drive to store all your document files, JPEG, MP3 and other personal data.

It is understood that your most important files are those that are difficult or virtually impossible to replace. For example, if Microsoft Word would to crash, you can always reinstall the application to make it work again. However, if your document files are corrupted by a virus or worm you may need to spend money and precious time trying to recover your data. Their organisation strongly impacts the maintenance required (e.g. moving files when a disk is full, recovering data upon disk failure) and the survivability to crashes (e.g. accidental reboot). A number of block device layers may be used to obtain a more flexible organisation than one device per physical disk.

Q.23 Explain key properties of Cloud computing.

Ans 23

The key properties of Cloud computing are:

- **User-centric:** Once the user gets connected to cloud, any data which is present there, such as images, videos, applications, becomes his/her property.
- **Task Centric:** In this, documents are given more priority than applications from which they are created.
- **Powerful:** Due to its computing power and mass data storage capability.
- **Self-Healing:** Backups of every document is created automatically in the cloud.
- **Multi-tenancy & Intelligence:** Multi-tenancy means sharing of data among a large number of users, by using data mining and analysis for accessing information in an intelligent manner.
- **Programmable:** Programming is associated with cloud computing, as processes such as backing up of data is done automatically, which requires programming.
- **Flexible:** It matches with the needs of user.

Q.24 Write short note on microSD memory card.

Ans 24

The microSD card is even smaller than the miniSD card. The microSD card is designed for use in cellular phones and small mobile devices. The microSD card can accessed in a SD card slot via an adapter.

Q.25 What is Miniature harddisk? Where it is used?

Ans 25

Miniature mobile storage media are rewriteable media usually in the forms of flash memory card, usb flash drive or smart card. Miniature mobile storage media allows mobile users to transport digital images, music or documents easily to and from computer and other devices. Used for both internal and external storage. Have form factors of 1.8 inch, 1 inch, and 0.85 inch. Used in some devices such as portable media players, digital cameras, and smart phones.

CHAPTER 4

Power Supply

4.1 POWER SUPPLY

A power supply is an internal hardware component that supplies components in a computer with power, sometimes abbreviated as PSU, which is short for Power Supply Unit. The power supply converts a 110-115 or 220-230 volt alternating current (AC) into a steady low-voltage direct current (DC) usable by the computer and rated by the number of watts it generates.

An electrical current is a movement of electrons through a copper wire or some other conducive property (more on this topic later). There are two types of electrical currents: alternating current (AC) and direct current (DC). Alternating current (AC) changes the direction of the electrical flow at a rate of about 60 times per second. The voltage changes from a positive charge to a negative charge, causing the electrical flow to change directions. The electrical flow in a direct current (DC) keeps a constant pace and flows in the same direction all the time. Direct current flows from a negative charge to a positive charge and does not fluctuate. DC is what the computer must have to operate properly. The computer needs DC power, but your wall outlet provides AC power Inside your PC is a module called the power supply, which converts the electricity in your household circuit (HC) from AC power into the DC power that the computer needs. All of the circuitry, the electronics on the motherboard, including the microprocessor, the disk drive motors, and all other electrical parts, require DC power to operate. It is the function of the power supply to convert the AC power to DC power. Electrical power tends to fluctuate in its voltage. While its normal operating range can vary, it is usually between 95 and 125 volts.

Power supply unit or PSU, the component that supplies power to a computer. Most personal computers can be plugged into standard electrical outlets. The power supply then pulls the required amount of electricity and converts the AC current to DC current. It also regulates the voltage to eliminate spikes and surges common in most electrical systems. Not all power supplies, however, do an adequate voltage-regulation job, so a computer is always susceptible to large voltage fluctuations.

Power supplies are rated in terms of the number of watts they generate. The more powerful the computer, the more watts it can provide to components. The power supply unit (PSU) in a PC regulates and delivers the power to the components in the case.

Standard power supplies turn the incoming 110V or 220V AC (Alternating Current) into various DC (Direct Current) voltages suitable for powering the computer's components.

Power supplies are quoted as having a certain power output specified in Watts, a standard power supply would typically be able to deliver around 350 Watts.

The more components (hard drives, CD/DVD drives, tape drives, ventilation fans, etc) you have in your PC the greater the power required from the power supply.

4.2 ELEMENTARY CONCEPTS OF POWER SUPPLY

Power supply plays a very important role in operation of computer devices, such as PCs (Personal Computers) and its peripherals. The power supply unit gets power from the wall socket and supplies it to the electrical and electronic circuit fitted in the PC. The power supply unit also contains a fan, to prevent the various chips in the SMPS (Switch Mode Power Supply) from overheating.

4.2.1 Voltage

When the two terminals of a battery are connected by a conductor, an electric current flows through the conductor due to *Voltage* difference at the two terminals, as one terminal continuously sends electrons into the conductor and the other terminal continuously receives electrons from it. The current flow is caused by the voltage difference between the two terminals. Voltage is measured in units called *volts*. Voltage is sometimes called *electromotive force* as it forces electrons to flow from higher level to lower level. Voltage can be of two types:

(a) Direct Voltage
(b) Alternate Voltage or Changing Voltage

4.2.2 Current

Current is the flow of electric charge through the conductor. The electric charge in a conductor is carried by electrons. Each electron carries a small electric charge. Thus, inside a copper wire, the flow of the charge is known as electric current. Batteries and generators are devices that produce electric current. Current can be also of two types. These types are:

(a) *Alternate Current* In Alternating Current (AC), periodically reverses direction because of the way it is generated.
(b) *Direct Current* In Direct Current (DC), the flow of electrons is in one direction. The convention for DC current is opposite to the flow of electrons.

The rate at which electric charge flows in a conductor is measured in *amperes*. One ampere of electric current is equal to about 6 billion electrons flowing per second.

4.2.3 Power

Power is the rate at which electrical energy is converted to another form of energy, such as movement, heat or an electromagnetic field. The common symbol for power is the *P*. The standard unit of power is the *Watt*.

Volt

The *volt* is the International System of Units (SI) units of electric potential or electromagnetic force (voltage).

Ampere

An *ampere* is a unit of measurement of the rate of electrons flow or current in an electrical conductor. One ampere of current represents one coulomb of electrical charge (6.24×10^{18}) moving past a specific point in one second. Generally, ampere is written as *A* or *amp*.

Watt

The *watt* is the standard unit of power. It is equal to the expenditure of 1 Joule of energy in 1 second. Watt is used to specify the rate at which electrical energy is radiated, absorbed or consumed.

4.3 RECTIFIER CIRCUITS

When we convert Alternate Current (AC) supply in to Direct Current (DC) supply, or unidirectional supply, the process is called 'rectification'. The devices used for rectification are called '*Rectifiers*'. Semiconductor diodes are used as rectifiers.

The rectifiers circuits are of two types:

(a) Half-wave rectifier circuit
(b) Full-wave rectifier circuit

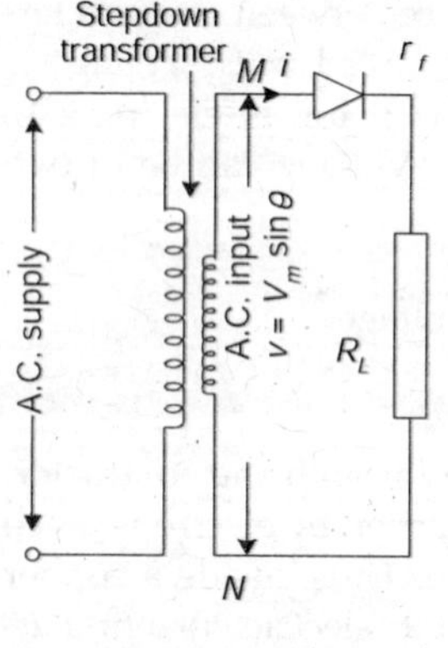

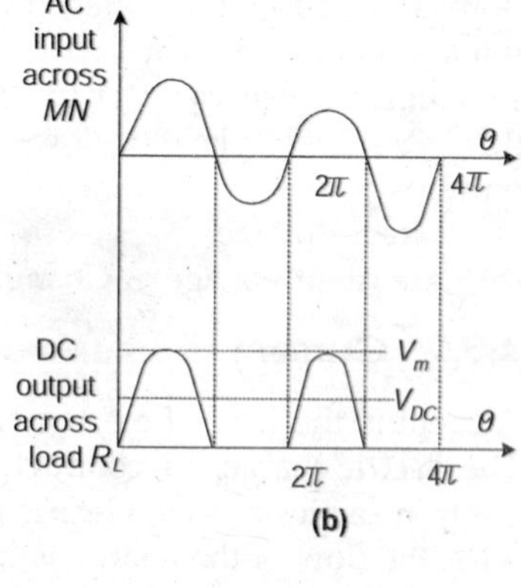

Figure 4.1 (a) Half-wave rectifier (b) Wave-forms at input and output voltages of the rectifier

☞ *A diode allows the current to pass only when it is forward biased. This property of a semiconductor is used for rectification of AC supply voltage into DC supply voltage.*

4.3.1 Half-Wave Rectifier

Figure 4.1 (a) shows the electric circuit for half-wave rectifier and Figure 4.1 (b) shows the waveforms at the input of the transformer and at the output of the load RL.

How does Half-wave Rectifier work?

The AC supply to the diodes is given through a stepdown transformer which brings down the voltage to be supplied to the diode. The output DC voltage is obtained across the load R_L (See Figure 4.1(a)).

When positive part of the AC input voltage appears across the diode, i.e., the end M is positive and end N is negative, the diode becomes forward biased and therefore it offers very little resistance to the applied voltage. Due to this reason, the whole +ve side of the AC voltage cycle appears across the load R_L.

When negative part of the AC cycle comes, i.e., end M becomes negative and N becomes positive, the diode is reverse biased and is open circuited. As a result, the whole AC Input of the negative cycle appears across the diode and output across the load is zero. The waveform across the load is shown in Figure 4.1 (b).

The efficiency of the half wave rectifier is about 50%. It is so because only positive half cycle voltage is rectified and negative cycle is dropped across the diode.

☞ *The DC output is not pure and such output DC voltage is pulsating because it still contains the value of voltage moving up from zero, rising to peak and then falling to zero.*

During the negative cycle, the diode is reverse biased. The whole negative cycle appears across the diode. The diode used for half-wave rectification should have high value of Peak Inverse Voltage (PIV).

Mathematically, efficiency $= \dfrac{\text{D.C. Power Output}}{\text{A.C. Power Input}}$

Example 1 The input AC power to the half-wave rectifier is 140 watts. The DC power output obtained is 60 watts. Calculate the efficiency of rectification in percentage.

Solution

$$\eta = \%\text{efficiency} = \frac{\text{D.C. Power Output}}{\text{A.C. Input Power}} = \frac{60 \times 100}{140}$$

$$= 42.8\%$$

4.3.2 Full-Wave Rectifier

There are two types of Full-wave (F.W.) rectifiers. These are:

(a) Centre tap F.W. Rectifier
(b) F.W. Bridge Rectifier

The difference is that in centre tap F.W. Rectifier, we use two diodes and in bridge rectifier, we use four diodes. The rectification efficiency is higher in full-wave rectifier.

Centre tap Full-Wave Rectifier

Circuit diagram for centre tap full-wave rectifier is shown in Figure 4.2 (a). It uses a Centre Tapped (C.T.) secondary transformer. This is a step down transformer. This means, that the secondary voltage at AB will be smaller than the applied AC voltage at CD.

Two diodes (P–N junction type) are connected across the secondary as shown in Figure 4.2 (a). One diode rectifies the positive half cycle and the other rectifies the negative half cycle.

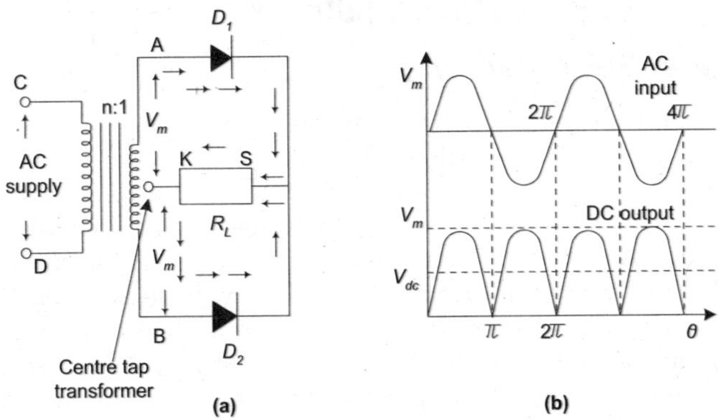

Figure 4.2 (a) Centre tap full-wave rectifier (b) Waveforms for AC input and DC output

Working of the Circuit

(a) During the positive half cycle, diode D_1 is forward biased as the end A is positive and B is negative. This makes diode D_1 forward-biased and D_2 reverse-biased. As a result, current flows through the diode D_1, and through the load R_L as shown by the directional arrows.

(b) During the negative half cycle, end B becomes positive and A negative in the secondary side of the transformer. This makes D_2 to conduct and current flows through D_2 and load R_L as shown by the arrow. The diode D_1 does not conduct during this negative half cycle.

☞ *The current through the load resistor R_L flows from S to K in both the half cycles. Thus, we get unidirectional current through the load R_L.*

Figure 4.2 (b) shows the waveforms for AC input and DC output. Also note the following points for this type of transforms:

(a) Both half cycles are rectified therefore, the efficiency is double that of half-wave rectifier discussed earlier.

(b) The DC output in this case also is not pure. But this is better than that of half–wave rectifier because rectification takes place for both the half cycles.

(c) The diodes used in this type of circuit should have high value of PIV which should be more than ($2 \times V_m$).

(d) It is difficult to get the centre of secondary winding of the transformer and hence the rectification is not very good as compared to bridge rectifier, being discussed next.

Full-wave Bridge Rectifier

It uses 4 diodes as connected in Figure 4.3 (a). The load R_L is connected between the two ends P and R of the bridge.

Working of the Circuit

During the positive half cycle of the secondary voltage, the end A of the secondary becomes positive and B becomes negative. As a result the diodes D_1 and D_3 become forward biased and conduct. The flow of current takes place from A to Q P R S B and back to A.

During the negative half cycle, the end A becomes negative and B becomes positive. The diodes D_2 and D_4 become forward biased and conduct in the manner B to S P R Q A and back to B.

The waveforms of the circuit are shown in Figure 4.3 (b). Note the following points:

(a) Each half of the cycle of AC voltage is rectified by two diodes simultaneously. Hence the output current is more than the centre tapped rectifier shown in Figure 4.2.

(b) The AC combination or ripple voltage is much less than half wave, or centre tapped-transformer rectifier.

(c) The diodes require lesser peak inverse voltage than in the case of centre tapped transformer.

(d) The two diodes simultaneously conduct in series, hence voltage drops in them equally. Thus, peak inverse voltage for each diode is half as compared to centre tapped rectifier diode.

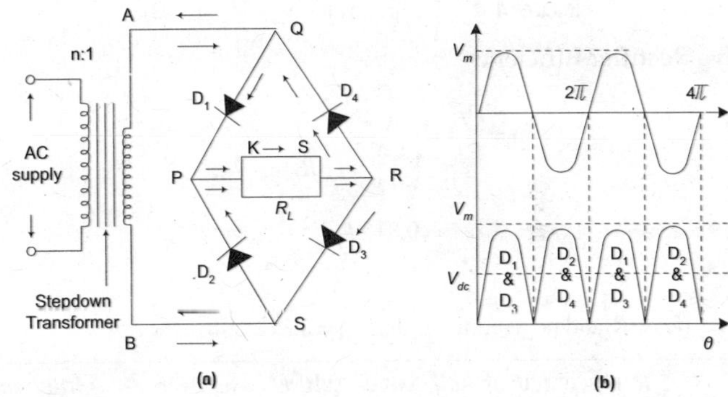

Figure 4.3 (a) Full-wave bridge rectifier (b) Waveforms

Efficiency of Full-wave Rectifier

(a) Let AC voltage rectified by the rectifier is represented as $v = V_m \sin(\theta)$ v = Voltage at any time.
where θ = Phase angle whose value changes from 0 to 360°.
V_m = Peak AC voltage.

(b) Let forward resistance of diode = r_f and load Resistance = R_L
The instantaneous current is given by

$$i = \frac{v}{r_f + R_L} = \frac{V_m \sin(\theta)}{r_f + R_L}$$

(c) *DC Output Power*
The current I_{DC} in a fully rectified circuit is given by:

$$I_{dc} = \frac{2I_m}{\pi} \text{ where } I_m \text{ is the maximum value of current}$$

$$\therefore \text{ DC power output } P_{DC} = I_{DC}^2 \times R_L = \left[\frac{2I_m}{\pi}\right]^2 R_L$$

(d) *AC Input Power*

$$I_{rms} = \left(\frac{\text{Peak current}}{\sqrt{2}}\right) = \left(\frac{I_m}{\sqrt{2}}\right)$$

where I_{rms} stands for root mean square current for AC input voltage

$$\therefore \text{ Input AC Power } P_{AC} = (I_{rms}^2)(r_f + R_L)$$

$$= \left(\frac{I_m}{\sqrt{2}}\right)^2 (r_f + R_L)$$

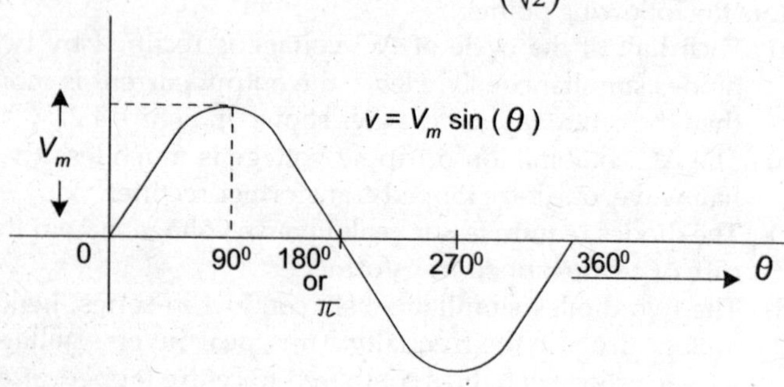

Figure 4.4 Diagram for $v = V_m \sin(\theta)$

(e) Rectifier Efficiency

$$\eta = \frac{P_{DC}}{P_{AC}} = \frac{\left(\frac{2I_m}{\pi}\right)^2 R_L}{\left(\frac{I_m}{\sqrt{2}}\right)^2 (r_f + R_L)}$$

$$= \frac{0.812\, R_L}{(r_f + R_L)}$$

If $r_f \ll R_L$ and neglecting r_f then $\eta = 0.812$ or 81.2%

☞ *The efficiency of half-wave rectifier was 40.6 %. Thus, the efficiency of full-wave rectifier is about 2 times that of half-wave rectifier.*

Example 2 A centre tap transformer uses 2 diodes each of forward resistance 20 Ω. The transformer secondary voltage from centre tap to each end of the secondary is 100 volts. Assume load resistance as 800 Ω. Find

(a) I_{DC} (b) I_{rms} (root mean square current)

Solution

$$\text{Given } r_f = 20\ \Omega$$

$$R_L = 800\ \Omega$$

$$\text{Max AC} = V_m = 100\sqrt{2}$$

$$= 142\text{V}$$

$$\therefore \text{ Maximum current } I_m = \frac{V_m}{r_f + R_L} = \left(\frac{142}{20 + 800}\right) \times 1000 \text{ mA}$$

$$= 173.17 \text{ mA}$$

(a) $$I_{DC} = \frac{2I_m}{\pi} = \frac{2 \times 173.17}{3.14} = 110.30 \text{ mA (Ans)}$$

(b) $$I_{rms} = \frac{I_m}{\sqrt{2}} = \frac{173.17}{1.41} = 122.8 \text{ mA (Ans)}$$

4.4 INTRODUCTION TO REGULATED OR LINEAR POWER SUPPLY

4.4.1 Basic Theory

In Linear power supply, the incoming AC voltage is stepped down to a lower AC voltage. For example, 120V ac is stepped down to 24V ac. The 24V ac is then rectified through a full-wave bridge rectifier, usually with a high-current, low-voltage bridge. A filter capacitor is used to maintain a constant dc level with minimum ripple. The output voltage is controlled by a power transistor operating in its linear region. It acts as a variable resistor in series with the load. The power transistor receives its control from a circuit that senses output voltage. The control circuit modifies the transistor bias to maintain a constant voltage output, regardless of changes in the load current.

Advantages

(a) Easily available in the market
(b) Relatively noise free
(c) Reasonably reliable
(d) Easy to design
(e) Inexpensive to manufacture

Disadvantages

(a) Because of the large transformers required, linear power supplies are generally heavy.
(b) Linear power supplies relates to the power transistor used to regulate the load. Because the power transistor operates in its linear region, and all the output current must pass through it, it requires large heat sinks to dissipate energy loss.

4.4.2 Features of Linear Power Supply

(a) Linear power supplies use a transformer operating at the mains frequency of 50 Hz in India. This low-frequency transformer is larger in size and heavier.
(b) Linear power supplies regulate the output by using a higher voltage in the initial stages and then expending some of it as heat to produce a lower, regulated voltage. This causes voltage drop and it is necessary and can not be eliminated by improving the design.
(c) A linear supply regulates the output voltage or current by converting excess power as heat.

(d) A linear regulator consists of a power transistor, voltage regulating IC (Integrated Circuit) and a noise filtering capacitor that are costly.

(e) Linear power supply units do not produce much interference and thus are used to supply power where radio interference must not occur.

(f) Inexpensive linear Power Supply Units (PSUs) with poor regulation may experience a small AC voltage "riding on" the DC output at twice mains frequency (100 Hz). These "ripples" are of the order of millivolts, and can be suppressed with larger filter capacitors or better voltage regulators. Thus, quality linear PSUs suppress ripples much better.

(g) Linear power supply units give off a faint, low frequency hum at mains frequency.

(h) Linear power supply units have low power factors.

4.5 POWER SUPPLY FILTER

Power supply filter includes a inductor with coil configurations allowing differential mode current from a DC source to pass through, so that the noise does not reach the DC source.

4.5.1 Uses of Power Supply Filter

(a) An active power supply filter effectively eliminates power supply noise using a resistive element and a capacitive element coupled at a node, and a switch with a control terminal controlled by the node.

(b) The active power supply filter is suitable for high frequency operation of a voltage-controlled oscillator.

(c) The active power supply filter removes Voltage Controlled Oscillator (VCO) noise.

(d) The active power supply filter is similarly useful in applications, such as microprocessors in which removal of substantial amounts of noise from the power supply is useful.

4.6 THREE TERMINAL REGULATOR

The best choice for a voltage regulator is the simple 3-terminal regulator. 78XX is 3-terminal regulator type which is used for regulating DC current. The pinout for a three terminal (pin) voltage regulator is as follows:

(a) Voltage in
(b) Ground
(c) Voltage out

4.6.1 Terminologies used in 3-Terminal Regulator

(a) *Output Voltage:* This is the most important characteristic of a 3-terminal regulator. The upper-limit and lower-limit values of the output voltage are specified under given conditions of junction temperature, input voltage, and output current. When designing your system using a 3-terminal regulator, make sure that the conditions of the output voltage of the regulator are satisfied.

(b) *Line Regulation:* This is the maximum value of changes in the output voltage when the input voltage varies in a specific range at constant conditions of junction temperature and output current. The lower the Line regulation, the higher the stability of the output voltage of an IC, i.e., integrated circuit.

(c) *Regulators Load Regulation (Output Stability):* This is the maximum value of changes in the output voltage when the output current (load current) varies in a specific range at constant conditions of junction temperature and input current.

☞ *The lower the load regulation, the higher the stability of the output voltage of an IC.*

(d) *Quiescent Current:* This is the current necessary for an IC to operate, which is specified as a current flowing from an input pin to a GND (Ground) pin.

(e) *Ripple Rejection:* This is the ratio expressed in decibels dB at which the alternate current component is included in an input voltage which attenuates before it is produced as an output voltage.

☞ *The higher the ripple rejection, the better the performance as changes in the input voltage do not appear as the output voltage.*

(f) *Dropout Voltage:* This is the difference between the input voltage and output voltage required for an IC to produce a stable output voltage. The product of the input and output voltage difference and the output current is the input-output loss of the 3-terminal regulator.

☞ *Therefore, the lower this value is, the lower the loss of the 3-terminal regulator.*

(g) *Peak Output Current:* A 3-terminal regulator has an internal overcurrent restriction circuit. The peak output current is an output current value at which the overcurrent restriction circuit starts operating. If an attempt is made to flow a current exceeding the peak output current, the output voltage drops. For example, if the input voltage is high or if the chip temperature is high, the restriction circuits may operate, lowering the output voltage, even when the output current is less than rated value say 1 Amp.

(h) *Short Circuit Current:* This is the current output from the output pin if the output short-circuited with ground by accident. This value is determined by the characteristics of the overcurrent restriction circuit. That is, the higher the input voltage and the higher the chip temperature, the more the current is restricted.

4.6.2 Regulated Power Supply using Three Terminal Regulator

A regulated linear power supply contains four basic components:

(a) transformer
(b) rectifier
(c) filter capacitor
(d) A 3-terminal regulator.

The regulated linear power supply solves all of the problems of the unregulated supply. But it is not as efficient because the 3-terminal regulator will dissipate the excess power in the form of heat which must be accommodated.

☞ *The output voltage has negligible ripple, very small load regulation, and high reliability, thus making it an ideal choice for use in low power electronic applications.*

4.7 TYPES OF POWER SUPPLIES

Depending on the mode of operation of the semiconductor used in PSU, the converters can be linear or switching and accordingly we have two categories of Power Supplies namely :

(a) **Linear Power Supply** : Linear power supplies are simpler, requiring only a few steps to convert AC electricity into DC electricity. They expend energy constantly and normally dump excess energy as heat and will require larger components for high power delivery. This limits them mostly to smaller power applications.

(b) **Switched Mode Power Supply** : A switched mode power supply, on the other hand, has an internal switch that controls the flow of electricity going into the rest of the power supply. While this adds complexity, it has a couple of benefits. The first is that the power supply uses less electricity than a linear power supply. The second is that the switching action generates high-frequency AC electricity, which in turn allows some components, such as inductors and transformers, to be smaller.

4.8 LINEAR POWER SUPPLY

Linear power supplies are widely used because of the advantages they offer in terms of overall performance. Linear power supplies are often used in exacting situations where the regulation and removal of noise is foremost. While linear power supplies may not be as efficient as other types of power supply technology, they offer the best performance and are therefore used in many applications where noise is of great importance. Often audio amplifiers and many other items of electronic equipment use linear power supplies to obtain the best performance.

Linear power supplies as the name suggest uses linear, i.e. non-switching techniques to regulate the voltage output from the power supply. The term linear power supply implies that the power supply is regulated to provide the correct voltage at the output. Sometimes the sensing of the voltage may be accomplished at the output terminals, or on some occasions it may be achieved directly at the load.

4.8.1 Block diagram of linear power supply architecture

The main elements of the linear power supply are:

(a) **Input transformer**: As many power supplies take their source power from an AC mains input, it is common for linear power supplies to have a step down or occasionally a step up transformer. This also serves to isolate the power supply from the mains input for safety.

(b) **Rectifier**: A rectifier converts AC power to DC power. The primary task of the power supply is to rectify the AC power of the power source into the DC power used by the computer. As the input from an AC supply is alternating, this needs to be converted to a DC format. Various forms of rectifier circuit are available.

(c) **Smoothing**: Once rectified from an AC signal, the DC needs to be smoothed to remove the varying voltage level. Large reservoir capacitors are used for this.

(d) **Linear regulator**: Once a smoothed supply is available, this can then be applied to the linear regulator. This will provide a properly regulated output.

(e) **Series regulator**: This is the most widely used format for a linear power supply. As the name implies a series element is placed in the circuit, and its resistance varied via the control electronics to ensure that the correct output voltage is generated for the current taken.

(f) **Shunt regulator**: The shunt regulator is less widely used as the main element within a voltage regulator. For this form of linear power supply, a variable element is placed across the load. There is a source resistor placed in series with the input, and the shunt regulator is varied to ensure that the voltage across the load remains constant.

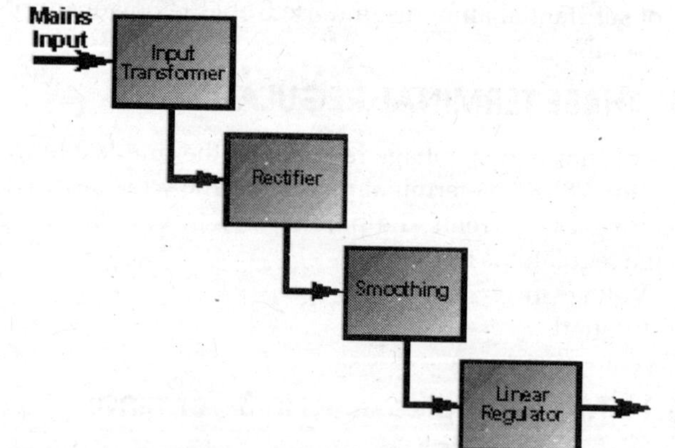

Figure 4.5 Block diagram of linear power supply architecture

4.9 SMPS (SWITCHED MODE POWER SUPPLY)

Like a linear power supply, the switched mode power supply too converts the available unregulated ac or dc input voltage to a regulated dc output voltage. However in case of SMPS with input supply drawn from the ac mains, the input voltage is first rectified and filtered using a capacitor at the rectifier output. The unregulated dc voltage across the capacitor is then fed to a high frequency dc-to-dc converter. Most of the dc-to-dc converters used in SMPS circuits have an intermediate high frequency ac conversion stage to facilitate the use of a high frequency transformer for voltage scaling and isolation. In contrast, in linear power supplies with input voltage drawn from ac mains, the mains voltage is first stepped down (and isolated) to the desired magnitude using a mains frequency transformer, followed by rectification and filtering.

PC contains Integrated Circuits (ICs) and transistors which need regulated DC (Direct Current) voltage. These different types of DC voltages are produced by the Switched Mode Power Supply unit fitted in the PC. In Switched Mode Power Supply, the controlling circuit works like an ideal switch which is either ON or OFF.

☞ *By controlling the ratio of the duration of ON time and OFF time of a power transistor, the AC (Alternating Current) voltage is converted to DC voltage.*

In SMPS, the same current flow is regulated by chopping the input voltage and controlling the average current by means of the duty cycle. When a higher current is drawn by the load, the control circuit of the SMPS suitably increases the on-line duration to accommodate such change in load current. Since the switch always operates either in saturation or in cut-off mode except for a brief transition period between these two states, the switching regulator can achieve very good voltage regulation despite large fluctuations in input AC voltage and the output load variations.

Figure 4.6 SMPS

4.9.1 Block Diagram of SMPS Working

The oscillator in above figure allows the control element to be switched ON and OFF. The control element usually consists of a transistor switch, an inductor, and a diode. For each switch ON, energy is pumped into the magnetic field associated with the inductor which is a transformer winding in practice. This energy is then released to the load at the desired voltage level.

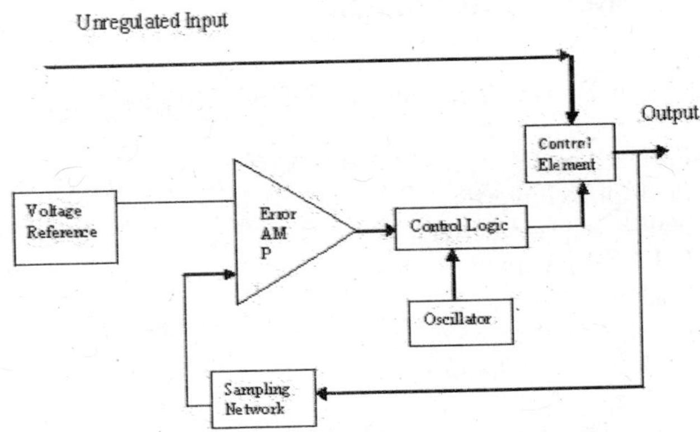

Figure 4.7 Block diagram of SMPS working

By varying the duty cycle or frequency of switching, we can vary the stored energy in each cycle and thus control the output voltage. Higher efficiency is obtained since only the energy required is pumped to maintain the load current hence no power dissipation.

Advantages

- In a SMPS, the active device that provides regulation is always operated in cut-off or in saturation mode.
- A switched mode power supply, has an internal switch that controls the flow of electricity going into the rest of the power supply. So SMPS power supply uses less electricity than a linear power supply.
- The switching action generates high-frequency AC electricity, which in turn allows some components, such as inductors and transformers, to be smaller. The high frequency transformer used in a SMPS circuit is much smaller in size and weight compared to the low frequency transformer of the linear power supply circuit.
- In switched mode circuit the unregulated portion of the voltage is removed by modulating the switch duty ratio. The switching losses in modern switches are much less compared to the loss in the linear element.
- Another advantage with SMPS is that the switching can be modulated in various ways, depending on the load conditions. The power supply output is regulated with a feedback circuit which adjusts the timing.

Disadvantages

- The switching creates a lot of noise that needs to be filtered in the output and possibly shielded to prevent leakage.
- The transient spikes due to the switching action can migrate into other areas of the circuits if not properly filtered. These can cause electromagnetic or RF interference affecting other nearby items of electronic equipment, particularly if they receive radio signals.
- The costs of a switch mode power supply is calculates before designing or using one. Additional filtering further adds to the cost.

4.9.2 SMPS Classification

SMPS can be classified into the following types as shown below:

(a) Forward and flyback converter
(b) Push-pull converter
(c) Half-bridge converter
(d) Full-bridge converter
(e) Buck regulator
(f) Boost regulator
(g) Buck-boost regulator
(h) Cuk regulator

Regulated DC voltage is required for semiconductor devices such as ICs and Transistors to function. Regulated voltage can be generated from commercial AC lines with an AC to DC power supply or from DC power source (such as Batteries) with a DC to DC converter. Each type is further classified to one that is isolated between primary (Input) circuit and secondary (Output) circuit or non-isolated. Over the past 15 years, there have been significant changes in the design of power supplies. The most important of these has been widespread change from linear regulator to switch mode power supplies (SMPS). The principal reason for the move to switch mode power supplies is their much greater efficiency typically 65 - 90% as opposed to 25 - 50% for the linear regulator. This greatly reduces the cooling requirement, and allows a much higher power density.

Forward and flyback converter : A power switching circuit which uses a centertapped transformer and two power switches which are driven ON and OFF alternatively. This circuit does not provide regulation by itself. Forward converter and flyback converter are methods of transfer of energy from primary to secondary source. The forward converter transfers energy when the switching transistor is ON (ON-ON converter), but flyback converter transfers the energy when transistor is OFF (ON-OFF converter).

Push-pull converter : A power switching circuit which uses a centertapped transformer and two power switches which are driven ON and OFF alternatively. This circuit does not provide regulation by itself.

Half-bridge converter : A power switching circuit similar to the full bridge converter except that only two transistors are used, with the other two replaced by capacitors.

Full-bridge converter : A power switching circuit in which four transistors are connected in a bridge configuration to drive a transformer

Buck regulator : In buck regulators, the output voltage will be of the same polarity but always lower than the input voltage. One supply line must be common to both input and output. This may be either the positive or negative line, depending on the regulator design. In other words, the buck converter is a commonly used in circuits that steps down the voltage level from the input voltage according to the requirement. It has the advantages of simplicity and low cost. Efficiency is about 90% Buck regulator is very simple and it requires only one transistor (switch). It has large tolerance of line voltage variation. Its disadvantage includes only unidirectional output is available. High output ripple. Slow transient response.

☞ *In the buck regulator, the average output voltage is less than the supply voltage.*

Boost regulator : In boost regulators, the output voltage will be of the same polarity but always higher than the input voltage. One supply line must be common to both input and output. This may be either the positive or negative line, depending on the design. In other words, A boost converter (step-up converter) is a power converter with an output DC voltage greater than its input DC voltage. It is a class of switching mode power supply (SMPS) containing at least two semi-conductors switches (a diode and a transistor) and at least one energy storage element. Filters made of capacitors (sometimes in combination with inductors) are normally added to the output of the converter to reduce output voltage ripple. It can step up the output voltage without a transformer. High efficiency due to single switch. Its disadvantages includes high peak current flows through to switch. Output voltage is highly sensitive to changes in duty cycle.

☞ *The boost regulator provides higher output voltage than the input voltage. It is like step-up chopper.*

Buck-boost regulator : In buck-boost regulators, the output voltage is of opposite polarity to the input, but its value may be higher, equal, or lower than that of the input. One supply line must be common to both input and output, and either polarity is possible by design.

Cuk regulator : The Cuk converter is used for getting the output voltage with different polarity. That means output voltage magnitude can be either larger or smaller than the input, and there is a polarity reversal on the output. The inductor on the input acts as a filter for the dc supply, to prevent large harmonic current. Unlike the previous converter topologies where energy transfer is associated with the inductor. Energy transfer for the cuk converter depends on the capacitor.

4.9.3 Topologies of SMPS

Topologies of SMPS are categorized into different types such as AC-DC converter, DC-DC converter, Forward Converter and Flyback converter. The working of a switch mode power supply topologies is discussed below.

DC-DC Converter SMPS Working

DC converters are power electronic circuits that convert a DC voltage to a different voltage level. There are different types of conversion method such as electronic, linear, switched mode, magnetic, capacitive. In this power source, a high voltage DC power is directly acquired from a DC power source. Then, this high voltage DC power is switched usually in the range of 15KHz-5KHz. And, then it is fed to a step down transformer unit of 50Hz. The o/p of this transformer is fed to the rectifier, then this rectified o/p power is used as a source for loads, and the oscillator ON time is controlled and a closed loop regulator is formed.

A few applications of interest of DC-DC converters are where 5V DC on a personal computer motherboard must be stepped down to 3V, 2V or less for one of the latest CPU chips; where 1.5V from a single cell must be stepped up to 5V or more, to operate electronic circuitry. In all of these applications, we want to change the DC energy from one voltage level to another, while wasting as little as possible in the process.

AC-DC Converter SMPS Working

This type of SMPS has an AC i/p and it is converted into DC by using rectifier & filter. This unregulated DC voltage is fed to the power factor correction circuits as it is affected. This is because around the voltage peaks, the rectifier draws short current pulses having significantly high-frequency energy that affects the power factor to reduce.

Fly-back Converter SMPS Working

The SMPS circuit which has very low o/p power (less than 100W) is called as fly-back converter SMPS. This type of SMPS is very low and simple circuit compared with other SMPS circuits. This type of SMPS is used for low power application.

Forward Converter type SMPS Working

This type of SMPS is almost same to the fly back converter type SMPS. But, in this type of SMPS a control is connected at the o/p of the secondary winding of the transformer to control the switch. As compared to the fly back converter, the filtering and rectification circuit is complicated.

4.9.4 Additional signals of SMPS

Nearly all newer PCs have energy efficiency tools and power management functions to help reduce the amount of electrical power consumed by the PC. Most power supplies have the ability to take 110V AC or 220V DC and have a two-position slide switch on back of the power supply near the fan grill that is used to select the power source voltage. If this switch is on 220V, it will not harm the system to plug it into a 110V source. The power supply will not be getting as much power as it believes it should be and will not function at all. So, if a PC seems to not have power the first time you plug it in, the first thing to check is the voltage selector.

After rectification, one of the power supply's most important functions is sending the POWER_GOOD (or PWR_OK) signal to the motherboard. The POWER_GOOD signal tells the motherboard that the power supply has completed its cycle-up process and is now able to provide clean power in the voltages needed by the PC. Should there be a problem with the power or with the power supply, no signal is sent and the boot process never completes. The power supply performs a self-test when the power is switched on that checks the incoming power for the required voltages. If all is well, the POWER_GOOD signal wire is set high (turned on) to indicate that the power supply is able to supply a good power stream in the right voltages. If there are any problems with the power source or the power supply's ability to produce a certain voltage stream, the POWER_GOOD signal is not set.

The motherboard uses the PS_ON (power supply on) signal over one of the wires connecting it to the power supply. This signal can turn the power supply on or off via software. It is sometimes known as the soft power feature. PS_ON is more evident when you use it with an operating system (OS) Such as Windows that supports the Advanced Power Management (APM) or Advanced Configuration and Power Interface (ACPI) specification. When you shut down a PC from the Start menu, Windows automatically turns off the computer after it completes the OS shutdown sequence due to this feature.

4.9.5 Form Factor

The form factor of a power supply defines its physical shape, how it fits into a case, and the amount of power it produces. In most situations, the power supply's form factor is the same as that of the system case and the motherboard. Since the power supply is normally bought already installed in the case, there are rarely any matching issues. It is only when you need to replace a power supply, or when you buy a case without a power supply, that form factor issues ever arise. There are newer power supplies that are compatible with several form factors, and there are cases that can fit several different power supply form factors. However, the most important part of matching the power supply to the system is to match the motherboard's power requirements to the capabilities of the power supply. Most AT class power supplies, which include the AT, Baby AT, ATX, and a few others, differ only in their size and mounting requirements; their power capabilities are roughly the same. The capabilities of the power supply are directly related to the size and shape of it case. Mid- and full-sized tower cases are typically larger (in both height and width) and use more power for cooling its interior components. Because of its size, a mid- or full-size tower case usually has more components installed inside the case. On the other hand, a desktop or a smaller tower case typically has fewer interior components, which means they need less power from the power supply. The more demand on the power supply, the larger the power supply needs to be.

Here is a quick overview of the most common power supply form factors:

The original Advanced Technology or AT design was developed in the early PC years with the IBM compatible systems. As the power requirements and layouts changed, the industry developed a new definition called Advanced Technology Extended or ATX. This specification has been used for many years. In fact it has undergone a large number of revisions through the years to deal with various power changes. Now a new format has been developed over the years called ATX12V. This standard is officially known as ATX v2.0 and above.

ATX : The ATX form factor was a major change from the form factors based on the PC XT and PC AT. The ATX is considered the de facto form factor standard for all PCs, whether desktop or tower. Physically, the ATX power supply was identical to the Baby At/LPX form factor, with the exception that the monitor pass-through connectors was now completely gone. Big changes occurred in both the output voltages and connectors. A single 20-pin connector replaced the two separate connectors, P8 and P9. The ATX was the first power supply to provide 3.3 volts, and it introduced the first "soft power" switch, which allowed software to turn the computer on and off.

mini ATX/micro ATX/ SFS form factor: All these form factor describes a single form factor that's physically smaller than the ATX and doesn't have a -5 vol signal, which is only needed by some older expansion bus (ISA) cards. The power supplies defined by smaller form factors, such as the micro-ATX and the LPX, are much smaller than those used for a full AT or ATX form factor PC.

WTX form factor : This form factor is usually only seen on larger, more powerful system (the W in WTX stands for workstation). The WTX is completely different from all earlier form factors. It's designed for multiple-CPU and multiple-drive systems such as server and high end engineering workstations.

ATX12V form factor : A superset of the ATX is called AT12V and was created for systems using pentium4 and higher end Athlon processors. The ATX12V adds an extra +12v power connector (called Auxillary power connector) that enables the delivery of more current to the high-end, processor-based boards. If you see a +12v four pin connector, you have an ATX12V power supply. If you don't find a +12v four-pin connector, your power supply is an ATX version. The newest styles of ATX12v have a 24-pin connector, combining the old 20-pin ATX connector and the auxiliary connector. If your motherboard only has a 20-pin connector, most 24-pin power supplies come with an adapter to fit your 20 pin motherboard. ATX12V is a 20pin power connector. ATX12V ver2 is a 24pin power connector. Current standard ATX12V ver2.2 is a 20/24pin power connector.

4.10 SMPS SPECIFICATION

In order to standardize the design of the system, specifications standards were developed for desktop computers that define the various dimensions, layouts and electrical requirements so that parts could be easily changed between vendors and systems. Since all computer system require electrical power that is converted from high voltage wall outlets to the low voltage currents used by the components, power supplies have very clear specifications. Desktop design specifications have been given a variety of names of the years. The original Advanced Technology or AT design was developed in the early PC years with the IBM compatible systems. As the power requirements and layouts changed, the industry developed a new definition called Advanced Technology Extended or ATX. This specification has been used for many years. In fact it has undergone a large number of revisions through the years to deal with various power changes. Now a new format has been developed over the years called ATX12V. This standard is officially known as ATX v2.0 and above. The different specification parameters for computer SMPS units are give below:

Feature	Typical Value
Standard	ATX 12 V
Power	600 W
Connectors	PCI, SATA, Molex
+12 rails	4 numbers
PCIe Connectors	2 X 8 pin
Fan Diameter	140 mm

An ATX power supply is typically controlled by an electronic switch. Instead of a hard switch at the main power input, the power button on an ATX system is a sensor input monitored by the computer. ATX systems allow the Operating System to control the final "off" signal to the power supply; this gives the OS time to save all information and complete important tasks before turning off the power supply using a dedicated output signal (PS_ON#). ATX power supplies also support lower power modes. They have an additional "Standby" power output (5VSB) that stays on to power standby devices whenever the system goes into low-power mode.

4.11 POWER SWITCHES

Most newer systems now have their two main switches, the power switch and the reset switch, on the front panel. If the power switch is not on the front panel, it is likely either on the right rear corner or near a corner on the back of the PC. Three main types of power switches are used on PCs. They can be described as follows:

- Front panel motherboard-controlled switch (ATX and newer)
- Front panel power supply AC switch (AT/LPX; obsolete)
- Integral power supply AC switch (PC/XT/AT; obsolete)

All ATX and newer power supplies that employ the 20- or 24-pin motherboard connector use the PS_ON signal to power up the system. In this design, the power supply runs in standby mode when plugged in with the system off. The PS_ON signal is routed from the power supply through the motherboard to a low-voltage momentary contact DC switch on the front panel. As a result, the remote power switch does not physically control the power supply's access to the 120 V AC power, as in older-style power supplies. Instead, the power supply's on or off status is toggled by the PS_ON signal received on the ATX Main power connector. This is sometimes called a soft-off switch because this is the name of the Advanced Configuration Power Interface (ACPI) state when the system is off but still receiving standby power. The PS_ON signal can be manipulated physically by the computer's power switch or electronically by the motherboard under software control. PS_ON is an active low signal, meaning the power supply voltage outputs are disabled (the system is off) when the PS_ON is high (greater than or equal to 2.0 V). This excludes the +5 VSB (Standby) on pin nine of the ATX main power connector, which is active whenever the power supply is connected to an AC power source. The power supply maintains the PS_ON signal at either 3.3 V or +5 V. This signal is then routed through the motherboard to the remote switch on the front of the case. When the switch is pressed, the PS_ON signal is grounded. When the power supply sees the PS_ON signal drop to 0.8 V or less, the power supply (and system) is turned on. Thus, the remote switch in a system using an ATX or newer power supply carries up to only +5 V of DC power, rather than the full 120 V-240 V AC current like that of the older AT/LPX form factors. The actual power switch used in ATX systems is normally a tiny momentary contact push button switch, which is connected to the motherboard front panel header via a tiny two-pin connector. When the button is pushed, the motherboard then grounds the PS_ON signal in the main 20/24-pin power connector, causing the power supply to turn on.

4.11.1 Colour Specification

The switch was connected to the power supply via a four-wire cable, and the ends of the cable were fitted with spade connector lugs, which plugged onto the spade connectors on the power switch. The cable from the power supply to the switch in the case contained four color-coded wires. In addition, a fifth wire supplying a ground connection to the case was sometimes included. The switch was usually included with the power supply and heavily shrink-wrapped or insulated where the connector lugs attached, to prevent electric shock.
The output wires from SMPS are colour standardized and contain the four or five wires are usually color-coded as follows:

- Brown and blue-These wires are the live and neutral feed wires from the 120 V power cord to the power supply. These are always hot when the power supply is plugged in.
- Black and white-These wires carry the AC feed from the switch back to the power supply. These leads should be hot only when the power supply is plugged in and the switch is turned on.
- Green or green with a yellow stripe-This is the ground lead. It should be connected to the PC case and should help ground the power supply to the case.

4.12 SMPS USED IN PCs

SMPS is a stabilized power supply device which takes care of the computer system from fluctuations from the main power supply. It gives a continuous power supply to the motherboard at low voltage which is accepted by the computer system, i.e., 5V and/or 9V for the proper functioning of the various other components of the motherboard and hard disk connected in a PC.

4.12.1 Supply to Hard Disk Drive

To give power supply, we use a 9V special connector. This connector takes 9V from SMPS and gives this supply to hard disk so that the motor can be rotated easily. In addition, 5V DC is also given for proper functioning of the electronic circuits. Both the supplies are ON as soon as PC is switched ON. The hard disk starts working immediately on receiving its DC power supply.

4.12.2 CD/DVD (Compact-Disk/ Digital Versatile Disk) Drive

A CD-ROM drive uses a low-power laser beam to read information (binary data) that has been encoded in the form of tiny pits on an optical disk. The drive then feeds the data to a computer for processing. DVD stores large volume of data.

For proper functioning of the device, 9V and 5V power supply given from the SMPS.

☞ *Notice that the connectors are same whether the power is given to hard disk drive or to a DVD. The maximum units you can connect at one time to a PC is 3 or 4 depending the wattage of the SPMS.*

4.13 GENERAL SMPS TROUBLESHOOTING APPROACH

The following sections provide a set of guidelines for attacking SMPS problems.

(a) Categorize the problem, i.e., startup problem, catastrophic failure, incorrect outputs, or excessive ripple or noise.
(b) Determine what the proper output voltages should be. Identify the main (regulated) output.
(c) Disconnect the supply from the equipment it is powering. This will prevent the possibility of expensive damage. If this is not possible, you will need to be extra careful - always use a Variance to bring up the input slowly and monitor the main output at all times.
(d) Determine an appropriate load for the outputs. A typical SMPS will want a minimum of 5% to 20% of full load current at least on the main output to regulate properly. Others may not need any load - it depends on the design.

4.13.1 Safety

The input side of the AC supply is directly connected to the AC line and will have large electrolytic capacitors with 320 V or greater DC when powered and for some time after being unplugged. There is risk of instantly destroying expensive parts of the supply like the switch mode power transistor if your short something either directly or by killing the feedback circuit. The precautions given below are to protect you from potentially deadly electrical shock hazards as well as the equipment from accidental damage.

(a) Always keep one hand in your pocket when working around a powered line-connected or high voltage system.
(b) Wear rubber bottom shoes or sneakers.
(c) Set up your work area away from possible grounds that you may accidentally contact.

(d) If you need to probe, solder, or otherwise touch circuits with power off, discharge (across) large power supply filter capacitors with a 2 W or greater resistor of 5-50 ohms/V approximate value.
(e) Connect/disconnect any test leads with the equipment unpowered and unplugged. Use an isolation transformer if there is any chance of contacting line connected circuits.

4.13.2 Test Equipment

If the SMPS is capable of producing voltages beyond 1,000 V, make sure you use a proper high voltage probe or high voltage meter.

4.13.3 Using Handy Widgets

Some gadgets and homemade testers are useful for many repair situations. Here are just a few of the most basic types:

(a) *Series light bulb* for current limiting during the testing of monitors, switching power supplies, audio power amplifiers, etc.
(b) *Variac:* Variac is an autotransformer. It does not need to be large - a 2 A Variac mounted with a switch, outlet and fuse will suffice for most tasks. However, a 5 amp or larger Variac is better.
(c) *Isolation Transformer*: This is very important for safely working on live chassis equipment like line connected switchmode power supplies. Isolation transformer is used for final test where confirmation is needed that the inrush from a direct line connection will not damage the newly repaired supply.

4.13.4 Voltage Checkers

A voltage checker is used mostly to just produce a quick indication of the presense of voltage, its polarity, and other basic parameters. One use is a quick, but reliable indication of the status of the charge on a BIG capacitor.

4.13.5 Series Light Bulb Trick

When powering up a monitor that has had work done on any power circuits, it is desirable to minimize the chance of blowing your newly installed parts should there still be a fault. There are two ways of doing this:

(a) Use of a Variac to bring up the AC line voltage gradually
(b) Use of a series load to limit current to power semiconductors.

4.13.6 SMPS Failure Modes

SMPS may fail in many ways. The following are some common reasons:

(a) *Faulty primary-side components:* Rectifier diodes, filter capacitor(s), MOVs, and other parts located before the switchmode (chopper) transistor(s) may short due to a surge or lightning. Main fuse will blow instantly indicating the fault.

Symptoms: Totally dead supply, fuse blows instantly. Test all components on line side of high frequency transformer for short circuit failures with a multimeter.

(b) *Shorted switchmode transistor:* It may take out additional parts, such as fusable flameproof resistors in collector or emitter circuits of bipolar transistors or source or drain circuits for MOSFETs as well as gate components like the 15 or 18 V protection zener.

☞ *Main fuse will blow unless protected by fusable resistors and one or more of them blows first.*

Symptoms: Totally dead supply, fuse blows instantly (vaporizes or explodes unless fusable resistor has opened).

(c) *Shorted rectifier diodes in secondary circuits*: These are high frequency high efficiency diodes under a fair amount of stress.

Symptoms: In a very basic supply without overcurrent protection, the failure of one or more of these diodes may then overload the supply and cause a catastrophic failure of the switchmode power transistor and related components. Thus, these should be checked before reapplying power to a supply that had a shorted switchmode transistor.

(d) *Bad startup circuit*: Initial base (gate) drive is often provided by a high value, high power resistor or resistors from the rectified AC voltage. These can simply open for no good reason.

Symptoms: In this case the supply will appear totally dead but all the semiconductors will check out and no fuses will blow. Check the startup resistors with an ohmmeter

(e) *Dried up capacitors:* Dried either input or output side of capacitor.

Symptoms: The main filter capacitor may dry up or open and cause the output to be pulsing at 50 or 100 Hz and all kinds of regulation problems. Measure voltage across main filter capacitor(s). If the reading is low and drops to a much lower value or 0 instantly upon pulling the plug, then one of these capacitors may be open or dried up.

(f) *Bad connection/dry solder joints* - Defective solder connections are very common especially around the pins of high power components like transformers, power resistors and transistors, and connectors.

Symptoms: Almost any kind of behaviour is possible. The unit may be erratic, intermittent, or totally dead. Visually inspect the solder side of the circuit board with a bright light and magnifying glass if necessary. Gently twist the circuit board with an insulating stick to see if the problem can be made to change.

(g) *Regulation problems*: Outputs high or low.

Symptoms: Voltage has changed and adjustment pot meter if one exists has no effect or is unable to set voltage to proper value. Check components in the feedback regulator, particularly the opto-isolator and its associated circuitry. A weak opto-isolator may allow for excessive output voltage. A shorted photodiode in the opto-isolator may prevent startup. An open photodiode may lead to a runaway condition.

4.13.7 Sounds that SMPSs Make

Most switchmode power supplies when operating normally produce little or no detectable sound. The switching frequencies are usually well above the range of human hearing. However, under various fault conditions, and sometimes when lightly loaded, there may be tell-tail audible indications of the SMPS's state of working. The cause may be in the SMPS itself or its load.

(a) Tweet-tweet-tweet or chirp-chirp-chirp (sometimes flub-flub-flub) - Short circuit or current overload. This is usually an indication of a shorted secondary-side rectifier.
(b) High pitched, but audible, whine - Excessive load. This may be caused by shorted components.
(c) Tick-tick-tick - Too little or no load. In a monitor using an SMPS, this is likely due to a lack of horizontal drive or a blown fuse or fusable resistor in the horizontal deflection system. The power supply is in a repeating cycle of starting up, being unable to limit the regulated voltage to a safe value. Attempting to power up an SMPS without an adequate dummy load may result in these symptoms.
(d) Hissing or white noise - possibly from inductors - This may be normal under certain conditions.

4.13.8 Troubleshooting SMPS using Discrete Controllers

The following paragraphs apply mainly to SMPS using discrete circuitry:

(a) *Startup problems* - Check the power on the switchmode transistor and work back from there. Check for open fusable resistors. Check for open startup resistors, bad connections, blown parts in the controller circuitry.
(b) *Blows fuses* - Check primary side components, switchmode transistor(s), and all other semiconductors for shorts. Then check for open fusable resistors and bad connections. Finally, check the electrolytic capacitors for reduced capacity and leakage.
(c) *Power cycling* - Monitor current and voltage sensing signals to determine if they are actually signaling a fault. Open or out of tolerance resistors may result in incorrect sensing. With the series light bulb and/or Variac, disable each of these inputs by bypassing the appropriate components.
(d) *Regulation or ripple/noise problems* - Check main HV filter capacitor and other filter capacitors for decreased value or opens. Check regulation components including shunt regulators and zener diodes.

4.13.9 Most Common Problems

The diagnosis of problems in switch mode power supplies is sometimes made complicated due the interdependence of components that must function properly for any portion of the power supply to begin to work. Depending on design, SMPS may or may not be protected from overload conditions and may fail catastrophically under a heavy load even when supposedly short circuit proof. There is particular stress on the switching devices (they are often 800 V transistors) which can lead to early or unexpected failure. Also, SMPS may fail upon restoration of power after a blackout if there is any kind of power spike since turn-on is a very stressful period - some designs take this into account and limit turn on surge. Problem could be harddisk and fan simultaneously failing to spin or overheating due to fan failure. Small brownouts that cause the system to reset. However, the cause of many problems are immediately obvious and have simple fixes - the blown chopper transistor or dried up main filter capacitor.

Some quick checks on a faulty SMPS are discussed below:

Problem 1: The Power doesn't come on.

- Check the external connections of the power supply. This is the first step in checking any electrical equipment that shows no signs of life.
- Confirm that the power supply cord is plugged into a functioning outlet.
- Verify the position of the On/Off switch.
- Examine the power cord for good connection at the rear of the unit.
- One simple test you can perform on a power supply is to check the output voltages. This shows whether a power supply is operating correctly and whether the output voltages are within the correct tolerance range. Note that you must measure all voltages with the power supply connected to a proper load, which usually means testing while the power supply is still installed in the system and connected to the motherboard and peripheral devices.
- Check the Power switch of the Cabinet and Front Panel of MotherBoard
- Check the SMPS without connecting it to the motherboard, you could see the two wire green and black which you have to short them (using any piece of wire/paper clip) in the 24 pin motherboard connector of the SMPS.

Problem 2: The absence of the lights and the fan operation.

- Check the Power switch of the Cabinet
- A portion of the power supply has failed, or is being overloaded. One or more of the basic voltages supplied by the power supply is missing while the others are still present.

Problem 3: SMPS partially working Sometimes the SMPS is only partially working: it may start for a fraction of a second and than shut down, or it may pulsate trying to start every few seconds and shutting down after a fraction of a second, or it may produce a wrong output voltage.

- Here, probably all power semiconductors are good, so the first thing to check are the capacitors
- Than, there may be something wrong with the feedback circuit: a good trick is to apply an external adjustable DC voltage to the SMPS output (the SMPS being not connected to the mains).

Problem 4: The PC Powers on beeps and stops. NO Power On Self Test (POST)messages.

- Check with another SMPS
- This may be a Motherboard Problem.

Problem 5: The PC Powers on runs POST but there is no display.

- Check the Monitor and the VGA Cable Connections
- Check with another SMPS
- This may be a Display Card Problem

Problem 6: There is a squealing/whistling/whining noise from SMPS when the PC starts.

- Check the SMPS Fan. If system noise is a problem, models with special fans can run more quietly than the standard models. These power supplies often use larger-diameter fans that spin more slowly, so they run more quietly but move the same amount of air as the smaller fans.
- Component problem with SMPS. Replace it

Problem 7: The PC freezes or reboots suddenly

- Check the SMPS Fan (May be overheating Problem) due to fan failure.
- Some of the available replacement power supplies have higher-capacity cooling fans than the originals, which can greatly prolong system life and minimize overheating problems-especially for the newer, hotter-running processors.

The diagnosis of problems in switch mode power supplies is sometimes made complicated due the interdependence of components that must function properly for any portion of the power supply to begin to work.

Depending on design, SMPS may or may not be protected from overload conditions and may fail catastrophically under a heavy load even when supposedly short circuit proof. There is particular stress on the switching devices (they are often 800 V transistors) which can lead to early or unexpected failure.

SMPS may fail upon restoration of power after a blackout if there is any kind of power spike since turn-on is a very stressful period - some designs take this into account and limit turn on surge.

The cause of many problems in SMPS are immediately obvious and have simple fixes:

(a) The blown chopper transistor
(b) Dried up main filter capacitor

☞ *Note that you can easily turn a simple repair (e.g., bad solder connections) into an expensive mess if you use inappropriate soldering equipment and/or lack the soldering skills to go along with it.*

4.13.10 How to choose the best SMPS for your PC?

Three things that should be kept in mind before choosing an SMPS for your PC.

(a) The load to be put on computer
(b) The motherboard of computer
(c) The architecture of computer.

An SMPS should be chosen keeping in view the load that has to be put on computer. The very first thing to look for is a 12 volt amperage reading. PSUs have a power output range from 200 watts to 1800 watts. A higher watt PSU will supply more power for more heavy work. If the maximum power combined of your system is 300 watts, a 600 watt PSU would be a good match and if total design power of your system is 700 watts then a PSU of 1200 watts will work well. You can go for a lower or higher efficiency capacity unit depending on your need to expand your system in future. An efficient PSU is always better.

In addition to output, manufacturers also specify the number of +12v rails their PSUs have. A single rail power system has a single +12v rail to supply power to the system; while a double rail unit bifurcates its output in two or more +12v rails. Single rail can supply much more power to your components as compared to multi rail, but can lead to major melt down if serious overload occurs. In general both are safe to use.

It is better to go with a branded SMPS depending upon the motherboard of your computer. A branded 300 watt SMPS can easily beat a 500-600 watt cheap SMPS.

Depending on the type of computer SMPS are of 3 types

(a) **AT SMPS**: 'Advanced Technology' SMPS are old SMPS. With a 12-pin power connector they were used in Pentium-I, Pentium-MM X, Pentium-II, and Pentium III CPUs.
(b) **ATX SMPS**: 'Advanced Technology Extended' has a 20-pin power connector called ATX power connector. They were used in Pentium-III, Pentium IV and AMD CPUs.
(c) **BTX SMPS**: 'Balanced Technology eXtended' SMPS have a 24-pin power connector and are also called BTX power connectors. It has a 15-pin SATA power connector and is used in dual core, core2duo, quad-core, i3, i5, i7 and the latest AMD CPUs.

These were some of the main points you need to keep in consideration while choosing an SMPS (Switch Mode Power Supply) unit or you can say PSU for your computer. For modern day computers, BTX technology SMPS are the best. However, if you have an old PC and want to replace its SMPS, you can opt for the ones mentioned in the above list

4.14 BATTERY

Battery is a device that converts energy stored in chemicals into energy in the form of electricity. It consists of two or more electric cells connected in series or parallel. Every battery has a cathode, or positive electrode, and an anode, or negative electrode. These electrodes must be separated by and are often immersed in an electrolyte that permits the passage of ions between the electrodes (See Figure 4.8). The electrode materials and electrolyte are arranged in the way so that sufficient electromotive force (voltage) and electric current (amperes) can be developed between the terminals of a battery to operate lighting device like electric bulb, machines, etc. The active parts of a battery are encased in a box (or jacket). These parts also cover system that keeps air outside and the electrolyte solvent inside and thus provides a structure for the assembly.

4.15 TYPES OF BATTERIES AND THEIR APPLICATIONS

Batteries are divided into two general groups. These are:

(a) Primary batteries
(b) Secondary or storage batteries

4.15.1 Primary Batteries

Primary batteries are designed to be used until the voltage is too low to operate a given device and then discarded.

Zinc Dioxide Systems

The anode of this system of batteries is a zinc alloy sheet or the alloy containing small amount of lead, cadmium, and mercury. The electrolyte consists of a saturated aqueous (watery) solution of ammonium chloride containing roughly 20 percent zinc chloride. The cathode is made of impure manganese dioxide. The zinc chloride cell is capable of greater continuous service. Its use is also increasing because it can provide satisfactory performance without mercury in the zinc alloy.

Uses These cell systems are the most commonly used world-wide in:

(a) Flashlights
(b) Toys
(c) Radios
(d) Tape recorders
(e) Flash cameras

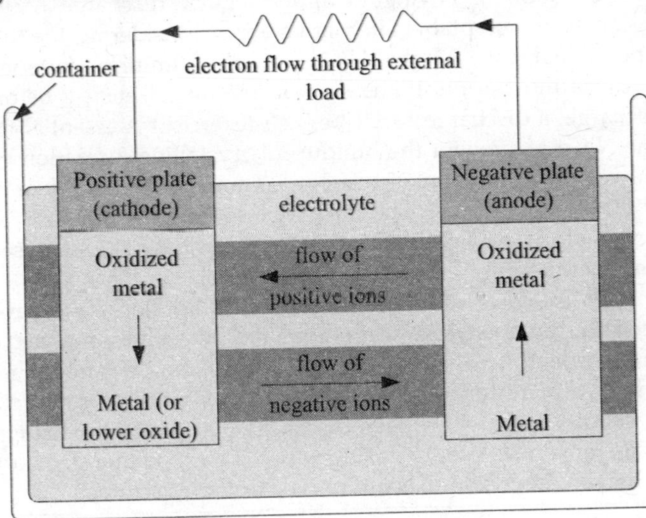

Figure 4.8 Ideal Cell in a Battery

Magnesium Dioxide Cell

This system functions well for specialized applications. It is much like the zinc chloride cell but has 0.3 volt more per cell. Magnesium dioxide cells have:

(a) Long shelf life
(b) High energy density are
(c) Lightweight

They are especially attractive for use as power packs for portable military radios. The one drawback of these cells is that they do not function nearly as well at below-freezing temperatures as at higher temperatures.

Mercuric Oxide Cell

This is an alkaline-electrolyte battery system. It has long been used in the form of button-sized cells for hearing aids and watches. Its energy density approximately four times greater than that of the alkaline zinc dioxide cell. Since the mercuric oxide cell provides an extremely reliable 1.35 volts, it serves as a standard reference cell.

Silver Oxide Cell

Silver oxide cell has the capacity to tolerate relatively heavy current load pulses and has a high, nearly constant, 1.5-volt operating voltage. The silver oxide cell is commonly used in:

(a) Watches
(b) Cameras
(c) Hearing aids

☞ *Inspite of its high cost, the outstanding current-carrying capability of this cell has resulted in its use as military applications.*

Air-depolarized Cells

A very practical way to obtain high energy density in a cell is to employ the oxygen in air for a liquid cathode material. If paired with an anode, such as zinc, long cell life at low cost per watt-hour (for a dry cell) can be obtained because a given cell volume may be devoted more completely to anode and electrolyte material. The cell, however, must be constructed in such a way that the oxygen is prevented from reaching the anode, which it will attack.

Zinc-air systems are commercially available in the form of very small cells and relatively large box like batteries. Their principle and design are simple.

4.15.2 Secondary Batteries

Secondary batteries have many special design features, as well as particular materials for the electrodes, that permit them to be reconstituted (recycled) after partial or complete discharge. They can be recharged by DC voltage and current to their original state. But the original state is not restored completely.

Lead-acid Battery

The lead-acid secondary battery has long been the most widely used rechargeable portable power source. These batteries are constructed with lead plates, or grids. One of the grids, the positive electrode, is coated with lead dioxide in a particular crystalline form, along with additives, such as calcium sulfate.

The electrolyte, composed of sulfuric acid, participates in the electrode reactions where lead sulfate is formed and carries current in moving ions.

☞ *The lead-acid battery has 20 times as much capacity as either the nickel-cadmium or nickel-iron alkaline rechargeable battery.*

The lead-acid battery system has been as successful as it has because of the following features:

(a) Large capability range for high or low current demand over ambient temperature.
(b) Good cycle life with high reliability for hundreds of cycles, especially with good recharge control.
(c) Relative low cost, comparatively good shelf life for a rechargeable system when stored.
(d) High cell voltage at 2.04 volts per cell.
(e) Ease of fabricating lead components by casting, welding, or rolling.
(f) High degree of recovery at low melting temperatures.

Lead-acid batteries are classified into the following three groups:

(a) *Starting-Lighting-Ignition (SLI) batteries:* The automotive SLI battery is the best known portable rechargeable power source. High current can be obtained.
(b) *Traction batteries:* Traction batteries are employed in industrial lift trucks, delivery trucks, and other vehicles. While some are readily portable, others may be very heavy.
(c) *Stationary batteries:* Stationary batteries have heavier grid structures and other features to give them long shelf life. They are used to power emergency lights and in uninterruptible power systems for hospitals, factories and telephone exchanges.

Alkaline Storage Batteries

In secondary batteries of this type, electric energy is derived from the chemical action in an alkaline solution.

Nickel (hydroxide) Cadmium Battery *Nickel (hydroxide) cadmium battery* systems are the most common small rechargeable battery type for portable appliances. The sealed cells are equipped with jelly roll electrodes, which allow high current to be delivered in an efficient way. These batteries are capable of delivering exceptionally high currents. They can be rapidly recharged many times, and are tolerant of abuse, such as over discharging or overcharging. In comparison of many primary batteries and even lead-acid batteries, nickel cadmium cells are heavy and have comparatively limited energy density. They last longer and perform better if fully discharged each cycle before recharge.

Nickel (hydroxide) Iron Batteries *Nickel (hydroxide) iron batteries* can provide thousands of cycles but do not recharge with high efficiency, generating heat and consuming more electricity than is generally desirable. They have been used extensively in the mining industry.

Alkaline Zinc Manganese Dioxide Rechargeable Battery Alkaline zinc manganese dioxide rechargeable cells have been developed as a substitute for other systems that provide moderate amounts of electricity for certain applications. Their high energy density and low cost encourage further engineering work and commercial introduction.

Silver (oxide) Zinc Batteries *Silver (oxide) zinc batteries* are expensive but are employed where high power density, good energy-cycling efficiency low weight, and low volume are critical. They are also employed in portable radar units and communications equipment, as well as in aircraft and space vehicles.

4.15.3 Regular Maintenance of Battery

Regular battery maintenance does the following:

(a) Prolongs battery life
(b) Keeps the battery in good working condition
(c) Provides the user with confidence.

The notion of having to apply regular discharge cycles becomes an acceptable alternative when considering the low operational cost of the NiCd (nickel-cadmium) batteries. Because most applications do not use up all energy before recharge, a discharge to 1V per cell (exercise) is essential for the NiCd to prevent the buildup of crystalline formation on the cell plates known as "memory,". This robs the battery of its ability to hold charge. The capacity loss caused by memory is reversible. If used daily, the NiCd battery should be exercised once per month.

If no exercise (discharge, recharge) is applied for several months, the crystalline formations fix themselves, making it more difficult to dissolve. In such a case, exercise is no longer effective in restoring a battery and recondition is required. Recondition is a slow, deep discharge that drains the battery of its remaining energy during which the crystalline structure is broken down and the battery is commonly restored.

☞ *By applying exercise, 45% battery failure will reduce to 15%.*

Exercise and recondition are most effective when applied while the batteries are still in reasonably good condition. Once the crystalline formation has advanced beyond a certain stage, restoration becomes difficult, even with recondition.

Battery Maintenance System

Most organizations service their batteries either when they no longer hold charge or when the equipment is sent in for repair. As a result, the system becomes unreliable over time, and battery-related failures become frequent. On a routine day, a marginal battery may hold out charge but during an emergency, when more energy is required, a poorly performing battery cannot provide the extra power that is needed and the system subsequently fails.

☞ *Implementing a battery maintenance plan requires some effort on behalf of management in sorting the batteries to be serviced and collecting them in one place without disrupting the operation.*

Certain organizations service the batteries in-house with their own battery analyzers. A set of spare batteries will be required to replace those that have been removed. After service, the batteries are marked to identify the date of service. One simple method is to attach a colour dot, each colour indicating the month of service. A different colour dot is applied when the battery is reserviced the following month.

☞ *A key to successful battery maintenance is a good battery analyzer that automatically print a label with date, company inscription and battery capacity when the battery is removed.*

One analyzer, for example, evaluates the condition of a battery and applies a recondition cycle to restore the battery's capacity if a preset performance level cannot be reached.

For NiCd users, the battery maintenance serves two functions:

(a) To prevent memory from occurring.
(b) To maximize the service life of a battery.

There is a time when a battery must be retired, and the battery maintenance system helps to determine when the time is right. With proper battery maintenance, the number of batteries discarded are fewer, a direct cost savings. More important, well-managed batteries provide the user with a level of confidence that is essential when working with today's hand-held equipments.

EXERCISE

1. Explain the basic principle of operation of linear and switched mode power supplies.
2. Identify the basic elements in a regulated power supply.
3. Compare the merits and demerits of SMPS and linear power supplies.
4. Write a short note on SMPS.
5. What do you mean by power supply? What are the main requirements of power supply unit used for PC?
6. What troubleshoot you do for *Startup problems* in SMPS?
7. Discuss working Principle of SMPS.
8. What do you mean by rectification?
9. Write short note on Flyback converter.
10. Why Regular Maintenance of Battery is required?
11. Discuss two types of Batteries.
12. Troubleshoot the problem of SMPS -"The PC Powers on beeps and stops. NO Power On Self Test (POST)messages".

REVIEW QUESTIONS WITH ANSWERS

1. Multiple Choice

1.1 Regulated DC voltage is required for semiconductor devices such as _______ to function.

a. ICs b. Transistors
c. ICs and Transistors d. None of these

Ans (c)

1.2 In First Stage SMPS conversion the input ___ voltage is directly rectified and converter in high voltage ____.

a. DC AC b. DC DC
c. AC DC d. AC AC

Ans (c)

1.3 In Second Stage of SMPS Conversion rectified high voltage ____ is stored in a capacitors.

a. DC b. Both AC & DC
c. AC d. None of these

Ans (a)

1.4 DC-DC converter DC - DC converters are power electronic circuits that convert a dc voltage to a different voltage level. Different types of conversion method

a. electronic , magnetic b. linear , switched mode
c. capacitive d. All of these

Ans (d)

1.5 The Full form of PSU

a. power supply unit b. power series unit
c. power stable unit d. None of these

Ans (a)

1.6 The hardware of computer works as per the instructions contained in

a. Software (OS) b. Power supply
c. Processor d. All of the above

Ans (a)

1.7 Which memory module has small, removable flash memory card format originally based on the ScanDisk TransFlash card format?

a. SIMM b. DIMM
c. MicroSD d. RIMM

Ans (c)

1.8 DIMMs are available in

a. 72-pin-DIMMs b. 200-pin-DIMMs
c. 168-pin-DIMMs d. All of the above

Ans (d)

1.9 Which out of the following is the SMPS failure mode?

a. Shorted Switchmode transistor
b. Bad startup circuit
c. Faulty secondary-side component
d. All of the above

Ans (b)

1.10 Regular battery maintenance does the following:

a. prolongs battery life
b. keeps the battery in good working condition

c. provides the user with confidence.
d. all of the above

Ans (d)

1.11 Which of the following is the most important characteristics of three-terminal regulator?

a. line regulation b. output voltage
c. ripple rejection d. quiescent current

Ans (b)

1.12 Step down transformer can be use for

a. doorbells b. power supply
c. toy electric trains. d. All of the above

Ans (d)

1.13 The hardware of computer works as per the instructions contained in

a. Software (OS) b. Processor
c. Power supply d. All of the above

Ans (a)

1.14 The data transfer between CPU and other devices takes place in chunks of 8 bits, 16 bits or 32 bits depending upon the width of

a. Data bus b. Address bus
c. Control bus d. None of the above

Ans (a)

1.15 Main component of linear power supply are:

a. power transistor b. voltage regulating IC
c. noise filtering capacitor d. All of the above

Ans (d)

2. State whether the following statements are True or False

2.1 Fly-back converters have been widely used because of the irrelative simplicity and their excellent performance for multi output applications.

Ans True

2.2 The output of the buck-boost converter can be either higher or lower than the input voltage.

Ans True

2.3 ATX-2 Power Supply is commonly in used today.

Ans True

2.4 SMPS can fail in many different ways, the most common being no output power at all.

Ans True

2.5 Rectification - turning the AC into DC.

Ans True

2.6 The POWER_GOOD signal tells the motherboard that the power supply has completed its cycle-up process and is now able to provide clean power in the voltages needed by the PC.

Ans True

2.7 Variac is an autotransformer.

Ans True

2.8 Impedance represents the relationship between voltage and current in which a device is capable of accepting or delivering electrons flow.

Ans True

2.9 When we convert alternate current into direct current, then the process is called rectification.

Ans True

2.10 A faulty capacitor can be open or short-circuited.

Ans True

2.11 Passive heat sinks can cause quick overheating of the microprocessors.

Ans False

2.12 Linear power supply units do not produce much interference.

Ans True

3. Match the following:

3.1	Linear power supplies	a.	series regulator element is either on or off.
3.2	The switching action means	b.	is used in dual core, core2duo, quad-core, i3, i5, i7 and the latest AMD CPUs
3.3	AT 'Advanced Technology' SMPS	c.	non-switching techniques
3.4	ATX SMPS	d.	old SMPS.
3.5	BTX SMPS	e.	used in Pentium-III, Pentium IV and AMD CPUs
3.6	SMPS	f.	Filter capacitor
3.7	Signal Rectification	g.	uses PWM
3.8	Electric current	h.	Diode
3.9	CMOS devices	i.	Ampere
3.10	A regulated linear power supply contains	j.	Low power dissipation

Ans 3.1 c 3.2 a 3.3 d 3.4 e 3.5 b
3.6 g 3.7 h 3.8 i 3.9 j 3.10 f

4. Fill in the blanks

4.1 The SMPS circuit which has very low o/p power (less than 100W) is called as _______ converter SMPS.

Ans fly-back

4.2 The _______ is a commonly used in circuits that steps down the voltage level from the input voltage according to the requirement.

Ans buck converter

4.3 A _______ (step-up converter) is a power converter with an output DC voltage greater than its input DC voltage.

Ans boost converter

4.4 The _____ converter is used for getting the output voltage with different polarity.

Ans Cuk

4.5 _______ means smoothing the ripple of the rectified voltage(s).

Ans Filtering

4.6 ________ is used to prevent the various chips in the SMPS from overheating.

Ans Fan

4.7 When we convert alternate current into direct current, then the process is called ________.

Ans rectification

4.8 In __________, the incoming AC voltage is stepped down to a lower AC voltage.

Ans Linear power supply

4.9 __________ contains an arrangement of resistances, inductances and capacitors in series, parallel or mixed grouping.

Ans AC circuit

4.10 By applying ____________, 45% battery failure will reduce to 15%.

Ans maintenance

Q.5 (a) Write short notes on the following

(i) PSU

(ii) Fly-back Converter SMPS Working

Ans 5(a)(i)

A power supply is an internal hardware component that supplies components in a computer with power, sometimes abbreviated as PSU, which is short for Power Supply Unit. The power supply converts a 110-115 or 220-230 volt alternating current (AC) into a steady low-voltage direct current (DC) usable by the computer and rated by the number of watts it generates.
Power supplies are rated in terms of the number of watts they generate. The more powerful the computer, the more watts it can provide to components. The power supply unit (PSU) in a PC regulates and delivers the power to the components in the case.

Ans 5(a)(ii)

Fly-back Converter SMPS Working

The SMPS circuit which has very low o/p power (less than 100W) is called as fly-back converter SMPS. This type of SMPS is very low and simple circuit compared with other SMPS circuits. This type of SMPS is used for low power application.

Q.6 Write advantages of Linear Power supply.

Ans 6
Linear power supply advantages

- **Low noise**: The use of the linear technology without any switching element means that noise is kept to a minimum.
- **Established technology**: Linear power supplies have been in widespread use for many years and their technology is well established and understood.

Q.7 Explain the terms Volt, Ampere adn Watt.

Ans 7
Volt
The *volt* is the International System of Units (SI) units of electric potential or electromagnetic force (voltage).
Ampere
An *ampere* is a unit of measurement of the rate of electrons flow or current in an electrical conductor. One ampere of current represents one coulomb of electrical charge (6.24×10^{18}) moving past a specific point in one second. Generally, ampere is written as *A* or *amp*.
Watt
The *watt* is the standard unit of power. It is equal to the expenditure of 1 Joule of energy in 1 second. Watt is used to specify the rate at which electrical energy is radiated, absorbed or consumed.

Q.8 How to choose the best SMPS for your PC?

Ans 8
Three things that should be kept in mind before choosing an SMPS for your PC.

- The load to be put on computer
- the motherboard of computer
- and the architecture of computer.

Q.9 How working of linear power supply is different from switched mode power supply?

Ans 9
Like a linear power supply, the switched mode power supply too converts the available unregulated ac or dc input voltage to a regulated dc output voltage. However in case of SMPS with input supply drawn from the ac mains, the input voltage is first rectified and filtered using a capacitor at the rectifier output. The unregulated dc voltage across the capacitor is then fed to a high frequency dc-to-dc converter. Most of the dc-to-dc converters used in SMPS circuits have an intermediate high frequency ac conversion stage to facilitate the use of a high frequency transformer for voltage scaling and isolation. In contrast, in linear power supplies with input voltage drawn from ac mains, the mains voltage is first stepped down (and isolated) to the desired magnitude using a mains frequency transformer, followed by rectification and filtering.

Q.10 Write disadvantages of Linear Power Supply.

Ans 10

Linear power supply disadvantages

- **Efficiency**: Linear power supply is highly inefficient if it has to work over large variations in input voltage, is more bulky because of the use of low frequency transformer and filter elements (inductors and capacitors).
- **Size**: The use of linear technology means that the size of a linear power supply tends to be larger than other forms of power supply.
- **Heat dissipation**: The use of a series or parallel (less common) regulating element means that significant amounts of heat are dissipated and this needs to be removed.

Q.11 Write Symptoms of a Failing Power Supply.

Ans 11

Symptoms of a Failing Power Supply

(a) Strange noises may emit from the back of the computer case where the cord is located.

(b) When the computer is turned on, nothing happens. Sometimes this may coincide with a flashing light on the front of the computer or an indicator on the back of the PSU (if equipped).

(c) The computer turns on for a couple of seconds and then turns right back off. While this can be a power supply issue, it may also indicate motherboard failures.

Q.12 Write few SMPS Trouble shooting Tips.

Ans 12

(a) First, determine that it is not something casual like a blown fuse due to a legitimate overload.

(b) Take the appropriate measurement to determine the reason of failure.

(c) Examine all electrolytic capacitors properly. See carefully one or more capacitors maybe damaged, loose etc. Replace accordingly.

(d) Once again, you need to see there's any sign of decayed glue on the components. If you see some on the capacitors, diodes, resistors etc then promptly clean them off.

(e) Now once you've taken care of the problem, don't fix the SMPS to the main CPU now. Be sure to test it on a 'dummy CPU'. This is to protect the main CPU in case over voltage issue persists.

Q.13 What do you mean by alternate current? What are its properties?

Ans 13

Certain sources of electricity produce voltages alternating in polarity, reversing positive and negative over time. Either as a voltage switching polarity or as a current switching direction back and forth. This kind of electricity is known as *Alternating Current (AC)*. The power supply coming from state electric Board's is AC supply.

AC source of electrical power changes constantly in amplitude and regularly changes polarity. The changes are smooth and regular, endlessly repeating in succession of identical cycles. This forms a sine wave. Because the changes are so regular, alternating voltage and current have a number of properties associated with any such waveform. These basic properties include the following points:

Frequency: One of the most important properties of any regular waveform identifies the number of complete cycles it goes through in a fixed period of time. For standard measurements, the period of time is one second, so the frequency of the wave is commonly measured in cycles per second (cycles/sec). In normal usage, it is expressed in units of Hertz (Hz). It is represented in mathematical equations by the letter '*f*.'

Period: If we need to know the amount of time required to complete one cycle of the waveform, then this is called period. Thus, period is the time duration of one cycle of the waveform. It is measured in seconds/cycle. AC power at 50 Hz will have a period of 1/50 = 0.02 seconds/cycle.

Wavelength: Because an AC wave moves physically as well as changing in time, when we need to know how far it moves in one cycle of the wave, rather than how long that cycle takes to complete. This depends on how fast the wave is moving as well. Electrical signals travel through their wires at nearly the speed of light, which is very nearly 3×10^8 meters/second. This is represented mathematically by the letter 'c.' The Greek letter (lambda) is used to represent wavelength. Thus:

$$\lambda = c/f.$$

Amplitude: Another thing we have to know is just how positive or negative the voltage is, with respect to some selected neutral reference. With DC, this is easy because the voltage is constant at some measurable value. But AC is regularly changing, and yet it still powers a load. In an AC power system, amplitude is the rating that would cause the same amount of work to be done (the same effect) as the same value of DC voltage or current would cause.

Q.14 Discuss the various components which are needed for a typical SMPS.

Ans 14

Switch Mode Power Transformers are an integral part of Switch Mode Power Supplies (SMPS) and DC/DC Converters, as well as other types of applications. It is used to change amplitude of high-frequency pulses by the turns ratio and to provide isolation between the circuits. It cannot transfer DC component of the voltage through. Ideally SMPS transformer transfers all energy instantaneously from one winding to another while wasting no or little energy in the process. This type of transformer operates at high frequencies, from 200kHz to 2MHz.

There are four different types of magnetic components that are needed for the typical SMPS. They are as follows.

(a) *Output Transformer:* Output Transformer or Main Transformer takes the input voltage that is supplied to its primary winding and then transforms the input voltage to one or more voltages that are the output of the secondary winding or windings.

(b) *Output Inductors:* Output Inductors are used to filter the output voltage so that the load current is DC value.

(c) *Input Inductors:* Input Inductors filter out the noise generated by the switching transistors so that this noise is not emitted back to the source.

(d) *Current Sense Transformer:* Current Sense Transformers are used to help regulate the SMPS so that when the load changes, the SMPS adjusts the power it is delivering to the load accordingly.

Q.15 Explain the detail description of SMPS troubleshooting?

Ans 15

Safety

The input side of the AC supply is directly connected to the AC line and will have large electrolytic capacitors with 320 V or greater DC when powered and for some time after being unplugged. There is risk of instantly destroying expensive parts of the supply like the switchmode power transistor if your short something either directly or by killing the feedback circuit. The precautions given below are to protect you from potentially deadly electrical shock hazards as well as the equipment from accidental damage.

(a) Always keep one hand in your pocket when working around a powered line-connected or high voltage system.

(b) Wear rubber bottom shoes or sneakers.

(c) Set up your work area away from possible grounds that you may accidentally contact.

(d) If you need to probe, solder, or otherwise touch circuits with power off, discharge (across) large power supply filter capacitors with a 2 W or greater resistor of 5-50 ohms/V approximate value.

(e) Connect/disconnect any test leads with the equipment unpowered and unplugged. Use an isolation transformer if there is any chance of contacting line connected circuits.

Test Equipment

If the SMPS is capable of producing voltages beyond 1,000 V, make sure you use a proper high voltage probe or high voltage meter.

Using Handy Widgets

Some gadgets and homemade testers are useful for many repair situations. Here are just a few of the most basic types:

(a) *Series light bulb* for current limiting during the testing of monitors, switching power supplies, audio power amplifiers, etc.

(b) *Variac:* Variac is an autotransformer. It does not need to be large - a 2 A Variac mounted with a switch, outlet and fuse will suffice for most tasks. However, a 5 amp or larger Variac is better.

(c) *Isolation Transformer*: This is very important for safely working on live chassis equipment like line connected switchmode power supplies. Isolation transformer is used for final test where confirmation is needed that the inrush from a direct line connection will not damage the newly repaired supply.

Voltage Checkers

A voltage checker is used mostly to just produce a quick indication of the presense of voltage, its polarity, and other basic parameters. One use is a quick, but reliable indication of the status of the charge on a BIG capacitor.

Series Light Bulb Trick

When powering up a monitor that has had work done on any power circuits, it is desirable to minimize the chance of blowing your newly installed parts should there still be a fault. There are two ways of doing this:

(a) Use of a Variac to bring up the AC line voltage gradually

(b) Use of a series load to limit current to power semiconductors.

Sounds that SMPSs Make

Most switchmode power supplies when operating normally produce little or no detectable sound. The switching frequencies are usually well above the range of human hearing. However, under various fault conditions, and sometimes when lightly loaded, there may be tell-tail audible indications of the SMPS's state of working. The cause may be in the SMPS itself or its load.

(a) Tweet-tweet-tweet or chirp-chirp-chirp (sometimes flub-flub-flub) - Short circuit or current overload. This is usually an indication of a shorted secondary-side rectifier.

(b) High pitched, but audible, whine - Excessive load. This may be caused by shorted components.

(c) Tick-tick-tick - Too little or no load. In a monitor using an SMPS, this is likely due to a lack of horizontal drive or a blown fuse or fusable resistor in the horizontal deflection system. The power supply is in a repeating cycle of starting up, being unable to limit the regulated voltage to a safe value. Attempting to power up an SMPS without an adequate dummy load may result in these symptoms.

(d) Hissing or white noise - possibly from inductors - this may be normal under certain conditions.

CHAPTER 5

Cabinet Types

5.1 PARTS OF PERSONAL COMPUTER (PC)

Various parts of a PC are described in the following sub-sections.

(a) Front panel,
(b) Rear panel, and
(c) Inside the system unit.

5.1.1 Front Panel

Various parts of the front panel of a PC are shown in Figure 5.1.

5.1.2 Rear Panel

If you look at the rear panel of the system unit of your PC, you will see certain holes and slots fitted with different cables. Details of such parts are explained in Figure 5.2.

5.1.3 Inside the System Unit

Inside the system unit are the electronic components that run the programs, handle typed instructions and determine the result. Some of the common components are given in Figure 5.3.

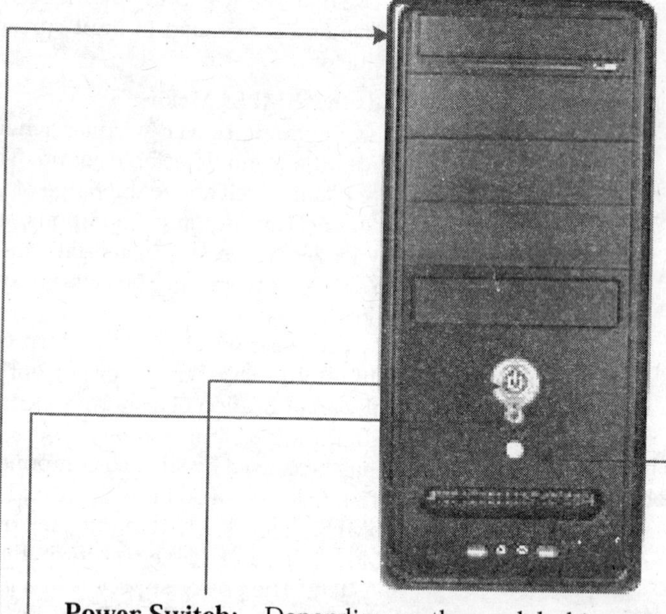

Power Switch: Depending on the model, this switch is located either in the front or at the side of the system unit and it is used to switch the system ON or OFF.

Reset Button: This is a switch which can be used to restart the PC without switching off the mains power supply.

Indicator Lights Computer unit may have colored lights to indicate the working of the PC. These lights also glow whenever data is recorded onto or read from CD, USB Drive or hard disk.

DVD Drive: It accepts CD and DVD and if the drive is capable of it, it might also write to writeable CDs & DVDs.

Figure 5.1 Parts of front panel of system

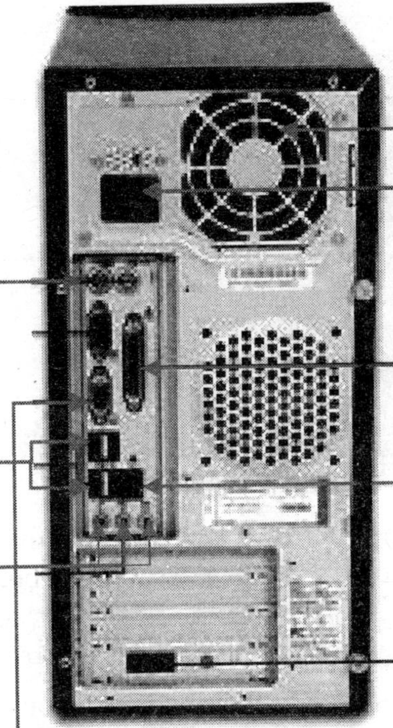

Video Port for Monitor: This is a 5 pin socket used to connect a monitor with the system unit.

PS/2 Port: This is used to connect the keyboard and mouse with the system.

Power Sockets: Cables plugged into these sockets carry electric power supply from the electrical outlet to your system unit and from the system unit to your monitor.

Parallel Port or Sockets: These ports or sockets are used for expanding the capability of your PC. For example, you can connect a printer, mouse, modem or some other peripheral to your system unit by using these ports.

Fan Housing: The power supply fitted inside the system unit has a small fan to take the heat out of the machine.

USB Port: These small rectangular slots accept Universal Serial Bus (USB) cables. Many types of devices use USB interfaces, including scanners, digital cameras, Mouse, Keyboard, Pen drive and printers.

Sound Connectors: Sound connectors are built-in but, in some systems they are on a separate in an expansion slot. There are three identical round rings i.e. output for speakers, input for microphone, and input for other devices.

Network Interface: It is a RJ-45 connector. It is used to connect the network wire in the system.

Figure 5.2 Parts of the rear panel of system

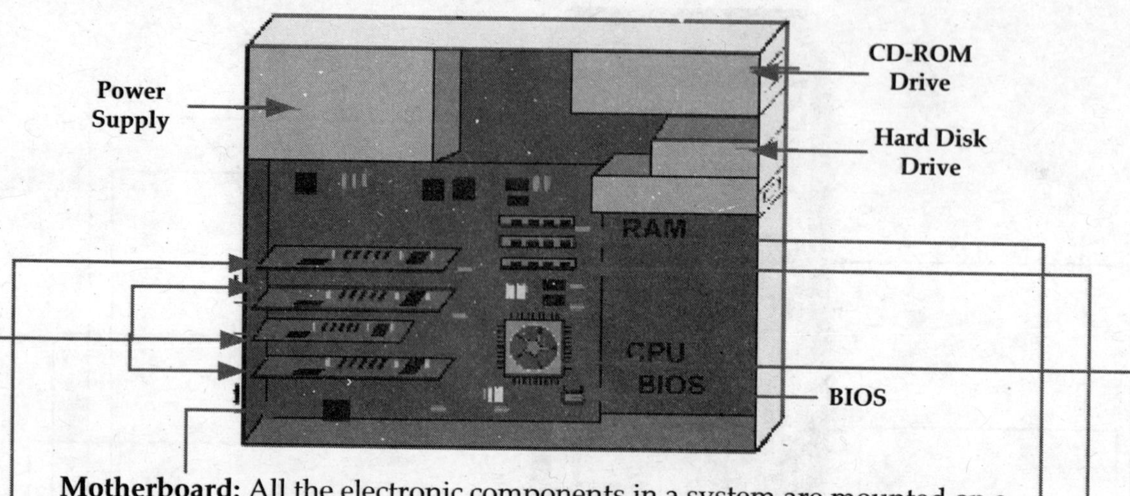

Motherboard: All the electronic components in a system are mounted on a piece of fiberglass called the motherboard. Fiberglass is used because it is a nonconductor of electricity . Thin metal lines on the fiberglass connect pins from one component to another, forming the computer's electrical circuits.

RAM (Random Access Memory) Chips: RAM chips consist of black plastic integrated circuit (IC) chips with a row of pins on each side. They may be inserted onto a printed circuit board.

ROM Chips: ROM chips such as BIOS contain data written on them during manufacture. It stores important instructions such as instructions that tell the CPU what to do immediately when you switch on your PC.

Display Adapter Card (Video Graphics Card): Display Adapter Card provides the link between the CPU and the Monitor. It converts binary form of information into human readable form.

Disk Interface Card: Disk Interface Card is necessary for communicating with a hard disk and other peripherals, such as floppy disk drives.

Input/Output Interface Card: Input/Output Interface Card is for input output devices such as printers or modems. It usually has one or two parallel ports, one or two serial ports and a joystick port.

Expansion Slots: Expansion Slots are long narrow connectors that allow you to plug in adapter cards, which offer extra options not available on a normal PC mother board. For example, one can plug sound card, network card etc. into these slots to enhance the capability of a PC.

Microprocessor: A microprocessor executes all the program instructions and is truly the heart of the personal computer. It consists of a silicon chip on which tiny circuits are engraved through a photochemical process.

CPU Support Chips: These chips help the CPU in managing different parts of the computer. Intel chip set is the one used on motherboard for supporting other devices.

Battery: Rechargeable, small capacity battery provides a small amount of constant power to the motherboard so that the items that always need to be on can stay even when the PC is unplugged from the main power supply.

Figure 5.3 Inside the System Unit

5.2 WHAT IS CABINET?

A computer case, also known as a computer chassis, tower, system unit, cabinet, base unit, or simply case, is the enclosure that contains most of the components of a computer (usually excluding the display, keyboard and mouse). Cabinets come in a variety of sizes, colors and styles and may contain baffles and fans to facilitate cooling and minimize recycled and bypass airflow. The terms rack and cabinet are often used interchangeably. However, a rack refers to the frame for actually mounting computers and other electronic equipment, while a cabinet is fitted with doors and side panels and may enclose a rack.

A well-designed computer or server cabinet should provide significant segregation between cool air supply and hot air return. To prevent bypass air, blanking panels may be used. The computer case serves mainly as a way to physically mount and contain all of the actual components inside of a computer, like the motherboard, hard drive, optical drive, etc. They typically come bundled with a power supply. (See Figure 5.4).

Figure 5.4 Cabinet

5.2.1 Important Computer Case Facts

Motherboards, computer cases, and power supplies all come in different sizes called *form factors*. All three must be compatible to work properly together. Many computer cases, especially ones made of metal, contain very sharp edges.

☞ *The computer case is also known as a tower, box, system unit, base unit, enclosure, housing, chassis, and cabinet.*

5.2.2 Why a Computer Case is Important?

A PC cabinet or computer case is a house for all your major computer components that includes processor, motherboard, ram, psu, hard disks, graphics card etc. A good cabinet with good airflow can certainly increase the lifespan of your components and also prevents them from overheating.

There are several reasons why we use computer cases. One is for protection against dust, animals, toys, liquids, etc. can all damage the internal parts of a computer if the hard shell of a computer case doesn't enclose them and keep them away from the outside environment. Another good reason to use a computer case is to keep the area cool. Proper airflow over the computer components is one more benefit to using a computer case. While the case has special vents to allow some of the fan air to escape, the rest of it can be used to cool down the hardware, which would otherwise get pretty hot and possibly overheat to the point of malfunction. Keeping noisy computer parts, like the fans, in a closed space within the computer case is one way to reduce the noise that they make. The structure of the computer case is also important. The different parts can fit together and become easily accessible to the user by being compacted in a case to hold it all together. For example, USB ports and the power button are easily accessible and the disc drive can be opened at any time.

5.2.3 Computer Case Description

The computer case itself can be constructed from any material that still allows the internal devices to be supported. This is usually steel, plastic or aluminum. Plastic tends to cool off faster and be more lightweight. Aluminum and steel tend to be strong. Most computer cases are rectangular and black. Case modding is the term used to describe the styling of a case.

The front of the computer case contains a power button and sometimes a reset button. Small LED lights are also typical, representing the current power status, hard drive activity and sometimes other internal processes. These buttons and lights connect directly to the motherboard which is secured to the inside of the case. Cases usually contain multiple 5.25 inch and 3.5 inch expansion bays for optical drives, hard drives and other media drives. These expansion bays are located at the front of the case so that, for example, the DVD drive be easily reached by the user when in use. At least one side of the case, perhaps both, slide or swing open to allow access to the internal components.

The rear of the computer case contains small openings to fit the connectors contained on the motherboard which is mounted inside. The power supply is also mounted just inside the back of the case and a large opening allows for the connection of the power cord and use of the built-in fan. Fans or other cooling devices may be attached to any and all sides of the case.

5.3 WHAT IS DRIVE BAY?

A drive bay is a system unit space reserved for the installation of any drive or other computer accessory. A drive bay is a standard-sized area for adding hardware to a computer. Most drive bays are fixed inside of a case, but some can be removed. Thus, the number of drive bays in a computer determines how many mass storage devices can be internally installed.

In addition, bays are described as either internal or exposed. An internal bay cannot be used for removable media, such as CD or DVD drives. Some manufacturers use the terms hidden and accessible in place of internal and exposed. The number of drive bays in a computer determines the total number of internal mass storage devices it can handle.

Figure 5.5 The Drive Bay

5.3.1 External Drive Bays

Since external means "outside" and these drive bays are certainly inside the case. However, they are called "external" because they allow access to the device from the outside. Any drive that uses removable media or has controls that must be operated manually must go in an external drive bay. The number of external 5.25" bays that the case holds will have an impact on what can be installed in the computer. These are the bays used for CD-ROM, DVD and Blu-ray optical drives and removable-storage drives.

5.3.2 Internal Drive Bays

These bays are entirely within the case and are not accessible from the outside. If a device does not require any access from the outside it is preferable to use an internal bay, and save the case's external bays for drives that need them. In practical terms, this means that internal drive bays are usually used for hard disk drives and solid state drives, which do not require any access by the user.

5.4 COMPUTER CASES

A computer case, also termed as computer chassis or cabinet, is a small enclosure or box into which all the major computer components and peripherals are fitted. The most common system case type is the tower. Depending on the specific number of internal drive bays and the height of the tower, these cases can be further classified into mini-size, mid-size and full-size tower cases. One of the biggest considerations when choosing between case sizes is the number of slots and the number of devices we would like to add to those cases.

5.4.1 Full Tower Case

These cases are commonly employed in the design of servers, mainframes, and advanced workstations that can handle multiple applications. Full-sized cases are generally huge with a height that is equal to or more than 30 inches (more than 76 cm). The number of internal drive bays inside these cases can be anywhere between 6 and 10. Also, these cases contain a similar number of externally accessible drive bays. Additionally, a great amount of space is present inside these cases and can be used for placing any number of hard drives, CD ROMs, and PCI cards.

Figure 5.6 Full Tower Case

Features of Full Tower Case

- These are the biggest and the tallest cabinets.
- Full Tower cabinets are the preferred choice for gamers, heavy duty users and servers.
- These cabinets can be 22 inches or more in height and they have ample room for every kind of component you have.
- These cabinets have extra internal and external drive bays so that you can put extra Hard Disks and DVD drives in it.
- The airflow in the full tower cabinets is excellent because of extra room and vents in the cabinet. The number of intake fan in any cabinet is generally one but the number of exhaust and side fan depends on the cabinet as different cabinets have different specifications.
- For ATX motherboards full tower cabinets are the ones to go for because it can easily accommodate a full sized ATX board, and for an Extended ATX motherboard only Full Tower cabinets can accommodate them.

5.4.2 Mid Tower Case

These cases are bigger than mini-towers and can be placed either below or above the computer desk without much inconvenience. Mid-tower cases are the most widely used computer cases. Mid Tower cases are about 18 to 24 (45 to 60 cm) inches high and they usually contain 2 to 4 internal drive bays and a similar number of external bays for CD/DVD readers etc. These cases can be easily expanded or upgraded to higher versions depending on the need and requirement. Interestingly, these cases are ideally suitable for any type of computer irrespective of whether it is a simple, business, or any advanced system.

Figure 5.7 Mid Tower Case

Features of Mid Tower Case

- Mid Tower cabinets are of medium size and are smaller than Full Tower cabinets.
- These cabinets are around 18 inches in height and are a perfect balance between space, price and performance.
- These cabinets also have good airflow and are suitable for most of the users who do not want big and bulky cabinets in their room.
- A mid-tower case can also a fit a full sized ATX motherboard but not an extended ATX motherboard.
- The number of exhaust and side fans also depends on the manufacturer.
- They can also be used for building a gaming PC.

5.4.3 Mini Tower Case

These cases are slightly bigger than the desktop cases and usually have 3 internal drive bays. Expendability is again a problem with these cases. Mini-cases normally stand at a height of 12-18 inches.

Figure 5.8 Mini Tower Case

Features of Mini Tower Case

- These are the smallest cabinets and they can be 14 to 16-inches tall. These cabinets are only suitable for micro-ATX motherboards and are meant for people who have space limitations in their room or office.
- The airflow in these cabinets in not good and there may be increase in the temperature of the components (cpu, hard disk, motherboard, graphics card etc.) if you use your PC for longer time.
- You cannot put a full sized graphics card in it and also some power supplies do not fit in mini-tower cabinets because of space limitations.
- Mini tower cabinet is not good if you are building a PC for gaming purpose or going to use it for longer intervals.

5.4.4 Slim Line Case

Slim line cases are simply tower cases turned on their sideways. They can hold a monitor on top of the case. The term tower is associated with them because these cabinets stand tall on the ground or hard surface and cannot be mounted.

- These are slimmest and smallest PC cabinets available.
- They support micro-ATX and mini-ITX motherboards only.
- They are very compact in size and are used in places where there is too much space limitation.
- Besides being small these cabinets are narrower too which makes it difficult for it to accommodate other components.
- The air flow in these cabinets is very poor and your components temperature will be much higher when they are inside slim tower cabinets.

Figure 5.9 Slim line Tower Case

5.4.5 Small Form Factor (SFF) Case

Small form factor or SFF cases are custom cases that are designed to minimize the spatial volume of a desktop computer. SFFs are available in a variety of sizes and shapes.

Figure 5.10 Small Form Factor (SFF) Case

5.4.6 All-in-One PC

All-in-One PCs are self-contained: components are mounted behind a display, with screen sizes ranging between 18 and 27 inches. Since there are no cords to manage or peripherals to juggle, setting up your new all-in-one PC can be as simple as pulling the machine out of the box and plugging it in.

5.4.7 Full tower heavy-duty cabinets

Poor quality cabinets tend to vibrate when fans, drives and other moving components start running. The end result is a very noisy cabinet. When you're spending a large sum of money on a new computer, it's right to spend a little more than the leftovers on a cabinet.

5.4.8 HAF (High Air Flow) Cabinets

HAF cabinets are built in a manner so as to deliver high ventilation and air flow for components attached. These are used for supporting pheripheral cards that generate high heat such as games controller cards.

Main consideration for selecting Cabinet size

The Features and Specifications to consider includes accessibility and expendability for both present and future system needs.

Form Factor: This term simply means size and shape. Be sure that the case can accommodate the internal components; conversely, when considering adding components, case-size is a key consideration. A full tower may accommodate just about any motherboard or PSU on the market, but the standard and mini towers will not.

Power Supply Unit: Often referred to as "PSUs," this is where, the electricity comes from. Different cases offer options for the power supply. A case with the PSU provided makes the build process a little simpler, but may ultimately reduce options. Consider how many and which kind of internal components will be used, as well as their relative power needs, and choose a PSU accordingly. Also consider the quality of the PSU; convenience in the short-term may mean replacement in the near future.

External 5.25" Drive Bays: The number of external 5.25" bays that the case holds will have an impact on what can be installed in the computer. These are the bays used for DVD and Blu-ray optical drives. For a computer that will be used as a Home Theater PC, consider a case with at least two of these bays, minimum.

Internal and External 3.5" Drive Bays: Nowadays one might find memory card readers, for example, in the external expansion spaces. The internal bays, on the other hand, are where you'll be putting your permanent hard disk and solid state drives. Specify a case that has enough 3.5" bays of both the internal and external variety for the computer to perform the functions you need. Also consider a case that has more than what is needed now to accommodate the addition of components in the future.

Room for the Graphics Cards : If you have a very large graphics card, make sure that the computer case has enough room for it. The graphics-intensive needs of some of today's computer users has resulted in some very large graphics cards. Make sure the case has plenty of room for space between and around the graphics cards, space for the number of cards to be used, and enough space to ensure adequate dissipation of the heat generated by more powerful components.

Cooling Options : Some cases have fans built-in, others do not but have places to mount one or multiple fans. Depending on how hard the computer will be pushed, cooling options need to be taken into account. Intake fans are placed near hard drives-more drives naturally generate more heat. Rear fans push the hot air out, away from the components. Adding fans can be helpful, but also keep in mind that you may hear them.

Larger fans are quieter and more efficient at a slower rate, and, therefore, more desirable. The gaming experience takes its toll on a system and causes it to heat up quite significantly. Because of this, make sure there are enough integrated fans or places to add fans as well as a side air duct for proper heat dissipation. In addition to cooling, the power supply unit will also be of concern to gamers. Standard PSUs often do not provide adequate power for higher-performing components. Consider a case that does not provide a power supply. This will give you the option of installing the power supply that is powerful enough to keep up with your gaming needs. Consider buying a case with an integrated power supply from a reputable manufacturer.

Number of Front Panel Ports : The number of front panel ports on the case is as important as the number of computer ports on the motherboard (the rear panel). Almost all cases come standard with at least two USB ports in the front. Also, find a computer case that has ample USB ports. You'll want a minimum of four rear USB ports considering a mouse, printer, and keyboard cable will each take one port. Front ports for mobile device charging will also be important. In addition to these data-transfer ports, cases also usually offer headphone and microphone jacks. Take into consideration what external devices will be connected to your computer and how many of each. Front panel connectivity is one of the key usability options of a computer, and choosing one with the right configuration will increase satisfaction with your case in the long run.

Cable Management: As mentioned briefly in the PSU section above, internal cable management is important when building a computer. Some cases have features that improve cable management. Not only does proper cable management make a computer look better (especially if it has a side window), but it also allows for better airflow and cooling. Make sure your new case is large enough for space behind the motherboard to route cables. Some cases come with hidden areas for the extra cables or cable length. If a case does not specify this feature, you'll need to do the cable management by hand.

5.5 ATX MOTHERBOARDS

The Advanced Technology Extended (ATX) motherboard, developed by Intel in the 1990's, replaced the AT-style motherboard that ruled the PC world for many years. One of the major aspects of this new style is that the processor and memory slots are placed in such a way that the system can run cooler. It's also engineered so that the processor and memory slots are to the right of the expansion slots, allowing users to throw in full-length expansion cards (e.g. cards that will span the length of the inside of the computer case).

5.5.1 Features of the ATX motherboard

- The ATX motherboard includes advanced control facilities, where the BIOS program continually checks the CPU temperature and voltages, the cooling fans RPM, etc. If overheating occurs, the PC will shut down automatically.
- The ATX motherboard has a stacked I/O connector panel mounted on the motherboard.
- On a socket 7 ATX motherboard, the socket has been placed a further distance from the expansion slots, allowing for long boards to be placed in easier.
- ATX 2.01 includes a single keyed, Molex internal power supply connector which cannot be placed improperly. However, its standby voltage needs to be greater than 720 mA.
- Relocation of the memory and the CPU allows for better ventilation and easier installation.
- Power management is now possible with proper BIOS support.
- The PC can also be turned on by a modem or network signal, since the power supply is controlled by the main board.
- The computer cannot be turned off as the computer boots. However, if the computer freezes as it is turning on you can turn off the computer by holding the power button for five seconds.

5.6 BTX MOTHERBOARDS

Short for Balanced Technology Extended, BTX is a motherboard form factor first announced by Intel on September 17, 2003 as a replacement for ATX.

5.6.1 Features of BTX Motherboards

- BTX form factor has the faceplate on the opposite side, hole positions are different and the processor socket is slightly rotated.
- The BTX motherboard will only fit within a computer case that is designed for a BTX motherboard.
- The BTX features a low profile, more efficient layout to facilitate cooling, a scalable board to accommodate different system sizes, and support for high-mass motherboard components.

5.6.2 Form Factor

Motherboards, computer cases, and power supplies all come in different sizes called form factors. There's one important consideration we need to be aware of when choosing the case size and that is the size of the motherboard. They need to match. The size of the motherboard is often called the Form Factor and there are several standards. The form factor identifies the size of the circuit board, the location of the slots as well as the location of the faceplate that comes out the back of the computer. The form factor also identifies the location of the holes that are used to mount the motherboard into the system case. For example, the full tower has more than enough room to fit an ATX motherboard. Mid-tower case can also accommodate an ATX motherboard in most cases.

When choosing a system case, other than considering the size of the computer that we want, the most important thing is to match the motherboard form factor with the form factor supported by the computer case. The most common system case type is the tower. Tower cases are: Full tower, Mid tower and Mini tower. Slim line cases are simply tower cases turned on their sideways. Small form factor or SFF cases are custom cases that are designed to minimize the spatial volume of a desktop computer. The size of the motherboard is often called the Form Factor. The most common form factor for a motherboard is the ATX form factor. When considering the size of ATX we differentiate Full ATX, Mini ATX, Micro ATX. When comparing with ATX, BTX form factor has the faceplate on the opposite side, hole positions are different and the processor socket is slightly rotated. The BTX motherboard will only fit within a computer case that is designed for a BTX motherboard.

5.6.3 ATX Desktop

Short for Advanced Technology eXtended, ATX is a specification used to outline motherboard configuration and dimensions in an effort to improve standardization. Probably the most common form factor for a motherboard is the ATX form factor. The standard, ATX desktop cases are designed to hold motherboards with the ATX form factor. These allow the easiest interchangeability of parts. These cases also usually accommodate motherboards that keep the basic rear layout but reduce the size of the board and the number of expansion slots. If you want a desktop case, the ATX desktop case will likely be your computer case of choice.

Figure 5.11 Standard ATX

5.6.4 ATX Bench Case

ATX bench cases are open-air computer cases, meaning the internal components are visibly exposed. A strength of this design is the ease of accessibility when switching out devices; optimum heat ventilation is another. One obvious concern for this design, however, is protection-this type of case must be located in a secure area.

5.6.5 ATX Mini Tower

A mini-ATX motherboard is a slightly smaller variation of the full ATX size. As the name suggests, this is the type of computer case needed when using an ATX micro motherboard. A micro motherboard will fit perfectly into these cases, and, since the cases are small, they won't take up much desk space.

Figure 5.12 A mini-ATX motherboard

5.6.6 ATX Mid Tower

ATX mid tower cases are designed with the ATX motherboard form factor in mind. However, unlike a full size tower, a mid-size tower will work in a smaller space. If large or extra componentry is not needed, or if the location for this computer is limited, this case will likely be preferable.

5.6.7 ATX Full Tower

These cases, like the kind mentioned just above, have been designed for motherboards with the ATX form factor. With a full tower, there is a generous amount of space inside for large components and/or multiple graphics cards.

5.6.8 ATX Super Tower

An ATX super tower is the largest computer case available on the market at this time. While they are available to any consumer, they are generally meant for computer enthusiasts. These cases are usually quite large and most are able to support two CPUs. These computer cases also can have as many as nine expansion card slots, with room for an ATX-XL motherboard.

5.6.9 Home Theater Computer Case

An "HTPC" can be a great addition to your custom home theater. Consider this type of case if the objective is to build a computer specifically for great audio and video reproduction. Optical drive support as well as general external appearance of the case will likely be important factors in choosing a case in this category.

A HTPC is a Home Theater Personal Computer. These are computers which you would normally buy or build yourself which is solely designed to connect to your television. A HTPC is basically an all-in-one entertainment system. A basic home theater media pc should allow you to: watch live HD television, watch movies (all formats), record television, play games, view videos/photos, and listen to music. Even a cheap home theater pc will have all of these features.

5.6.10 BTX Form Factor

There are a few main differences with the BTX form factor. Faceplate is on the opposite end. Another difference is that the hole positions are different. Also, the processor socket is slightly rotated so that it is at an angle to the system board. This rotation is to aid in the airflow across the processor to assist in cooling the processor. The BTX motherboard will only fit within a system case that is designed for a BTX motherboard. In many cases this means that an ATX system case will not work with a BTX system board, although there are system cases that are able to accommodate both the ATX and the BTX form factors. The BTX form factor has not been widely adopted despite its improvements over ATX and related standards. As a result, the availability and variety of BTX-compatible components is limited.

5.6.11 ITX motherboards

Short for Information Technology eXtended, ITX is a small motherboard form factor from VIA Technologies that was first introduced in November 2001 with the Mini-ITX. Later versions of ITX include the Nano-ITX released in March 2003, the Mobile-ITX released in March 2004, and the Pico-ITX released in April 2007. With the compact configuration of ITX motherboards, they are typically used in low-cost small setups found in cars, network devices, set-top boxes, and other small computers. Below is a comparison of all of the ITX motherboards.

5.6.12 Mini-ITX

The Mini-ITX motherboard form factor that measures 17 cm x 17 cm (6.75" x 6.75") in size. They typically have two memory (RAM) slots, 1 PCI-Express or mini-PCI slot, several USB ports, and one network port. Some Mini-ITX motherboards include an onboard VGA port and an HDMI port. An important feature of a Mini-ITX motherboard is its low power consumption, using less than 25 watts of power, with some as few as five watts.

5.6.13 Nano-ITX

The Nano-ITX motherboard form factor measures 12cm x 12cm (4.7" x 4.7") and has removed the legacy ports, moved to mini-PCI and SODIMM. Pico-ITX. The Nano-ITX motherboard form factor measures 7.2cm x 10cm (2.8" x 3.9") and is 75% smaller than the Mini-ITX form factor. The motherboard supports any processor that uses VIA's NanoBGA2 technology with speeds up to 1.5 GHz with 128 KB L1 and L2 cache.

Figure 5.13 The Nano-ITX motherboard

5.6.14 Pico-ITX

Pico-ITX uses DDR2 400/533 SO-DIMM memory with support for up to 1 GB and AGP video with built-in MPEG-2, 4, and WMV9 decoding acceleration. Mobile-ITX (2.4" x 2.4").

Figure 5.14 The Pico-ITX motherboard

5.6.15 Mobile-ITX

The Mobile-ITX motherboard form factor measures 7.2cm x 10cm (2.8" x 3.9") and has no computer ports unless an I/O carrier board is used. The Mobile-ITX design is intended for medical, transportation and military embedded markets. Sometimes referred to as the mATX, the microATX is a motherboard

5.6.16 How to Clean Your Computer Case

Keeping a desktop computer clean is essential to long-lasting and optimal performance. Fans and heatsink will function normally, keeping the system from overheating and ruining vital and expensive components. Data and power connectors will continue to operate well, and replacement and upgrade efforts will require minimal effort. When cleaning a computer, remember to follow guidelines such as these:

- Shutdown and unplug the computer before opening the case.
- Use an air compressor on a lower setting, or use a can of compressed air designated for cleaning computers and electrical components.
- Do not use a vacuum cleaner on the internal components of the computer.
- Do not blow off stickers that may be required for warranty verification.
- Keep compressed air cans upright so as to avoid accumulation of moisture and blowing into a computer.

- For cleaning fans, processor and/or heatsink use compressed air to blow off/out any visible dust. Use alcohol and cotton swabs to remove remaining dust and for general cleaning.
- After a complete cleaning, make sure all the parts are dry. Use the cloth to carefully wipe dry any damp areas or components.

5.7 TYPICAL SPECIFICATION OF A CABINET FOR GAMMING PURPOSE

If you use your computer for gaming CAD, or video rendering, you may want to look into overclocking your CPU and graphics card(s). This can be accommodated with air cooled accessories, like CPU coolers, that require a fair amount of room inside the case. Essentially this a large heatsink with many rows of fins that you bolt to your CPU with fans that blow across it to remove the heat from your processor. Make sure that you have enough entrance and exhaust fans to deal with the amount of waste heat generated inside your computer.

Buying a new desktop can be exhaustive task. It's confusing to compare the models, specifications and prices with so many options in the market. There are a lot of questions to which there is no clear answer. Here are a few things you can consider before getting yourself a new computer:

5.7.1 Usability

The first question you should ask yourself is 'How much will I use my system and what for?' You should think long term while choosing the right configuration. The wide variety of products always gives you the option of an upgrade later. You should have a good understanding of the components and choose wisely for optimum performance.

5.7.2 Processor

Choosing the right processor is the key element in building a desktop. It forms the core of your machine and will decide the performance as well. If you are a light user wherein your major usage such as browsing and using Microsoft Office then an Intel i3 would be an perfect choice. If you are a moderate user with gaming and use of media tools then Intel i5 is good for you. And if you're a heavy user with some intense graphic gaming and a number of software then an Intel i7 is the best that can handle all that.

☞ *Note higher the configuration of the processor, the higher the amount of heat it will generate.*

5.7.3 Motherboard

The motherboard is the base of your computer. The alignment and functionality of your processor, RAM and graphics card depend on it. The first thing to keep in mind while choosing a motherboard is that it should be future proof. You can upgrade all the other elements very easily but only if your motherboard supports them. The main aspects to look for are the amount of RAM slots, USB ports and a built-in-audio.

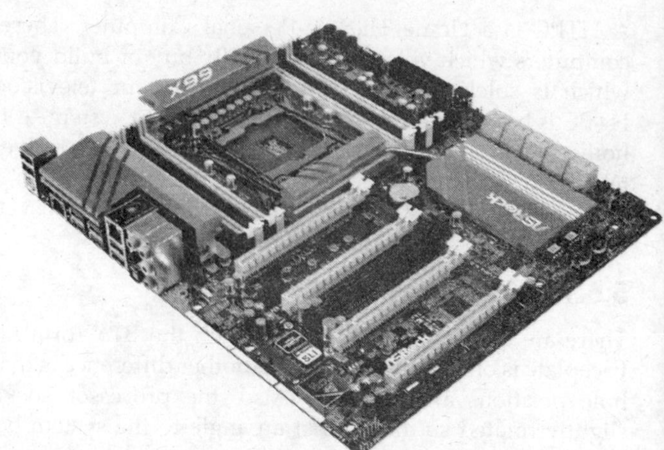

Figure 5.15 The motherboard

5.7.4 Memory

The amount of RAM in the system allows you to run the processes smoothly and determine their speed as well. More RAM will allow you to run more programs simultaneously and generally improve the performance of the machine. An ideal desktop these days uses 4 GB of RAM though some budget systems may limit them to 2-3 GB. If you tend to multi-task or play games then the minimum requirement would be 8 GB which can be further expanded

5.7.5 Graphics Card

A graphics card is responsible for what you see on your display, whether you're playing games or watching videos. If you aren't interested in gaming then the integrated graphics built on the motherboard is more than enough. On the other hand, if you're a gamer and an keen user of graphic-related software then investing in a graphics card is a must.

5.7.6 Hard Disk

Even the most basic of systems consist of a 320GB hard disk. The space really depends on your usage. The internal hard drive should be of a decent capacity so that the system runs smoothly. Nowadays, a lot of systems come with 1 or 2 TB hard disks. To further enhance the speed of your system, you can invest in a SSD (Solid State Drive) which can be used to store applications and OS.

5.7.7 PSU (Power Supply Unit)

The PSU is the most undervalued part in the system and yet a lot of functions depend on it. It affects the performance and reliability of the system. While buying a power supply, you need to determine the amount of wattage required according to your configuration. The efficiency rating is also important as higher efficiency units tend to have better components, waste less power, and generate less heat. Cooler Master is the local favourite as they build good quality PSUs with lesser power consumption.

5.7.8 Cabinet

Some cabinets may seem fancy from the outside but will not provide you with adequate space to store your components. They come in different types of sizes and formats. The most essential thing in a cabinet is its sturdiness. Poor quality cabinets tend to vibrate when fans and drives start running which leads to a very noisy atmosphere. Look for cabinets that have an adequate-sized fan in one spot and provision for more fans in other locations for optimum cooling.

5.7.9 Mouse and Keyboard

Last but not least, the mouse and keyboard are also essential parts of assembling a desktop. They come in different categories liked USB wired and wireless. The most important factor in choosing a mouse is how it feels. Size and grip play key roles. There are basic mouses available along with some precision mouses that have a higher DPI , sensitivity and are recommended for gamers.

Keyboards also come in various varieties. You should choose the one with an adjustable height and raised keys, however this is just a preference. Some extra navigation controls like the volume buttons would also add to the ease of your functions.

5.8 INTRODUCTION TO SERVER CABINETS

A server in its most simple form is just a PC running software that is responsible for coordinating some form of communication between nodes on a network. There are four requirements for a server Computer Hardware, Operating System (OS), Server Software and Connections between the devices on the network. The hardware can be as simple as a standard desktop PC or as complex as a blade server rack mounted in a large server farm. The minimum requirement for the OS is that it must support networking. It must have a software program running that "serves" something. The final requirement is a connection to the devices that are to use the services provided by the server.

In many ways server hardware really isn't all that different from desktop PC hardware. Both use the same basic components such as memory, CPUs, and power supplies. In spite of these similarities however, server hardware are more advanced than the components that are found in desktop computers. Servers may also make use of redundant and / or how swappable components. Occasionally PCs might have redundant or even hot swappable components, but such features are much more common on servers.

Servers are usually accessed over a network, these high end systems are isolated and kept in a separate area of the office building called the "Server Room". Computer server hardware has historically been dedicated to managing a single functional purpose; therefore, the server hardware can range widely in size, performance, cost, capability, and environmental impact. Dedicated server functions include: application servers, file servers, game servers, mail servers, print servers, database servers, and many more. Several servers are typically required to enable a computer to properly interact with other network clients due to this dedicated nature of a server. A collection of servers is referred to as a server farm or server cluster and the facility used to house the server farm and associated components is referred to as a data center.

The server cabinet has good technical performance. The server cabinet should have anti-vibration, impact resistance, corrosion resistance, dust, water, radiation and other properties

5.9 SERVER FORM FACTOR

The term form factor describes the physical dimensions and standards used by various system components and by the computer as a whole. To give you a more concrete example, many PCs use a form factor called standard ATX. A standard ATX case can physically accommodate any standard ATX system board and power supply, even if they are made by a different vendor.

Another common PC standard is Micro ATX. Many standard ATX computer cases are designed to accept either standard ATX or Micro ATX system boards, but a Micro ATX case would not be able to accommodate a standard ATX system board because Micro ATX cases use a smaller form factor.

Form factors apply to server hardware also. There are several different form factors used for network servers, but the three most common form factors are *tower servers, rack servers* and *blade servers*.

5.9.1 Tower Servers

Tower servers look a lot like PCs. Each tower server is a standalone machine that is built into an upright case. They are very powerful and have bundled software tools to manage them.

The problem with Tower Severs is the space they occupy, management personnel they require, and cost of operating them (power, network, etc.). Tower servers are used mostly in smaller datacenters. Larger datacenters typically avoid the use of tower servers because of the amount of physical space that they consume and because they tend to be noisy. Another disadvantage to using tower servers is that the cabling can get messy. Server racks and blade server chassis usually have features that are designed to manage cables, but tower servers have no such features.

5.9.2 Rack Server

As the name implies, rack servers are servers that are mounted within a rack. The rack is of a uniform width and servers are mounted to the rack using screws. Each rack can accommodate multiple servers and the servers are typically stacked on top of each other. A single rack can contain multiple servers stacked one above the other, consolidating network resources and minimizing the required floor space. The rack server configuration also simplifies cabling among network components. In an equipment rack filled with servers, a special cooling system is necessary to prevent excessive heat buildup that would otherwise occur when many power-dissipating components are confined in a small space.

A rack server, also called a rack-mounted server, is a computer dedicated to use as a server and designed to be installed in a framework called a rack. The rack contains multiple mounting slots called bays, each designed to hold a hardware unit secured in place with screws. A rack server has a low-profile enclosure, in contrast to a tower server, which is built into an upright, standalone cabinet.

Because racks are designed to accommodate standard sized components, many hardware vendors offer rack mountable networking components other than servers. For example there are rack mountable network appliances (such as hardware firewalls) and rack mountable switches. Rack mount components follow a form factor that is referred to as a rack unit. A standard rack mount server is referred to as a 1U server meaning that it is 1 rack unit in size. A 2U server consumes two rack units of space within the rack. Some vendors also offer 4U and 1/2U servers. The larger form factors are usually used when the server needs to be able to accommodate a large amount of storage.

Figure 5.16 Rack Server

Rack Server PROS

Cable management - Rack servers require a lot of cables, but they are relatively easy to organize due to management tools built into the rack.

Failure containment - Identifying, removing, and replacing a malfunctioning rack server is generally simple and has little effect on other servers.

Cost - Rack servers offer a substantial amount of computing power at a relatively low cost.

Rack Server CONS

Power usage - Rack servers often require attendant equipment like a cooling system to function properly, driving up the power consumption of a single server.

Size - Depending on your needs, the larger size of rack servers could take up all your available space.

Maintenance - Taking care of routine maintenance tasks on a rack packed tightly with servers can be time consuming and cumbersome, especially in larger server rooms.

5.9.3 Rack Types

There are three primary types of racks: open frame racks, rack enclosures and wall-mount racks.

Open frame racks are just that-open frames with mounting rails, but without sides or doors. They're typically used for applications where the rack does not need to control airflow or provide physical security. Open frame racks are good for network wiring closet and distribution frame applications that have high-density cabling because they provide convenient access and lots of open space for cable management.

Rack enclosures have removable front and rear doors, removable side panels and four adjustable vertical mounting rails (posts). They're also called rack cabinets. The front and rear doors are typically ventilated to encourage ample airflow from front to back, through any installed equipment. Rack enclosures are ideal for applications that require heavier equipment, hotter equipment and higher wattages per rack. Since the doors and side panels lock, they also provide physical equipment security at the rack level (as opposed to the room level). Enclosures are a popular choice for high density data centers and server rooms.

Wall-mount racks are designed to be attached to the wall, saving floor space and fitting in areas where other racks can't. They can be open frame racks or enclosed cabinets. They're usually smaller than their floor-standing counterparts and can't support as much weight. The cabinets can be adapted to floor-standing applications by adding rolling casters.

5.9.4 Blade Server

Like rack servers, blade servers also adhere to a standard size and mount inside a special "rack". In the case of a blade server however, the rack is known as a chassis. A blade server can be considered a stripped-down rack mounted server. Blade servers have a modular design and do not include many components typically found in traditional rack servers to save space, and minimize power consumption. The removed components are found in the blade enclosure, which can hold multiple blade servers and provides services such as power, cooling, and various interconnects and management.

Different blade server manufacturers include different components in the blade itself. Blade servers tend to be vendor proprietary. You can't for example insert a Dell blade server into an HP chassis. The reason why blade server design is

Figure 5.17 Blade Server

proprietary is because unlike a rack server, which is fully self-contained, blade servers lack some of the components that they need to function. For example, blade servers do not have power supplies.

Blade Server PROS

Size - Blade servers are the smallest type of server available and allow you to fit a significant amount of computing power into a minimal amount of space.
Centralized management - You can connect to all of your blade servers through a single interface, making maintenance and monitoring tasks easier.
Cabling - Blade servers require significantly less cabling than rack servers, meaning that they are easier to set up and can keep your server room more organized.

Blade Server CONS

Heat - The small size and compact arrangement of blade servers makes heat dispensation a challenge. Failing to address this issue can compromise the function of the servers.
Cost - The price of blade servers has decreased in recent years and is lower but are typically more expensive than rack servers for comparable amounts of computing power.
Power requirements - Blade servers require power to be off to complete certain tasks. Many data center experts cite this as an inconvenience.

Difference between Rack and Blade Servers

Rack servers are essentially stand alone computers on which applications are run. In a rack server, all components like hard drives, a network card, etc. are contained in a case. Rack servers are also known as traditional servers. They are essentially stand alone computers on which applications are run. All the components like hard drives, a network card, etc. are contained in a case. A blade server is a stripped down computer server that is based on a modular design. It minimizes the use of physical space.
Rack servers are specially designed to be stored in racks, hence the name rack server where as Blade comes from the word "blade" indicating the restricted format).
Blade servers require significantly less cabling than rack servers

Blade servers are gaining more popularity over the rack servers.

5.9.5 KVM Switch

KVM Switches allow access to and control of nearby computers and servers - across the room, in another room, on another floor of the building. IP KVM Switches access the same type of equipment, but they can remotely access and control them from anywhere in the world with an internet connection. KVM Switch manages Computers/File Servers, Domain Servers, Print Servers, and Blade Servers.

5.9.6 Back Plane

Back planes are typically used on blade servers to attach hot swappable hard drives. There are also "butterfly" back planes that can allow the connection of devices to both sides of circuit board.

5.9.7 Blade Encloser

Enclosure (Chassis) perform many of the non-core computing services found in most computers. Server gets self-operating/self-admin component support from enclosure; it does not hold the component on itself. It should be kept in mind that, since shared components within blade enclosure and enclosure costs are additional costs for blade servers.
A blade enclosure contains following components generally according to project demands Blade Servers, SAN modules, Network modules, Power supplies, and Fans. All above components cover an individual place in the cabinet in rack type systems whereas they come in enclosure in blade servers. In rack type systems, all components should be cabled, cooled and powered as redundant separately. Regardless of number of server, in blade systems you only power up the enclosure, only enclosure must be cooled, it has all redundant network and SAN connection points on the enclosure.
A server chassis is a metal structure that is used to house or physically assemble servers in various different form factors. A server chassis makes it possible to put multiple servers and other storage and peripheral equipment in a single physical body. A server chassis can also be called a server casing or server case. A server chassis is primarily designed to reduce the amount of physical space consumed by a standard server. Generally, a server chassis in used in environments where multiple parallel servers are needed to work on a core business application. Server chassis come in various forms, including rack and pedestal (tower). They can be classified according to their physical dimensions and are termed as being a 1U, 2U and up to 20U and more, where U represents the number of units. Typically a 1U server can house up to two servers in rack or tower form/enclosure. A server chassis can easily be upgraded/expanded to add more servers such as upgrading from 1U to 2U and above.

EXERCISE

1. What is Tower Servers? Write its advantages.
2. Write short notes on Server cabinets.
3. What are the main considerations for selecting Cabinet size?
4. Write features of the ATX motherboard.
5. Discuss different ITX motherboards.
6. What is drive bay?
7. Write features of Mid Tower Case.
8. How rack servers are different from blade servers?
9. Write features of BTX Motherboards.

REVIEW QUESTIONS WITH ANSWERS

1. Multiple Choice

1.1 Use a KVM Switch to manage:

a. Computers/File Servers b. Print and Blade Servers
c. Domain Servers d. All of these

Ans (d)

1.2 Full form of SFF is

a. Small Form Factor b. Slim Form Factor
c. Small Face Factor d. None of these

Ans (a)

1.3 Identify form factor(s)

a. ATX b. Mini ATX
c. Micro ATX d. All of these

Ans (d)

1.4 Essential feature(s) of a cabinet

a. Drive bays b. USB support
c. Fans and vents d. All of these

Ans (d)

1.5 Rack Server CONS

a. Power usage b. Maintenance
c. Size d. All of these

Ans (d)

2. State whether the following statements are True or False

2.1 Blade servers are the smallest type of server available and allow you to fit a significant amount of computing power into a minimal amount of space.

Ans True

2.2 Blade servers require significantly more cabling than rack servers.

Ans False

2.3 Rack servers require a lot of cables, but they are relatively easy to organize due to management tools built into the rack.

Ans True

2.4 Tower servers take up a lot of space and require individual monitors, keyboards, etc.

Ans True

2.5 Computer chasis ack like dust magnets.

Ans True

2.6 Case modding is the term used to describe the styling of a case.

Ans True

2.7 An internal bay can be used for removable media.

Ans False

2.8 The number of drive bays in a computer determines the total number of internal mass storage devices it can handle.

Ans True

2.9 The number of exhaust and side fans depends on the manufacturer.

Ans True

2.10 Back planes are typically used on blade servers to attach hot swappable hard drives.

Ans True

3. Match the following:

3.1	Server Racks	a.	Keyboard Video Mouse
3.2	One rack unit	b.	19 inch
3.3	KVM	c.	RU
3.4	Enclosure	d.	Stripped down
3.5	Blade Server	e.	Chasis

Ans 3.1 b 3.2 c 3.3 a 3.4 e 3.5 d

4. Fill in the blanks

4.1 ______ servers allow more processing power in less space which simplifies cabling, storage, and maintenance.

Ans Blade

4.2 A blade server most importantly ______ power consumption and improves power management.

Ans reduces

4.3 Blades can be scaled up as needed by just simply adding a new server ______

Ans blade

4.4 A server ______ is a metal structure that is used to house or physically assemble servers in various different form factors.

Ans chassis

4.5 ______ is a standalone machine that is built into an upright case.

Ans Tower server

4.6 ______ bays are usually used for hard disk drives

Ans Internal drive

4.7 ______ servers are also known as traditional servers.

Ans Rack

4.8 Shutdown and ______ the computer before opening the case.

Ans Unplug

4.9 ______ are typically housed in Sever cabinets.

Ans Server

4.10 A ______ essentially houses all the equipment of the computer system.

Ans Cabinet

Q.5 (a) Write short notes on the following:

(i) KVM Switch

(ii) Rack Servers

Ans 5(a)(i)

KVM Switches allow access to and control of nearby computers and servers - across the room, in another room, on another floor of the building. IP KVM Switches access the same type of equipment, but they can remotely access and control them from anywhere in the world with an internet connection.

Ans 5(a)(ii)

Rack Servers are designed for compact vertical arrangement within a rack or cabinet, rack servers use space efficiently and offer centralized cable and server management. When a rack is stacked with multiple servers, a cooling system is necessary to avoid heat buildup that may occur when these power dissipating servers are confined to a small space. Rack servers are typically preferred by groups that need to maximize their computing power without compromising space.

Q.6 What are advantages of Blade Systems?

Ans 6

Blade Systems have many advantages such as; they cover fewer places, they reach much high hardware, they can change function immediately, they can interfere with the hardware without closing all enclosure, they have full-redundant power supply, fans, and network interfaces and data paths. Besides that, they have flexible integrated process power with virtualization infrastructure and memory pool.

- Quick and easy installation.
- First purchase cost is relatively low as compared to rack-type servers having the same processor and memory.
- Operation costs are relatively lower than rack-type servers.
- Needs smaller place than Rack/Tower form factor servers.
- Being the platform that is preferred for virtualization and consolidation choices and integration simplicity.
- It provides a dense server area and flexibility due to arranged blade enclosure and avoids cable tangle.
- Being unrivalled due to full-redundant component and flexible structure in business continuity field.
- Lower power consumption and cooling cost as compared to rack/tower form factor servers.

Q.7 What does Server Chassis mean?

Ans 7

A server chassis is a metal structure that is used to house or physically assemble servers in various different form factors. A server chassis makes it possible to put multiple servers and other storage and peripheral equipment in a single physical body. A server chassis can also be called a server casing or server case.

Q.8 Why it is important to choose good quality cabinet?

Ans 8

The server cabinet has good technical performance. The server cabinet should have anti-vibration, impact resistance, corrosion resistance, dust, water, radiation and other properties. They come in different types of sizes and formats. The most essential thing in a cabinet is its robustness. Poor quality cabinets tend to vibrate when fans and drives start running which leads to a very noisy atmosphere. Look for cabinets that have an adequate-sized fan in one spot and provision for more fans in other locations for optimum cooling.

Q.9 What are disadvantages of Tower servers?

Ans 9

Tower servers look a lot like PCs. Each tower server is a standalone machine that is built into an upright case. Tower servers are used mostly in smaller datacenters. Larger datacenters typically avoid the use of tower servers because of the amount of physical space that they consume and because they tend to be noisy.

Another disadvantage to using tower servers is that the cabling can get messy. Server racks and blade server chassis usually have features that are designed to manage cables, but tower servers have no such features.

Q.10 Write advantages of rack server.

Ans 10

A rack server, also called a rack-mounted server, is a computer dedicated to use as a server and designed to be installed in a framework called a rack. The rack contains multiple mounting slots called bays, each designed to hold a hardware unit secured in place with screws. A rack server has a low-profile enclosure, in contrast to a tower server, which is built into an upright, standalone cabinet.

- A single rack can contain multiple servers stacked one above the other, consolidating network resources and minimizing the required floor space.

- The rack server configuration also simplifies cabling among network components.
- Many rack servers support large amounts of RAM.

Q.11 Write Features of Full Tower Case.

Ans 11

Features of Full Tower Case

- These are the biggest and the tallest cabinets.
- Full Tower cabinets are the preferred choice for gamers, heavy duty users and servers.
- These cabinets can be 22 inches or more in height and they have ample room for every kind of component you have.
- These cabinets have extra internal and external drive bays so that you can put extra Hard Disks and DVD drives in it.
- The airflow in the full tower cabinets is excellent because of extra room and vents in the cabinet. The number of intake fan in any cabinet is generally one but the number of exhaust & side fan depends on the cabinet as different cabinets have different specifications.
- For ATX motherboards full tower cabinets are the ones to go for because it can easily accommodate a full sized ATX board, and for an Extended ATX motherboard only Full Tower cabinets can accommodate them.

Q.12 Discuss about External Drive Bays.

Ans 12

Since external means "outside" and these drive bays are certainly inside the case. However, they are called "external" because they allow access to the device from the outside. Any drive that uses removable media or has controls that must be operated manually must go in an external drive bay. The number of external 5.25" bays that the case holds will have an impact on what can be installed in the computer. These are the bays used for CD-ROM, DVD and Blu-ray optical drives and removable-storage drives.

Q.13 Which type of cleaning solutions or solvents are used in maintenance of computer system? Describe.

Ans 13

Solvents come either as aerosols (spray solvents) or as liquids. They are used for cleaning purposes. Various types of solvents are available in market. These are :

(a) *Non-Lubricating cleaners:* These type of cleaners are used to remove dust from circuit boards, mechanical assemblies and parts like magnetic tape heads.

(b) *Lubricating cleaners:* These type of cleaners should not be used for applications in which lubricant is likely to attract dust after its application, as the dust creates friction in moving parts. Lubricating cleaners are preferred in potentiometers and switches.

(c) *Foam type cleaners:* They are specially made from compounds, which are packed as spray. These compounds contain mild abrasives in high density base.

Q.14 What is Nano-ITX?

Ans 14

The Nano-ITX motherboard form factor measures 12cm x 12cm (4.7" x 4.7") and has removed the legacy ports, moved to mini-PCI and SODIMM. Pico-ITX. The Nano-ITX motherboard form factor measures 7.2cm x 10cm (2.8" x 3.9") and is 75% smaller than the Mini-ITX form factor. The motherboard supports any processor that uses VIA's NanoBGA2 technology with speeds up to 1.5 GHz with 128 KB L1 and L2 cache.

CHM–O Level

MODULE–H2

PC ARCHITECTURE

CHAPTER 6

Introduction to Microprocessor

6.1 BASIC CONCEPTS OF MICROPROCESSOR

Present day PCs operate using microprocessors. A microprocessor is a semiconductor chip, which is manufactured using the Large Scale integration (LSI) or Very Large Scale Integration (VLSI), which comprises Arithmetic Logic Unit, Control unit and Central Processing Unit (CPU) fabricated on a single chip. The invention of microprocessor has created a revolution in the reduction of *price* and the *size* of PCs.

☞ *A microprocessor is a controlling unit of a micro-computer, fabricated on a small chip capable of performing Arithmetic Logical Unit (ALU) operations and communicating with the other devices connected to it.*

A microprocessor is a combination of arithmetical, logical unit and control unit on a single integrated chip (See Figure 6.1). A microprocessor requires power supply, clock system and main memory to function as a complete personal computer (PC). A microprocessor works using binary digits 0 and 1. The CPU of a less powerful computer may contain a single microprocessor. The CPU of a large sized workstation may contain a number of micro-processors on one or more motherboards.

Figure 6.1 Microprocessor

6.2 EVOLUTION OF MICROPROCESSOR

The first microprocessor was the Intel 4004, introduced in 1971. The 4004 was not very powerful; it was primarily used to perform simple mathematical operations in a calculator. The 4004 contained only 2300 transistors and performed 60,000 calculations per second.

☞ *Intel 4004, a 4-bit CPU released by Intel Corporation in 1971, is considered as the first commercial microprocessor.*

It was quickly succeeded by the 8008, which was twice as powerful. In 1978, Intel released the 16-bit 8086 processor. The 8088, also a 16-bit chip, followed less than a year later. The 8088 incorporated technologies designed to make it backward-compatible with the 8-bit chips that were still in wide use at the time. IBM chose the 8088 chip to power their original Personal Computer. And so it was that IBM, Intel, and a little startup company called Microsoft brought computing to the masses. In the early 1990's, Intel released the i386 processor. The 386 was the first commercially available 32-bit microprocessor. For the first time, it made multitasking (running more than one program at a time) possible on desktop computers. The i486 added an onboard math co-processor, improved data transfer, and an onboard memory cache, all of which were stunning advances in technology in that era. The Intel Pentium processor, released in 1993, was the first commercially available microprocessor capable of executing two instructions for every clock cycle. Later releases in the Pentium line revolutionized everything from the way data is moved about on the chips, to the way that multimedia content is handled. Those improvements have since been eclipsed, however, by Intel's line of multi-core, 64-bit processors, such as the popular Core(tm) series.

Today Intel has three major brands for mainstream consumer PC's, Core(tm) 2, Core(tm) i7 and Core(tm) i5. The Core 2 family was introduced in 2006 and is available in dual core (Core 2(tm) Duo) as well as quad core (Core 2(tm) Quad) configurations. Intel's Core 2 processors are offered with varying clock speeds, cache sizes and bus speeds. The Core i7 and Core i5 are based on what is known as the Nehalem architecture and are very different from the Core 2 based processors.

6.3 MAJOR PARTS OF MICROPROCESSOR

The major parts of a Microprocessor are: (See Figure 6.2)

(a) Arithmetic Logical Unit (ALU)

(b) Control Unit (CU)

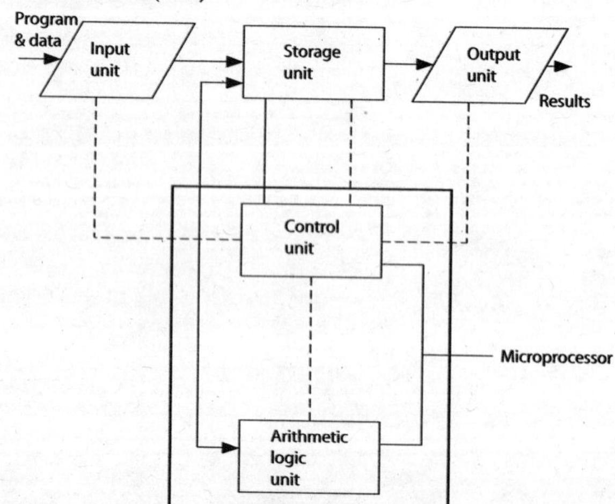

Figure 6.2 Major Parts of Microprocessor shown in thick black lined block

These are further elaborated as follows:

Arithmetic and Logic unit (ALU): The arithmetic logic unit (ALU) of a computer system is the place where the actual execution of instructions takes place during the processing operation. To be more precise, all calculations are performed and all comparisons including logical are made in the ALU.

Control unit: Control unit is responsible for controlling the entire functioning of the ALU. It receives instructions from the main memory and executes them after decoding. The timing and control signals are generated by this unit and sent to other units for execution of the program. It also transfers data between memory and input/output devices.

☞ *A **microprocessor** contains a control unit and an arithmetic and logic unit (ALU). When main memory is added to a microprocessor, it forms a CPU.*

6.4 CHARACTERISTICS OF MICROPROCESSOR

Three basic characteristics of microprocessor are discussed below:

Instruction Set : The set of instructions that the microprocessor can execute are called instruction set.

Word Length : The number of bits that a computer can manipulate or process *at a time* is called its *word length.* The commonly used word lengths are: 8, 16, 32 or 64 bits. It is a measure of the computing power of a computer. Computers with longer word lengths are more powerful. When we talk of a 32-bit computer, it means that its word length is 32 bits.

Clock Speed : In a computer, *clock speed* means the number of pulses per second generated by an oscillator that sets the number of times the processor processes and operates on data in a second. Clock speed is a measure of how quickly a computer completes basic computations and operations. Clock speed is generally measured in MHz (megahertz or million pulses per second) and GHz (gegahertz or billion pulses per second).

6.5 PROCESSORS ON PCs

A *Processor* is a logical circuit that functions as the processing unit of digital computers and other digital devices. It also provides computational control.

6.5.1 Single Processor

PC with *Single processor* have only one socket on the motherboard so that they can work with only one processor. Such PCs with single processor are relatively slow for manipulating large volume of data.

6.5.2 Dual Processors

Computer with *dual processors* have two sockets on the motherboard for connecting two microprocessors working together. However, at a time, only one processor is active. When one processor is idle, the other is automatically active. This increases the speed of processing large volume of data. This type of computers reduces the possibility of data loss even if one processor fails to work.

6.5.3 Multiple Processors

Computers fitted with *multiple processors* have several sockets on the motherboard to install more than one processors working together. Such computers are very powerful but highly expensive.

6.6 CLASSIFICATION OF MICROPROCESSORS

Microprocessors are classified into different types on the basis of the number of bits of operations at a time. Based on bits of operation at a time, microprocessors are also classified into the following types:

6.6.1 8-Bit Microprocessor

An *8-bit microprocessor* can handle a combination of 8-bits at a time. These bits are formed by 0s and 1s such as 10011000, 01110001, etc. The most popular 8-bit microprocessor was Intel 8085. But such processors are now superceded by more powerful ones.

6.6.2 16-Bit Microprocessor

A *16-bit microprocessor* manipulates 16 bits at a time. Thus, a *16 bit computer* means that the word length of this computer is 16 bits and processor manipulates 16 bits of data. Examples of 16 bit microprocessor is Intel 80286.

6.6.3 32-Bit Microprocessor

When we talk of a *32-bit computer,* it means that its word length is 32 bits. The processor it uses is a 32-bit microprocessor. Some examples are Intel 80386, 80486, Intel Pentium, Celeron, AMD Sempron, etc. These types of microprocessors are widely used in PCs. Windows XP and Linux operating systems are designed for these processors.

6.6.4 64-Bit Microprocessor

64-bit microprocessors are used in powerful workstations and mini computers. An important 64-bit microprocessor based computer is DEC's Alpha Server. 64-bit microprocessors are mostly used in servers, minicomputers and high-end workstations. An example of 64-bit microprocessor is AMD Athlon. Operating systems such as Windows 7, Windows 8, Linux, BSD and Mac OS X also run on 64-bit microprocessor. These operating systems fully utilize the capabilities of such processors.

Based on the instruction set, microprocessors are also classified into:

(a) CISC (Complex Instruction Set Computing): These types of processors are used in desktops, laptops and high end servers used in business.

(b) RISC (Reduced Instruction Set Computing): These types of processors are commonly used in ovens, air conditioners, etc.

(c) EPIC (Explicitly Parallel Instruction Computing): It is a computer architecture that combines the best feature of RISC and CISC.

6.7 CISC

CISC stands for Complex Instruction Set Computer. CISC computers are designed with a full set of computer instructions as needed to give processing capabilities in the most efficient way. However, CISC processors are very complex and expensive to produce but they have large sized instruction sets and different variety of addressing modes. Therefore, such processors make the job of programmers easy in writing complex codes speedily.

☞ *The Cyrix 6x86 supporting CISC architecture is a sixth-generation, 32-bit x86-compatible microprocessor. It was manufactured by IBM and SGS-Thomson.*

In CISC processor, a microprogram is executed for each instruction using the sequence of micro-instructions. When a micro-instruction is executed, a set of control signals are produced for the execution of instruction. For each micro-instruction, there is a microcode which is stored in the ROM. Thus, the availability of micro-code in a ROM enables checking of micro-instruction to be carried out more easily. If there is an error in any micro-instruction then the designer can change that micro-instruction in the ROM easily rather than changing the whole program instruction.

A CISC processor has the following properties:

(a) CISC processors have relatively large instruction sets.
(b) CISC machines have variable-length instruction formats.
(c) Many addressing modes are used in CISC machines
(d) The CISC machines use microprogramming.
(e) CISC machines are more complex and less efficient.
(f) Small numbers of general-purpose registers are employed in CISC machines.

☞ *The micro-instructions of a microprogram in CISC based PC system are executed one by one, and in turn, the necessary control signals are produced in steps for the execution of an instruction.*

6.8 RISC

RISC refers to Reduced Instruction Set Computer. It is the opposite of CISC (Complex Instruction Set Computer). In this type of microprocessor, most of the instructions for computer processing are relatively simple and computers are designed to handle those simple instructions extremely fast.

☞ *The term RISC was coined by David Patterson. He is also known as one of the innovators of the Redundant Arrays of Independent Disks (RAID) and Network of Workstations (NOW).*

RISC microprocessors are used extensively in high-end workstations and other expensive computer systems. Popular RISC microprocessor families include Sun Microsystems' SPARC (Scalar Processor ARChitecture), Intel's i860, and Motorola's 88000. A RISC processor has the following properties:

(a) RISC microprocessors have relatively small instruction sets
(b) RISC machines have fixed and easily decoded instruction formats.
(c) Few addressing modes are used in RISC machines
(d) Hardwired controls are used in RISC machines
(e) RISC machine is 5 to 10 times faster than a CISC machine.
(f) Several general-purpose registers are employed in RISC machines.

☞ *Software packages developed for RISC microprocessors provide a larger but simpler instruction set than software developed for CISC systems.*

6.9 EPIC

EPIC (Explicitly Parallel Instruction Computing) is a computer architecture that combines the best feature of RISC and CISC. A EPIC processor has the following properties:

(a) EPIC does not use fixed with instruction, rather aims at parallel processing of instructions.
(b) Programs must be written using sequential semantics with explicitly laid out parallelism.
(c) It uses a bundle of complex instructions that in addition to basic instruction also contain information on how to run the instruction in parallel with other instructions.

6.10 COMMONLY USED PROCESSORS

6.10.1 Intel Series

Pentium is a high speed microprocessor developed by Intel corporation of USA. It has 32-bit address bus and 64-bit data bus. The clock frequencies of its different versions vary in the range of MHz. It is mainly used in personal computers. It is suitable for multitasking/multiuser systems also. The original Pentium includes processor and co-processor on one chip.

Pentium Pro processor contains cache memory also. The cache memory is closer to the processor and thus speeds up the working of computer's main memory. It has 32-bit CISC processor. Pentium Pro was designed for high-end PCs and workstations and server where high speed data processing is required.

Pentium II contains all the features of Pentium Pro with MMX technology. MMX stands for Multi-Media eXentsions. This technology has been developed to handle the multimedia applications such as motion video, 3D images and sound. Among the Pentium II's features are a 512 KB level two (L1 and L2) cache memory twice that of the Pentium Pro processor. The L2 cache can include error correcting code.

Pentium III was introduced in 1999 as the improved version of Pentium II. It is faster than Pentium II. It means it can run 3D image, streaming video, speech recognition and audio applications more quickly. It can support floating point arithmetics as well as integer calculations. It also supports SIMD (Single Instruction Multiple Data) Instructions. This means, it can allow the data of a single instruction to be modified in multiple memory location simultaneously.

Pentium 4 is designed by Intel Corporation of USA as successor to its *Pentium III*. It has a clock speed of 1.7 GHz (gigahertz) and contain about 42 million transistors. It has a rapid execution engine which doubles the frequency and execute each instruction in a half clock cycle. It possesses a 400 MHz system bus, improved floating point calculations, improved multimedia and advanced dynamic executions. All these features enable faster processing for especially demanding applications such as digital video, voice recognition and online gaming.

ITANIUM is the latest processor from Intel Corporation. It is a 64 bit processor. It is mainly designed for e-commerce and ISP (Internet Service Provider) based servers.

Core i3: Core i3 is Intel's latest budget processor. Core i3 processors do support 64-bit versions of Windows. Core i3 processors includes dual core base, hyper threading support, and virtualization. By taking advantage of Intel's new chipset and 32nm technology, Core i3's have even been known to perform closely to lower end Core 2 Quad processors. If you use your computer for basic tasks such as word processing, email, surfing the web, etc., a Core i3 processor is more than enough to handle all of that with ease. A Core i3 processor is a solid, affordable choice for the heavy majority of people.

Core i5: Core i5 is the latest mid-range processor by Intel. There are two main types of Core i5 Processors. These are dual core and quad core.

Dual Core i5 processors have 32nm technology, hyper threading support, virtualization support, and Turbo Boost technology.

Quad Core i5 processors have 45nm technology, virtualization support and Turbo Boost technology, but do not have hyper threading support.

Core i5 processor is a great, mid-range priced processor for people who use their computers frequently and often multi task. To edit multiple files in Adobe Flash, with virtualization software, the Core i5 is snappier.

Core i7: Intel Core i7 is an Intel brand name for several families of desktop and laptop 64-bit processors. The Core i7 brand is mainly targeted for business and high-end consumer markets for both desktop and laptop computers.

6.10.2 Intel Celeron

Celeron is the low-end (low cost) microprocessor from Intel Corporation that is based on its Pentium Pro architecture. Although it is based on the same architecture as Pentium II, it lacks some high performance features of the Pentium II. Celeron includes L1 and L2 cache memory on the micro chip. It means cache memory is accessed at the same clock speed as the processor operates. Celeron L2 cache memory is smaller (128 KB) than the Pentium II (512 KB). Intel is marketing this processor as a chip for the basic PC at low price.

6.10.3 Cyrix

Cyrix is a low cost microprocessor designed for personal computer and information appliances like automatic washing machines and others. It competed, along with AMD (Advanced Micro Device) processors and Intel processors for the low cost microprocessor marketed by them. It has the maximum size of 32-bit microprocessor.

6.10.4 AMD Series

AMD is the second largest microprocessor manufacturing company after Intel Corporation in the USA. It has developed 32-bit microprocessors: K5, K6, K6-MMX, K6-2, K6-3 and K7. The processor K6-MMX is a multimedia processor. It is suitable for server computers also. AMD also makes integrated circuits for networking devices.

AMD-K6 is the microprocessor from AMD that competes with Intel's Pentium microprocessor. The successor of K6 is Athlon. It is much cheaper yet more powerful than Intel Pentium 4 processor.

Athlon (code or development name is "K7") microprocessor, introduced in 1999. It is the first microprocessor to supports 200 MHz system bus and 1 GHz (gigahertz) clock speed. It includes a superscalar pipelining floating point unit and a programmable L1 and L2 cache memory.

AMD Thunderbird: The latest AMD processor, this processor is the socket version.

6.10.5 Xeon

Xeon Pentium microprocessor is designed by Intel Corporation of USA which is used for servers and high-end workstations. It is also designed to work with a new and faster AGP (Accelerated Graphics Port) and PCI (Peripheral Component Interconnect) bus to carry data between the processors, RAM and input/output devices. It has a faster cache which runs at 400 MHz clock speed. It has extended server memory architecture that provide 36-bit address.

☞ *Xeon is mainly designed for Internet and large transactional database servers as well as for engineering, graphics and multimedia applications that need transferring a large amount of data from one place to another.*

6.10.6 Intel Mobile

Intel offers processors for mobile phones and chipsets to meet the growing needs of all mobile PC segments including high performance, low power devices. Intel created first mobile version of Pentium II in April 1998. After this, Intel launched a Mobile Pentium III. Its clock speed is 1.2 GHz and cache memory is 32 kb level 1 and 256 Level 2.

Pentium 4 is design to achieve higher performance than Pentium III. In its Pentium 4 version of Mobile, Intel increased the clock speed and shrink the size of transistors. Shrinked size consumes less power and generates lesser heat. Pentium 4 Mobile processor was launched at a speed of up to 1.7 GHz. In addition to this, Intel corporation adds a large cache memory buffer i.e. 512 kb L2 cache.

Now, Java-enabled audio, visual and multimedia applications will appear on mobile devices using Intel's Xscale-based processors, following a deal between Intel and Sun Microsystems. Sun's Connected Limited Device Configuration (CLDC) HotSpot Implementation will be ported for use in mobile devices such as phones and PDAs running Intel processors.

6.10.7 Mac Series

Similar to IBM PC systems, there is another class of PCs called Mac series. When Apple Corporation designed the Macintosh, they took a different approach than IBM. The computers of Mac series have a proprietary architecture. This means that other computer manufacturers cannot produce Mac "clones".

6.11 TYPES OF PROCESSOR

6.11.1 Pentium MMX Processor

Intel released its newest processor, Intel Pentium with MMX (Multimedia eXtension) Technology in January 1997 (See Figure 6.3). It is an evolutionary design, adding some enhancements and new capabilities to the "classic" Pentium. The main difference between the Pentium with MMX and the Pentium Classic is the inclusion of the MMX instruction set extensions. Running software on a Pentium MMX will result in a significant increase in performance over the regular Pentium at the same clock speed.

The Pentium with MMX is pin-compatible with the regular Pentium and goes in a Socket 7 just like the old chip. However, there is one important difference between the two: the Pentium with MMX uses split-rail voltage, i.e., 3.3 volts for the external voltage and 2.8 volts for the core.

Features of Pentium MMX Processor

MMX processor has the following enhancements over the previous generation of x86 processors (80486):

- **Doubled Primary Cache:** The Pentium with MMX has 16 KB for each of the level 1 data and instruction caches (Regular Pentium processor had 8 KB code and 8 KB data cache).
- **Improved Cache Mapping:** The primary cache is now 4-way set associative instead of 2-way.
- **Deepening of Internal Pipelines:** Both of the internal integer executions units are increased from 5 to 6 stages.
- **Better Use of Internal Pipelines:** More types of instructions can be run in parallel down the two execution pipes than on the older Pentium, so more use is made of the second pipe.
- **Improved Branch Prediction Unit:** Branch prediction was enhanced in comparison with Pentium processors.
- **Improved Instruction Decoder:** The instruction decoder is more efficient than the Pentium's decoder.

Figure 6.3 Pentium MMX processor

6.11.2 Dual Core Processor

Dual core refers to a CPU that includes two complete execution cores per physical processor. It has combined two processors and their caches and cache controllers onto a single integrated circuit (Silicon Chip). Dual core processors are well suited for multitasking environments because there are two complete execution cores instead of one, each with an independent interface to the front side bus. Since each core has its own cache, the operating system has sufficient resources to handle most compute intensive tasks in parallel.

Multicore is similar to dual core in that it is an expansion to the dual core technology which allows for more than two separate processors. In a single core or traditional processor the CPU is fed strings of instructions executes it and then selectively store in its cache for quick retrieval. When data outside the cache is required, it is retrieved through the system bus from Random Access Memory (RAM) or from storage devices. Accessing these slows down performance to the maximum speed the bus, RAM or storage device will allow, which is far slower than the speed of the CPU. In a dual core processor, each core handles incoming data strings simultaneously to improve efficiency. Now when one is executing the other can be accessing the system bus or executing its own code. To utilize a dual core processor, the operating system must be able to recognize multithreading and the software must have Simultaneous Multithreading Technology (SMT) written into its code. SMT enables parallel multi threading wherein the cores are served multi-threaded instructions in parallel. Without SMT the software will only recognize one core. Adobe Photoshop is an example of SMT-aware software. SMT is also used with multiprocessor systems common to servers. A dual core processor is different from a multiprocessor system. In the multiprocessor there are two separate CPUs with their own resources. In the dual core processor, resources are shared and the core resides on the same chip. A multi processor system is faster than a system with a dual core processor, while a dual core system is faster than a single core system. Dual core processors do not require a new motherboard, but can be used in existing boards that feature the correct socket. For the average user the difference in performance will be most noticeable in multitasking until more software is SMT aware. Servers running multiple dual core processors will be seen an appreciable increase in performance.

Features and Benefits

Outstanding Dual Core Performance With its two execution cores, the Intel Core Duo processor is optimized for multi-threaded applications and multitasking. We can simultaneously run multiple demanding applications, such as graphics intensive games or serious number-crunching programs while downloading music or running virus scanning security programs in the background.

Power Efficiency Demand for greater power efficiency in computing is on the rise from desktop to laptop PCs. With an Intel Core Duo processor, we get a balance of great dual core computing capabilities and power savings. Its enhanced voltage efficiency supports cooler and quieter system designs as compared to traditional desktop and laptop PCs. And thanks to the innovative energy efficient technologies built-in, the Intel Core Duo processor is able to transfer power only to those areas of the processor that need it, thereby enabling laptops to save power and desktops to have thinner, sleeker designs.

A Vibrant Media Experience The Intel Core Duo processor enables Intel Viiv technology and Intel Centrino Duo mobile technology multimedia experience to be all the more vibrant. Featuring Intel Digital Media Boost, the Intel Core Duo processor enables accelerating technologies for applications, such as CAD (Computer-Aided Design) tools, 3D (Three Dimension) and 2D (Two Dimension) modeling, video editing, digital music, digital photography and gaming. This is one of the key ingredients that help Intel Viiv technology and Intel Centrino Duo mobile technology to give you a truly rich multimedia experience.

Smarter, More Efficient Designs The Intel Core Duo processor features Intel smart Cache which helps deliver a smarter and more efficient cache and bus design to enable enhanced dual-core performance, and power savings.

☞ *The Intel Core Duo processor is Intel's first mobile dual-core processor and a key component of the new Intel Centrino Duo mobile technology platform.*

6.11.3 Intel Core 2 Duo Processor

The latest generation of Intel x86-compatible processor, Core 2 Duo microprocessor family. It was introduced on July 27, 2006. The Core 2 Duo processors include two cores, each core having 32 KB L1 data and 32 KB L1 code caches, and both cores having shared 2 or 4 MB L2 cache. The Core 2 Duo CPUs run at lower frequency than Pentium 4 processors, but they offer excellent performance due to more efficient architecture:

- Each processor's core can execute up to 4 instructions per cycle.
- Shared L2 cache allows the same copy of data to be used by both cores. Another advantage of shared L2 cache is that more heavily loaded core can use bigger portion of L2 cache - up to the full size of the cache.
- 128-bit SSE instructions can be executed at sustained rate of one 128-bit instruction per cycle.

Core 2 Duo architecture includes other performance enhancing features. One of these features is a "macrofusion". This feature allows the processor to load and execute common instruction pairs as one instruction.

The performance of Core 2 Duo family is much higher than the performance of Pentium 4. Lower processor speed of Core 2 Duo and Extreme processors are also translated into lower power consumption. Core 2 Duo E6600 and E6700 processors have thermal design power 65 Watt (75 Watt for Core 2 Extreme x6800), while less efficient Pentium 4 Extreme Edition 3.73 GHz has thermal design power of 115 Watt.

The Intel Core 2 Duo divided into desktop processors and mobile processors. The desktop processors are split into three code names. Conroe, which uses the 65-nanometer and made in August 2006. Allendale 65-nm, in January 2007 and Walfdale, in January 2008 (See Figure 6.4).

Figure 6.4 Intel Core 2 Duo processor

Types of Core 2 Families

Core 2 Duo: Core 2 Duo was the first family of desktop-class microprocessors based on Core microarchitecture. The first Core 2 Duo processors had much lower core frequency and approximately the same FSB (Front Side Bus) frequency and level 2 cache size as Pentium D microprocessors. They had better performance than the fastest Pentium D 960 due to much more efficient microarchitecture.

Core 2 Quad: Core 2 Quad microprocessors are essentially two Core 2 Duo CPUs in one package - two cores are located on one die, two other cores are on another die, and both dies are packaged together. The level 2 cache on these processors is shared between two cores. These CPUs have higher (about 50% higher) Thermal Design Power than dual-core microprocessors running at the same frequency. The quad core CPUs have the same performance as the Core 2 Duo processors in single-threaded applications, and are faster or considerably faster in multi-threaded applications. Performance difference in games between quad and dual core microprocessors is highly dependent on the game, and varies from no difference at all to 20% performance advantage for quad core CPUs.

Core 2 Extreme is a brand name for the best performing desktop Core 2 microprocessors. These processors were always faster than other Core 2 Duo and Core 2 Quad. Only Extreme processors had higher core frequency, they also had unlocked clocked multiplier which allowed to increase their frequency above nominal. Extreme processors had other features that increased their performance even further. Higher bus frequency, twice as many cores, and/or large level 2 cache. Being faster than any other Core 2 Duo and Core 2 Quad on the market, these CPUs were almost twice more expansive than the most expensive Core 2 Duo/Quad microprocessor.

Core 2 Solo is a family of low power microprocessors based on Core microarchitecture. These processors have only one core. Like other mobile Core 2 families, the Core 2 Solo CPUs have additional low-power modes along with Dynamic Acceleration technology. Solo processors have much lower Thermal Design Power than Core 2 Duo mobile microprocessors - 5.5 Watt versus 25 or 35 Watt.

Main Features and Benefits

Each Intel Core 2 Duo CPU has its two cores placed on a single die, which is a wafer of semiconductor material. The 65-nm chips are bigger than the 45-nm ones. The Core 2 Duo division has a 1.06 to 3.33 GHz processing speed range, 533 to 1,333 MHz data bus speed range; a 2MB, 3MB, 4MB or 6MB Level 2 cache, or secondary memory bank; and a maximum power consumption range of 10 to 65 watts. The mobile processors tend to be the less powerful but more energy efficient Core 2 Duo chips.

6.11.4 Intel Core i3 Processor

Core i3 Core-branded microprocessors was introduced on January 7, 2010. It is originally based on Westmere (enhanced Nehalem) micro architecture, Core i3 CPUs were eventually transitioned to Sandy Bridge, and later to Ivy Bridge architecture. Common features of all Core i3 generations are dual-channel DDR3 memory controller, HD-capable graphics controller, and separate DMI interface to peripheral devices (See Figure 6.5).

Figure 6.5 Inter Core i3 processor

All processors have per-core 256 KB level 2 cache, large level 3 cache shared between two cores, as well as support for basic and some advanced microarchitecture features, such as SSE4 instructions, and Virtualization and HyperThreading technologies. Sandy Bridge and Ivy Bridge CPUs also added support for Advanced Vector Extensions.

Intel Core i3 currently consists of desktop and mobile Core i3 families. Desktop Core i3 microprocessors are packaged in 1155- and 1156-land Land Grid Array (LGA) packages, and require socket 1155 or socket 1156 motherboards. Mobile Core i3 CPUs are manufactured in 1023-ball BGA (Ball Grid Array), 1288-ball BGA or 988 micro-PGA packages. BGA processors are soldered directly on motherboards, and PGA processors utilize socket G1 or G2.

Basic Features of i3

The basic feature of the i3 features are highly improved as compared to previous version of the processor by Intel. i3 processors have 3.06 GHz and 2.93 GHz core speed which is very high as compared to the previous configurations of Intel processors. They have four processing threads that enables multithreading and multitasking. 4 MB additional Cache memory is also provided inside the processor. Double channeled DDR (Digitalized-Image Data Record) with 1333 MHZ memory sequence. Some of the popular and leading features of i3 processors are listed below.

- i3 processors is featured with accuracy and high performance. The users with the high throughput rates, and also reduced time in executing the programs by the processor.
- It is fully equipped by the latest HD graphics with powerful and advanced video engine that provides smooth high quality display along with the 3D graphics capabilities.

- It also provides hyper threading technology to its users which enable the multitasking capability of both user and the system. The systems with i3 processors can perform execution and compilation of two tasks simultaneously without causing the executing delays and debuggers errors. They are so responsive that output of the programs can be generated at the same time too. More than seven applications can run simultaneously on the system with i3 processor built on the motherboards.
- i3 processors are smarter, faster and more adaptive in all kinds of networking scheme. They can be used with any of the hard disk configurations.
- They are also famous in the markets by the name of desktop processor because of the great quality resolution. Integrated components on the motherboards also makes i3 processors unique in their architecture and circuit installations.

Advantages of i3

The advantages that are of great use in the field of computers and technology. Some of them are listed below.

- Dual core processing has the ability to run two independent programs with one hardware.
- i3 processors have improved Pentium base, they have totally new architecture with more integrations and high speed performance structure.
- Hyper threading technology also enables user to enjoy the high speed and better performance with more reliable outputs. It has 4 tasking threads that allows user to easily execute 3 to 4 programmes at a time.
- Smart memory and cache sequence allow user to enjoy the optimized and efficient data access both direct and sequentially. Effective shortcuts have reduced the access time of the file and system.
- HD graphical features also make these processors distinguished from the others because they are considered as best in their resolution.

6.11.5 Intel Core i5 Processor

Intel Core i5 microprocessor family, released in September 2009, is a family of processors with medium-level performance as compared to Core i7. The i5 processors include many features found in Core i7 CPUs. It is single-die(IC) quad-core design, on-die(IC) DDR3 memory controller, point-to-point protocol used to communicate with I/O devices, 256 KB level 2 cache (per core), large shared level 3 cache, SSE4 instructions, and support for such features as Virtualization technology and Turbo Boost technology (See Figure 6.6).

Basic Features of Intel i5 Processors

As i5 processors are more advanced as compared to the i3 or all the previous versions of the processors. It has lot of features that deals the advanced technologies in a very respectable way. Some of the basic key Intel i5 features are as follows:

- Basically i5 processors are introduces to do the intelligent networking and enhance the performance of different purposes, such as for gaming, faster procession, reliable data transmission, etc.
- One of the important feature of the i5 processors is that it automatically manages the power supply where needed and does not break the speed and the performance of the system.
- It also allows the user to enjoy the heavy applications with the higher rate such as HD video and music composing.
- It also provides the opportunity to the users to use the system with multitasking.
- It also able to increase the memory of the system and help users to work with the high bandwidth and great performance.
- A big feature of the i5 processors is that they have ability to run two multitasking processors together that are generally called as dual processors and can increase the working performance of the system efficiently.
- Turbo Boost technology of i5 processors is the key beneficial feature of the i5 processors that allow the users to do their regular and important working with the help of heavy applications.
- It also consists of Hyper Threading technology that enables the users for multitasking and improves their business or working by working on the two different tasks at the same time.

Advantages of i5 Prccessors

There are many more benefits of the i5 processors because they are advanced form of the processing units. Some more important benefits of the i5 processors are given below.

- Providing high quality visualization for advanced applications.
- High performance with the help of dual processor technology.
- HD graphics enhance the video graphics and applications related to the same architecture.

Figure 6.6 Intel Core i5 processor

6.11.6 Intel Core i7 Processor

Intel developed different types processors for the users for the sake of faster working as compared to the previous versions. After the development of i3 and i5 processor, Intel introduces a new version, i.e., i7 processor that is comparatively a lot more faster than the old ones. Basically i7 processors were designed to meet the challenges of the intelligent and the fastest working performance of the computer system. They were designed in 2008 and were announced in 2009 just after the i5 processors. i7 processors have ability to handle all the problems and working of the latest computer systems and provide the quality systematic to technological world (See Figure 6.7).

Features of i7 Processors

There are many features of i7 processors that are more advanced as compared to the previous or the old versions of the processors invented by the Intel Company. Some of the latest technological features of the i7 features are as follows:

Figure 6.7 Core i7 processor

- With the help of i7 processors, users can enjoy the high speed working with the additional feature of the multitasking, i.e., using two different documents or the files at the same time.
- Dual core technology is also a part of i7 processors that provide reliable and high data rate working performance to the customers.
- It is the Turbo Boost technology. This technology provides the high performance to the system to the users to overcome the work load of different applications on the system and maintain the speed of the system.
- Like i5 and i3 processors, i7 also have a feature of Hyper threading technology enhances the activity and the speed of the system by managing the multitasking, work load and different types of heavier applications of the users.
- i7 processors are so advanced to deal with the integrated memory of system and have ability to increase the memory up to 1066 MB and provide the working speed of 25.6 GB/sec.

Technical Specifications of i7 Processors

Some technicalities specifications of i7 processors that encourages the customers to buy the processing units are as follows:

- i7 processors have integrated memory up to 1066 MB and can provide the faster working for applications.
- i7 processors are also able to supports cache that is very important for the high rate performance and can support up to 8 to 12 MB.
- Highest clock speed of the newt poking of the i7 processors is 3.2 GHz. That is why these are very famous among the users to meet the requirements of the latest technological/professional world.
- There are many other technologies that really make the processors and the system powerful, such as high visualization, and can support up to 64 bits, with the help of these specifications system maintains the working of the BIOS (Basic Input/Output System) and other chipset devices.
- There are different types of cores involved on the manufacturing of the Intel i7 processors but the common cores that are involved are Bloomfield or Lynnfield etc.

Advantages of i7 Processors

i7 is latest processors for the systems that are able to support dual processors technology and provide the fastest and the convenient working performance to the users. Due to its advancement, i7 processors has many advantages, some of them are listed below:

- They are faster from the old versions of the processors given by the Intel and can support dual processor technology.
- Provide high data visualization technology to the users to view the high quality images and video graphics. Better then i3 and i5 family processors.

On top of all advantages, the only major disadvantage of the i7 processors is that they are very expensive to install in systems. And people who have specific requirements in profession they use it, i7 are not used that commonly.

6.12 CONCEPT OF PROCESSOR SPEED

A processor, or "microprocessor," is a small chip that resides in computers and other electronic devices. Its basic job is to receive input and provide the appropriate output.

The processor is a unit of computer system that interprets instructions and executes them. The microprocessor is the heart of the computer. A PC's (Personal Computers) performance depends on the capability and speed of the microprocessor. The processing speed of a microprocessor is usually measure in Millions Instructions Per Second (MIPS). The MIPS rating is used to specify the integer computation performance of a processor. The processing speed of a microprocessor for floating point computation is measured in Millions of Floating

Point Instructions Per Second (MFLOPS). It speed is the rate at which a processor can complete a processing cycle. It is typically measured in Megahertz (MHz) or Gigahertz (GHz). One megahertz is equal to one million cycles per second, while one gigahertz equals one billion cycles per second. This means a 1.8 GHz processor has twice the clock speed of a 900 MHz processor.

A microprocessor is a combination of arithmetical logical unit and control unit on a single integrated chip. It requires power supply, clock system and the main memory to function as a complete PC. Microprocessor is also used in many other digital devices besides PCs and workstations. It works on the binary digits 0 and 1. The CPU of a less powerful computer may contain a single microprocessor. The CPU of a bigger workstation may contain a number of microprocessors on one or more motherboards. The major parts of a microprocessor includes:

(a) Arithmetic Logical Unit (ALU)
(b) Control Unit (CU)

☞ *The combination of ALU and CU is known as a microprocessor.*

Processors are, distinguished from each other by the following criteria:

- The architecture, the presence and size of cache memory, the inclusion of a floating point math co-processor, etc.
- The size of data that can be manipulated at one time: 16 bits, 32 bits, or 64 bits. The word bit means binary digit.
- The size of the external bus, that is, the width of the path data. For instance, with 64 bits bus, 8 characters can be sent simultaneously, while a 16-bit bus requires four separate operations to perform the same data transfer.
- Maximum addressable memory, which limits the amount of memory that can be installed in the computer.
- The internal and external clock frequency, that is, the speed at which the processor itself works and the speed at which it can communicate with other components.

6.13 PROCESSOR SPECIFICATION

Processors can be identified by two main parameters: how wide they are and how fast they are. The speed of a processor is a fairly simple concept. Speed is counted in megahertz (MHz) and (GHz), which means millions of cycles per second and billons cycles per second. The speed of a computer's processor chip (technically known as its "clock speed") in measured in gigahertz (GHz), with the fastest modern processors currently running at up to 4.7GHz. However, for most computing tasks including web browsing, sending e-mails, word processing and spreadsheet work any processor running at 1GHz or more remains perfectly sufficient. Where higher processor speeds become more important is for applications such as video editing, 3D graphics work and playing computer games. Alongside clock speed, the architecture of a processor is the most important factor to determine its performance, and refers to its basic design and complexity. In addition to clock speed and architecture, a processor's cache and front side bus (FSB) speed also determine a computer's overall power. In brief, cache is a form of very fast memory integrated into the processor chip, and used to store up instructions (work for the processor) so that it has to slow down as little as possible between tasks. Cache is measured in megabytes (MB), with (for example) low-end Celeron processors having as little as 0.25MB of cache (256KB), and high-end Itaniums having up to 24MB. The simple message is, the more cache the better -- though high levels of cache still come at a very significant price. Front side bus (FSB) speed is a measure of how fast a microprocessor communicates with the computer's main circuit board (or "motherboard") into which it is physically connected. Again, the higher the measure the better for overall performance, with FSB speeds currently ranging from 533MHz (still perfectly sufficient for the vast majority of applications) up to 1600Mhz.

The width of a processor is a little more complicated to discuss because there are three main specifications in a processor that are expressed in width.

(a) Data bus
(b) Memory address bus
(c) Internal registers

6.13.1 Data Bus

The most common way to describe a processor is by the speed at which it runs and the width of the processor's external data bus. This defines the number of data bits that can be moved into or out of the processor in one cycle. A bus is a series of connections that carry common signals.

A typical computer system has several internal and external buses. The processor bus discussed most often is the external data bus-the bundle of wires (or pins) used to send and receive data. The more signals that can be sent at the same time, the more data can be transmitted in a specified interval and, therefore, the faster (and wider) the bus. A wider data bus is like having a highway with more lanes, which allows for greater throughput.

6.13.2 Memory address bus

The address bus is the set of wires that carries the addressing information used to describe the memory location to which the data is being sent or from which the data is being retrieved. As with the data bus, each wire in an address bus carries a single bit of information. This single bit is a single digit in the address. The more wires (digits) used in calculating these addresses, the greater the total number of address locations. The size (or width) of the address bus indicates the maximum amount of RAM that a chip can address. The highway analogy can be used to show how the address bus fits in. If the data bus is the highway and the size of the data bus is equivalent to the number of lanes, the address bus relates to the house number or street address.

The data bus and address bus are independent, and chip designers can use whatever size they want for each. Usually, however, chips with larger data buses have larger address buses. The sizes of the buses can provide important information about a chip's relative power, measured in two important ways. The size of the data bus is an indication of the chip's information-moving capability, and the size of the address bus tells you how much memory the chip can handle.

6.13.3 Internal Registers

The size of the internal registers indicate how much information the processor can operate on at one time and how it moves data around internally within the chip. This is sometimes also referred to as the internal data bus. The register size is essentially the same as the internal data bus size. A register is a holding cell within the processor; for example, the processor can add numbers in two different registers, storing the result in a third register. The register size determines the size of data the processor can operate on. The register size also describes the type of software or commands and instructions a chip can run.

6.14 PROCESSOR MODES

Processor modes refer to the various operating environments and affect the instructions and capabilities of the chip. The processor mode controls how the processor sees and manages the system memory and the tasks that use it. Four different modes of operation possible are:

(a) Real mode
(b) Protected mode
(c) Virtual Real mode
(d) 64 Bit Extension Mode

6.14.1 Real mode

The original IBM PC included an 8088 processor that could execute 16-bit instructions using 16-bit internal registers and could address only 1 MB of memory using 20 address lines and the original versions of DOS created to work on it were designed with this in mind. All original PC software was created to work with this chip and was designed around the 16-bit instruction set and 1MB memory model. Later processors such as the 286 could also run the same 16-bit instructions as the original 8088, but much faster. In other words, the 286 was fully compatible with the original 8088 and could run all 16-bit software just the same as an 8088, but, that software would run faster. The 16-bit instruction mode of the 8088 and 286 processors has become known as real mode. All software running in real mode must use only 16-bit instructions and live within the 20-bit (1MB) memory architecture it supports. Software of this type is normally single-tasking, which means that only one program can run at a time. There is no built-in protection to keep one program from overwriting another program or even the operating system in memory, which means that if more than one program is running, it is possible for one of them to bring the entire system to a crashing halt.

☞ *In the real mode, the memory address ability is limited to 1MB and it cannot take advantage of additional hardware support for virtual memory etc because interrupts are disabled.*

6.14.2 Protected mode

The name "protected" actually derives from the fact that processes run in different address spaces and that they are essentially protected from one another. If a process tries to access another's address space, it traps to the MMU hardware. In this mode, the full hardware support is enabled, and the processor can address the entire 32 bit address space.

The 386, was the PC industry's first 32-bit processor. Protected mode is also sometimes called 386 Enhanced Mode, since it became mainstream with that family of processors. This chip could run an entirely new 32-bit instruction set. The 32-bit instruction set, required a 32-bit operating system and a 32-bit application. This new 32-bit mode was referred to as protected mode, which refer to the fact that software programs running in that mode are protected from overwriting one another in memory. Such protection helps make the system much more crash-proof, as an erratic program cannot very easily damage other programs or the operating system. In addition, a crashed program can be terminated, while the rest of the system continues to run unaffected. This is a much more powerful mode of operation than real mode, and is used in all modern multitasking operating systems. The advantages of protected mode (compared to real mode) are:

(a) Full access to all of the system's memory. There is no 1 MB limit in protected mode.
(b) Ability to multitask, meaning having the operating system manage the execution of multiple programs simultaneously.
(c) Support for virtual memory, which allows the system to use the hard disk to emulate additional system memory when needed.
(d) Faster (32-bit) access to memory, and faster 32-bit drivers to do I/O transfers.

In protected mode, the processor uses segmented (non-linear) addressing, as opposed to linear addressing. Segmented addressing means that memory (physical and virtual memory) is divided into 64K blocks. This is the maximum value for the Instruction Pointer (IP) register. The IP register works with the Code Segment (CS) register to point to the memory location from where the microprocessor should fetch its next instruction.

6.14.3 Virtual Real mode

The third mode, which is called the Virtual Real mode was created to enable programs that were designed to work with the older real mode to work. Whenever you run a DOS program from Windows, the processor switches to the Virtual Real mode and back to the same constraints of real mode. This is also the reason why boot loaders are small because they have to run in real mode.

The third mode of processor operation is actually an additional capability, an enhancement, of protected mode. Virtual real is essentially a virtual real mode 16-bit environment that runs inside 32-bit protected mode. Protected mode is normally used to run graphical multitasking operating systems such as the various flavors of Windows. When you run a DOS prompt window inside Windows, you have created a virtual real mode session. Because protected mode allows true multitasking, you can actually have several real mode sessions running, each with its own software running on a virtual PC. This can all run simultaneously, even while other 32-bit applications are running. In brief, it emulates real mode from within protected mode, allowing DOS programs to run. A protected mode operating system such as Windows can in fact create multiple virtual real mode machines, each of which appear to the software running them as if they are the only software running on the machine.

6.14.4 64 Bit Extension Mode

This mode is also called Long Mode. 64 bit extension mode is the mode where a 64 bit application can access the 64 bit instruction and registers while 32 bit and 16 bit programs are executed in a compatibility sub mode.

6.14.5 Processor Performance

Measure the performance of a central processing unit or computer processor by determining the number of computations the processor can perform per second and the number of individual processors in the chip itself. When purchasing a processor or desktop computer, you often look at the clockspeed. Calculated in megahertz and gigahertz, or MHz and GHz. CPU clock speed, or clock rate, is measured in Hertz - generally in gigahertz, or GHz. A CPU's clock speed rate is a measure of how many clock cycles a CPU can perform per second. For example, a CPU with a clock rate of 1.8 GHz can perform 1,800,000,000 clock cycles per second. To measure a computer system's performance is to test the system using the actual software applications you use and not just by considering the clock frequency of the CPU.

Computer performance is the amount of work accomplished by a computer system. Depending on the context, high computer performance may involve one or more of the following: Short response time for a given piece of work. High throughput (rate of processing work) Low utilization of computing resource(s).

Originally, CPUs had a single core. That meant the physical CPU had a single central processing unit on it. To increase performance, manufacturers add additional "cores," or central processing units. A dual-core CPU has two central processing units, so it appears to the operating system as two CPUs. A different process can be using each core at the same time. This speeds up your system, because your computer can do multiple things at once. With a multi-core CPU, it can use other cores for such background tasks to avoid slowing your programs down.

6.14.6 Processor Features

With on-going developments, new features are continually added to the CPU architecture to help improve everything from performance to the reliability of the CPU as a whole. Let's take a look at some of these technologies.

System Management Mode (SMM)

System Management Mode (SMM) is an operating mode on x86 and x86-64 processors, intended for use by Firmware/BIOS to perform low-level system management operations while an OS is running. SMM is intended to be used for advanced power-management features and other operating-system-independent functions. The chipset is programmed to recognize many types of events and timeouts.

Superscalar Execution

Superscalar describes a microprocessor design that makes it possible for more than one instruction at a time to be executed during a single clock cycle . In a superscalar design, the processor or the instruction compiler is able to determine whether an instruction can be carried out independently of other sequential instructions, or whether it has a dependency on another instruction and must be executed in sequence with it. The processor then uses multiple execution units to simultaneously carry out two or more independent instructions at a time. Superscalar design is sometimes called "second generation RISC".

A superscalar processor is a CPU that implements a form of parallelism called instruction-level parallelism within a single processor. It therefore allows for more throughput (the number of instructions that can be executed in a unit of time) than would otherwise be possible at a given clock rate.

The fifth-generation Pentium and newer processors feature multiple internal instruction execution pipelines, which enable them to execute multiple instructions at the same time. The 486 and all preceding chips can perform only a single instruction at a time. Intel calls the capability to execute more than one instruction at a time superscalar technology. This technology provides additional performance compared with the 486.

MMX Technology

MMX technology was originally named for multimedia extensions. Commercially introduced in January 1997, the MMX technology is an extension of the Intel architecture that uses a single-instruction, multiple-data execution model that allows several data elements to be processed simultaneously. Applications that benefit from the MMX technology are those that do many parallelizable computations using small integer numbers. Examples of these kinds of applications are 2-D/3-D graphics, image processing, virtual reality, audio synthesis and data compression.

MMX is a Pentium microprocessor from Intel that is designed to run faster when playing multimedia applications. According to Intel, a PC with an MMX microprocessor runs a multimedia application up to 60% faster than one with a microprocessor having the same clock speed but without MMX. In addition, an MMX microprocessor runs other applications about 10% faster, probably because of increased cache.

SSE, SSE2, SSE3 and SSE4

Streaming SIMD (Single Instruction Multiple Data) Extensions, MMX plus 70 additional instructions for graphics and sound processing. SSE (Streaming SIMD Extensions), additional graphics and sound instructions built in to the PIII. SSE was subsequently expanded by Intel to SSE2, SSE3, SSSE3, and SSE4.

SSE2 (Streaming SIMD Extensions 2), is one of the Intel SIMD (Single Instruction, Multiple Data) processor supplementary instruction sets first introduced by Intel with the initial version of the Pentium 4 in 2001. It extends the earlier SSE instruction set, and is intended to fully replace MMX.

SSE3, Streaming SIMD Extensions 3, also known by its Intel code name Prescott New Instructions (PNI), is the third iteration of the SSE instruction set for the IA-32 (x86) architecture. Intel introduced SSE3 in early 2004 with the Prescott revision of their Pentium 4 CPU.

SSE4 (Streaming SIMD Extensions 4) is a SIMD CPU instruction set used in the Intel Core microarchitecture and AMD K10 (K8L).

3DNow!, Enhanced 3DNow! and 3DNow Professional

3DNow! is an extension to the x86 instruction set developed by Advanced Micro Devices (AMD). It adds single instruction multiple data (SIMD) instructions to the base x86 instruction set, enabling it to perform vector processing, which improves the performance of many graphic-intensive applications. 3DNow! technology enables faster frame rates on high-resolution video scenes, better physical modeling of real-world environments, sharper and more detailed 3D imaging, smoother video playback, and theater-quality audio. One advantage of 3DNow is that it is possible to add or multiply the two numbers that are stored in the same register. With SSE, each number can only be combined with a number in the same position in another register. This capability, known as horizontal in Intel terminology, was the major addition to the SSE3 instruction set. A disadvantage with 3DNow is that 3DNow instructions and MMX instructions share the same register-file, whereas SSE adds 8 new independent registers.

3DNow and Enhanced 3DNow are sets of instructions that extend the multimedia capabilities of the AMD chips beyond MMX. This allows greater performance for 3D graphics, multimedia, and other floating-point-intensive PC applications. Actually 3DNow originally came out in the K6 series before Intel released SSE in the Pentium III, and then AMD added Enhanced 3DNow to the Athlon and Duron processors. AMD licensed MMX from Intel and all its K6 series, Athlon, Duron, and later processors include full MMX instruction support.

3DNow Professional is a trade name used to indicate processors that combine 3DNow technology with a complete SSE instructions set (such as SSE1, SSE2 or SSE3). The Athlon XP was the first processor to carry the 3DNow Professional trade name, and was the first product in the Athlon family to support the complete SSE1 instruction set.

Dynamic Execution

Dynamic execution enables the processor to be more efficient by manipulating data in a more logically ordered fashion rather than simply processing a list of instructions, and it is one of the hallmarks of all sixth-generation processors. The way software is written can dramatically influence a processor's performance. For example, performance will be adversely affected if the processor is frequently required to stop what it is doing and jump or branch to a point elsewhere in the program. Delays also occur when the processor cannot process a new instruction until the current instruction is completed. Dynamic execution allows the processor to not only dynamically predict the order of instructions, but execute them out of order internally, if necessary, for an improvement in speed.

Dynamic execution is first used in the P6 or sixth-generation processors. It is an innovative combination of three processing techniques designed to help the processor manipulate data more efficiently. Those techniques are multiple branch prediction, data flow analysis, and speculative execution.

Multiple Branch Prediction Multiple branch prediction predicts the flow of the program through several branches. Using a special algorithm, the processor can anticipate jumps or branches in the instruction flow. It uses this to predict where the next instructions can be found in memory with an accuracy of 90 percent or greater. This is possible because while the processor is fetching instructions, it is also looking at instructions further ahead in the program.

Data Flow Analysis Data flow analysis analyzes and schedules instructions to be executed in an optimal sequence, independent of the original program order. The processor looks at decoded software instructions and determines whether they are available for processing or are instead dependent on other instructions to be executed first. The processor then determines the optimal sequence for processing and executes the instructions in the most efficient manner.

Speculative Execution Speculative execution increases performance by looking ahead of the program counter and executing instructions that are likely to be needed later. Because the software instructions being processed are based on predicted branches, the results are stored in a pool for later referral. If they are to be executed by the resultant program flow, the already completed instructions are retired and the results are committed to the processor's main registers in the original program execution order. This technique essentially allows the processor to complete instructions in advance and then grab the already completed results when necessary.

Dual Independent Bus Architecture

Dual Independent Bus (DIB) is a bus architecture. It has two separate or independent bus systems incorporated into the processor chip. One bus connects to the main memory and the other connects with the L2 cache. Both buses can be used simultaneously rather than singly to increase program execution speed.

Dual Independent Bus Architecture was created to improve processor bus bandwidth and performance. Having two (dual) independent data I/O buses enables the processor to access data from either of its buses simultaneously and in parallel, rather than in a singular sequential manner (as in a single-bus system).

The key to implementing DIB was to move the L2 cache memory off of the motherboard and into the processor package. L1 cache has always been directly a part of the processor mold, but L2 was larger and had to be external. By moving the L2 cache into the processor, the L2 cache could run at speeds more like the L1 cache, much faster than the motherboard or processor bus. To move the L2 cache into the processor initially, modifications had to be made to the CPU socket or slot. The processor reads and writes data to and from the Level 2 cache using a specialised high-speed bus. Called the backside bus, it's separate from the CPU to main memory system bus (now called the frontside bus). The DIB architecture allows the processor to use both buses simultaneously.

The Dual Independent Bus architecture was first implemented in the sixth-generation processors from Intel and AMD.

Hyper-Threading Technology

Intel Hyper-Threading Technology, commonly referred to HT Technology, increases processor efficiency by allowing multiple threads to run on each processor core within the chip. Hyper-Threading is a technology used by some Intel microprocessors that allows a single microprocessor to act like two separate processors to the operating system and the application programs that use it. It is a feature of Intel's IA-32 processor architecture. This is the architecture that is the basis for all current Intel Core i3, i5 and i7 processors. Before hyper-threading and multi-core CPUs came around, people attempted to add additional processing power to computers by adding additional CPUs. This requires a motherboard with more than one CPU socket - multiple CPUs are inserted into different sockets. The motherboard also needs additional hardware to connect those CPU sockets to the RAM and other resources. There's a lot of overhead here - there's additional latency if the CPUs need to communicate with each other, systems with multiple CPU will consume more power, and the motherboard needs more sockets and hardware.

Dual-core Technology

Originally, CPUs had a single core. That meant the physical CPU had a single central processing unit on it. To increase performance, manufacturers add additional "cores," or central processing units. A dual-core CPU has two central processing units, so it appears to the operating system as two CPUs. A different process can use each core at the same time. This speeds up your system, because your computer can do multiple things at once. Unlike hyper-threading, a dual-core CPU literally has two central processing units on the CPU chip. A quad-core CPU has four central processing units, an octa-core CPU has eight central processing units, and so on. The more CPUs or cores a computer has, the more things it can do at once. This helps improve performance across everything you do - even if you're just doing one thing at a time, the computer needs to perform background tasks. With a multi-core CPU, it can use other cores for such background tasks to avoid slowing your programs down. The advent of dual-core CPUs offered a dramatically better desktop experience to PC users. Dual-core refers to a CPU that includes two complete execution cores per physical processor. It has combined two processors and their caches and cache controllers onto a single integrated circuit (silicon chip).

6.15 INTERFACE

Today, there is a wide availability of types of interface the CPU may connect to. Below is a listing of each of the interfaces and a brief description on each of them.

6.15.1 Slot

The slot was first used and introduced by Intel when they released the Pentium II processors. This slot was designed to allow users to install the processor easily into the computer. Computers that have the Slot are the Intel Pentium II and early versions of the Intel Pentium III. The AMD processors use the Slot A interface.

6.15.2 Socket

Socket, which is a slot card, can be used to connect a socket or FPGA processor. This is not an actual interface but can be an option for users who have a slot adapter with a computer that supports speeds of a socket or FPGA processor. When looking at the interface of the CPU, it must match that of what is on the motherboard unless it is possible to use a Socket.

Processor Socket and Slot Types

When referring to a processor, a CPU socket or processor socket is a connection that allows a computer processor to be connected to a motherboard. For example, the Socket 370 is an example of such a socket. The processor socket helps determine what computer processors your computer motherboard is capable of accepting. For example, a socket 1 processor is not compatible with a Socket 370 because of the pin layout and the technology differences used in each socket.

After socket 0, Intel released socket 1, which had the same pinout as socket 0 with the addition of a key pin. It also adopted the ZIF standard, allowing the installation of several different types of processors on the same socket (i.e., on the same motherboard). Other socket standards were released for the 486 family after socket 1 (socket 2, socket 3, and socket 6) in order to increase the number of CPU models that could be installed on the CPU socket. Thus, socket 2 accepts the same CPUs accepted by socket 1 in addition to some more models, and so forth. Even though the socket 6 was designed, it was never used. Thus, we usually call the pinout used by 486-class processors as "socket 3" . Socket 7 uses the same pinout as socket 5 with the addition of one key pin, accepting the same processors accepted by socket 5 plus new CPUs, especially CPUs designed by competing companies.

All Slot 1, Slot A, Socket 8, Socket 370, and Socket A, processors have automatic voltage detection, where the system will detect and set the correct voltage by reading certain pins on the processor. Some motherboards, such as those made by Intel, do not allow any changes to these settings manually.

☞ *The cpu socket is where you will be installing your cpu. You simply need to make sure to match your motherboard socket type with your cpu socket type to ensure that they are compatible.*

Socket 478

The Socket 478 is a CPU socket that utilizes the pin grid array and was used by Intel for the Pentium 4 and Celeron processors. Socket 478 was a replacement for Socket 423, which was found to be inadequate for processor speeds above 2.0 GHz. Intel released these processors in response to AMD's Socket 462 processors. Socket 478 processors ranged in speed from 1.4 GHz to 3.4 GHz. Intel eventually replaced the Socket 478 with LGA 775.

Socket T

Socket 775, also called Socket T or LGA775, is designed specifically for the Intel Socket 775 (Socket T) range of processors, including Intel Core 2 Duo and Intel Core 2 Quad, Core 2 Duo Extreme CPUs. The CPU cooler features a large aluminum heatsink that maximizes dissipation of the heat around the CPU, as well a low-noise 95mm fan that provides up to 50 CFM of air circulation, helping to keep the CPU cooler for optimized performance. The Socket 775/T cooler/fan offers simple installation, providing tool-less clips for easy connection to the motherboard. The socket LGA775 supports Intel CPUs from 1.8 to 3.8 GHz with Front-Side Bus frequencies ranging from 533 MHz to 1600 MHz. This socket superseded socket 478.

6.15.3 CPU Operating Voltages

The benefits of lower voltage are that with lower voltage comes lower overall power consumption. By consuming less power, the system is less expensive to run, but more importantly for portable or mobile systems, it runs much longer on existing battery technology. The second major benefit is that with less voltage and therefore less power consumption, less heat is produced. Processors that run cooler can be packed into systems more tightly and last longer. The third major benefit is that a processor running cooler on less power can be made to run faster. Lowering the voltage has been one of the key factors in enabling the clock rates of processors to go higher and higher. This is because the lower the voltage, the shorter the time needed to change a signal from low to high.

☞ *A voltage regulator built into the motherboard converts the power supply voltage into the various levels the processor core requires.*

6.15.4 Heat and Cooling Problems

It is highly recommended that all processors have a heat sink. The heat sink helps to allow for the processor to remain cool and therefore run more efficiently. Heat sinks with fans are referred to as active heatsinks.

When looking at a processor, also consider the heat sink that will be attached to that processor and ensure that the processor being purchased is compatible with that heat sink. A computer processor with a missing, bad or failing heat sink will cause the computer to lock up, cause errors or encounter other issues.

☞ *The power supply also powers the fans, or a liquid cooling system, which prevents the computer from overheating.*

6.15.5 Math Co-processor

Co-processor is a special purpose microprocessor which is used to speed up main processor job by taking over some of the main processor's work. Most common type of co-processor are math co-processor and graphic co-processor. A math co-processor helps main processor in performing mathematical calculations. Different mathematical operations performed by math co-processor are long division, trigonometric functions, roots and logarithms etc. A graphic co-processor help the main processor in carrying out video/graphic related operations.

Old system required a co-processor chips to be inserted into special socket on the motherboard, but the current generation of CPU's have math co-processor built inside the main processor itself.

6.15.6 Cache memory

A CPU cache is a cache memory used by the CPU of a computer to reduce the average time to access main memory. The Cache is a smaller, faster memory as the memory which stores copies of the data from the most frequently used main memory location.

The high-speed memory used for the Cache purpose is very costly that is the reason it is not used as the main memory of the computer. The information frequently required by the processor is kept in the Cache memory by the Cache controller. This Cache controller always tries to make sure that the data required by the processor in the next memory access is available in the Cache memory. This improves the speed of the computer very much because if the required data is in the cache memory it is made available to the CPU without any wait state. When the required data is available in the cache it is called a hit. In case of a cache hit the processor immediately reads or writes the data in the data cache line. The proportion of accesses that result in a cache hit is known as the hit rate, and is a measure of the effectiveness of the cache. When the required data is not available in the cache memory it is called a miss. In case of cache miss, most caches allocate new entry, which comprises the tag just missed and a copy of the data from memory. The reference can then be applied to the new entry just as in case of a hit. Misses are comparatively slow because they require the data to be transferred from main memory. This transfer incurs a delay since main memory is much slower than cache memory.

☞ *Cache memory is a very high speed memory built in the processor and it is used between main memory (RAM) and the processor.*

The performance of the cache depends on the following:

(a) Speed and size of the Cache memory
(b) The logic used to read data around the memory area read by the CPU.
(c) The logic used to guess next required data by the processor.
(d) Most of the new micro processors have the Cache memory added in the CPU chip itself to speed up the process even further. Even on these CPUs with built in internal Cache, you can add external Cache.

6.16 ARCHITECTURE OF MICROPROCESSOR

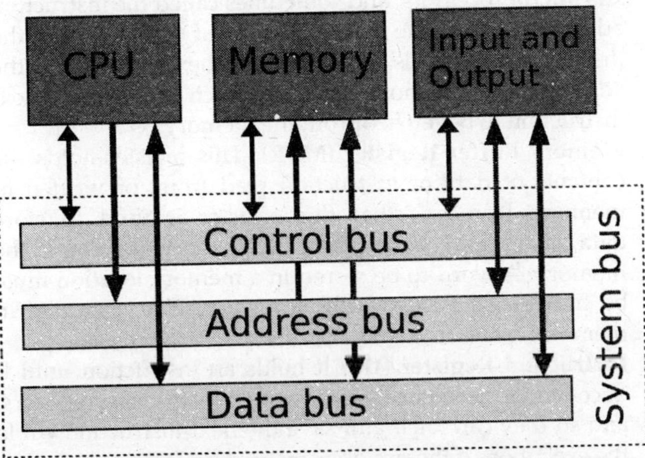

Figure 6.8 Architecture of Micoprocessor.

The architecture of microprocessor chip is a description of the physical layout of the various elements that form it. It directly affects how information and electrical current flows throughout the chip. A microprocessor can either have a CISC, or complex instruction set computer, architecture or a RISC, or reduced instruction set computer, architecture. The CISC architecture is more complex and has the ability to perform complex commands. The RISC architecture is simpler, smaller and faster. Microprocessor architecture has evolved from single core processors to multi-core processors. Processors with two or more cores are faster because they can process multiple pieces of information simultaneously. The basic components of microprocessor architecture include:

6.16.1 CPU

The CPU ("central processing unit," synonymous with "microprocessor," or even simply "processor") is often referred to as the "brain" of the computer. It does the bulk of the processing and co-ordinates all of the other pieces of hardware so your computer works as it should do.

A microprocessor is a computer processor which incorporates the functions of a computer's central processing unit (CPU) on a single integrated circuit (IC), or at most a few integrated circuits. A microprocessor is a controlling unit of a microcomputer, fabricated on a small chip capable of performing Arithmetic Logical Unit (ALU) operations and communicating with the other devices connected to it. The central processing unit is responsible for handling instructions passed to it by programs and input devices. The arithmetic logic unit handles the arithmetic and logic functions. The control unit is responsible for processing instructions that come from the computer's memory and activating the other components of the computer.

6.16.2 Input/Output Devices

Inputting refers to the process of entering data into the computer. Outputting: refers to the process of showing the information or data to the user. Input-output devices are also called as peripherals. The data is retrieved from memory or taken from an input device and the result of processing is stored in the memory or delivered to an appropriate output device, all as per the instructions.

☞ *Input/output instructions are the instructions used for interacting with user, i.e., getting data from the user or showing data to the user through monitor or printer.*

6.16.3 Memory

It stores both the instructions to be executed (i.e., the program) and the data involved. It usually consists of both RAMs (random-access memories) and ROMS (read-only memories).

6.17 INSIDE A MICROPROCESSOR

A microprocessor is a semiconductor chip, which is manufactured using the Large Scale integration (LSI) or Very Large Scale Integration (VLSI), which comprises Arithmetic Logic Unit, Control unit and Central Processing Unit (CPU) fabricated on a single chip.

6.17.1 Busses

A collection of wires through which data is transmitted from one part of a computer to another. Busses allow exchange of words between the blocks. A bus has a wire or line for each bit and thus allows exchange of all bits of a word in parallel. The processing of bits in the microprocessor is also in parallel. The busses can thus be viewed as data highways. You can think of a bus as a highway on which data travels within a computer. When used in reference to personal computers, the term bus usually refers to internal bus. This is a bus that connects all the internal computer components to the CPU and main memory. All buses consist of two parts - an address bus and a data bus. The data bus transfers actual data whereas the address bus transfers information about where the data should go. The control bus is used by the CPU to direct and monitor the actions of the other functional areas of the computer. It is used to transmit a variety of individual signals (read, write, interrupt, acknowledge, and so forth) necessary to control and coordinate the operations of the computer.

The size of a bus, known as its width, is important because it determines how much data can be transmitted at one time. For example, a 16-bit bus can transmit 16 bits of data, whereas a 32-bit bus can transmit 32 bits. The width of a bus is the number of signal lines that constitute the bus. Over the address bus, the microprocessor transmits the address of that I/O device or memory locations which it desires to access. This address is received by all the devices connected to the processor, but only the device which has been addressed responds. The data bus is used by the microprocessor to send and receive data to and from different devices (I/O and memory) including instructions stored in memory. Obviously the address bus is unidirectional and the data bus is bidirectional. The control bus is used for transmitting and receiving control signals between the microprocessor and various devices in the system.

6.17.2 ALU

All calculations including comparisons are made by the ALU. The data and instructions, stored in the primary memory prior to processing, are transferred to the ALU where processing takes place.

Results generated in the ALU are transferred to the primary memory. After completion of processing, the final results available in the primary memory are sent to an output device, such as printer or monitor.

ALUs are designed to perform the four basic arithmetic operations—add, subtract, multiply, divide—and logic operations or comparisons such as less than, equal to, or greater than.

6.17.3 Register

Registers are used to quickly accept, store, and transfer data and instructions that are being used immediately by the CPU. There are various types of registers those are used for various purpose. Among of the some mostly used registers named as AC or Accumulator, Data Register or DR, the AR or Address Register, Program Counter (PC), Memory Data Register (MDR), Index Register, Memory Buffer Register.

These registers are used for performing the various operations. While we are working on the system then these registers are used by the CPU for performing the operations. When we give some input to the system then the input will be stored into the registers and when the system gives us the results after processing then the result will also be from the registers. So that they are used by the CPU for processing the data which is given by the user.

The number of registers that a CPU has and the size of each (number of bits) help determine the power and speed of a CPU. For example, a 32-bit CPU is one in which each register is 32 bits wide. Therefore, each CPU instruction can manipulate 32 bits of data. The number of registers varies from computer-to-computer, there are some registers common to all computers. Functions of these registers are described below.

1. **Memory Address Register (MAR):** This register holds the memory addresses of data and instructions. This register is used to access data and instructions from memory during the execution phase of an instruction. Suppose CPU wants to store some data in the memory or to read the data from the memory. It places the address of the required memory location in the MAR.
2. **Program Counter (PC) Register:** The Program Counter (PC), commonly called the Instruction Pointer (IP) in Intel x86 microprocessors, and sometimes called the instruction address register. The PC keeps track of the address of the instructions which is to be executed next. So it holds the address of the memory location, which contains the next instruction to be fetched from the memory.
3. **Memory Buffer Register (MBR):** This register holds the contents of data or instruction read from, or written in memory. It means that this register is used to store data/instruction coming from the memory or going to the memory. A word to be stored in a memory location must be transferred first to MBR from where it is written in memory.
4. **Instruction Register (IR):** It holds an instruction until it decoded. Some computers have two instruction registers, and so they can fetch and save the next instruction while the execution of the previous instruction is going on.

5. **Index Register (IR):** A hardware element which holds a number that can be added to (or, in some cases, subtracted from) the address portion of a computer instruction to form an effective address. Also known as base register. An index register in a computer's CPU is a processor register used for modifying operand addresses during the run of a program.
6. **Accumulator Register (A):** This register is used for storing the results those are produced by the system. When the CPU will generate some results after the processing then all the results will be stored into the AC register.
7. **Input/Output Register:** It is used to communicate with input/output devices. All input information such as instructions and data are transferred an input device is found in this register. Similarly, all output information to be transferred to an output device is found in this register.

6.17.4 Control Unit

The control unit is responsible for processing instructions that come from the computer's memory and activating the other components of the computer.

☞ *Control unit holds the circuitry that controls the process of executing, decoding and fetching program instructions.*

How does the input device know that it is time for it to feed data into the storage unit? How does the ALU know what should be done with the data once they are received? And how is it that only the final results are sent to the output device and not the intermediate results? All this is possible because of the control unit of the computer system. By selecting, interpreting, and conforming to the execution of the program instructions, the control unit is able to maintain *order* and *direct* the working of the entire working of the computer system. Although it does not perform any processing on the data, the control unit acts as the central nervous system for all other components of the computer. It coordinates the entire computer system.

EXERCISE

1. What do you mean by the term microprocessor? How many types of microprocessors are available for use in a PC?
2. What is the difference between single and dual processors installed on the motherboard? For high-end PCs and mini computers, which one would you prefer and why?
3. What is the role played by the clock speed in a computer system? What is the typical value of clock frequency for a high-end PC.
4. Write the basic characteristics used to differentiate microprocessors.
5. What is the purpose of system clocks?
6. Differentiate between CISC and RISC.
7. Write an example of 64-bit microprocessor.
8. Define computer architecture.
9. Write short note on EPIC.
10. What is the use of Math Co-processor.
11. Discuss different processor modes.
12. What is difference between Data Bus and Address Bus?
13. What do you mean by Internal register?
14. Discuss different generations of microprocessor.

REVIEW QUESTIONS WITH ANSWERS

1. Multiple Choice

1.1 Add, Subtract, Divide, Multiply and Logic operations are performed by

a. Registers b. Control unit
c. ALU d. None of these

Ans (c)

1.2 Logical operations in a computer are done by

a. Registers b. Control unit
c. ALU d. None of the above

Ans (c)

1.3 A microprocessor works using digit(s):

a. 1 b. 0
c. 0 and 1 d. All of the above

Ans (c)

1.4 Characteristics of RISC

a. Pipelining b. Hardwired control
c. Instructions executes in one clock cycle d. All of the above

Ans (d)

1.5 Characteristic(s) of microprocessor

a. Instruction set b. Clock speed
c. Word Length d. All of the above

Ans (d)

1.6 MMX technology acronym for

a. Multimedia Extensions b. Matrix Math Extensions
c. Both (a) & (b) d. None of these

Ans (c)

1.7 The data transfer between CPU and other devices takes place in chunks of 8 bits, 16 bits or 32 bits depending upon the width of

a. Data bus b. Address bus
c. Control bus d. None of the above

Ans (a)

1.8 Which of the following is wrong statement in context with computer's main memory?

a. It is made up of DRAM chips.
b. It is made up of SRAM chips.
c. It losses its contents if power supply if off.
d. None of the above.

Ans (d)

1.9 The CPU of a computer understands which of the following language?

a. Machine b. Basic
c. English d. Hypertext Markup

Ans (a)

1.10 A physical memory divides the storage area into:

a. pages b. segments
c. sectors d. blocks

Ans (a)

2. State whether the following statements are True or False

2.1 Fetching of an instruction for execution is done by the control unit.

Ans True

2.2 The Dual Independent Bus (DIB) architecture was first implemented in the sixth-generation processors.

Ans True

2.3 DIB was created to improve processor bus bandwidth and performance.

Ans True

2.4 Chipset reduce the size of motherboard which is very much suitable for Personal Computers.

Ans True

2.5 Contents of SRAM (Static RAM) remain permanent as long as power is given to it.

Ans True

2.6 Cache memory holds copies of instructions and data that it gets from RAM to provide high speed access by the processor.

Ans True

2.7 RISC stands for Reduced Instruction Small Computer.

Ans False

2.8 AMD stands for Advanced Micro Devices.

Ans True

2.9 Passive heat sinks can cause quick overheating of the microprocessors.

Ans False

2.10 If data is permanently stored, even when power supply is off then memory is called volatile memory.

Ans False

2.11 At the cache level a chunk is called a memory page.

Ans False

2.12 Flash memory is used in digital camera, cellular phones, LAN switches etc.

Ans True

2.13 Socket 1 supports microprocessor that have 237 pins.

Ans False

2.14 Motherboard is also known as expansion board.

Ans False

3. Match the following:

3.1	Font side bus	a.	coupled to the speed of the processor core.
3.2	Back side bus	b.	coupled to the speed of the motherboard
3.3	Core i7 and Core i5	c.	Central Processing Unit (CPU)
3.4	Microprocessor	d.	Nehalem architecture
3.5	POST	e.	track 0, sector 1
3.6	Boot sector	f.	ROM-BIOS
3.7	Register	g.	a slot card
3.8	Cache	h.	memory locations inside the memory used in CPU
3.9	Co-processor	i.	High speed memory in the processor
3.10	Socket	j.	special purpose microprocessor

Ans 3.1 b 3.2 a 3.3 d 3.4 c 3.5 f
3.6 e 3.7 h 3.8 i 3.9 j 3.10 g

4. Fill in the blanks

4.1 The set of instructions that the microprocessor can execute are called ________.

Ans Instruction set.

4.2 Final results of processing, before releasing, to output unit are held in ________ unit.

Ans Memory

4.3 A control unit acts as ________ for all components of a computer.

Ans Central nervous system

4.4 A general purpose ________ holds data and intermediate result during the execution of a program.

Ans Register

4.5 The ________ memory is directly addressed by the CPU.

Ans Main

4.6 A ________ contains a small processor that holds certain information.

Ans Smart card

4.7 ________ holds the circuitry that controls the process of executing, decoding and fetching program instructions.

Ans Control unit

4.8 A ____________ is larger than the registers but smaller than the main memory.

Ans Cache memory

4.9 Socket 1 supports microprocessor that have ________ pins.

Ans 169

4.10 ______ is a Pentium microprocessor from Intel that is designed to run faster when playing multimedia applications.

Ans MMX

Q.5 (a) Write short notes on:

(i) Dynamic execution

(ii) Protected mode

Ans 5(a)(i)

Dynamic execution is first used in the P6 or sixth-generation processors. It is an innovative combination of three processing techniques designed to help the processor manipulate data more efficiently. Those techniques are multiple branch prediction, data flow analysis, and speculative execution.

Ans 5(a)(ii)

The name "protected" actually derives from the fact that processes run in different address spaces and that they are essentially protected from one another. If a process tries to access another's address space, it traps to the MMU hardware. In this mode, the full hardware support is enabled, and the processor can address the entire 32 bit address space.

Q.6 Write short note on microprocessor.

Ans 6
A Microprocessor is a CPU minus memory on a single chip. A microprocessor requires a power supply, clock and memory in order to function as a complete computer.

Q.7 What is Clock speed?

Ans 7
Clock speed is a measure of how quickly a computer completes basic computations and operations.

Q.8 Discuss important features of a RISC microprocessor.

Ans 8
RISC is an abbreviation for Reduced Instruction Set Computer. The important features of a RISC microprocessor are as follows:

- There are few instruction types and few addressing modes.
- Instruction set is simpler so that the processor runs faster. RISC machines have fixed and easily decoded instruction formats. All instructions are decoded by hardware.
- Most instructions are executed in a single cycle.
- Most RISC instructions involve only register-to-register operations. Memory access is limited only to load and store instructions.
- Several general-purpose registers and large cache memories are employed.
- Hardwired controls are used. Microprogramming is not used. In other words microcodes are not employed to generate instructions.

Q.9 Write properties of EPIC processor.

Ans 9
EPIC (Explicitly Parallel Instruction Computing) is a computer architecture that combines the best feature of RISC and CISC. A EPIC processor has the following properties:

- EPIC does not use fixed with instruction, rather aims at parallel processing of instructions.
- Programs must be written using sequential semantics with explicitly laid out parallelism.
- It uses a bundle of complex instructions that in addition to basic instruction also contain information on how to run the instruction in parallel with other instructions.

Q.10 What is the function of ALU?

Ans 10
Arithmetic and Logic unit (ALU): The arithmetic logic unit (ALU) of a computer system is the place where the actual execution of instructions takes place during the processing operation. To be more precise, all calculations are performed and all comparisons including logical are made in the ALU.

Q.11 How does Intel Core Dual Processor differ from multi-processor system?

Ans 11
A dual core processor is different from a multi-processor system. In the multi processor there are two separate CPUs with their own resources. In the dual core processor, resources are shared and the core resides on the same chip. A multi-processor system is faster than a system with a dual core processor, while a dual core system is faster than a single-core system. Dual core processors do not require a new motherboard, but can be used in existing boards that feature the correct socket.

Q.12 Define computer architecture.

Ans 12
Computer architecture is defined as the functional operation of the individual hardware unit in a computer system and the flow of information among the control of units.

Q.13 Compare RISC with CISC based machines.

Ans 13
Comparison of RISC and CISC is shown below.

	RISC	CISC
1.	RISC is an abbreviation for Reduced Instruction Set Computer.	CISC is an abbreviation for Complex Instruction Set Computers.
2.	The examples of RISC machines is Motorola PowerPC based computer.	The examples of CISC machines are: Intel 80486, Pentium, Motorola 68030, 68040 based computers.
3.	RISC microprocessors have relatively small instruction sets	CISC processors have relatively large instruction sets.
4.	RISC machines have fixed and easily decoded instruction formats.	CISC machines have variable-length instruction formats.
5.	Few addressing modes are used in RISC machines	Many addressing modes are used in CISC machines
6.	Hardwired controls are used in RISC machines	The CISC machines use microprogramming.
7.	RISC machine is 5 to 10 times faster than a CISC machine.	CISC machines are more complex and less efficient.
8.	Several general-purpose registers are employed in RISC machines	Small numbers of general-purpose registers are employed in CISC machines.

Q.14 What is the role of MAR and MDR?

Ans 14

The MAR (Memory Address Register) is used to hold the address of the location to or from which data are to be transferred and the MDR (Memory Data Register) contains the data to be written into or read out of the addressed location.

Q.15 What is the role of IR and PC?

Ans 15

Instruction Register (IR) contains the instruction being executed. Its output is available to the control circuits, which generate the timing signals for controlling the processing circuits needed to execute the instructions.

The Program Counter (PC) register keeps track of the execution of the program. It contains the memory address of the instruction currently being executed. During the execution of the current instruction, the contents of the PC are updated to correspond to the address of the next instructions to be executed.

Q.16 How can you say that CPU is the brain of the computer?

Ans 16

A CPU is the brain of a computer. Its primary function is to execute programs. Besides executing programs, the CPU also controls the operation of all other components such as memory, input and output devices. Under its control, programs and data are stored in the memory and outputs are displayed on the monitor screen or printed on paper, once processing has taken place.

A microprocessor contains a control unit and an arithmetic and logic unit (ALU). When main memory is added to a microprocessor, it forms a CPU.

☞ *The CPU of a small computer has a single microprocessor. But, the CPU of a large computer may contain a number of microprocessors on one or more circuit boards. Each microprocessor in a large CPU performs a specific task.*

Q.17 What is Heat sink?

Ans 17

It is highly recommended that all processors have a heat sink. The heat sink helps to allow for the processor to remain cool and therefore run more efficiently.

☞ *A computer processor with a missing, bad or failing heat sink will cause the computer to lock up, cause errors or encounter other issues.*

When looking at a processor, also consider the heat sink that will be attached to that processor and ensure that the processor being purchased is compatible with that heat sink.

Q.18 Write short note on Socket 478.

Ans 18

The Socket 478 is a CPU socket that utilizes the pin grid array and was used by Intel for the Pentium 4 and Celeron processors. Socket 478 was a replacement for Socket 423, which was found to be inadequate for processor speeds above 2.0 GHz. Intel released these processors in response to AMD's Socket 462 processors. Socket 478 processors ranged in speed from 1.4 GHz to 3.4 GHz. Intel eventually replaced the Socket 478 with LGA 775.

Q.19 What is SSE2?

Ans 19

SSE2 (Streaming SIMD Extensions 2), is one of the Intel SIMD (Single Instruction, Multiple Data) processor supplementary instruction sets first introduced by Intel with the initial version of the Pentium 4 in 2001. It extends the earlier SSE instruction set, and is intended to fully replace MMX.

Q.20 How dual processor is dual processor is different form single processor?

Ans 20

Computer with *dual processors* have two sockets on the motherboard for connecting two microprocessors working together. However, at a time, only one processor is active. When one processor is idle, the other is automatically active. This increases the speed of processing large volume of data. This type of computers reduces the possibility of data loss even if one processor fails to work.

PC with *Single processor* have only one socket on the motherboard so that they can work with only one processor. Such PCs with single processor are relatively slow for manipulating large volume of data.

Q.21 Write short note on 64-Bit Microprocessor.

Ans 21

64-bit microprocessors are used in powerful workstations and mini computers. An important 64-bit microprocessor based computer is DEC's Alpha Server. 64-bit microprocessors are mostly used in servers, minicomputers and high-end workstations. An example of 64-bit microprocessor is AMD Athlon. Operating systems such as Windows 7, Windows 8, Linux, BSD and Mac OS X also run on 64-bit microprocessor. These operating systems fully utilize the capabilities of such processors.

Q.22 What is Superscalar Execution?

Ans 22

Superscalar describes a microprocessor design that makes it possible for more than one instruction at a time to be executed during a single clock cycle . In a superscalar design, the processor or the instruction compiler is able to determine whether an instruction can be carried out independently of other sequential instructions, or whether it has a dependency on another instruction and must be executed in sequence with it. The processor then uses multiple execution units to simultaneously carry out two or more independent instructions at a time. Superscalar design is sometimes called "second generation RISC".

CHAPTER 7

ARM Processor

7.1 INTRODUCTION TO ARM PROCESSOR

An ARM (Advanced RISC Machines) processor is one of a family of CPUs based on the RISC (Reduced Instruction Set Computer) architecture developed by Advanced RISC Machines (ARM). ARM makes 32-bit and 64-bit RISC multi-coreprocessors. RISC processors are designed to perform a smaller number of types of computer instructions so that they can operate at a higher speed, performing more millions of instructions per second (MIPS). By stripping out unneeded instructions and optimizing pathways, RISC processors provide outstanding performance at a fraction of the power demand of CISC (Complex Instruction Set Computing) devices. The ARM processor's smaller size, reduced complexity and lower power consumption makes them suitable for increasingly miniaturized devices. ARM processors are microprocessors and are widely used in many of the mobile phones. They are also used in personal digital assistants (PDA), digital media and music layers, hand-held gaming systems, calculators, and even computer hard drives. Nowadays, there are several embedded architectures in use such as ARM architecture developed by ARM Ltd, Atmel's ARV architecture, TI's MSP430 architecture and many more.

☞ *ARM processor finds applications in digital TVs, set-top boxes, smart phones, mobile, laptops etc.*

Figure 7.1 ARM Processor.

7.2 HISTORY OF ARM PROCESSORS

It all began in the 1980s when Acorn Computers Ltd., spurred by the success of their platform BBC Micro wished to move on from simple CMOS processors to something more powerful, something that could stand strong against the IBM machines launched in 1981.

The first ARM processor-based computer was the Acorn Archimedes, released in 1987. Apple Computer became involved with helping to improve the ARM technology in the late 1980s, with their work resulting in the ARM6 technology in 1992. Later, Acorn used the ARM6-based ARM 610 processor in their Risc PC's in 1994. Today, the ARM architecture is licensed for use by many companies, including Apple, Cirrus Logic, Intel, LG, Microsoft, NEC, Nintendo, Nvidia, Sony, Samsung, Sharp, Texas Instruments, Yamaha, and many more. The latest developed ARM processor families include ARM11 and Cortex. ARM processors capable of 64-bit processing are currently in development.

☞ *Advanced RISC machine (ARM) is the first reduced instruction set computer RISC processor for commercial use, which is currently being developed by ARM holdings.*

7.3 ARM CORTEX SERIES

The ARM Cortex series of cores encompasses a very wide range of scalable performance options offering designers a great deal of choice and the opportunity to use the best-fit core for their application without being forced into a one-size-fits-all solution. The Cortex portfolio is split broadly into three main categories:

(a) Cortex-A application processor cores for a performance-intensive systems.

(b) Cortex-R high-performance cores for real-time applications.

(c) Cortex-M microcontroller cores for a wide range of embedded applications.

Cortex-A, Cortex-R and cortex-M series is targeted for different requirements and for different applications. It is important to know the parameters and features that separate them as there could be applications where three of them can fit in.

7.3.1 Cortex-A

Cortex-A processors provide a range of solutions for devices that make use of a rich operating system such as Linux or Android and are used in a wide range of applications from low-cost handsets to smartphones, tablet computers, set-top boxes and also enterprise networking equipment.

Cortex-A Characteristics

- High performance
- Cortex A devices offers power efficient performance for the targeted applications. It can be realized in mobile smart phone, tablet devices and wireless infrastructure applications.
- Best suited for accessing internet through mobile supports.

☞ *Cortex-A series provides varieties of application processors and it offers solution for the devices having strong operating systems and user applications*

7.3.2 Cortex-R

Moving on from Cortex-A, the Cortex-R series is the smallest ARM processor offering in terms of derivatives and possibly the least well known. The Cortex-R processors target high-performance real-time applications such as hard disk controllers (or solid state drive controllers), networking equipment and printers in the enterprise segment, consumer devices such as Blu-ray players and media players, and also automotive applications such as airbags, braking systems and engine management. ARM Cortex R-Real-time Embedded Processors offer high-performance computing solutions for embedded systems where reliability, high availability, fault tolerance and/or deterministic real-time responses are needed. Cortex-R processors are used in products where performance requirements and timing deadlines must always be met. In addition, Cortex-R processors are used in electronic systems which must be functionally safe to avoid hazardous situations, for example, in medical applications or autonomous systems. Cortex-R5, providing an area and power efficient solution, and the Cortex-R52, offering advanced integrated functional safety features and virtualization support. The Cortex-R7 and Cortex-R8 deliver very high performance and coherency to address the requirements of applications such as modems and storage. Applications include:

- Automotive braking systems
- Powertrain solutions
- Mass storage controller

Cortex-R Characteristics

The ARM Cortex-R real-time processors offer high-performance computing solutions for embedded systems where reliability, high availability, fault tolerance, maintainability and real-time responses are required.

- High performance - fast processing combined with a high clock frequency.
- Real-time - deterministic operation to ensure responsiveness.
- Reliable - detects errors and maintains system operation.
- Cost effective - features for optimal for performance, power and area.

☞ *Cortex Real-time Embedded processors have been developed for deeply embedded real-time applications where the need for low power and good interrupt behaviour are balanced with exceptional performance and strong compatibility with existing platforms.*

7.3.3 Cortex-M

Cortex-M series processors have been developed primarily for the microcontroller domain where the need for fast, highly deterministic, interrupt management is coupled with the desire for extremely low gate count and lowest possible power consumption. Applications include:

- Microcontrollers
- Mixed signal devices
- Smart sensors
- Automotive body electronics and airbags

Cortex-M Characteristics

- They are optimized for low cost rather than high performance.
- They are generally combined with FLASH, RAM and peripherals into a micro-controller chip.

7.3.4 ARM architecture profiles

The ARM architecture profiles are:

Application profile (Cortex-A)

Application profiles implement a traditional ARM architecture with multiple modes and support a virtual memory system architecture based on an MMU. These profiles support both ARM and Thumb instruction sets.

Real-time profile (Cortex-R)

Real-time profiles implement a traditional ARM architecture with multiple modes and support a protected memory system architecture based on an MPU.

Microcontroller profile (Cortex-M)

Microcontroller profiles implement a programmer's model designed for fast interrupt processing, with hardware stacking of registers and support for writing interrupt handlers in high-level languages. The processor is designed for integration into an FPGA and is ideal for use in very low power applications.

7.4 ARM PROCESSOR FEATURES

ARM processor core is the engine within the system that fetches ARM (and possibly Thumb) instructions from the memory and execute them. ARM cores are very small typically occupying just a few square millimeters of the chip area. Modern VLSI technology allows a large number of additional system components to be incorporated on the same chip.

ARM processor features include:

- Load/store architecture.
- An orthogonal instruction set.
- Most instructions are executed in single cycle only.
- Enhanced power-saving design i.e., Low power consumption.
- 64 and 32-bit execution states for scalable high performance.
- Hardware virtualization support. ARM has hardware support for JAVA. JAVA code is directly processed by hardware. So power consumption is very much reduced.

7.5 THE ARM ARCHITECTURE

ARM processors are a completely different architecture than the traditional chips favoured by Intel and AMD. ARM's Reduced Instruction Set Computing (RISC) processors are physically simpler than x86 processors, which means they cost less and use less power.

The ARM architecture is a simple hardware design allowing things to left off the chip. It provides small die-shaped chip which helps in reducing cost. Its low cost simple pipeline construction adds the benefits to embedded application. ARM allows an instruction set called "Thumb", which comprises 32-bit instructions to 16-bits, enabling programs to be coded much more density than standard RISC instruction set. Processors enabled to execute "Thumb" also allow 32-bit instructions to run on the same hence allowing 16-bit and 32-bit instructions to mix together without affecting the performance maintaining powerful computing capabilities. The instruction set of in ARM processor are classified as ARM instruction set, Thumb instruction set and Jazelle mode. ARM mode is a standard 32-bit instruction set. A Thumb instruction set is a 16-bit compressed form that provides better performance than Complex Instruction Set Computer. Jazelle DBX allows some ARM processor to execute java byte codes.

An ARM processor consists of 31 general purpose 32-bit register. Sixteen registers namely R0-R15 are visible, which means they can be modified by the user whereas other registers help to speed up the execution process. Some registers play some special roles like R14 acts as a link register (LR), R15 acts as a Program Counter (PC) and R13 acts as a Stack Pointer.

The ARM processor is constructed from the following components:

7.5.1 Address Register

The register holds the 32 bit address which is released on the Address Bus to reference a memory location. The address in this register is incremented by a suitable value whereever the next word/half word / byte are to be accessed. Byte means 8 bits. Halfword means 16 bits (two bytes). Word means 32 bits (four bytes).

7.5.2 Register Bank

This is a group of 31 32 bit registers plus an additional 6 status registers which are bank switched depending on the mode of operation.

7.5.3 Multiplier

The multiplier factor has three 32-bit inputs and the inputs return from the register file. The multiplier output is only the 32 least significant bits of the product.

7.5.4 Barrel Shifter

This unit provides the rotate and shift operations for the CPU. Shifted data is presented to the ALU as one operand to realize more complex computations. Barrel Shifter preprocesses data, before it enters ALU. Barrel Shifter is basically a combinational logic circuit, which can shift data to left or right by arbitrary number of position in same cycle. Increment or Decrement logic can update register content for sequential access.

☞ *The arithmetic, logical, comparisons, and move instructions can all use the inline barrel shifter, which pre-processes the second register before it enters into the ALU.*

7.5.5 ALU

The ALU has two 32-bits inputs. The primary comes from the register file, whereas the other comes from the shifter.

7.5.6 Write Data Register

This register holds the data to be released to the output devices over the data bus lines.

7.5.7 Instruction Pipeline

A pipeline is the mechanism a RISC processor uses to execute instructions. Instruction Pipeline is the 3 stage instruction pipeline implemented in the ARM7TDMI. The pipeline's output is realised to the Instruction Decoder and control Logic unit.

7.5.8 Instruction Decoder & Control Logic Unit

The instruction decoder translates instructions before they are executed. Each instruction executed belongs to a particular instruction set. This unit also generates the control signals to sequence the instruction execution. This unit also generates the control signals needed for the processor core to interface with the memory units over the processor's internal buses. It also generates the required signals to manage the intrrupts and exchange data over the ARM High Performance Bus (AHB) and the ARM Peripheral Bus (APB).

The Advanced Microcontroller Bus Architecture (AMBA) was introduced in 1996 and has been widely adopted as the on-chip bus architecture used for ARM processors. The first AMBA buses introduced were the ARM System Bus (ASB) and the ARM Peripheral Bus (APB). Later ARM introduced another bus design, called the ARM High Performance Bus (AHB).

The ARM has seven basic operating modes:

- **User** : unprivileged mode under which most tasks run.
- **FIQ** : entered when a high priority (fast) interrupt is raised.
- **IRQ** : entered when a low priority (normal) interrupt is raised.
- **Supervisor** : entered on reset and when a Software Interrupt instruction is executed.
- **Abort** : used to handle memory access violations.

- **Undef** : used to handle undefined instructions.
- **System** : privileged mode using the same registers as user mode.

7.5.9 Important registers in ARM

There are two important registers in ARM, namely Current Program Status Register (CPSR) and Saved Program Status Register (SPSR). CPSR is similar to PSWR register in 8051 micro-controller, which indicate some important flag bits like carry bits and zero flag bits. Whereas SPSR is used in execution modes. Whenever exception occurs the content of CPSR are copied in SPSR.

7.5.10 ARM Processor Modes

The processor mode determines which registers are active and the access rights to the Current Program Status Register (CPSR) itself. There are seven modes of operations. These modes are categorized as user mode, prevailed mode and exception mode. User mode is a normal program execution mode in which the system resources are unavailable. If some exception occurs, then the mode is changed to the exception mode. In exception mode, all system resources are available.
Each processor mode is either privileged or nonprivileged: A privileged mode allows full read-write access to the CPSR. Conversely, a nonprivileged mode only allows read access to the control field in the CPSR but still allows read-write access to the condition flags. There are seven processor modes in total: six privileged modes (abort, fast interrupt request, interrupt request, supervisor, system, and undefined) and one nonprivileged mode (user).

7.6 ARM BUS TECHNOLOGY

Embedded systems use different bus technologies than those designed for x86 PCs. The most common PC bus technology, the Peripheral Component Interconnect (PCI) bus, connects such devices as video cards and hard disk controllers to the x86 processor bus. This type of technology is external or off-chip (i.e., the bus is designed to connect mechanically and electrically to devices external to the chip) and is built into the motherboard of a PC. In contrast, embedded devices use an on-chip bus that is internal to the chip and that allows different peripheral devices to be interconnected with an ARM core. The ARM processor core is a bus master-a logical device capable of initiating a data transfer with another device across the same bus. Peripherals tend to be bus slaves-logical devices capable only of responding to a transfer request from a bus master device. A bus has two architecture levels. The first is a physical level that covers the electrical characteristics and bus width (16, 32, or 64 bits). The second level deals with protocol-the logical rules that govern the communication between the processor and a peripheral. ARM is primarily a design company. It seldom implements the electrical characteristics of the bus, but it routinely specifies the bus protocol.

7.7 PROGRAMMER'S MODEL OF THE ARM

The ARM Instruction Set Architecture (ISA), also called the programmer's model provides 16 general purpose registers in the user mode. This ISA includes all the core ARM instructions as well as some of the newer features in the ARM instruction set.
All instructions in the ARM ISA are conditional with the normal execution instructions also being accompanied by condition AL. There are 14 conditions available excluding AL. The instruction set added many feathers to its cap as and when the generations grew.

7.8 ARM PROCESSOR FAMILY

Within each ARM family, there are a number of variations of memory management cache, and TCM processor extensions. ARM continues to expand both the number of families available and the different variations within each family. The postfix numbers 7, 9, 10, and 11 indicate different core designs. The ascending number equates to an increase in performance and sophistication. The numbers quoted can vary greatly and are directly dependent upon the type and geometry of the manufacturing process, which has a direct effect on the frequency (MHz) and power consumption (watts). ARM Processor has following family:

- ARM7
- ARM9
- ARM10
- ARM11
- CORTEX
- Specialized Processors

7.8.1 ARM7

The ARM7 family is a range of low-power 32-bit RISC microprocessor cores optimized for cost and power-sensitive consumer applications. The ARM7 family incorporates the Thumb 16-bit instruction set - enabling 32-bit performance at 8/16-bit system cost. Widely used in many applications such as palmtop computers, portable instruments, smart card. ARM processors up to ARM7 employ a simple 3-stage pipeline with stages like fetch, decode and execute.

- Fetch loads an instruction from memory.
- Decode identifies the instruction to be executed.
- Execute processes the instruction and writes the result back to a register.

Each instruction takes a single cycle to complete after the pipeline is filled. The three instructions are placed into the pipeline sequentially. (See Figure 7.2).

Figure 7.2 ARM7 Three-stage pipeline.

7.8.2 ARM9

The ARM9 family was announced in 1997. Because of its five-stage pipeline, the ARM9 processor can run at higher clock frequencies than the ARM7 family. The extra stages improve the overall performance of the processor. The memory system has been redesigned to follow the Harvard architecture, which separates the data and instruction. The ARM9 Family is 32-bit RISC Processor with ARM and Thumb instruction sets which supports five-stage pipeline. (See Figure 7.3).

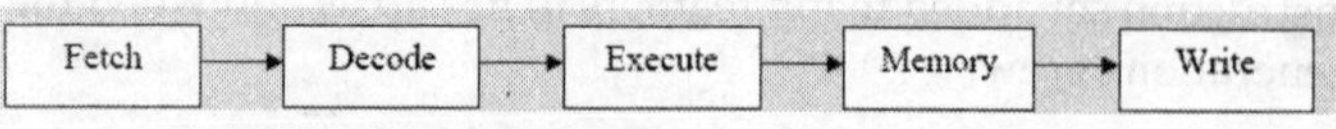

Figure 7.3 ARM9 Five-stage pipeline.

7.8.3 ARM10

The ARM10, announced in 1999, was designed for performance. It extends the ARM9 pipeline to six stages. It also supports an optional vector floating-point (VFP) unit, which adds a seventh stage to the ARM10 pipeline. The VFP significantly increases floating-point performance. (See Figure 7.4).

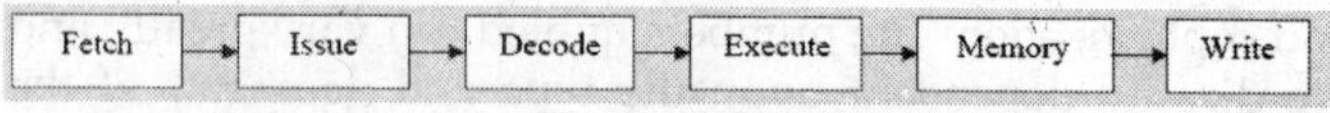

Figure 7.4 ARM10 seven-stage pipeline.

7.8.4 ARM11

The ARM11 Family is 32-bit RISC processor with ARM, Thumb and DSP instruction sets. It uses Harvard Architecture and supports eight-stage Pipelines except ARM1156T2 uses nine-stage pipeline. It is widely used in automotive and industrial control systems, 3D graphics, security critical applications.

7.8.5 CORTEX

ARM architecture has evolved over the time and ARM core also available in latest cortex series, again to reuse the term A R M. Cortex Series comes in three different profiles as ARM Cortex - A series, ARM Cortex - R series, ARM Cortex - M series.

Cortex - A series provides varieties of application processors and it offers solution for the devices having strong operating systems and user applications consisting of low-cost-handset.

Cortex - R series consists of Real Time Processors which offers high performance computing solution, very good fault tolerance, detect errors thereby maintain reliable system operation and real time response for embedded systems.

Cortex - M series consists of Microcontroller based processors having energy efficient upward compatible processor, code reuse facility and better connectivity.

7.8.6 Specialized Processors

StrongARM was originally co-developed by Digital Semiconductor and is now exclusively licensed by Intel Corporation. It is has been popular for PDAs and applications that require performance with low power consumption. It is a Harvard architecture with separate D+I caches. StrongARM was the first high-performance ARM processor to include a five-stage pipeline, but it does not support the Thumb instruction set. Intel's XScale is a follow-on product to the StrongARM and offers dramatic increases in performance. At the time of writing, XScale was quoted as being able to run up to 1 GHz.

7.9 INSTRUCTION SET DESIGN

7.9.1 ARM instruction set

ARM allows an instruction set called "Thumb", which comprises 32-bit instructions to 16-bits, enabling programs to be coded much more density than standard RISC instruction set. 32-bit instructions, support load-store architecture, conditionally execution, use 3-address format. Today many embedded applications like smart phones, set-top boxes, digital television, digital camera use ARM processors due to their cost effectiveness and low power consumption. ARM architecture is compatible with all four major OS i.e., Symbian OS, Palm OS, Windows and Android OS. ARM Instruction Set supports six different types of instructions:

Data Processing Instructions

Data Processing Instructions used to manipulate data in general-purpose registers, employ a 3-address format, support barrel shifter.

Arithmetic Instructions: ADD, ADC, SUB, SBC, RSB, RSC
Move Instructions: MOV, MVN
Bit-Wise Logical Instructions: AND, EOR, ORR, BIC
Comparison Instructions: TST, TEQ, CMP, CMN
Multiply Instructions: MUL, MLA

Branch Instructions

Branch Instructions change the flow of sequential execution of instructions and force to modify the program counter. Branch (B) jumps in a range of +/-32 MB. Branch with link (BL) suitable for subroutine call by storing the address of next instructions after BL into the link register and restore the program counter from the link register while returning from subroutine.

Load/Store Instructions

Load/Store Instructions transfer data between memory and registers. Single Register Transfer Instructions is used to move a single data item in and out of register. Multiple Register Transfer Instructions are any subset or all the 16 registers loaded from or stored to memory but increase interrupt latency.

Software Interrupt Instruction

The software interrupt instruction causes a software interrupt that forces the processor into SVC mode; this instruction invokes privileged operating system routines.

Program Status Register Instructions

The program status register instructions write and read to the CPSR and SPSR.

Co-processor Instructions

Co-processors can be attached to the ARM processor. A co-processor extends the processing features of a core by extending the instruction set or by providing configuration registers. More than one co-processor can be added to the ARM core via the co-processor interface. Co-processor used to extend the instruction set, to control on-chips functions (caches and memory management) and for additional computations.
There are three types of co-processor instructions:

Data-processing instructions These start a co-processor-specific internal operation.

Data transfer instructions These transfer co-processor data to or from memory. The address of the transfer is calculated by the ARM processor.

Register transfer instructions These allow a co-processor value to be transferred to or from an ARM register, or a pair of ARM registers.

7.9.2 Thumb instruction set

16-bit instructions, support load-store architecture, unconditionally execution (branch instructions), use 2-address format.

7.9.3 Jazelle instruction set

8-bit instructions, Javabyte code execution.

7.10 ARM PIPELINES

A pipeline is the mechanism a RISC processor uses to execute instructions. Using a pipeline speeds up execution by fetching the next instruction while other instructions are being decoded and executed. A 3 stage pipeline is the simplest form of pipeline that does not suffer from the problems such as read before write. In a pipeline, when one instruction is executed, second instruction is decoded and third instruction will be fetched. This is executed in a single cycle.
ARM processors up to ARM7 employ a simple 3-stage pipeline with stages like fetch, decode and execute i.e., a 3 stage pipeline fetches the instructions, then decodes it and then finally executes the instruction. ARM9 five-stage pipeline. ARM10 six-stage pipeline. The ARM10 increases the pipeline length still further by adding a sixth stage.

7.11 CORE EXTENSIONS

They improve performance, manage resources, and provide extra functionality and are designed to provide flexibility in handling particular applications. Core extensions speed up and organize main memory as well as extend the instruction set. There are three hardware extensions ARM wraps around the core: cache and tightly coupled memory, memory management, and the co-processor interface.

7.12 MEMORY MANAGEMENT

Embedded systems often use multiple memory devices. It is usually necessary to have a method to help organize these devices and protect the system from applications trying to make inappropriate accesses to hardware. This is achieved with the assistance of memory management hardware.
ARM cores have three different types of memory management hardware-no extensions providing no protection, a memory protection unit (MPU) providing limited protection, and a Memory Management Unit (MMU) providing full protection. Nonprotected memory is fixed and provides very little flexibility. It is normally used for small, simple embedded systems that require no protection from rogue applications. MPUs employ a simple system that uses a limited number of memory regions. These regions are controlled with a set of special co-processor registers, and each region is defined with specific access permissions. This type of memory management is used for systems that require memory protection but don't have a complex memory map.
The ARM Memory Management Unit (MMU) performs two primary functions: First, it translates virtual addresses into physical addresses. Second, it controls memory access by checking permissions. The MMU hardware which performs these functions consists of a Translation Lookaside Buffer (TLB), access control logic and translation table walking logic. The ARM MMU supports memory accesses based on either Sections or Pages. Memory management by sections is a one-level paging scheme. The level-1 page table contains section descriptors, each of which specifies a 1MB block of memory. Memory management by paging is a two-level paging scheme. The level-1 page table contains page table descriptors, each of which specifies a level-2 page table. The level-2 page table contains page descriptors, each of which specifies a page frame in memory and access control bits. The ARM paging scheme supports two different page sizes. Small pages consist of 4KB blocks of memory and large pages consist of 64KB blocks of memory. The ARM MMU also supports the concept of domains. A domain is a memory area that can be defined with individual access rights.

7.13 ARM NOMENCLATURE

ARM uses the nomenclature to describe the processor implementations. The letters and numbers after the word "ARM" indicate the features a processor:
ARM{x}{y}{z}{T}{D}{M}{I}{E}{J}{F}{-S}
x-family
y-memory management/protection unit
z-cache
T-Thumb 16-bit decoder
D-JTAG debug
M-fast multiplier
I-EmbeddedICE macrocell
E-enhanced instructions (assumes TDMI)

J-Jazelle
F-vector floating-point unit
S-synthesizible version

7.14 OVERVIEW OF THUMB MODE

The thumb mode has been featured by the processors from ARM7TDMI to help in improving the compiled code density. The 16 bit instructions are executed in this mode and they are mapped to the normal ARM instructions. The opcodes that are smaller in size show less functionality in thumb. Some opcodes cannot access all the registers and only the braches can be opted as conditional. Smaller opcodes are more efficient. Usually a very small amount of RAM is accessible with a datapath of 32 bit in embedded hardware. Rest of it is accessed by a 16 bit path. Therefore it becomes logical to use 16 bit thumb code and the wider instructions can be placed in a memory which is accessible by 32 bit. The ARM7TDI was the first process having a thumb instruction decoder.
The Thumb-2 technology was introduced on ARM1156 core and it was announced in the year 2003. It increases the breadth of the instruction set by adding 32 bit instructions to the limited 16 bit instruction set of the previously mentioned technology Thumb. The code density resembling the Thumb is achieved by the Thumb-2 and also its performance is similar to the ARM instruction set on a memory of 32 bit. The instruction set Thumb-2 is supported by all the ARMv7 chips. But some of the chips for example cortex-M3 only supports the Thumb-2 instruction set.
The ThumbEE first appeared in the Cortex-A8 processor. The instruction set is increased as compared to the Thumb-2 instruction set. Thumb EE is used for languages such as Python, Limbo, Java, C# and Perl etc., smaller codes are outputted by the JIT compilers and there is no significant impact on the performance.

7.15 JAZELLE

Besides the ARM and Thumb modes, a new technology has been introduced which allows the execution of Java bytecode in hardware. This technology is known as Jazelle. It is most prominently used in mobile phones so that the execution speed of Java EM games can be increased. The Java Virtual Machine performs the complicated operations in software while the Java bytecodes are usually run on hardware.

7.16 ADVANCED SIMD (NEON)

The advanced SIMD (Single Instruction Multiple Data) also known as the NEON technology, is a combination of 128 bit and 64 bit SIMD instruction set. It provides acceleration for the applications of signal processing and media. Its execution operations include decoding of MP3 audio on 10 MHz CPUs, and runs.

7.17 GSM AMR

GSM AMR (Adaptive Multi Rate) speech codec at 13 Mhz. It supports up to 64 bit integers and also handles games and graphics as well as audio/video processing. The SIMD in NEON can support 16 operations at a time.

7.18 LPC 2148 MICROCONTROLLER

The ARM processors have a less number of transistors because they have a reduced instruction set, which allows a smaller size for the IC. Thereby being space efficient also. Most of the electronic devices such as tablets, mobiles, smart phones and other mobile devices consist of these processors. By combining the ARM microprocessor with RAM, ROM and other peripherals in one single chip, we get an ARM microcontroller, for example, LPC2148.
LPC2148 is the widely used IC from ARM-7 family. It is manufactured by Philips and it is pre-loaded with many inbuilt peripherals making it more efficient and a reliable option for the beginners as well as high end application developer.
LPC2148 has 32kB on chip SRAM and 512kB on chip FLASH memory. This chip has built in support up to 2kB end point USB RAM. This memory is more than enough for almost all applications. The LPC2148 has 512kB flash memory. This memory may used for both code and data storage. The flash memory can be programmed by various ways:

- Using serial built in JTAG Interface.
- Using In-System Programming (ISP).
- By means of In-Application Programming (IAP) capabilities.

Features of LPC2148

- 8 to 40 kB of on-chip static RAM.
- 32 to 512 kB of on-chip flash program memory.
- 128 bit wide interface/accelerator enables high speed 60 MHz operation.
- In-System/In-Application Programming (ISP/IAP) via on-chip boot-loader software.
- Embedded ICE RT and Embedded Trace interfaces offer real-time debugging with the on-chip Real Monitor software and high speed tracing of instruction execution.
- USB 2.0 Full Speed compliant Device Controller with 2 KB of endpoint RAM. In addition, the LPC2146/8 provides 8 kB of on-chip RAM accessible to USB by DMA.
- Low power real-time clock with independent power and dedicated 32 kHz clock input.
- Vectored interrupt controller with configurable priorities and vector addresses.
- Multiple serial interfaces including two UARTs (16C550), two Fast I2C-bus(400 kbit/s), SPI and SSP with buffering and variable data length capabilities.

7.18.1 Architectural Overview

Over the last few years, the ARM architecture has become the most pervasive 32-bitarchitecture in the world, with wide range of ICs available from various IC manufacturers. ARM processors are embedded in products ranging from cell/mobile phones to automotive braking systems. A world wide community of ARM partners and third-party vendors has developed among semiconductor and product design companies, including hardware engineers, system designers, and software developers. ARM is an architecture which is used in many processors and microcontrollers. The ARM architecture licensed to companies that want to manufacture ARM-based CPUs or System-on-Chip products. This enables the companies to develop their own processors compliant with the ARM instruction set architecture. ARM7 is one of the widely used micro-controller family in embedded system application. LPC2148 is the widely used IC from ARM-7 family. It is manufactured by Philips and it is pre-loaded with many inbuilt peripherals making it more efficient and a reliable option for the beginners as well as high end application developer.

The ARM architecture is based on Reduced Instruction Set Computer (RISC) principles, and the instruction set and related decode mechanism are much simpler. This simplicity results in a high instruction throughput and impressive real-time interrupt response from a small and cost-effective processor core. Pipeline techniques are employed so that all parts of the processing and memory systems can operate continuously. Typically, while one instruction is being executed, its successor is being decoded, and a third instruction is being fetched from memory. The ARM7TDMI-S processor also employs a unique architectural strategy known as Thumb, which makes it ideally suited to high-volume applications with memory restrictions, or applications where code density is an issue. Various 32-bit timers, single or dual 10-bit ADC(s), 10-bit DAC, PWM channels and 45 fast GPIO lines with up to nine edge or level sensitive external interrupt pins make these microcontrollers particularly suitable for industrial control and medical systems.

LPC2148 provides 32kB of static RAM which may be used for code and/or data storage. It may be accessed as 8-bit, 16-bit and 32-bits.

LPC2148 has 512kB on chip FLASH memory. This chip has built in support up to 2kB end point USB RAM. This memory is more than enough for almost all applications.

It has Vectored interrupt controller (VIC) with configurable priorities and vector addresses. The Vectored Interrupt Controller (VIC) accepts all of the interrupt request inputs and categorizes them as Fast Interrupt Request (FIQ), vectored Interrupt Request (IRQ), and non-vectored IRQ as defined by programmable settings. The programmable assignment scheme means that priorities of interrupts from the various peripherals can be dynamically assigned and adjusted. Fast interrupt request (FIQ) has the highest priority. If more than one request is assigned to FIQ, the VIC combines the requests to produce the FIQ signal to the ARM processor. The fastest possible FIQ latency is achieved when only one request is classified as FIQ, because then the FIQ service routine does not need to branch into the interrupt service routine but can run from the interrupt vector location. If more than one request is assigned to the FIQ class, the FIQ service routine will read a word from the VIC that identifies which FIQ source(s) is (are) requesting an interrupt.

Device pins that are not connected to a specific peripheral function are controlled by the General purpose Parallel I/O (GPIO) registers. Pins may be dynamically configured as inputs or outputs. Separate registers allow setting or clearing any number of outputs simultaneously.

7.18.2 Analog-to-Digital (ADC) in LPC2148

Microcontrollers are very useful especially when it comes to communicate with other devices, such as sensors, motors, switches, memory and even other microcontroller. As we all know many interface methods have been developed over years to solve complex problem of balancing need of features, cost, size, power consumption, reliability etc. ADC is simple and efficient technique to read data from sensor.

☞ *An analog-to-digital converter (abbreviated ADC, A/D or A to D) is a device that converts a continuous physical quantity (usually voltage) to a digital number that represents the quantity's amplitude.*

Analog to Digital Converter (ADC) is used to convert analog signal/voltage into its equivalent digital number so that microcontroller can process that numbers and make it human readable. The ADC characterized by resolution. The resolution of ADC indicates the number of digital values. The ADC in LPC2148 ARM7 Microcontroller is 10-bit successive approximation analog to digital converter. In LPC2148 microcontroller have in-built 10-bit ADC. So for 10-bit ADC resolution is 10-bit and maximum value will be 210=1024. This means our digital value or discrete level lies between 0 to 1023. The features are listed as:

- LPC2148 has two inbuilt ADC Modules, named as ADC0 & ADC1.
- ADC operating frequency is 4.5 MHz (max.), operating frequency decides the conversion time.
- Supports power down mode.
- Burst conversion mode for single or multiple inputs.
- 10 bit successive approximation analog to digital converter.
- Optional conversion on transition on input pin or Timer Match signal.
- Global Start command for both converters

7.18.3 Digital-to-Analog (DAC) in LPC2148

DAC is Single 10-bit D/A converter provides variable analog output. Feature of DAC are

- 10 bit digital to analog converter.
- Resistor string architecture.
- Buffered output
- Power-down mode
- Selectable speed vs. power.

7.18.4 Universal Asynchronous Receiver & Transmitter (UART)

An UART, Universal Asynchronous Receiver & Transmitter is responsible for performing the main task in serial communications with computers. The device changes in coming parallel information to serial data which can be sent on a communication line. A second UART can be used to retrieve the information. The UART performs all the tasks, timing, parity checking etc., needed for the communication.

7.18.5 I2C-bus serial I/O controller

The LPC2148 contain two I2C-bus controllers. The I2C-bus is bidirectional, for inter-IC control using only two wires: a Serial Clock Line (SCL), and a Serial Data Line (SDA). Each device is recognized by a unique address and can operate as either a receiver-only device (e.g., an LCD driver or a transmitter with the capability to both receive and send information (such as memory)). Transmitters and/or receivers can operate in either master or slave mode, depending on whether the chip has to initiate a data transfer or is only addressed. The I2C-bus is a multi-master bus, it can be controlled by more than one bus master connected to it. It has following features:

- The I2C-bus implemented in LPC2148 supports bit rates up to 400 kbit/s.
- Bidirectional data transfer between masters and slaves.
- Arbitration between simultaneously transmitting masters without corruption of serial data on the bus.
- Serial clock synchronization allows devices with different bit rates to communicate via one serial bus.

7.18.6 SPI serial I/O controller

The LPC2148 each contain one SPI controller. The SSP controller is capable of operation on a SPI, 4-wire SSI, or Microwire bus. It can interact with multiple masters and slaves on the bus. However, only a single master and a single slave can communicate on the bus during a given data transfer. The SSP supports full duplex transfers, with data frames of 4 bits to 16 bits of data flowing from the master to the slave and from the slave to the master.

7.18.7 Crystal Oscillator

On-chip integrated oscillator operates with an external crystal in range from 1 MHz to 25 MHz. The Wake-up Timer monitors the crystal oscillator as the means of checking whether it is safe to begin code execution.

7.18.8 Power Control

The LPC2148 supports two reduced power modes: Idle mode and Power-down mode. In Idle mode, execution of instructions is suspended until either a reset or interrupt occurs.

EXERCISE

1. What is multicore processor?
2. Write features of LPC2148.
3. Write short note on Specialized Processors.
4. Briefly explain Jazelle technology.
5. How Cortex-M differ from Cortex-R series.
6. What is Thumb instruction set.
7. Explain ARM7 and ARM9 with a neat diagram.
8. Explain different ARM Processor family.
9. Write features of ARM Core.
10. Write benefits of reduce operating voltage for processors.

REVIEW QUESTIONS WITH ANSWERS

1. Multiple Choice

1.1 ARM is a family of instruction set architectures for computer processors based on
a. RISC b. CISC
c. Both (a) and (b) d. None of these
Ans (a)

1.2 ARM modes
a. User mode b. IRQ mode
c. FIQ mode d. All of these
Ans (d)

1.3 The features of LPC2148 Microcontroller:
a. Based on 16 bit/32 bit b. Supports 32 bit timers/counters
c. Supports PWM (six outputs) d. All of these
Ans (d)

1.4 It is used to reduce ripple factor of DC output available from rectifier end.
a. Transformer b. Rectifier
c. Filter d. Regulator
Ans (c)

1.5 It is used to regulate DC supply output.
a. Regulator b. Rectifier
c. Filter d. None of these
Ans (a)

2. State whether the following statements are True or False

2.1 The RISC processors are higher in speed because they perform a small number of instructions.
Ans True

2.2 ARM is well-known for the design of mobile, power-efficient processor designs.
Ans True

2.3 LPC2148 is manufactured by NXP Semiconductor (Philips).
Ans - True

2.4 ARM makes 32-bit and 64-bit RISC multi-core processors.
Ans True

2.5 The Cortex-A15 is the first processor from ARM to incorporate hardware support for data management and arbitration of virtualized software environments.
Ans True

2.6 Application profiles implement a traditional ARM architecture with multiple modes and support a protected memory system architecture based on an MPU.

Ans False

2.7 Jumpers are two-or three hole connectors that connect pins on the motherboard.

Ans True

2.8 PnP feature enables the system to automatically search for new hardware connected to the system.

Ans True

2.9 BIOS is encoded in the Read Only memory of a PC.

Ans True

2.10 Cartridge used in a printer contains ink for printing.

Ans True

2.11 Microprocessor are always inserted in specific sockets made for particular model.

Ans True

2.12 HT Technology converts a single physical processor into two virtual processors.

Ans True

2.13 SSE2 includes all the previous MMX and SSE instructions.

Ans True

2.14 80286 was the first CPU to have protected mode.

Ans True

2.15 A status register consisting of a few flip-flops called condition flags.

Ans True

3. Match the following:

3.1	IRQ mode	a.	all normal application run under this mode
3.2	FIQ mode	b.	vectored (priority based) interrupt handler
3.3	User mode	c.	all fast interrupt data transfer or channel process service
3.4	System mode	d.	converts AC supply into DC
3.5	Rectifier	e.	all operating related task

Ans 3.1 b 3.2 c 3.3 a 3.4 e 3.5 d

4. Fill in the blanks

4.1 _____ is one of the widely used micro-controller family in embedded system application.

Ans ARM7

4.2 Modes other than User mode are collectively known as _________.

Ans Privileged modes

4.3 ______ mode !entered after a data or instruction Prefetch Abort exception.

Ans Abort

4.4 ________ mode is protected mode for the operating system.

Ans Supervision

4.5 A ________ is a small device that controls other equipment.

Ans Microprocessor

Q.5 (a) Write short notes on

(i) Thumb mode

(ii) JAZELLE

Ans 5(a)(i)

The thumb mode has been featured by the processors from ARM7TDMI to help in improving the compiled code density. The 16 bit instructions are executed in this mode and they are mapped to the normal ARM instructions. The opcodes that are smaller in size show less functionality in thumb. Some opcodes cannot access all the registers and only the braches can be opted as conditional. Smaller opcodes are more efficient. Usually a very small amount of RAM is accessible with a datapath of 32 bit in embedded hardware.

Ans 5(a)(ii)

Besides the ARM and Thumb modes, a new technology has been introduced which allows the execution of Java bytecode in hardware. This technology is known as Jazelle. It is most prominently used in mobile phones so that the execution speed of Java EM games can be increased. The Java Virtual Machine performs the complicated operations in software while the Java bytecodes are usually run on hardware.

Q.6 What is ARM?

Ans 6

ARM-Advanced RISC Machine is a 32-bit RISC (Reduced Instruction Set Computer) processor architecture developed by ARM Holdings. ARM is an architecture which is used in many processors and microcontrollers. ARM is one of the major options available for embedded system developer. ARM processors are embedded in products ranging from cell/mobilephones to automotive braking systems.

Q.7 Differentiate between microcontrollers and microprocessors.

Ans 7

Microcontrollers (embedded processors) are processors (or specialized microprocessors) that have many peripherals to interact with real-world sensors and actuators. Microcontrollers are typically employed in scenarios that must have low power consumption, operate fan-less, thus must have low power dissipation. Also, often micro-controllers run relatively simpler set of instructions.

Microprocessors (Application processors) usually are for general-purpose applications, and rarely have many peripheral interconnect options. They target high performance applications, focus on computational power, and thus come with multiple level of caches, have very high clock speeds, have less to worry about power dissipation and power consumption. Often, they have little or no onboard RAM.

Q.8 Write characteristics of Cortex-R.

Ans 8

Cortex-R processors are designed for implementation on advanced silicon processes for applications where high-performance, real-time, safe and cost-effective processing is required.

- High performance - rapid execution of complex code and DSP functionality.
- Real-time - deterministic operation to ensure responsiveness.
- Reliable - detects errors and maintains system operation.
- Cost effective - fast time-to-market and customizable features.

Q.9 Why ARM processors have a less number of transistors?

Ans 9

The ARM processors have a less number of transistors because they have a reduced instruction set, which allows a smaller size for the IC. Thereby being space efficient also. Most of the electronic devices such as tablets, mobiles, smart phones and other mobile devices consist of these processors. By combining the ARM microprocessor with RAM, ROM and other peripherals in one single chip.

Q.10 Differentiate between ARM and Intel processors.

Ans 10

Intel processors found in desktop and laptop computers are sometimes referred to as x86 processors. The core difference between ARM and x86 chips is their instruction set. x86 chips are CISC, which stands for complex instruction set computing. CISC chips attempt to represent a given task in the fewest lines of assembly as possible, abstracting away basic functions. These more complex operations also need to run over multiple clock cycles

ARM chips are RISC, which stands for reduced instruction set computing. RISC chips include extremely rudimentary instruction sets, breaking every process down into extremely small, simple steps. Each of these smaller steps can be executed in a single clock cycle.

CISC chips execute commands over multiple clock cycles, while each instruction in a RISC chip is executed over a single clock cycle.

All of CISC's instructions and logic need to be stored in transistors. RISC chips can use less transistors because they need to store fewer instructions.

The lower number of transistors required by RISC allows for lower power usage. CISC chips can also operate directly on main memory while RISC chips can only operate on CPU registers.

The other core difference is power usage. RISC chips require less transistors to function. This means that fewer transistors need to be powered, leading to power savings and heat reduction. This has lead to ARM chips powering nearly all mobile devices. Intel and AMD's x86 chips are better for desktop machines where power consumption isn't as much of an issue. They are also included in laptops which are obviously battery-powered.

CHAPTER 8

Troubleshooting and General PC Problems

8.1 MAINTENANCE

Maintenance is the actions associated with equipment repair when it does not work properly. The dictionary defines maintenance "the work of keeping equipment in proper condition". This would imply that the maintenance should be the actions taken to prevent a device or component from failing. It is to repair normal equipment degradation experienced due to the operation of the device and to keep it in proper working order.

A computer system, like any mechanical or electrical system is likely to fail. There are many causes, including disk crash, power failure, software errors, a fire in the machine room, or even sabotage. Maintenance will be to prevent all such occurrences.

8.1.1 Types of Maintenance

Maintenance is divided into two types:

(a) Preventive maintenance

(b) Breakdown maintenance

Preventive Maintenance

Preventive maintenance can be defined as follows: Actions performed on a time or machine run based schedule that detect, preclude, or mitigate degradation of a component or system with the aim of sustaining or extending its useful life by controlling degradation to an acceptable level.

Preventive maintenance is a schedule of planned servicing action aimed at the prevention of breakdown and failures. The primary goal of preventive maintenance is to prevent the failure of equipment. It is designed to preserve and enhance equipment reliability by replacing worn out components before they actually fail.

The Personal Computer (PC) is a machine with electrical and electronic circuits as well as electro-mechanical assemblies. For reliable operation and long life, a PC should be handled carefully. Computer room should be cleaned and must be dust free. Preventive maintenance steps prescribed by the manufacturer should be done periodically using appropriate materials.

A good preventative maintenance program incorporates a comprehensive backup plan, measures to secure the system against malicious exploits, periodic hardware and software maintenance and steps to maintain general system tidiness. The goal of preventative maintenance is to reduce the likelihood of hardware failures, extend the useful life of the system, minimize system crashes caused by outdated driver and other software problems, secure the system against viruses and prevent data loss.

Breakdown Maintenance

Breakdown maintenance is the repair carried out once the PC stops working. Breakdown maintenance is also called corrective maintenance. Breakdown maintenance is a repair service and can be categorized into three classes.

(a) Routine repairs when the breakdown is seen as an inconvenience but does not affect usual service.

(b) Urgent repairs where vital facilities and services are disrupted.

(c) Emergency repairs where failure of an item can present an immediate danger.

8.2 BASIC COMPUTER MAINTENANCE

- **Backup**: Backing up your data just means saving your files to a separate location (like a CD-ROM, DVD, pen drive, or zip disk) so that in the event of disaster, you can easily copy your files back onto your computer.
- **Invest in an UPS (Uninterruptible Power Source)**: A UPS is a wonderful device that works as a surge protector and a battery backup all in one. Not only does it keep your computer safe from electrical spikes that can be traveling through the lines, but also it gives you time to save your work, and properly power down your computer in event of a power failure. You do not lose your work, and your computer gets to be shut down properly.
- **Never turn the computer off with the power switch**: The one exception to this rule is when your computer locks up and your hard drive is not running (the hard drive light is not blinking) then in this situation, you can turn the power off without harmful effects to the hard drive. As cutting the power can also result in lost data or Windows files.

  Doing this can help in prevent permanent hard drive damage caused by the hard drive heads contacting the surface of the drive disk. This can prevent a lots of Windows problems.

  Whenever possible, recover from crashed by pressing the Ctrl + Alt + Delete keys at the same time and going into your Task Manager. You can often find programs that are not responding in here, and choose to close them from this utility. Press Ctrl + Alt + Delete keys again to reboot your computer from this screen.

  Switch off the monitor, system unit and the printer before switching off the UPS.
- **Scan disk and defrag once a month**: These utilities help to keep your hard drive in optimal shape and error free.

- **Do not unplug peripheral devices while the power supply is on**: Unplugging devices such as your mouse, keyboard, printer, etc., with the power on can short out the connector socket or even the motherboard itself.
- **Remove programs from your startup**: Often when you install a program, it will ask you whether it should load up as soon as Windows loads (or just decide to do so on its own). The more programs you have trying to start up at the same time, the slower your Computer will start. Also, all those programs running in the background while you try to work will slow your computer's response time.
- **Run virus checks and adware/spyware scans regularly (at least once a week):** There are so many types and variations of viruses, spyware and adware floating around the Internet that at times it may seem daunting to even have Internet access on your computer. However, regular scans with your virus scanner, and adware scanners, can ensure your computer remains healthy.
- **Keep disks handy**: If the worst thing happens, and you need to format your system for one reason or another, then it is good idea to have all your driver disks, operating system disks, backup disks, etc., in a readily available place.
- **Keep your software updated**: Software developers are always writing and releasing patches that update the software you have already bought from them. A lot of these patches fix problems you may be experiencing yourself with a particular program.
  Other patches plug security leaks. Still other patches update reference files for your virus/spy/adware scanners to make sure you are scanning for as many variants as possible. So make sure you regularly update/patch your operating system, virus scanners, and various other applications.
- **Develop a schedule of maintenance practices**: All this advice is meaningless if you keep forgetting to do it, or only remember after something has gone wrong. Write yourself up a maintenance schedule, with a list of what tasks should be performed daily, weekly, and monthly.
  If you develop a routine and stick to it, then you should avoid the larger problems by always being on top of the smaller ones.

8.2.1 Why is Proper Computer Maintenance Important?

Proper computer maintenance is important because of the following reasons:

- It will increase the speed of your PC.
- Prevent errors, which will save money.
- Secure your data and information.
- Save time.

8.3 TOOLS FOR PC MAINTENANCE

Following types of tools used in PC maintenance:

Vacuum Cleaner

A vacuum cleaner is a device that uses an air pump to create a partial vacuum to suck up dust and dirt. The dirt is collected by a filtering system or a cyclone for later disposal.

A vacuum's suction is caused by a difference in air pressure. A pump reduces the pressure inside the tube. Atmospheric pressure then pushes the air and into the tube, and so the dust is literally pushed into the bag.

Brush

Brush refers to a variety of devices mainly with bristles, wire or other filament of any possible material used mainly for cleaning and other kinds of surface finishing. They are also used for painting.

Forceps

Forceps are a handheld, hinged instrument used for grasping and holding objects. Forceps are used when fingers are too large to grasp small objects or when many objects need to be held at one time while the hands are used to perform a task.

Mechanically, forceps employ the principle of the lever to grasp and apply pressure. There are two basic types of forceps:

(a) *Non-locking or thumb forceps:* Non-locking forceps also come in two basic forms, hinged at one end, away from the grasping end (colloquially such forceps are called tweezers and hinged in the middle, rather like scissors (though, unlike scissors, forceps meet on flat, grasping surfaces rather than in interposing blades).

(b) *Locking forceps:* Locking forceps are almost always hinged in the middle, though some forms place the hinge very close to the grasping end.

Screwdriver

Screwdriver is a device specifically designed to insert and tighten, or to loosen and remove, screws. The screwdriver comprises a head or tip which engages with a screw, a mechanism to apply torque by rotating the tip, and some way to position and support the screwdriver. A typical hand screwdriver comprises an approximately cylindrical handle of a size and shape to be held by a human hand, and an axial shaft fixed to the handle, the tip of which is shaped to fit a particular type of screw. The handle and shaft allow the screwdriver to be positioned and supported and, when rotated, to apply torque.

☞ *When tightening a screw with force, it is important to press the head hard into the screw, again to avoid damaging the screw.*

Some manual screwdrivers have a ratchet action whereby the screwdriver blade is locked to the handle for clockwise rotation, but uncoupled for counterclockwise rotation when set for tightening screws and vice versa for loosening. Whereas many screwdriver designs have a handle with detachable head (the part of the screwdriver which engages with the screw), called bits as with drill bits, allowing a set of one handle and several heads to be used for a variety of screw sizes and types.

Cutter

Cutter are essential tools for component lead cutting and removing insulation prior soldering. Cutter should be of side cutting. Preferably cutter should have insulated grips. They should be slim line and light weight for precision work. Cutter blades should be very well aligned so that cutting edges meet squarely and allow little or no light to pass through when held together. Cutter action should be smooth and clean. Cutter normally used to cut copper wire or leads of components.

Pliers

Pliers are hand tools, designed primarily for gripping objects by using leverage. Pliers are designed for numerous purposes and require different jaw configurations to grip, turn, pull, or crimp a variety of things. Many types of pliers also include jaws for cutting.

The handles are long relative to the shorter nose of the pliers. The two arms thus act as first class levers with a mechanical advantage, increasing the force applied by the hand's grip and concentrating it on the work piece.

The materials used to make pliers consist mainly of steel alloys with additives such as Vanadium and/or Chromium, to improve alloy strength and prevent corrosion. Pliers have insulated grips to ensure better handling and prevent electrical conductivity.

Stripper

Strippers are used to remove insulation from the wires. The most commonly used strippers are of cutting type. In strippers, there are two set of jaws: one set to hold wire and another one is used to hold sleeve of wire and pull it apart. It has two handles. The set of jaws operate when the jaw's handle is pressed together.

8.4 DUST CONTROL

Dust is very harmful for computer parts. Excess dust can cause mechanical failures, particularly on computer components with moving parts. The computers themselves should be regularly dusted (wiped with a dry cloth or duster) and if the computers are housed in a particularly dusty area, the use of dust covers (when the computers are turned off) is advised. In addition, when a computer case is opened for other repairs, the dust that has built up inside the case should be blown out. This works best with forced air. Different mechanical and electrical tools are available to compress air.

☞ *Cleaning your computer regularly will help you keep it working properly and avoid expensive repairs.*

8.5 MAINTENANCE OF CASE

Cleaning your case keeps the appearance of the computer looking new. While cleaning, if you see ventilation slots, these can be cleaned or cleared to help keep a steady airflow into the computer and keep all components cool. The plastic case that houses the PC components can be cleaned with a slightly damp lint-free cloth. For stubborn stains, add a little household detergent to the cloth. You should not use a solvent cleaner on plastics.

Make sure all vents and air holes are hair and lint free by rubbing a cloth over the holes and vents. It is also helpful to take a vacuum around each of the hole, vents, and crevices on the computer. It is safe to use a standard vacuum when cleaning the outside vents of a computer.

8.6 MAINTENANCE OF MOUSE

As you move the mouse on a flat surface and sends signals to the computer. The computer then translates these signals into the movement of the mouse pointer.

There are two main mouse types: optical and mechanical. Each is cleaned in basically the same way, although the mechanical mouse requires a bit more work.

Optical mouse require no internal cleaning because they do not contain any rotating parts; however, they can get sticky over time as dust collects near the light emitter. This can cause erratic cursor movement or prevent the mouse from working properly.

Mechanical mouse are especially susceptible to dust and particles that can accumulate inside the mouse, which can make it difficult to track or move properly. If the mouse pointer does not move smoothly, the mouse may need to be cleaned.

The optical mouse replaces the mouse ball with optical sensors that track the movement of the mouse over a surface. The fact that it does not need to be cleared internally is the biggest advantage that an optical mouse has over conventional mouse.

Unplug the mouse from the USB. Moisten a cotton cloth with rubbing alcohol, and use it to clean the top and bottom of the mouse.

If you have a mechanical mouse, remove the tracking ball by turning the ball-cover ring counter-clockwise. Then clean the tracking ball and the inside of the mouse with a cotton cloth moistened with rubbing alcohol. Allow all of the parts to dry before reassembling and reconnecting the mouse.

Cleaning your mouse pad with a damp cloth can also help improve a computer's mouse movement.

☞ *If you just want to give the mouse a quick cleaning, place it on a clean sheet of paper and move the mouse back and forth. Some of the dust and particles should rub off onto the paper.*

8.7 MAINTENANCE OF KEYBOARD

Dust, food, liquid, and other particles can get stuck underneath the keys on your keyboard, which can prevent it from working properly. The basic cleaning tips below can help keep your keyboard clean.

Shutdown your PC and remove the main plug. Unplug the keyboard and hold it upside down to release any debris from in between the keys (pressing the key is a good way to clean it).

Now, take one of the cotton buds and put a couple of drops of the cleaning fluid on it, use the cotton bud to clean the sides of the keys. Use a can of compressed air to clean between the keys.

After cleaning the sides of the keys take your free cloth and dampen it with your cleaning fluid. Do not put the liquid directly on the keyboard. Give the surface of the keyboard a good wipe over using the cloth to trace the contours of the keys. When you have finished, give the keyboard a wipe over with the dry cloth/duster. You should now have a nice clean keyboard.

☞ *Turn the keyboard upside down and gently shake it to remove dirt and dust.*

8.8 MAINTENANCE OF HEADPHONES

Headphones and headsets can be used by many different people and may need to be frequently cleaned to help prevent the spreading of germs. If the headphones being used are plastic or vinyl, moisten a cloth with warm water and rub the head and earpieces of the headphones. Headphones that have cushions also have the availability of having the cushions replaced. Replacing these cushions can also help keep the headphones clean.

8.9 MAINTENANCE OF MONITOR

The only part of the monitor worthy of cleanliness is the screen – the part where information is displayed. Start by spraying some window cleaner on a soft cloth. Then use the cloth to gently wipe the front of the monitor. Unlike a CRT computer monitor, the LCD or LED monitor is not glass and requires special cleaning procedures.

When cleaning the LCD or LED screen, it is important to remember that you do not spray any liquids onto the screen directly. Press gently while cleaning and do not use a paper towel, since it can scratch the screen.

To clean the LCD or LED screen, use a non-rugged microfiber cloth, soft cotton cloth, or Swiffer duster. If a dry cloth does not completely clean the screen, you can apply rubbing alcohol to the cloth and wipe the screen with a damp cloth.

☞ *Never spray cleaning solution directly on the screen.*

8.10 MAINTENANCE OF CD/DVD DRIVE

A dirty CD-ROM drive or other disc drives can cause read errors when reading discs. These read errors could cause software installation issues or issues while running the program.

The tray of CD/DVD drive is the main source from where dust reaches into the assembly of the CD/DVD drive. The accumulation of dust results into data reading error. However, you can avoid such problem with few precautions. These are:

- Never leave tray open. After using the CD/DVD drive, immediately, put the button to put back tray into the CD/DVD drive.
- Avoid touching the surface of tray with oily and dirty hands.
- Use CD cleaning kit on regular basis to clean the CD/DVD drive. You can purchase one such kit from market. It comes with a special CD. This CD contains small brushes on its surface. When CD is inserted into the CD drive, the brushes on its surface clean dirt in the CD/DVD drive.
- Use a cleaning kit or damp clean cotton cloth to clean CDs, DVDs, and other discs. When cleaning a disc wipe against the tracks, starting from the middle of the CD or DVD and wiping towards the outer side.

8.11 MAINTENANCE OF PRINTER

Cleaning the outside of a printer can help keep the printer's appearance looking good. First, make sure to turn off the printer before cleaning it. Dampen a cloth with water or rubbing alcohol and wipe the case and each of the buttons or knobs on the printer. As mentioned earlier, never spray any liquid directly onto the printer.

Every printer needs an occasional tune-up, particularly if it has not been used for a long time. The maintenance process consumes ink, so do not use it unless necessary. Maintenance tools are accessed through the printer driver. Once the procedure begins, let it run full cycle before shutting the printer off.

8.11.1 Nozzle check

When printouts become faint or certain colors fail to print, test whether the print heads are working properly. Use the utility that performs a nozzle check pattern. If the printout shows gaps, clean the nozzles.

8.11.2 Cleaning print heads

If the nozzle check indicates that a cleaning is needed, or if the printer is completely clogged, clean the print heads. The process removes blockages in the nozzles. Run additional nozzle checks since sometimes cleaning must be performed more than once to be successful. Some printers have a deep cleaning option.

8.11.3 Print Head Alignment

If lines and colours look out or there is banding, then align the print heads.

If cleaning and alignment do not solve a problem, contact the manufacturer for the cost of repair. If your printer is no longer covered under warranty, assess whether repair costs are worth it. Sometimes buying a new printer, particularly those that come with a full set of ink cartridges, is the better option.

☞ *Printing problems are common with every printer and laser printer is not an exception. However, with regular maintenance and preventive measures, we can easily keep a laser printer fit for years.*

Over time, particles of toner and paper will begin to accumulate inside the printer. This may cause print quality problems during printing. Cleaning the printer will eliminate or reduce these problems. You may undertake following steps to clean the printer:

(a) Turn off the printer and open the top cover of printer.
(b) Hold the cartridge from top and pull-out from the printer.
(c) With a dry, lint free cloth, wipe any residue from the paper path area and the toner cartridge cavity.
(d) Replace the toner cartridge and close the top cover. Plug in the power cable, and switch the printer on.

8.12 MAINTENANCE OF SCANNER

Flatbed scanners commonly become dirty with dust, fingerprints, and hair. When the scanner is dirty, the images may have distortions. !Clean a flatbed scanner's surface by spraying a window cleaner onto a paper towel or cotton cloth and wipe the glass until clean. As mentioned earlier, never spray a liquid directly onto the component.
The same towel or cotton cloth can also be used to clean the outside of the scanner.

8.13 ESSENTIAL ROUTINE HARD DISK CLEANUP, MAINTENANCE AND REPAIR TASKS

Hard disk drives need little or no preventive maintenance. If it is a fixed hard disk drive, it does not need preventive maintenance because it is a sealed unit that you must not open for any reason. However, they can be cleaned with software utilities to help it run fast and efficiently. Utilizing these utilities prevent the hard drive from slowing down.
Regular computer hard disk clean up is vital to prevent errors and to keep your PC in top form. A healthy hard drive will protect your data and will make your PC working fast by allowing fast access to files and folders.
Essential regular hard disk cleanup and maintenance tasks are as follows :

8.13.1 Scandisk

Scandisk is a PC tools available in Windows Operating System. This is a diagnostic and repair program that scans the data on your hard drive.

Scandisk PC tool can verify the file and directory structure of your data and can perform repairs when problems are found. Scandisk can further run a surface scan on your hard drive to determine whether or not any physical damage is present and attempt to move and affected data to another section of the hard drive.

By using this hard drive clean up tool, you can increase the speed of your PC, as this will enable faster access to files and folders.
If your hear a strange noise from the Hard Drive (tick tick sound) use Scandisk immediately. It is recommended to use scandisk once in every two months. However, increases the frequency if you are a regular PC user.
To run ScanDisk, in Windows 7 follow these steps.

(a) Double-click!My Computer.
(b) Highlight a local hard drive by clicking on it once.
(c) Right-click the highlighted local drive and select!Properties.
(d) Click on the!Tools!tab and click!Check Now!to check the drive for errors.
(e) The computer needs to restart to run ScanDisk without getting interrupted.

8.13.2 Disk Defragmenter

Disk Defragmenter consolidates fragmented files and folders on your computer's hard disk, so that each file occupies a single, contiguous space on the volume. As a result, your system can gain access to your files and folders and save new ones more efficiently. By consolidating your files and folders, *Disk Defragmenter* also consolidates the volume's free space, making it less likely for new files to be fragmented.

After some use, if you feel that your drive has started getting slow, DOS or Windows programs and data files take much more time to load, then most probably this could be due to a fragmentation problem.

Let us first understand this term. On a disk drive, any information is stored in clusters. When all the clusters of a file are stored in consecutive sectors, then it is not fragmented but when the clusters which make a file are scattered across the disk, the file or the disk is said to be fragmented.

As it takes the read/write head longer to read the file scattered across the disk surface, a fragmented file takes longer to load compared to an unfragmented file.

This can be compared with a real life situation: If your room is not in order, it takes you longer to find something compared to a room where everything is arranged properly.

The fragmentation occurs because whenever the operating system wants to write some information on the disk drive, it consults the FAT (File Allocation Table) to find an empty cluster. The FAT keeps a record of used, available and bad (unusable) areas on the disk surface.

After finding an empty cluster, the operating system writes to that area and updates the FAT. If the complete file could not be written in one contiguous empty area, then the operating system looks for other areas where the rest of the file can be written. The FAT keeps record of this chain of clusters taken up by the file. When a file is removed from the disk, the FAT is again updated to show the cluster taken up by the file as an empty area.

After some time, this removing of file and writing of new information produce a lot of holes, i.e., empty areas in between the data area, thus the files scattering across the disk surface. This is known as disk fragmentation.

File fragmentation increases disk access time and decreases the chances of salvaging a file when there is a problem. The disk defragmenter utility reads and rewrites the files on the disk to reorder them so that each file is once again stored contiguously on the disk surface and can be read much more efficiently by the hard disk drive.

☞ *Disk defragmenter moves the pieces of each file or folder to one location on the volume, so that each occupies a single, contiguous space on the disk drive.*

First part of Figure 8.1 shows a file fragmented across the disk surface and the second part shows the same file after it has been defragmented.

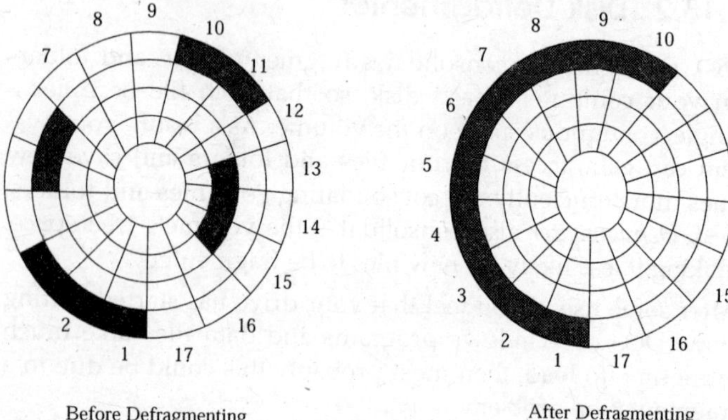

Figure 8.1 Parts of a file scattered across the disk surface before defragmenting and the same file after defragmenting

Because the defragmentation software moves the information stored on the disk surface, it is always better to take a backup of the information on the disk surface before using these software. These software are fully tested and the chances of data corruption are very remote, but a power loss during defragmentation or some other unexpected event may corrupt the data, so it is always better to have a current backup of all important information on the drive before using these programs.

Depending on the frequency of creating/editing/deleting of the files on the hard disk drive, you can defragment the drive once a week or once a month to keep the files in one place.

Defragmenting a drive also increases the drive's life as the read/write head will require to move less to get to the data on a properly defragmented drive. Another advantage is if the files are stored contiguously, it is easier to restore them in case of any accidental deletion. Files that are scattered makes it impossible to restore them.

Disk Fragmentation does not work in the following conditions:

(a) If the disk is formatted using file system other than NTFS (New Technology File System), FAT and FAT32.
(b) If a disk contains an error and not able to be repaired.
(c) Network locations cannot be defragmented.

It is recommended to use Defragmenter tool once in every two months. However, increase the frequency if you are a heavy PC user.

Let us now learn to use the Disk Defragmenter. But first, undertake the following steps to open the Disk Defragmenter window.

➡ **To open Disk Defragmenter, do this:**

1. Click **Start** button, Choose **All Programs**, highlight **Accessories**, highlight **System Tools**, and then choose **Disk Defragmenter.** Disk Defragmenter window will open up as shown in Figure 8.2.

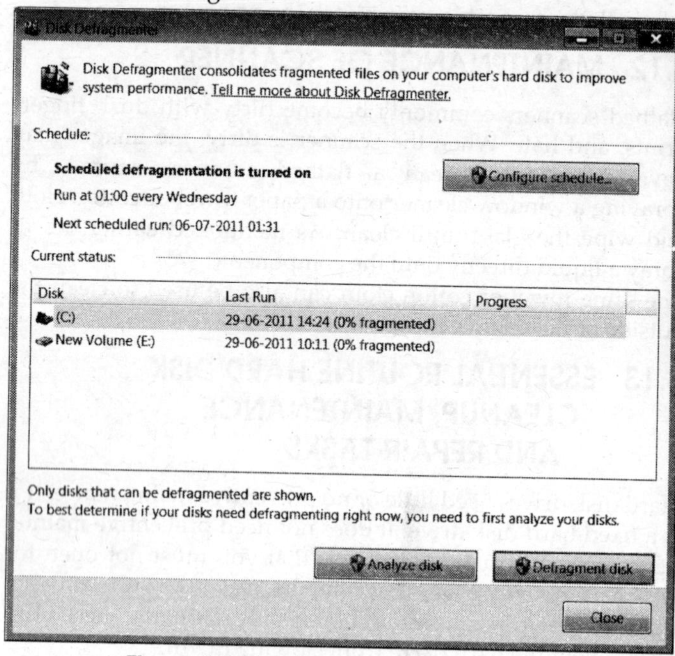

Figure 8.2 Disk Defragmenter window

2. To start defragmentation, under **Current status**, select the disk you want to defragment.
3. Click **Defragment** disk.

8.13.3 Delete Temporary Internet Files

Every time you go to a Web site, a copy of what you see on your monitor is stored in a special place on your computer. This makes your Web surfing go faster. If you return to a site you went yesterday (or last week), your Web browser just accesses the copy stored on your hard drive. After a while the file that holds the Temporary Internet files can get so big it slows your computer's performance.

To delete temporary file, from Internet Explorer, click on the Tools menu and select Internet options. Now choose the button marked as 'Delete Files'. Then put a check mark in the little white square that says 'Delete all offline content' and click OK. To really finish the job you need to close all open windows for Internet Explorer.

You can also delete the Temporary Internet files from the Control Panel by clicking on your Start button on your Desktop, select Settings & the Control Panel. Look for the icon named Internet Options and use the same procedure explained above.

Web pages are stored in Temporary Internet Files folder the first time in the hard disk using Web browser. The function of Web browser is to save temporarily the pages which you visited frequently. Internet Explorer can open them from the hard disk instead of from the Internet, if user tries to visit again.

To delete all temporary files from hard disk type '%temp%' in the RUN window.

☞ *Delete temporary Internet files in every 20-30 days.*

8.13.4 Disk Cleanup

The Disk Cleanup program frees up space on your hard disk drive by removing temporary and unused files (including Temporary Internet Files and files in the Recycle Bin). You can run Disk Cleanup manually, or you can set it up to run automatically.

Disk Cleanup is a convenient way to delete files you no longer need and free up hard disk space on your computer. When you schedule Disk Cleanup, it will first open and then prompt for you to make choices before deleting files from the computer.

Deleting temporary Internet files is also a part of disk clean up. But there are other temporary files, which are taking unnecessary disk space. This process is essential if you have a small hard drive and are constantly on the verge of running out of space.

➡ **To open Disk Cleanup, do this:**

1. Click **Start** button, Choose **All Programs**, highlight **Accessories**, highlight **System Tools**, and then choose **Disk Cleanup**.
2. **Disk Cleanup: Drive Selection** dialog box appears as shown in Figure 8.3.
3. Choose the drive which you want to clean and then click OK.
4. The **Disk Cleanup** dialog box appears for the drive which you have selected (See Figure 8.4).

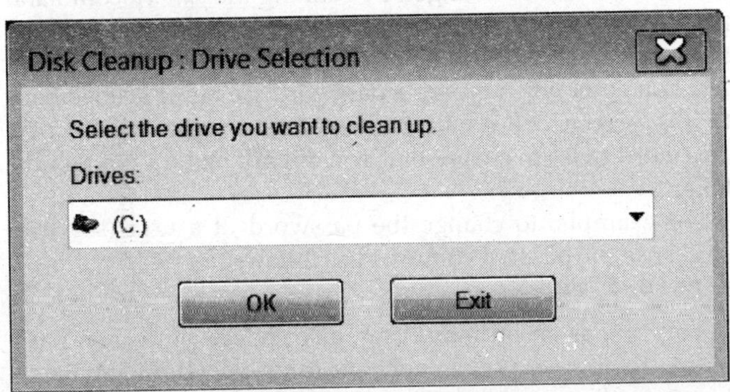

Figure 8.3 Disk Cleanup: Drive Selection dialog box

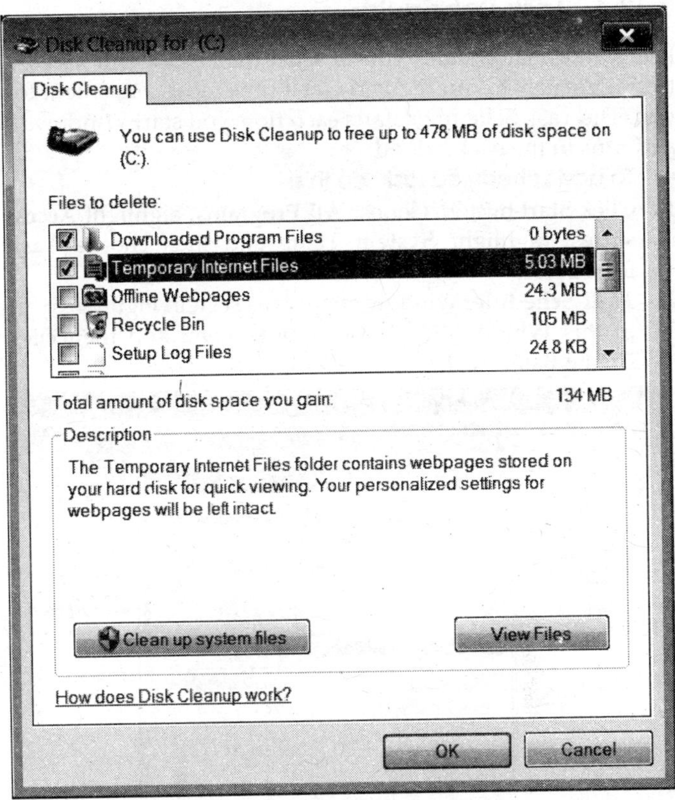

Figure 8.4 Disk Cleanup dialog box

☞ *Disk Cleanup helps to free up space on your hard drive. Disk Cleanup searches your drive, and then shows you temporary files, cache files, and unnecessary program files that you can safely delete. You can direct Disk Cleanup to delete some or all of those files.*

5. Under **Files to delete:** list, click the check box for each file that you want to delete.
6. Then click OK button.

8.13.5 Uninstall Unnecessary Programs

Many things happen when you install program. First, they sit on your hard drive taking up space, and they have installed files on your "Registry". Also some Dynamic Link Library files (these are little files needed for Windows to make the program run) run in your PC.

These go in a Windows initializing file called "system.ini". INI stands for Initialization File. When Windows starts it looks at the "system.ini" to see what programs have to be available so they will start when you want to use them.

Windows also reads the Registry to see what programs are on your Computer and what it has to do to make them work. Also, Windows reads your Startup Folders to see what has to start automatically and hide in the background. Also the "msconfig" is to place all these programs in your "Startup". All this will slow down the operation of your PC.

8.13.6 Task Scheduler

It is a tool that enables you to schedule tasks (such as Disk Defragmenter) to run regularly, at a time most convenient for you. The Task Scheduler starts each time you start Windows 7 and runs in the background.

➡ **To add scheduled task, do this:**

1. Click **Start** button, Choose **All Programs**, highlight **Accessories**, highlight **System Tools** and then choose **Task Scheduler.**
2. **Task Scheduler** window appears as seen in Figure 8.5.
3. In this Window, Click the **Action** menu and then click **Create Basic Task**.

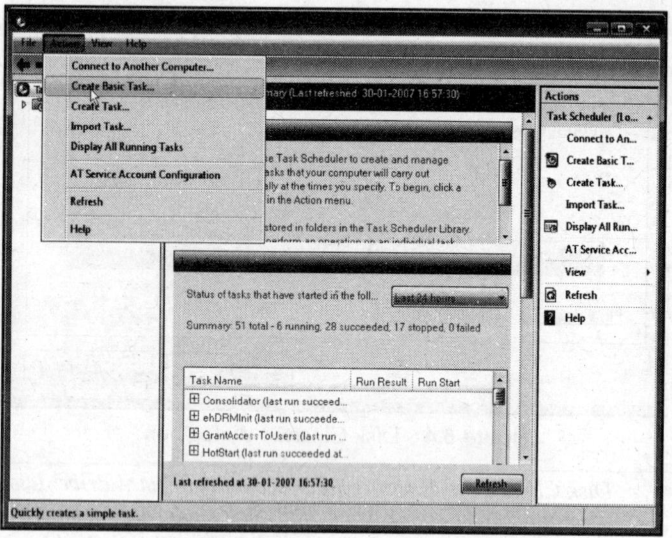

Figure 8.5 Task Scheduler window

4. In **Create Basic Task Wizard**, type a name for the task and give description, and then click **Next**.
5. In the next step, select an option from *When do you want the task to start?*, i.e., *Daily, Weekly*, etc., and then click **Next**.
6. In Next dialog box, specify the schedule which you want to use, and then click Next.
7. To schedule a program to start automatically, click **Start** a program, and then click **Next**.
8. Select a program from the list, or browse to the program you want to start, and then click **Next**.
9. Click **Finish**.

8.13.7 Keep Software Updated

There is an easy, free way to help to keep your PC safer and running smoothly. It is called Windows Update. All you have to do is turn it on, and you'll get the latest security and other important updates from MS automatically.

Setting up Windows Update is simple. If you have already got automatic updating turned on, Windows Update in Control Panel will open and show your update status. If it is not yet turned on, you'll be guided through the steps to do so. After that, all the latest security and performance improvements will be installed on your PC quickly and reliably.

➡ **To keep software updated:**

1. Open **Control Panel** and select **Windows Updated**.
2. In the left pane, click **Change settings.**
3. Under **Important updates**, choose the option that you want.
4. Under **Recommended updates**, select the *Give me recommended updates the same way I receive important updates* check box, and then click OK. Administrator permission required If you're prompted for an administrator password or confirmation, type the password or provide confirmation.

You can also choose if you want to allow anyone to install updates by selecting the *Allow all users to install updates on this computer* check box. This applies only to updates and software that are installed manually; automatic updates will be installed regardless of the user.

8.13.8 Changing Your Password

The combination of login name and password controls access to the system. An important aspect of maintaining the security of the system is to create passwords that are difficult to guess and to change them often. How often passwords should be changed depends on the circumstances at your site. However, the rules for creating strong passwords are normally the following:

1. It should contain atleast eight characters.
2. It should not be based on a dictionary word. Also avoid using your real name, login name, etc.
3. It should contain a variety of different types of characters, at least three of the following:
   (i) lower case letters
   (ii) upper case letters (Linux passwords are case sensitive)
   (iii) punctuation and other special characters
4. It should not contain easy to determine personal information, such as your birthday, anniversary, etc.

Also, as a general rule you should change your password the first time you log in and thereafter you should change it regularly.

Password can be changed by running the *passwd* command from the command line. Before the password can be changed, the current password must be supplied. Note that the characters you enter when typing a password are never echoed back to the screen. You will be expected to enter your new password twice to ensure that you did not make a typing mistake.

For example, to change the password of a user (say user *vivek*) use the **passwd** command as follows:

```
# passwd vivek
```

You can, as an ordinary user, also change your own password. In this case, you do not have to supply your login name. Just type the command **passwd** and the system will prompt for the new password.

By default, the system performs some checks to ensure that a weak password is not chosen. If you enter such a password, the system will return an error message and will ask you to try again.

To change your password using the graphical tool, run Applications->Preferences->Password.

To change your password using GNOME, navigate to System->Preferences->About Me and then click Password.

8.14 HANDLING OF HARD DISK DRIVE

8.14.1 Vibration and Shock Precaution

Every hard disk has a limited lifetime, meaning it is bound to fail ultimately. There are a number of moving parts in a hard disk drive, such as the read/write head and spindle motor. It is this type of part that suffers the most wear and tear. Here are some precautions you can take to give your drive(s) a safer and longer life.

It is especially dangerous when a hard disk drive receives a shock or jerk while it is operating. This can result in the read/write head scratching the disk surface. Since the head operates only a few micrometers above the disk surface, even a slight shock can cause the head to contact the disk and damage its outermost magnetic layer. Therefore, never vibrate PC or move it while operating.

8.14.2 Temperature and Humidity Precautions

There is also a risk from sudden temperature changes, which can create condensation of water inside the drive. This condensation can lead to the drive's read/write head(s) adhering to the disk surface(s), which will, in turn, stop the hard disk from rotating.

Sudden changes in temperature or air pressure can cause disk surface material to evaporate, which can also cause the head to adhere to the disk surface. This sometimes happens when a hard disk drive is left unused for a long period of time.

8.14.3 When Data is Lost or Corrupted

One possible reason for either losing or corrupting hard disk data may be the computer's application software. To minimize the risk of data loss or corruption, you should check your disk(s) regularly with a disk diagnosis utility, such as the Windows "Scandisk" utility. When using Windows, be sure to follow that OS' standard shutdown procedures before switching the computer OFF. Suddenly turning the computer power OFF may result in hard disk data loss, which may prevent Windows from being able to start up again.

8.14.4 Hard Disk Service Life

The average service life of a hard disk is usually given as "5 years or 20,000 hours." This means if a hard disk operates 24 hours a day, you will need to replace your drive with a new one every 1.5 to 2 years.

8.14.5 Data Backup

Backing up your data regularly is very important. Even if a drive failure is the result of a manufacturing defect, it is not guaranteed that you will be able to recover all your data.

8.14.6 Replace Your Hard Disks Regularly

Since every drive has a finite service life, it should be replaced periodically with new drive, according to the drive's service life rating. In addition, inspecting your drive(s) regularly will allow you to detect potential hard disk problems in advance, giving you the option of either fixing the current drive or replacing it with a new one. No part or device can be used forever and even under normal usage conditions, as your drive approaches the end of its service life, the chance of a breakdown will increase. Thus, periodic inspection and replacement of your drive(s) will help to prevent costly breakdowns and expensive downtime.

8.15 BACKUP

Backup is the activity of copying data, files, database systems so they will be preserved in the event of equipment failure or another catastrophic failure, such as corruption of the original disk or a natural disaster. You can use the CD or DVD burning software included on your PC to create backup discs of important information including personal files, e-mail messages, and Web site bookmarks. When writing data to a backup disc, you should use software that includes write verification functionality. This verification feature compares the data on your hard disk drive with the data copied to the disc to ensure it is an exact copy. Depending on your disc burning software, you may need to manually enable this feature.

Creating System Recovery Discs is a one-time step that you should perform while your PC is working properly. If you later encounter problems with your PC, you can restore it to its original configuration using the System Recovery discs that you create.

Backups are useful primarily for two purposes:

(a) To restore a computer to an operational state following a disaster called disaster recovery.

(b) To restore small numbers of files after they have been accidentally deleted or corrupted.

Database Backup is the activity of copying database to a permanent storage (such as magnetic tape) so that they will be preserved in case of equipment failure or other disasters. Equipment failures include system crashes, disk damage, etc. Disasters include fire, flood or earthquakes. The backup copy can then be used to restore data. The backup must be kept synchronized with the primary copy of the database, regularly. That is, one should copy the primary database onto the backup everyday, every week or every month depending on the need. Generally, the backup copy of the database is kept separated from the primary copy. This is because a disaster at the primary location should not damage the backup site.

Keeping a backup increases the availability of data. That is, data is available to the user in spite of system failures or environmental disasters. Latest copy of the backup is loaded from the tape to the system and thus the normal operations are restarted.

An important part of database planning is backup planning. Planning backup means to make sure that a current copy of the database is always available even in case of catastrophes. Any disaster, be it fire, flood, earthquake, terrorist or virus attacks, disk drive crash, power failure or accidental deletion may not block the normal functioning the system.

One major problem with backup activity is that while the database copy is being made, changes could still be made to the primary copy. New changes are made in the primary copy. That is, a backup copy just made can also become outdated. For all such cases, the Database Administrator has to determine how often to perform a partial backup. In a partial backup, recently made changes are stored in a log. The administrator also has to determine how often to perform a full database backup.

Partial backups are faster to create and requires less storage space but takes more time to restore, in case of disaster.

A schedule must be planned for backup activity and this schedule must be revised regularly. This is so because the log (partial backup area) may become full because of many changes at any time. In that case, backup has to be run earlier than scheduled. If such a situation occurs very often, the backup schedule must be modified.

8.15.1 Hardware Protection and Redundancy

Protection of hardware equipment is another important step towards enhancing security. Following are some of the measures to be followed in this direction:

(a) Highly critical hardware components, such as magnetic tapes, etc., must be placed in locked and secure rooms.
(b) Physical access to computers, network equipment and data storage areas should be limited.
(c) Database servers should be kept in a separate room and be made accessible only to the Database Administrator (DBA).
(d) Data transmission media (such as cables and connectors) should be kept covered and protected to ensure that they cannot be tapped.
(e) Organizations storing database in workstations should keep a spare computer for use in emergency. The backup computer may be an additional CPU (Central Processing Unit) or complete computer system that can be used if the main system goes down, due to any unforeseen reasons.
(f) Provision for auxiliary power supply, such as UPS (Uninterrupted Power Supply), that can be called upon if mains power fails, must be made.
(g) Arrangements must be made for fire extinguishers within the vicinity of the computer system. All people should be trained to operate fire extinguishers.

Computer hardware is relatively sensitive to heat and water. Tapes or disks used to store data also gets easily damaged by heat, moisture, etc. Keeping extra hardware, i.e., same components in two or more computer systems, can prove useful in emergency. The backup equipment can be placed internally within the company premises or adjustments can be made with such companies which are using similar equipments, to provide backup facilities. There are some companies that maintain spare computer equipments as backup protection for their clients. Their services could be utilized in case of emergencies.

8.16 TROUBLESHOOTING

General tips For Basic Troubleshooting

- **Write down troubleshooting steps**: Once you start troubleshooting, you should write down each step you take. This way, you will remember exactly what you have done and avoid repeating the same mistakes.
- **Take notes about error messages**: If your computer gives you an error message, be sure to write down as much information as possible.
- **Always check the cables**: If have problem with a specific piece of computer hardware, such as monitor, printer, mouse or keyboard, then an easy first step is to check all related cables to make sure they are connected properly.
- **Restart the computer**: When all else fails, restarting the computer is a good thing to try. This can solve a lot of basic issues you may experience with your computer.

8.16.1 Common Problems and Solutions

The power supply may not turn on to the CPU. The lack of power is often a problem with the PC machine. Check the following:

Power would not Turn On

- Find the power switch cable and make sure that it is connected to the motherboard. It is a possibility that simply reversing the lead will do the trick.
- Make sure the board is not touching the case.
- Make sure none of the screws that hold the board in place is touching any metal or any of the electrical pathways. If you have any doubt on this, you can remove each screw, one at a time and place washers on them. You do not need to remove the motherboard to do this.

PC Boots, but Beeping Sound is Heard

Beeping can indicate a serious problem, often a critical function failure. The codes are intended to inform you about what is going on when no visual signal is available. They originate from the BIOS of the computer.

When the monitor is working, the BIOS will normally display error messages on the screen. However, there are times when the video card is not activated or working or during a serious problem that the BIOS will send out a beep code to attract your attention.

Beep codes are not standardized. Different BIOS manufacturers use different beeps for the same thing. You need to find out what the beeps mean. To do this, you need to locate the name of the BIOS manufacturers, then get the information.

The two most popular BIOS manufacturers are Phoenix and American Megatrends. So their codes are the most common.

Fans come on, but there is no Video or Beeps.

This is because a key component may not be plugged in properly or may not be operational. Check the memory modules and the processor to be sure they are firmly installed. You might want to make sure the processor is actually working. To do this, unplug the processor fan and place you fingers on the processor. It should heat up quickly. On the other hand, should the processor remain at room temperature, then you may have a defective processor and it may need replacing. Sometimes, you may need to track down a problem component through a process of elimination. You may need to replace parts one by one and figure out the problem. Be sure you have the processor jumper settings set properly.

PC seems to be locked up and not responding.

Use the Windows Task Manager to close any programs not responding or to restart the PC. Press Ctrl, Alt and the Delete keys all together on the keyboard. Select the program that is not responding, and click End Task. Or Click Shut Down, and then click Restart.

PC date and time display is incorrect

The real-time clock (RTC) battery may need to be replaced. Battery life is approximately seven years. Before replacing the battery, try resetting the date and time in your operating system by using the Control Panel. If the problem persists, replace the battery.

Keyboard does not work

This one does not happen very often. However, if it does, the two trouble sources will be the keyboard itself or the keyboard controller on the motherboard.

Insufficient memory message displays

Close all open programs, and then try the desired task again, or restart your PC (click Start, Turn Off Computer, and then Restart). If the message displays again, consider purchasing and installing additional memory.

Monitor is blacked out

Make sure the monitor is turned on. Try pressing the power button on the monitor again. The computer may be in Sleep mode. Shake the mouse around or press the enter key to wake it. If the green light is not in front, check the power cord connecting the monitor into the outlet. If the green light is on, check the brightness level by using the buttons on the monitor. Check the cable connection from the monitor into the computer.

No Sound from speaker

Check the cord in the back of the computer to see if the speakers are plugged into the computer. Plug in your speaker cable and then try adjusting the volume control (the speaker icon) on the task bar. Make sure it is not set to mute. Click on the sliding tab should make a sound. Double click on the volume icon on the task bar and the volume control box appears. Make sure the mute button at he bottom is not checked.

Mouse starts acting unbalanced

If your mouse starts acting unbalanced, it could be insufficient memory problem. Reboot and see if that corrects the problem. If your mouse will only move one way, either vertically or horizontally, your mouse may need cleaning. Shut down your machine and unplug your mouse from the computer. Clean it with a soft cloth.

The computer is frozen or non responsive

When your computer locks up and will not respond to either keyboard strokes or mouse clicks, then your machine is frozen. If you are in the middle of running a particular application and this occurs, then hold down the Ctrl Key + Alt Key and Del key at the same time. It will display a dialog box say - Microsoft Word (not responding) If you see this, then highlight the name of the application by clicking on it and then select END TASK from the choices in the box below. It may take a few minutes to comply. You may see another box saying the application isn't responding. Click on END TASK and it will shut down that particular application. or other solution to this problem is - Press and hold the Power button. The Power button is usually located on the front or side of the computer, typically indicated by the power symbol. Press and hold the Power button for 5 to 10 seconds to force the computer to shut down.

Improving Slow Performance

Many of us have had an experience with a computer in which we open a program, and then find that we are waiting for over a minute for the program to actually open. Run the Antivirus program, May be some malware running in the background is slowing down things. Viruses, worms, spyware and adware are collectively known as malware. These undesirable programs, which are usually added without a user's knowledge, can significantly slow down the performance of a computer. Keeping antivirus software up to date and running scans on a regular basis are the best ways to prevent virus infections. Or, harddisk may be full so remove unwanted programs from the harddisk. Defragmenting can also become a regular maintenance task for heavily used computers to keep them performing well.

Excess or Unused Software, particularly if it is software that loads when the computer is booting up, can certainly slow performance. If a user is certain that a particular program is not used and is not needed for the computer to function properly, then this software can be deleted.

It is possible that a computer does not have sufficient RAM to perform the desired functions. This problem is most likely if the computer is rather old and has had a newer (and more memory demanding) operating system installed.

Out of Memory Errors

Out of memory error messages can be caused by a variety of problems, including memory glitches (that will be solved by rebooting), insufficient memory, poor memory management, not enough hard disk space, faulty memory and software problems. The user may be running too many programs at once. Try closing some of the open programs. If this doesn't work, the next step to try is to reboot the computer

The Blue Screen of Death

The Blue Screen of Death is the casual name given to the error code that occurs with Windows operating systems when a critical error has occurred that causes the system to shut down to prevent further errors.

Its nickname comes from the fact that the screen turns blue in color, and the computer "dies" or "crashes", meaning it is shut down. These errors are often caused by poorly functioning device drivers, hardware problems (such as with memory, power supplies or system overheating), or problems with the system software.

8.17 GENERAL PC SOFTWARE TROUBLESHOOTING

Software problems are tough to fix because dozens of programs are simultaneously running on your PC. Here are suggestions for solving the problem:

- Run Windows Update for the latest software versions.
- Use the Update Driver to ensure that you have the latest software drivers.
- Use System Restore
- If the computer runs fine in Safe Mode, the problem isn't with Windows itself.
- Regularly scan your PC for viruses and spyware.
- Use the Task Manager to determine which programs have stopped running.

8.17.1 CMOS Memory

CMOS is an abbreviation for Complementary Metal Oxide Semiconductor. It is an on-board semiconductor chip powered by a CMOS battery. CMOS uses a complimentary arrangement of both NMOS and PMOS, negative and positive Metal Oxide transistor circuits. CMOS memory draws a very little current (nano-amps). Values stored in it can be maintained for a very long period of time while the computer is off with a rechargeable lithium battery. The CMOS memory is used to store system configuration information, such as disk drive parameters, memory configuration, and the date-time, some of which you enter in the CMOS Setup program. It is used by the Basic Input Output System (BIOS), a program permanently stored in the Flash memory on recent motherboards and in Read Only Memory (ROM) on older motherboards, to configure the computer. The CMOS Setup is part of the BIOS program. The CMOS memory is usually located with the real-time clock in the motherboard chipset or in a separate real-time clock chip. It is located in the chipset on most recent motherboards.

CMOS memory is used to store the configuration information of your computer, and its electrical current is supplied by battery backup when your computer is turned off.

8.17.2 Real Time Clock (RTC) Circuit

The real time clock is the calendar and watch of the computer. It lets the PC keep track of the current data and time with the help of a battery and CMOS memory. This circuit maintains correct date and time even when the main AC supply to the computer is switched off.

The real time clock chip is a battery operated chip that maintains basic settings and the system time.

8.17.3 Memory (ROM and RAM)

Memories are one of the most important parts of a computer system. The term memory refers to any device that can be used for storage. There are two basic ways to store memory. One way is to store the memory within the actual circuitry of the computer, which allows for it to be quickly accessed by the central processing unit. These memory devices are generally used for temporary storage of data and programs that are currently used by the CPU. The second type of memory storage is to store the memory in external storage devices. They include hard drives (also known as hard disks), pendrives, DVDs and CDs. Programs and information that you are not currently using can be permanently stored on these devices. The term "memory" usually pertains to the devices stored within the circuitry of the computer. They are temporary, meaning that when the computer is turned off, they will be deleted. These devices are connected directly to the CPU and are very fast. On the other hand, the external storage devices are not considered part of a computer's memory.

There are basically two types of memory used in the computer :

(a) RAM (Random Access Memory)
(b) ROM (Read Only Memory)

RAM is an acronym for random access memory. It is used to temporarily store the programs currently in use by the user and by the main processing unit of the computer, the central-processing unit. When you first turn your computer on, the RAM is empty. There will be no data and no information in it until you open or load a program. These programs are originally permanently stored in the external storage devices, like a hard disk, a pen drive, or a CD-ROM. When you open up the program, it is copied from the external device it is located on to the RAM, which is directly connected to the CPU. This is because if the CPU was to directly access this program from the external storage device, it would be extremely slow. However, programs cannot be permanently stored on the RAM because the RAM, unlike hard drives, is not big enough to store all the programs a computer system contains. RAMs are also expensive.

The RAM is useful because it can feed information to the central processor at extremely high speeds. However, it does not permanently store information. The RAM is volatile, which means that when you exit out of a program or when the computer is turned off, all the information stored in it will be erased. This is why you need to save all of your work before you close a program. Once the program is closed, it is purged from the RAM, and if the information was not saved to a permanent location like the hard drive, or a pen drive, CD or which are non-volatile (meaning that the information stored on them will not be deleted when the computer is shut off), then it will be lost forever.

The RAM is a read-write memory. The information in a read-write memory can be read, and the new information can be written into the memory.

The ROM is a read only memory. This means that you can only read its contents, but you cannot write over it and you cannot change or alter it in any way. A computer needs some sort of instructions when it is first turned on. These instructions are stored in the ROM. The ROM is also used to store certain information not needing to be changed, and it is non-volatile, meaning that the information it stores is not erased when you turn the computer off.

Like the RAM, the ROM also has a spreadsheet layout. However, unlike the RAM, the ROM does not have capacitors in the cells where the columns and rows meet. Instead, it uses a diode. A diode allows an electrical current to flow in one direction. If a diode is present in a certain cell, then an electrical charge will be conducted through the cell to the ground, and the bit in the cell will be a 1. However, if there is no diode, then the cell will store a 0. ROMs are very cheap and reliable, but unfortunately, they are read-only.

8.18 DIAGNOSTICS SOFTWARE

Diagnostic software can help troubleshoot problems when your computer malfunctions or you suspect problems with an upgraded component or an entirely new system built from scratch. Several types of diagnostic software are available for PCs. Some diagnostic functions are integrated into the PC hardware directly, whereas others take the form of operating system utilities or separate software products.

A diagnostic program is written for examining the state, or locating problems with the hardware, or operating system environment that it is running on/in. Computer diagnostic software takes many forms. Some focuses on diagnosing hardware while other allows you to improve a computer's performance. In addition, computer repair tools are available for monitoring heat, recovering data, and wiping data from hard disks permanently.

The desktop computer comes with several sophisticated diagnostic programs. Technicians use these tools to find the causes of erratic behavior in the computer, slow operation and other problems. These programs consist of software that is built into hardware drivers and components of the Windows operating system. Unlike previous versions of the Windows operating system, the DirectX Diagnostic Tool is now included by default and can help diagnose issues related to the multimedia performance of your system. Apart from general system information such as the processor type and amount of memory, the Diagnostic Tool also contains information about the display, sound and input of the computer.

Computer errors can occur due to either hardware or software issues and often requires time consuming trial-and-error troubleshooting to diagnose. Windows 8 includes a few diagnostic tools that can assist you and save you money in the process. The diagnostic tools cover the usual culprits such as memory, hard drives, video cards and software, allowing you to pinpoint the source of your computer troubles. In instances where the tools cannot outright repair the errors, the information provided can be key to determining what has to be replaced.

System Diagnostics included with Windows 8 is the Performance Monitor application, which features a system diagnostics option. The Performance Monitor is accessible by typing "Perfmon" (without the quotation marks) on the Start screen and pressing "Enter." Performing the system diagnostics test provides you with a report about the status of hardware and resources. If any issues are encountered, you'll see a warning along with information on how to resolve the problem. The operating system, hard disks, security and system services of the computer are also checked as part of the diagnosis.

8.18.1 Software and Hardware Diagnostic Tools

Diagnostic software, the kind that comes with your computer as well as the types of available third-party software, is vitally important to you any time your computer malfunctions or you begin the process of upgrading a system component or adding a new device. Even when you attempt a simple procedure, such as adding a new adapter card, or begin the sometimes tedious process of troubleshooting a hardware problem that causes a system crash or lockup when you are working, you need to know more about your system than you can learn from the packing list sent with the system. Diagnostic software provides the portal through which you can examine your system hardware and the way your components are working.

Several types of diagnostic software are available for PC-compatible systems. The diagnostic programs include the following:

8.18.2 POST

The Power-On Self Test (POST) is a built in diagnostic program that checks PC hardware to ensure that everything is present and functioning properly, before the actual booting begins. The most important job of the BIOS is to give the microprocessor its first instructions and to load the operating system when the computer is switched on. It then performs a POST, or Power-On Self Test. This is an inspection to check that everything in the PC is working and functioning properly.

If everything is found to be working properly during the POST, the BIOS will then try to boot the computer from the hard disk drive. This is the process of launching the operating system.

8.18.3 Manufacturer supplied diagnostics software

Major manufacturers such as Dell, HP, and IBM, develop special diagnostics software that consist of a number of tests to thoroughly examine your PC. These diagnostics software usually come along with the system or you may need to download it from the manufacturer's Web site. At times, you may even need to purchase the software.

8.18.4 Aftermarket diagnostics software

There are a number of manufacturers making general purpose diagnostics software for PC-compatible systems. This includes utilities--Symantec's Norton Utilities, PC-Technician and others--that provide detailed diagnostics of any PC-compatible systems.

8.18.5 Peripheral diagnostics software

Many peripheral devices such as printers, scanners, sound cards, and network adapters are shipped along with special diagnostics software to test their specific functions. Peripheral-specific diagnostic software usually are included on the disk that contains the driver to run the peripheral on the system. Many hardware devices ship with specialized diagnostics software designed to test their particular functions. RAID adapters, for example, include configuration and diagnostic functions in the card's ROM BIOS that you can access with a keystroke at boot time. Other devices or adapters might provide a diagnostic program or disk, usually included with the drivers for the device.

8.18.6 Operating system diagnostics software

Windows operating systems equipped with a number of different PC diagnostic utilities. These utilities enable you to monitor the performance of various PC components and identify any problems occurring in them. Windows includes a number of utilities, tools, and error-reporting programs that make it quite easy for you to determine the reason behind an error.

8.18.7 Commercial Diagnostics Software

A large number of commercial third-party diagnostics programs are available for PC systems. These commercial programs are used by technicians to perform testing of new systems (often called burn-in testing) or testing of existing systems either in the shop or in the field.

8.18.8 Free/User Supported Diagnostics

Numerous free or user supported diagnostic programs are available, covering everything from processors to memory, disk drives, and virtually all other components in a PC.

8.19 BOOT PROCESS

Booting is a process in which your computer gets initialized. This process includes initilizing all your hadware components in your computer and get them to work together and to load your default operating system which will make your computer operational.

The normal startup sequence for Windows 7 is:

(a) Power-on self test (POST) phase.

(b) Initial startup phase.

(c) Windows Boot Manager phase.

(d) Windows Boot Loader phase.

(e) Kernel loading phase.

(f) Logon phase

To begin the boot process, turn on the computer. This is called a cold boot. When the computer is powered on, it performs a Power On Self Test (POST). POST stands for Power On Self Test. POST checks all the hardware devices connected to a computer like RAM, hard disk etc and make sure that the system can run smoothly with those hardware devices. If the POST is a failure the system halts with a beep sound. Boot process are reported by a series of audible tones, called beep codes.

After POST, now BIOS checks the boot priority. The BIOS locates and reads the configuration settings that are stored in the CMOS memory. The boot device priority, is the order in which devices are checked to locate the operating system. The boot device priority is set in the BIOS and can be arranged in any order. The BIOS boots the computer using the first drive that contains an operating system. Hard drives, network drives, USB drives, and even removable magnetic media, such as Compact Flash or Secure Digital (SD) cards can be used in the boot order, depending on the capabilities of the motherboard. Some BIOS also have a boot device priority menu that is accessed with a special key combination while the computer is starting but before the boot sequence begins. You can use this menu to select the device to boot, which is useful if multiple drives can boot the computer.

Windows Boot Loader and Windows Boot Manager in Windows 7. When the drive storing the OS is located, the BIOS finds the Master Boot Record (MBR). At this point, Windows Boot Manager (BOOTMGR) controls several installation steps. For instance, if more than one OS is present on the disk, BOOTMGR gives the user a chance to select which one to use. If there are no other operating systems, or if the user does not make a selection before the timer expires, the following process occurs:

- WinLoad uses the path specified in BOOTMGR to find the boot partition.
- WinLoad loads two files that make up the core of Windows 7: NTOSKRNL.EXE and HAL.DLL.
- WinLoad reads the Registry files, chooses a hardware profile, and loads the device drivers.

At this point, the NT kernel takes over. The NT kernel is the heart of all Windows operating systems. The name of this file is NTOSKRNL.EXE. It starts the login file called WINLOGON.EXE and displays the Windows Welcome screen.

8.19.1 BIOS (Basic Input Output System)

BIOS is an abbreviation of Basic Input output system. BIOS is an essential set of solutions stored in a chip that provides an interface between the operating system and the hardware of a PC.

BIOS is a set of instructions built in to your computer to control how information and data flow in and out of your computer.

The BIOS software has a number of different roles, but its most important role is to load the operating system. When you turn on your computer, the microprocessor tries to execute its first instruction, it has to get that instruction from somewhere. It cannot get it from the operating system because the operating system is located on a hard disk. The BIOS provides those instructions. Some of the other common tasks that the BIOS performs include:

- A Power-On Self-Test (POST) for all of the different hardware components in the system to make sure everything is working properly.
- Activating other BIOS chips on different cards installed in the computer, for example SCSI (Small Computer System Interface) and graphics cards often have their own BIOS chips.
- Providing a set of low-level routines that the operating system uses to interface to different hardware devices. It is these routines that give the BIOS its name. They manage things like keyboard, screen, and serial and parallel ports especially when the computer is booting.
- Managing a collection of settings for the hard disks, clock, etc. The BIOS is special software that interfaces the major hardware components of your computer with the operating system. It is usually stored on a Flash memory chip on the motherboard, but sometimes the chip is another type of ROM.

Booting sequence for PC is as follows:

- The first thing is BIOS working, as soon as PC is switched on.
- The BIOS checks the CMOS for the settings that you have specified for operating system (such as background, font, etc.). CMOS is an acronym for Complementary Metal Oxide Semiconductor. It is a ROM chip that stores basic information about PC and configurations. The BIOS will check this to find out the type of hard drive, CD drive, floppy disk drive, etc., in the computer and how much memory is there.
- The BIOS loads in the main memory, interrupt handlers, which are the programmes that act like translators. It loads the device drivers, which are software identifying hardware components like a keyboard, mouse, and hard disk. It will check the motherboard ports to make sure that all these devices are working properly.
- The BIOS also performs the POST to make sure that everything is working properly.
- It will finally display system settings.

8.19.2 BIOS Setup Utility

BIOS setup utility enables the user to modify the PC settings and store them in the CMOS. This utility also enables to control the booting sequence. This utility can be used to change the BIOS to correct any hardware problem error.

To enter the BIOS setup utility, do the following:

Start the system: To enter or to modify the CMOS setup, you should press a key or combination of keys during the initial startup sequence. Most PC systems use "Esc", "Del", "F1", "F2", "Ctrl+Esc" or Ctrl+Alt+Esc keys" to enter setup.

Once you have entered setup, you will see a set of text screens with a number of options.

Some of these are standard, while others vary according to the BIOS manufacturer. Common options include the following:

- System Time/Date - Set the system time and date.
- Boot Sequence - The order that BIOS will try to load the operating system.
- Plug and Play - A standard for auto-detecting connected devices. You should set it to "Yes" if your PC and operating system both support it.
- Mouse/Keyboard - " Enable Num Lock, " "Enable the Keyboard, " "Auto-Detect Mouse".
- Drive Configuration - Configure hard drives, CD-ROM and floppy disk drives.
- Memory - Direct the BIOS to shadow to a specific memory address.
- Security - Set a password for accessing the computer if need be.
- Power Management - Select whether to use power management, as well as set the amount of time for standby and suspend.
- Exit - Save your changes, discard your changes or restore default settings.

After you have finished with changes, you should choose "Save Changes" and exit. The BIOS will then restart PC so that the new settings take effect.

Press Esc key to exit without saving the new changes. A dialog box appears confirming if you want to exit without saving. Enter "Y" and press Enter key to exit without saving.

8.19.3 Setting the Standard and Advanced Setup CMOS Setup

Standard CMOS setup page enables you to set the basic settings of the system, such as the date and time. You can enter the hard disk setting using the options on this page. You can also enable and set the sequence of booting from HDD to CD Drive. The Advanced Setup page enables you to access the advanced function of the BIOS. You can modify the settings in this page to increase or decrease the time taken to boot the system. You can also specify the order of the devices that the operating system must search for the system files while booting the system.

8.19.4 Setting the Power Management

The Power management page enables you to control the power setup of the system. The power management enables PC to automatically switch off the power supply to the devices such as the hard disk or the monitor, when it is not used. This saves power and also increases the life of the system. To return the system to the normal working state you may have to press a key on the keyboard or move the mouse. However, you must first check that the operating system that you use support the different power management modes such as the Standby and the Suspend mode, otherwise the PC may not function properly.

8.19.5 Setting the Plug and Play (PnP) Feature

The PnP feature is available on newer PC systems and enables the system to automatically search for new hardware connected to the PC. It also install new any special drivers to use the new device.

8.19.6 Applying Optimal Settings

The Optimal Settings feature enables you to set the BIOS options to the default options. This keeps the system settings at the minimum level and is recommended when the system does not function properly or crashes frequently.

8.19.7 Applying Best Performance Settings

The Best Performance Settings feature enables you to set the BIOS options to make the system perform at the best level, such as increasing the processing speed. This setting boosts the hardware and makes the system work at the maximum possible level. This setting may put an extra load on the system and is recommended only on PC systems having high-performance hardware installed on them.

8.19.8 Setting the Features Setup

The motherboard has numerous built-in components, such as the serial port, parallel port, PS/2 port, and sound card. The Features setup page enables you to control these components by setting their properties. You can also enable and disable the components that you do not use, such as if you connect your keyboard and mouse to the serial port on the system then you can disable the PS/2 ports that are not being used. This allows you to free up IRQ (Interrupt Request) lines that can be used by other devices.

8.19.9 Setting the CPU PnP Setup Page

The Central Processing Unit (CPU) Plug-and-Play (PnP) setup page displays the details of the microprocessor installed on the motherboard. You can also change the microprocessor settings, using this page.

8.19.10 Setting the Hardware Monitor

The Hardware Monitor displays the system hardware details, such as voltage used by the system, CPU fan speeds, power, system and CPU temperatures. These options are useful as they enable you to monitor the system to check that the system does not get overheated.

8.19.11 Setting the BIOS Password

The BIOS password is used to protect the settings stored in the CMOS. You should enable the password option from the Advanced Setup page. When enabled, the system prompts user to enter the password before accessing the Setup Utility. To set the BIOS password you should remember the following points when changing the password:

- Make it a habit to change password regularly.
- The password can have a maximum of six alphabets or numerals.
- Use a password that you find easy to remember but difficult for others to guess.

8.19.12 Upgrading the BIOS

By updating the BIOS, you can add additional functions and can fix all the errors and bugs. You must also upgrade the BIOS if the software or hardware that you installed needs an updated version of the BIOS. You can get updated BIOS by removing the old motherboard and installing a new motherboard in your PC. However, if the BIOS is not permanently soldered on the motherboard, you can remove the BIOS chip and install a newer version of the chip on the PC motherboard.

You can also update the BIOS if your system has an Electronically Erasable Programmable Read Only Memory (EEPROM) for the BIOS. This enables you to change the BIOS using software. You can download the BIOS from the motherboard companies website. Some motherboards have a flash recovery jumper that you can use to restore the system if BIOS upgrade using the BIOS upgrade software does not work properly.

8.19.13 BIOS Error Codes

When a computer is first switched on, the hardware runs a Power-On Self Test (POST). If errors are encountered during this POST test, they are displayed via an audio beep or in the form of a code number flashed across the screen. With this audio code in hand, you can determine what part of the system is having problems and accordingly find a solution. The pattern of beeps whether it is the number of beeps or the length of those beeps will give you an indication of the actual problem. Beep sound is a distress signal from the PC in a morse code like pattern.

8.20 WHAT IS PRINTER?

Printers are the most popular output device. It provides information in a permanent readable form. It produces printed output of results, programs, and data. Printers can be divided into two categories:

- Impact printers
- Non-impact printers

8.20.1 Impact Printers

In these printers, there is a mechanical contact between the printhead and paper. The impact printers are further classified into the following categories:

(a) Line printers
(b) Character printers

Line printers

A line printer prints one line of the text at a time. Printing speeds may vary from 300–3000 lines per minute. Different types of line printers are–*Drum printer* and *Chain printer*.

Drum Printer A drum printer consists of a cylindrical drum on which characters are emobossed. One complete set of characters is embossed for each and every print position on a line. The drum is rotated at a high speed. There is a magnetically-driven hammer in each character position of the line. A character is printed by striking a hammer against the embossed character on the surface.

The printer receives all characters to be printed in one line of the text from the processor. The hammers hit the ribbon and paper against the desired character on the drum when it comes in the printing position. Its noise level is high and speed varies from 200 to 2000 lines per minute. They are expensive also.

Chain Printer A chain printer uses a rapidly, rotating chain which is called print chain (See Figure 8.6). Magnetically-driven hammers are located in each print position. To print a line, the characters in the line are transmitted from the memory to printer buffer. The band is rotated at a high speed. With the rotation of the band, a hammer is activated when the desired character comes in front of it. Thus, for a printer with 132 characters per line, 132 hammers will be positioned to strike the ribbon.

The noise level of the printer is high and its speed lies in the range of 400-2400 lines per minute.

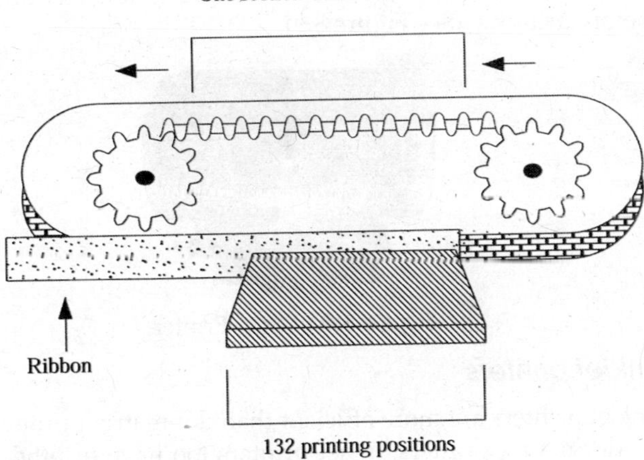

Figure 8.6 Chain printer

Character Printers (Serial Printer)

A character printer prints one character of the text at a time. They are low-speed printers. Their printing speed lies in the range of 30-600 characters per second. Different types of character printers are–*Dot matrix printers* and *Letter quality printers.*

Dot matrix printer A dot matrix printer is the most popular serial printer. The printhead contains a vertical array of pins. As the printhead moves across the paper, selected pins fire against the ribbon to form a pattern of dots on the paper.

The printhead contains a vertical array of 7,9,14,18 or even 24 pins.

A dot matrix printer is faster than a letter quality printer. These printers operate at two or three speeds. The lower the speed the better is the printing quality. Higher speed is for draft printing and lower speed is for Near-Letter quality (NLQ) printing, i.e., the printing is as good as that of a letter quality printer. Many dot matrix printers are bi-directional, i.e., they print one line of text from left to right and then the next line from right to left. Dot matrix printers do not have fixed character fonts. They can print special characters and graphics. There are 80 column and 132 column dot matrix printers available in the market.

☞ *Dot matrix printers are common in accounts department, warehouses and have many administrative purpose, including mailing labels, etc.*

Letter Quality printers These printers print full characters, which means that a character is not made up of dots. The most popular printer of this type is daisy-wheel printer. In a daisy-wheel printer, the pirnthead resembles a daisy flower, with its print arms appearing like the petals of the flower. The character to be printed is sent to the printer buffer. The hub is continuously rotating at high speed and a hammer strikes the appropriate character when it is in position. The daisy-wheel printer has a speed up to 90 characters per second. These are no more in use today.

8.20.2 Non-Impact Printers

Non-impact printers are thermal, chemical, electrostatic, laser beam, or inkjet technology for printing. Usually a non-impact printer is faster than an impact printer. These printers are categorized as:

(a) Electromagnetic printer
(b) Thermal printer
(c) Label Printer
(d) Photo Printer
(e) Inkjet printer
(f) Multi-function Printer
(g) Laser printer

Electromagnetic Printer

This printer uses magnetic recording techniques. By using this technique, the required output is written on a drum surface. Then this surface is passed through magnetic powder which adheres to the charged areas. The powder is then pressed onto the paper.

Thermal printer

Thermal transfer prints with the use of a ribbon. Heat from the print head melts ink from the ribbon onto special thermal transfer paper or synthetic label media that is specially treated for thermal transfer use. There are advantages and disadvantages to both thermal transfer and direct thermal printers. Thermal printers use hot needles that leave an impression on the thermally sensitive paper. When the paper passes over the thermal print head, images or text is created in black and other colors through the use of temperature variations. In order to print, the paper is inserted between the print head and the roller, and the printer sends an electrical current to the thermal head to generate the images and text. The thermo-sensitive paper reacts and changes color where the paper was heated. (See Figure 8.7).

Thermal printers work in two ways. For older models, heat sensitive paper is used by placing a roll in a container inside the machine and the end of that roll is stuck into a slot that takes the paper between the print head and the roller. The heat that has built up in the machine reacts with the heat-sensitive paper and the pigments transfer the image to the sheet.

For newer machines, tape cartridges are placed in the printer. There is a waxy material inside the cartridges. When the printer is in use, the paper is fed through the groove between the print head and roll. Heat causes the substance to stick to the paper.

Thermal printers are inexpensive, but the print quality is low and images tend to fade over time with climatic conditions. These printers are very fast, small, durable and perfectly transportable. They are very easy to use and use very little power during operation which keeps them noise free. However, there are some relative disadvantages of thermal printers. One of the inefficiencies of thermal printers is that because these machines need heat to start working, if the machine becomes very hot, it will use more ink so that printing will not always be stable and accurate. Another disadvantage is that because the paper is sensitive to heat, even the human touch can cause the paper to react by causing smudges and stains.

Thermal printers are used effectively in many areas. These printers are widely used in stores, kiosks, petroleum stations, POS systems, ATM machines, restaurant bill counter, credit card swipe unit etc.

Figure 8.7 Thermal printer

Label Printer

A label printer is a computer printer that prints on self-adhesive label material and/or card-stock (tags). A label printer with built-in keyboard and display for stand-alone use (not connected to a separate computer) is often called a label maker. Label printers are different from ordinary printers because they need to have special feed mechanisms to handle rolled stock, or tear sheet (fanfold) stock. (See Figure 8.8).

Common connectivity for label printers include RS-232 serial, Universal Serial Bus (USB), parallel, Ethernet and various kinds of wireless. Label printers have a wide variety of applications, including supply chain management, retail price marking, packaging labels, blood and laboratory specimen marking, and fixed assets management.

Figure 8.8 Label printer

Photo Printer

Photo printers are specifically designed to create photographs that rival any 35mm film print. Some photo printers print just one or two sizes of photos. Others print up to letter size, legal size or ever larger. Some photo printers have built-in LCD color screens, allowing users to view and enhance the photo before printing. (See Figure 8.9).

Figure 8.9 Photo Printer

Inkjet printers

Inkjet printers are more efficient than dot matrix printers. Just as dot matrix printers, inkjet printers too have printhead but inkjet's printhead does not have metal pins that come out from the printhead. Instead, the inkjet's printhead has many tiny nozzles that spray ink into the paper. Each nozzle is thinner than human hair. (See Figure 8.10).

Inkjet printers use a continuous stream of ink drops to print characters on paper. Droplets of ink are electrically charged after leaving a nozzle. The droplets are then guided to the proper position on the paper by electrically charged deflection plates. The print quality is good because the character is formed by dozens of tiny ink dots. These printers produce better quality of text and graphics and are faster. Almost all inkjets offer a color option as standard, in varying degrees of resolution. Inkjet printers are capable of producing high quality print which almost matches the quality of a laser printer. A standard inkjet printer has a resolution of 300 dots per inch, although newer models have improved on that.

Figure 8.10 Inkjet Printer

☞ *Inkjet printers are ideal for small business, home computers and individual computer office.*

Multi-function Printer

A multi-function printer (sometimes abbreviated to MFP) is a compact all-in-one machine that incorporates a photocopier, scanner and fax machine as well as a printer into one machine. A multi-function printer offers the convenience of additional features. For example, if you normally do not send or receive many fax messages, you may not have invested in a separate fax machine. However, a multi-functional printer that includes fax capabilities allows you to send or receive the occasional fax without an added expense. In addition, the ability to scan an image and then print that image using the same machine offers another level of convenience by saving you the time of walking to two separate devices. (See Figure 8.11).

Figure 8.11 Multi-function printer

Advantages Space Savings : One of the greatest advantages of a multi-functional printer includes the space savings. Rather than having to find space for a printer, a copier, a fax machine and a scanner, you can have the same functionality in a single machine. This space savings may benefit those trying to make the most of their home office space or those working with significant space constraints.

Cost Savings : Another advantage of a multi-functional printer includes the cost savings of purchasing one device that performs multiple functions. Although the purchase price for an all-in-one printer may exceed that of a traditional printer, the overall cost typically remains less than purchasing multiple machines.

Power Savings : Multi-function printers typically require one cord to power the entire device. Not only does this reduce cable congestion, it lowers the electricity required to run the device. This power savings also leads to increased cost savings.

Laser Printer

Laser printers are non-impact type printers. They print one page at a time. These printers use laser or some other light source to produce an image on a photosensitive drum. The computer controls the laser beam to turn it on and off when the laser beam is sent back and forth across the drum. An image is produced following the raster scan principle. The laser-exposed areas attract toner (an ink powder). Thereafter the drum transfers the toner to the paper. The paper then moves to a fusing station where the toner is permanently fused on the paper with heat or pressure. After this the drum is discharged and cleaned. Now the drum is ready for processing the next page. Laser printers are quiet and produce high-quality output. These printers are expensive and require periodic maintenance. Low-speed laser printers produce 10 pages or more per minute and are used with microcomputers. High-speed laser printers producing upto 30 pages per minute are used with mini and large computers. Laser printers have become popular for voluminous printing work. They are mainly used for desktop publishing work. (See Figure 8.12).

Figure 8.12 Laser Printer

Laser printer Vs Inkjet printer

The laser printer is different from an inkjet printer in a number of ways:

(a) The toner or ink in a laser printer is dry. In an inkjet printer, it is wet.
(b) Inkjet printer is about ten times more expensive to operate than a laser printer, because ink needs replenishing more frequently.
(c) The printed paper from an inkjet printer will smear it wet, but a laser printed document will not.

(d) If your printing needs are minimal, an inkjet printer is sufficient. But if your printing volume is high, consider buying a laser printer.

8.20.3 Classification of Printers

Printers are also classified by the following characteristics:

Quality of Type

The output produced by printers is said to be either letter quality (as good as a typewriter), near letter quality, or draft quality. Only daisy-wheel, inkjet and laser printers produce letter-quality type. Some dotmatrix printers also claim letter-quality print.

Speed

Measured in *characters per second* or pages per minute. The speed of printers varies widely. Daisy-wheel printers tend to be the slowest, printing about 30 Cps. Line printers are fastest (up to 3,000 lines per minute). Dotmatrix printers can print up to 500 Cps, and laser printers range from about 4 to 20 text pages per minute.

Impact or Non-impact

Impact printers include all printers that work by striking an ink ribbon. Daisy-wheel, dotmatrix and line printers are impact printers. Non-impact printers include laser printers and inkjet printers. Impact printers are much noisier.

Graphics

Some printers (daisy-wheel and line printers) can print only text. Other printers can print both text and graphics.

Fonts

Some printers, like dotmatrix printers, are limited to one or a few fonts. In contrast, laser and ink-jet printers are capable of printing and almost unlimited variety of fonts. Daisy-wheel printers can also print different fonts, but you need to change the daisy-wheel.

While buying a printer, the four main aspects to look at are as follows:

Resolution

The printers resolution is the sharpness at which the graphics or text appear on the paper when the print is removed. This resolution is generally measured in dots per inch. General printers will give you a resolution of about six hundred dots per inch. This resolution would be adequate enough for normal everyday print jobs.

Speed

In a workplace or if a person requires many print outs day in and day out the speed at which the printer functions becomes a crucial aspect. The normal everyday printers are capable of removing about three to six printed sheets of paper every sixty seconds. However, this number reduces if you are removing colour print outs. The printer that cost more ar capable of removing print outs, both colour and black an white, at a faster rate.

Colour

You would need a colour printer if your work demands tha coloured images be part of the print outs. With colour print ers, you have the best of both worlds, because they can also b programmed to give print outs in only black and white.

☞ *Depending on the manufacturer and model of the printer, in cartridge comes in various combinations, such as separat black and colour cartridges. Colour and black in a single car tridges or even a cartridge for each ink colour.*

Memory

Printers have a small quantity of memory storage space However the user can make this bigger. Increasing the memory is beneficial and also makes the printer quicker wher it has to give printouts of large number of graphics.

8.21 INTERFACE SIGNALS AND CABLES

A port is a connector for attaching cables or peripherals to a computer. The I/O (Input /Output) ports and cables connect the input and output devices to the PC. Accepting input and producing output are the basic functions of a PC. The I/O ports and cables provide the means to establish connections to external devices. Different types of I/O ports are as follows: (See Figure 8.13)

(a) Serial port
(b) Parallel port
(c) USB port

8.21.1 Serial port

The serial port is used for the computer to communicate with a device one bit at a time. The data moves serially 1 bit at a time from one device to another. Serial port connects to devices, such as modems, printers, digital cameras. Serial port is the oldest kinds of ports in use (See Figure 8.13).

To communicate using serial communication, two communicating devices must use the same communication parameters, such as the communication mode, baud rate (bit per second), parity bits etc. Serial ports enables data flow in both directions. Most PCs have two serial port connectors: a compact 9-pin connector and a larger 25-pin connector. A 25-pin connector was introduced with the PC system, but as not all 25-pins are used for data transmission, IBM (International Business Machines), introduced 9-pin connectors with the PC system.

8.21.2 Parallel Port

Parallel ports transmit data in a parallel manner. Parallel ports are wide in size to enable parallel transmission of data. This port is also known as the 'printer port' because it is commonly used for the printer interfacing. Parallel ports are much faster han serial ports. Scanner, tape backup, portable CD-ROM rives, etc. are also designed to use the parallel port (See Figure 8.13).

Serial Vs Parallel Ports

Serial and parallel ports are two different types of connecting devices. They can be used to connect all sorts of peripherals like *modems, mice,* and *printers*. The major difference between serial and parallel ports is that serial ports transfer data one bit at a time, while parallel ports can transfer data 8 bits at a time. Serial ports have to take apart the 8 bits in a byte, and transfer them one by one. On the other hand, the newer parallel ports line up the 8 bits and can transfer them all at once.

Because serial ports can only transfer data 1 bit at a time, it is pretty obvious that they are much slower than the parallel ports that can transfer data eight bits at a time. However, serial ports are also smaller and also require fewer wires. This is because parallel ports need eight wires to be able to transfer all eight bits at one time. Also, serial ports are much cheaper than parallel ports.

8.21.3 USB Port

Universal Serial Bus (USB) port are included on most computers sold today. USB makes it easier to connect peripherals to computers and eliminates the need to configure Interrupt Request (IRQ) settings or Dual Inline Package (DIP) switches. USB can be used to connect various peripherals includes keyboard, mouse, joysticks, scanners, printers, monitors, modems and digital camera. USB is very fast and becoming a popular replacement for serial and parallel ports. This is because USB is highly advanced, fast, and simple to use. USB devices are hot pluggable, i.e. you can add devices to your computer easily without having to shut down the computer. External devices can be connected any time, even when the computer is running.

The I/O cables connect the PC to different I/O devices. The I/O cables are very important to the connections formed by a PC. There are different types of cables available, such as Shielded Twisted Pair (STD), Unshielded Twisted Pair (UTP) and Fiber optic cables (See Figure 8.13).

Serial port, used to connect the mouse

Parallel port, used to connect the printers

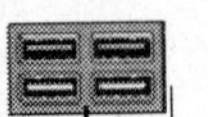
USB port is used to connect the mouse, pen drive, printers, etc.

Figure 8.13 Ports for connecting

> ☞ *USB port allow you to connect up to 127 peripherals to your computer, using USB hubs.*

> ☞ *FireWire is yet another device that can be used to connect peripherals to your computer system, while it is much faster than USB, FireWire can connect fewer devices.*

8.22 PRINTER DIP SWITCHES

DIP switches are located at the back of the printer. The DIP switches are read after the initialization process either by turning the power switch on or inputting the INITIAL signal of the parallel interface.

> ☞ *The printer's power must be turned OFF before making any DIP switch changes.*

In some cases, jumpers (jumpers are two or three hole connectors that connect pins on the motherboard) are replaced by blocks of sliding, or flip-flop, DIP switches. These blocks are labeled SW and followed by a number, as in SW1, SW2 etc. Each DIP switch is set to either ON or OFF.

An individual DIP switch is designed by its block number followed by its position within the block. For example, the fourth switch of block 2 is called SW 2-4. The configurations in the illustration are referred to as follows:

	1.1	1.2	1.3	1.4	1.5	1.6	1.7	1.8
SW1	OFF	OFF	OFF	OFF	OFF	OFF	ON	ON
SW2	OFF	ON	OFF	OFF	OFF	ON	ON	OFF

Never turn the printer off while it is writing the new setting to memory. Always wait until *'DIP SW setting complete !!'* is printed before turning the power off.

8.22.1 Printer Port

A port is used to connect the system and a device together, using a connecting cable, so that they can communicate together. Different ports available are located at the back of the system case.

The parallel port connector has 25 pins to connect devices, such as printer. So parallel port is also called printer port. Newer systems feature on Enhanced Capabilities Port (ECP) able to provide duplex operation and higher data rates.

> ☞ *ECP provides increased data communication speed between the system and the printer.*

8.22.2 Printer Driver

A driver is a program that controls the behaviour of device connected to a computer. It provides a connection between peripheral devices and the operating system. All devices, such as monitors, modems and printers require drivers for their functioning. Drivers for certain devices, such as the keyboard form a part of the operating system. Other devices like printers need to have their drivers installed separately.

8.22.3 Printer Head and Ribbon

In dot matrix printer or other impact printer, a printer head is the pins that strike the ink ribbon against the paper to generate the printed image. Since, the impact printers strike the media to create an impression, they can print not just through a ribbon but also through several sheets of papers and carbon sheet to print multiple carbon copies in a single pass.

Dot matrix printer uses a matrix of metal pins on a print head to create dots on the print. The head of dot matrix printer has a number of small print pin mechanisms. A print pin mechanism is a combination of permanent magnet, electro-magnet, spring and print pins.

The number of metal pins in the print head determines the quality of output of a dot matrix printer. The number of metal pins in the dot matrix printers varies from 9 to 24 pins. The best quality dot matrix printers have 24 metal pins.

When a line of character is to be printed, the print head moves horizontally across the paper and print pin strikes the paper through an inked ribbon. The print head of the dot matrix printer runs repeatedly across the surface of the page being printed. The metal pins on the print head of the printer are driven by electromagnets. Dot matrix printers can be monochrome or colour printers. The colour printers use a multi-coloured striped ink ribbon to print.

In the inkjet printer, a printer head is the nozzal that places the ink on the printer. Inkjet uses liquid ink to spray characters on to the page. Non-impact printers do not strike any ribbon or paper to produce the image. Instead, they use ink spraying, electrostatic magnetization or heat process to produce the required image. As the inkjet printers do not use any ribbon and the ink is directly released to the paper, the image looks much smoother then the image generate using dotmatrix impact printer.

☞ *Non-impact printer cannot be used to print carbon copies or multiple copies in a single pass.*

8.23 PRINCIPLES OF OPERATION OF INKJET PRINTER

In the inkjet printing mechanism, the print head has several tiny nozzles, also called jets. As the paper moves past the print head, the nozzles spray ink onto it, forming the characters and images. An inkjet printer can produce from 100 to several hundred pages, depending on the nature of the hard copy, before the ink cartridges must be replaced. There is usually one black ink cartridge and one so-called color cartridge containing ink in primary pigments (cyan, magenta, and yellow). Some inkjet printers use a single cartridge with cyan, magenta, yellow, and black ink. A few models require separate cartridges for each primary pigment, along with a black ink cartridge.

Inkjet printer works in the following manner:

1. An ink-filled print cartridge attached to the inkjet's print head moves sideways across the width of a sheet of paper. This sheet of paper is fed through the printer below the print head.
2. The print head is made up of small ink-filled chambers, each attached to a nozzle smaller than a human hair.
3. An electrical pulse flows through a heating element, i.e., a thin resistors located at the back of the ink chambers.
4. When an electrical current flows through the resistor, the resistor heats a thin layer of ink at the bottom of the chamber to more than 900°. Fahrenheit for a very-very short duration. This makes the ink to boil and forms a small bubble of vapor.
5. At this vapor bubble expands, it pushes ink through the nozzle to form a droplet at the tip of the nozzle.
6. When the bubble further expands, the ink droplet overcomes the surface tension and the pressure of the bubble forces the droplet onto the paper forming a small dot.
7. A typical character is formed by a number of these tiny dots.
8. As the resistor cools, the bubble collapses and the resulting pulls fresh ink from the attached reservoir into the ink chamber.
9. For colour printing multiple cartridges of three basic colour Cyan, Magenta and Yellow are used. The colour output of the Inkjet printers are of very high quality because there is no ribbon to fade the colour, ink is directly deposited on the paper. In addition, by mixing different colours on the paper Inkjet printers can provide millions of colours.
10. Most of the good quality inkjet printers provide one additional black cartridge other than three basic colour cartridges. This black cartridge is used to print black text or other black color images. Mixing of the three basic colors to produce black gives very faded black colour.

☞ *In Piezoelectric technology, pressure, not heat is used to eject ink on the paper. Now most of the inkjet printers use this technology.*

8.23.1 Various Components of Inkjet Printers

An inkjet printer is made up of several parts that accept, support and move the paper during the process of printing. All these parts have to work in co-ordination so that the printer works properly. If any of these components gets spoilt then will hold up the printing process.

The various inkjet parts are categorized into two main groups: These are:

(a) Print Head Assembly
(b) Paper Feed Assembly

The parts that fall into the print head assembly category are as follows:

Print Head Assembly

Print Head The first and most obvious part is the print head itself. The print head is the soul of any ink jet printer. The print head is a device that is made up of several nozzles whose purpose is to spray small droplets of ink on to the paper. Without this component the ink jet printer would be completely useless.

Cartridge The second most important part in this category is the ink cartridges. Cartridge contains ink for printing. The type of ink cartridge will differ depending on which manufacturer you buy from. Different manufacturers make ink cartridges with a variety of different combinations. For example, you can purchase ink cartridges that come with individual cartridges for black ink and coloured inks or with a single cartridge for both kinds of ink. You can even purchase an individual ink cartridge for every different colour. There are some ink cartridges available for inkjet printer that come built in with the print head.

☞ *Cover of cartridge provides a cover for the ink cartridge. Thus cover is removed only when a cartridge has to be replaced.*

Printer Head Stepper Motor Another important part of the inkjet printer is the Print Head Stepper Motor. The printer comes built in with a stepper motor. The function of the stepper motor is to move the print head assembly, which consists of the ink cartridges and the print head, forward and backward from corner-to-corner of the page.

Belt The belt is another part of the print head assembly. A belt is used to attach the print head assembly to the stepper motor.

Stabilizer Bar The print head assembly also makes use of a stabilizer bar. The function of the stabilizer bar is to make sure that the printing process goes through with precision, control and accuracy.

Paper Feed Assembly

Paper Tray/Feeder The main part in this category is the paper tray/feeder. Almost all the models of the Inkjet printer consist of a tray into which you load the paper. Others make use of a feeder in place of a tray. Feeder accepts the paper and forwards individual sheets as printing progresses. The feeder pulls open at an angle and is placed at the back of the printer. However, there is a disadvantage with paper feeders. They cannot hold as much paper as a normal paper tray.

Roller The function of a roller is to pull the page from the paper tray or paper feeder and send it ahead into the printer once the print head system is all set to print.

The other important parts of the printer are as follows:

Power Supply While earlier printers often had an external transformer, most printers sold today use standard power supply that is incorporated into the printer itself.

Control Circuitry The Control Circuitry a tiny but significant piece of circuitry that is built into the printer. The main function of this circuitry is to oversee and manage the mechanical phases of the printing process. The other function it has to carry out is to decode all kinds of information that is given by the computer to the printer for any print jobs.

Interface Port The last component is actually a group of devices combined and put under one category, which are called the Interface Ports. The parallel port is still used by many printers. The newest range in Interface Ports amongst printer owners is the USB ports.

8.23.2 Trouble Shooting of Inkjet Printers

There are many problems that can arise during the working of the printer. Inkjet printers are easy to maintain. The general problems that can occur with inkjet printers are blank printouts, white streaks on a printout and messy printout.

Printout from the Printer are Blank

This type of problem may be due to faulty ink cartridge. Check if the plastic cover has been removed from the ink cartridge. There may be a possibility of air entrapment inside the cartridge. To undo any such fault, cover the cartridge in a tissue and shake it gently. Replace faulty cartridge with another ink cartridge. This helps to locate fault in the cartridge and also to find out if the cartridge is empty.

Colour Printout are Faulty

If an inkjet printer is not properly printing colour printouts, it may be due to result of a faulty ink cartridge. Leaky cartridges can cause a great deal of problems in printing. It also leads to unnecessary wastage of ink. In this case, lay the ink cartridge on a wet tissue. The print head should touch the tissue so that the excess ink can be absorbed.

Printer Lights are flashing

Flashing lights can indicate one of many problems. The printer uses this signal to indicate some internal problem. It could be a paper jam or damaged system board. There are different patterns for flashing lights. Each indicates a different problem.

If print cartridge status is flashing then first of all check whether top cover printer is open? If it is open close it. If everything is fine with the top cover go after cartridge inspection. There could be possibility that cartridge are not installed properly. One more reason could be one cartridge is missing or running out of ink. Replace the faulty cartridge with a good cartridge.

Resume light is flashing then printer may be out of paper. Put appropriate number of pages in the tray to complete the printing task. If sheets of paper are there in the tray then printer may be printing the second side of a two-sided document and due to which resume light is flashing. Wait for sometime and let the printer complete the printing task. If none of the listed problem is causing the problem then there must be paper jam. Clear the paper jam and resume printing.

Power light is flashing then printer is preparing to print the document. The light stops flashing when printer receives all data.

Horizontal White Lines in a Printout

If lines and dots are appearing in the printout then cartridge needs cleaning. Either clean cartridges manually or automatically. To clean the printer.

(a) Turn off the printer
(b) Check the manual for cleaning instructions. If instructions are provided, follow them.
(c) If the manual does not have cleaning instructions, clean the printer contacts with a moist soft cloth.
(d) To clean the print head or cartridges, use the cleaning button on the printer if it is there.
(e) Print a test page.

No Power to Printer

Fuse Has Blown Check the fuse with a meter and replace the fuse. Ensure the correct voltage and amperage.

Internal Power Supply has Failed Most common fault. Repair yourself only if you know what you are doing.

AC (Alternating) Power Supply has Failed Most AC adapters are sealed. Repair yourself only if you know that you are doing. Chances are there is multiple damage, replacing one or two components will only allow power to circulate temporarily causing greater damage.

Main Logic Board is Shutting Down the Power Repair the logic on the main logic board and in some cases, when damage is too extensive or parts are unavailable (custom chipsets), the main logic board will require replacement.

Power available but Not Printing

Printer Cable not Installed Properly Ensure that both ends of the cable are correctly installed.

Printer Cable is Faulty Check for possible pin damage and replace if necessary.

No Paper or Paper Not Installed Properly No paper will result with the printer going into alarm, not coming "online" or "ready". Install some paper. If there is paper, ensure it is correctly installed. Ensure that the "online" button has been selected. There are sensors along the paper path, if these are defective they will cause the printer not to print. Check the sensors along the paper path and replace if necessary.

Printer Port Connection at PC is Faulty Try printing plain text via DOS (you can even use the "print screen" command on your keyboard while you are in the DOS). If still not printing, refer to your printer's owner manual and perform a "self test" of your printer. If the printer prints OK, the fault is more that likely going to be with the printer cable or computer, not with the printer.

8.24 PRINCIPLES OF OPERATION OF LASER PRINTERS

The term laser stands for *light amplification by simulated emission of radiation.* A laser printer operates on the principle of electro-photography used in photocopy machine. The laser printer uses a beam of laser for the purpose of printing. The basic functioning of the laser printer is the principle of static electricity. Electric charge that accumulates on an insulated object is called static electricity. Since oppositely charged atoms (positive and negative) are attracted to each other, objects with opposite static electricity fields get attached to each other. The laser printer uses this property to combine ink powder and paper.

The laser printer consists of a revolving cylinder that is made up of photoconductive material. At initial drum is given a positive charge with the help of a wire and the drum starts revolving. This wire is known as *Corona Wire.* The wire has electric current passing through it. The laser printer works in the following manner:

1. In a laser printer, the photosensitive drum or the Organic Photo Conductive (OPC) drum is the main component for the image formation system. It is the center of the complete image formation process. The photo conductive drum is given a positive or negative charge by the charge corona wire.
2. As the drum starts revolving, the printer shines a laser beam on the surface of drum to create some discharge points. In this way laser draws letters and images to be printed as pattern of electrical charge. In order to draw the pattern on drum, the laser receives the page data (tiny dots that make up text and images) one horizontal line at a time. Also, the laser does not move the beam itself, instead it emits the beam on a movable mirror. The mirror moves and shines the beam through series of lenses on the surface of the drum.
3. After the pattern is set, the printer coats the negatively charge surface of the drum with toner–a type of fine black powder. Since the toner is positively charged, it sticks only on negative discharged points on the drum.
4. With powder pattern attach, the drum rolls over the sheet of paper coming from paper tray. This paper sheet is positively charged. The positive charge is strong enough to attract the negatively charged toner particles from the drum. The toner particles leave the drum and go onto the paper. At this point, the image is on the paper, however, the particles are held only by their opposite charge.
5. The printer passes the pages through the fuser, a pair of heated rollers. As the paper passes through these rollers, the loose toner power melts, fusing with the fibers in the paper. This makes the image permanent. The fuser rolls the paper to the output tray and you get the finished

page. Printouts from laser printers are warm because they pass through the fuser before coming out. However, the paper moves at a very high-speed and therefore, it does not get burned. The fuser rollers must be coated with Teflon, which is non-stick material. Thus, material prevents the collection of toner on the fuser.

6. Lastly, the drum is cleaned to remove any toner particles left on it. Then the drum surface passes the discharge lamp. The bright light of the lamp exposer the entire surface of the drum, erasing the pattern of electric charge. Then corona wire reapplies the positive charge to the drum, making drum ready for next printing job.

8.24.1 Various Components of Laser Printer

The basic parts that a laser printer consists of are a toner hopper, corona wire, discharge lamp, laser scanning unit, fuser, developer roller and a photoreceptor drum assembly. Each of these parts have a very important role to play in the printing process (See Figure 8.14).

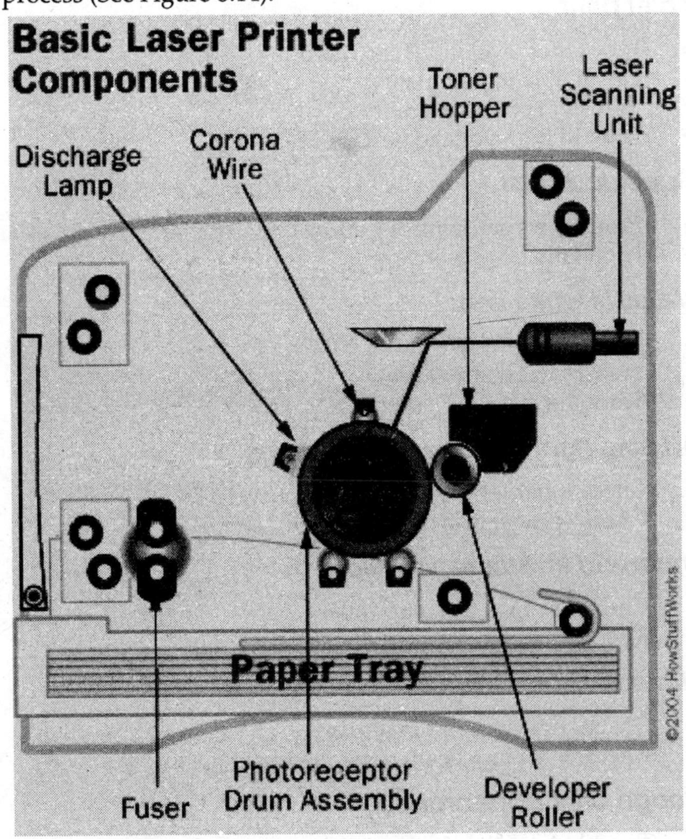

Figure 8.14 Components of Laser printer

Toner hopper

The toner of the laser printer is stored in a little compartment that is known as the toner hopper. This toner hopper section is basically a small little container that is built into a removable casing, so that it can be removed filled and put back into the laser printer without any sort of trouble.

Corona Wire

An initial storage of the printing, a light sensitive drum is given a positive charge with the help of a wire and the drum starts revolving. This wire is known as *corona wire.*

Discharge lamp

The bright light of the lamp exposes the entire surface of the drum, erasing the pattern of electric changes.

Laser scanning unit

Laser scanning unit is capable of radiating heat generated by a light source.

Fuser

Fuser is a device which basically compromises of two rollers, which are heated. The heat element in the fuser is a very important aspect of finishing the printing job. When the paper goes in between these two rollers that are heated, the toner powder that has remained loose will melt and will combine with the fiber that are present in the paper. After this the fuser simply passes the paper into the output tray.

Photoreceptor

The most important part of the laser printer without which it cannot function is something known as the photoreceptor. The photoreceptor basically consists of a cylinder or a drum that revolves, using highly photoconductive material that is dispersed by light photons.

8.24.2 Stages Involved in Printing Process of Laser Printer

Let us now see the steps performed by the laser printer during the print process.

Charging

This step cleans the surface of the cylindrical photosensitive drum. The drum is prepared for use and corona wire passes electric charge to the drum.

Writing

The laser beam and movable lens together write an image of document on the surface of drum.

Developing

During this step, the toner (fine black powder) gets attached to the positive points of the drum.

Transferring

Image made with dry toner powder on the drum surface gets transferred to the paper.

Detaching

This step removes the paper, along with the dry toner image on the paper surface, from the drum.

Fusing

It is the job of the fusing section to melt the toner and fuse it on the printing media by applying heat and pressure. This makes the image permanent.

Cleaning

In this process toner is cleaned from the drum. The cleaning blade remover of any toner that remains on the drum after the transfer process. The toner that the cleaning blade removes is collected in a separate waste toner compartment within the toner cartridge. Waste toner cannot be reused for printing because it can be contaminated with dust and paper fibers. A quality printed image requires, clean toner.

8.24.3 Trouble Shooting of Laser Printers

To initiate automatic cleaning by a printer software do this steps:

(a) In Windows operating system, Open the Control Panel. Click printer and faxes. In printer and faxes dialog box. In the printer task pane. Click Troubleshoot printing.

(b) You can then follow the instructions on the screen.

(c) If the results are not satisfactory, repeat the cleaning process.

The supreme quality of laser printing is due to the delicacy of the particles of toner and the means used to arrange the toner into super-sharp images is by applying a static charge to a roller, which then presses the toner to the paper. These two properties make toner a real problem when it comes to cleaning up a spill.

The best way to clean a toner is with a rag if possible or with compressed air for those tricky bits but always be aware of how to use compressed air safely. For large spills, you should be able to use a trusty dustpan and brush for the bulk of the spill.

As there are many individual parts which make up a complete printer, economic repairs of laser printers are more commonplace. Diagnosis is typically aided by an error description or number displayed on an LCD (Liquid Crystal Display) panel on the printer and/or by the image on the paper. Reference to the user manual should be made for the former and the following lists should help in diagnosing the latter. To supplement the manual, below are suggestions on how to respond to error messages:

"Warming-up" message continuously shows

- Faulty data cable
- Faulty interface circuit

"Paper Out" message

- If paper is actually present, improperly positioned paper tray
- Non-working tray sensors

"Toner Low" message always appears or never appears

- Suspect EP (Electro Photographic) cartridge
- Faulty high voltage power supply

"Paper Jam" message

- Poor quality paper
- Worn pickup assembly
- Fuser unit problem

"Error" message

- Suspect scanner unit
- A bad connection between scanner and hardware driver

"Service" message

- Generally concerned with fuser problems

Blacked-out paper

- Primary corona in EP cartridge
- Electronic logic fault

Faint print

- Low toner level in EP cartridge
- Unsuitable paper quality
- Transfer corona assembly
- Fault in high voltage power supply

Speckled print

- Primary corona control grid
- High voltage power supply

Vertical white lines

- EP Cartridge
- Transfer corona assembly
- Scanning and laser assembly

Missing right hand or distorted text

- Check toner level or replace EP cartridge
- Check scanner and optical alignment

Incorrect Image registration

- Check or replace pickup rollers
- Check or replace drive train

Horizontal black lines

- Check connectors from sensor
- Check or replace beam detect sensor

Rough print appearance

- Troubleshoot the electronic logic circuit

Smeared print

- Check fusing roller and cleaning pads
- Check or replace static discharge comb
- Check the drive train and paper path

Distorted images

- Check paper path
- Check or replace the scanner unit

Vertically repetitive effects

- Check and clean all rollers and belts
- Check or replace EP cartridge

Print Quality Poor

Toner Cartridge Faulty Remove the toner cartridge and check to see if the toner cartridge appears to be leaking, damaged or rotation has seized. Replace the toner cartridge.

Drum Unit Faulty Some laserjet printers have a separate drum unit. Remove the drum unit being careful not to allow direct sunlight or continuous exposure to daylight and do not touch it even if it appears to have residue of toner on it.
It is probably faulty anyway but if it is not, then touching will damage it.

Transfer Corona Assembly Faulty

Depending on the brand of your laserjet, this item will be either a roller assembly or a wire assembly. Remove, clean thoroughly, replace and test.
If yours is the roller assembly type, make sure that you do not touch the roller, the oil on your hand will damage it.

Fuser Unit Assembly Faulty

Probably the most common place to cause poor print quality and paper jamming. Inspect the fuser unit assembly for scratches on the fuser roller. Ensure that the printer has been turned off for at least one hour as extreme temperatures exist within this item.

If scratches are in evidence, replace the entire assembly. You can be sure that the thermistors, thermoswitches, gearing and lamp will fail next. It is always better to replace the entire assembly.

High Voltage Power Supply Faulty

Classic signs are blank pages, black pages or faint print. Replace the high voltage power supply.

Laser Scanner Unit Assembly & Optical Fiber Cable

Missing print, faint print. Try cleaning the mirror, the front of the scanner unit assembly and then test it.

Most of the time this procedure should work. If this procedure fails to rectify the fault, replace the scanner unit assembly.

It is also good practice to replace the optical fiber cable as well.

No Power to Printer

Fuse Has Blown Check the fuse with a meter and replace the fuse. Ensure the correct voltage and amperage.

Faulty Power On-Off Switch Check the switch with a meter and replace the switch. Ensure the correct voltage and amperage.

AC Power Supply has Failed Replace the AC power supply. Try to repair only if you are sure about what you are doing. Chances are there is multiple damage, replacing one or two components will only allow power to circulate temporarily causing greater damage.

PC Interface/Main Logic Board in Shutting Down the Power Supply

Repair the logic on the PCA (Printed Circuit Assembly) interface/main logic board and in some cases, when damage is too extensive or parts are unavailable (custom chipsets), the PCA interface/main logic board will require replacement.

DC Controller is Shutting Down the Power Supply

Repair the logic on the DC controller and in some cases, when damage is too extensive or parts are unavailable (custom chipsets), the DC controller will require replacement.

DC Power Supply is Faulty

Repair or replace the DC power supply. DC power supply feeds the DC controller. Quite often if this is the culprit, then damage to the DC controller could have occurred.

Power is On but not Printing

Printer Cable not Installed Properly Ensure that both ends of the cable are correctly installed.

Printer Cable is Faulty Check for possible pin damage and replace if necessary.

No Paper or Paper not inserted Properly No paper will result with the printer going into alarm, not coming, "on-line" or "ready". Insert some paper. If there is paper, ensure it is correctly installed. Ensure that the "on-line" button has been selected. There are sensors along the paper path, if these are defective they will cause the printer not to print. Check the sensors along the paper path and replace if necessary.

Printer Port Connection at PC is Faulty Try printing plain text via DOS (you can even use the "print screen" command on your keyboard while you are in the DOS environment). If the printer OK, the fault is more than likely going to be with the printer cable or computer, not with the printer.

Self Test is OK and PC Printer Port is OK Faulty PCA interface/main logic board. Repair input/output circuit on PCA interface/main logic board. Extensive damage may require that the main logic board is to be replaced.

Grinding Noises

Obstruction Along Paper Path There might be something caught along the paper path.

Gear Train Assembly Worn Out or Damaged Inspect the gear train assembly. If worn out or damaged, replace the gear train assembly.

Toner Cartridge is Faulty Remove the toner cartridge and inspect its gearing and rotation replace if necessary.

Main Motor Faulty Inspect the main motor's gearing and rotation and replace if found to be faulty. More often than not, damaged gearing attached to the main motor will not be available as a separate entity, meaning that the entire main motor assembly will require replacement.

Fuser Unit Assembly Faulty As with faults with poor print quality and paper jamming, the fuser unit assembly will also cause grinding noises. Grinding noises coming from the fuser unit assembly is a sure sign of worse things to come. Replace the fuser unit assembly. It is always better to replace the entire assemblies as well as meshing gears that it links up with.

Cooling Fans Grinding noises coming from the cooling fans tell you only one thing, it is about to stop.

Seized fans will overheat the printer and cause possible extensive damage.

Replace the faulty fan immediately when this occurs.

Paper Jamming/Misfeeding

Paper Quality Poor Ensure that the paper you introduce into your printer meets with the standards of the printer manufacturer and replace if necessary. This is especially important when dealing with transparencies and labels.

Obstruction Along Paper Path There might be something caught along the paper path.

Toner Cartridge is Faulty Remove the toner cartridge and inspect its gearing and rotation replace if necessary.

Fuser Unit Assembly Faulty As with faults with poor print quality and paper jamming, the fuser unit assembly is one of the most common faults regarding paper jamming. It is always better to replace the entire assemblies as well as the meshing gears that it links up with.

Sensors Faulty Faulty sensors along the paper path will not provide the printer with the correct information about the paper's position in the printer and hence the printer will fall into a false paper jam mode. Inspect and test the sensors and replace if necessary.

Paper Registration Assembly Faulty This fault will prevent the paper from being "picked up" in the first instance. Replace the paper registration assembly and it is a good idea to replace the paper path sensors as well.

Clutch Drive Assembly Faulty Causes internal paper jamming to occur. Replace both the entire clutch drive assembly and the gear train assembly.

Paper Delivery Assembly Faulty Causes internal paper jamming to occur. Replace both the paper delivery assembly and the gear train assembly.

Fuser Malfunction/Error 50

Fuser Unit Assembly Faulty A Fuser Malfunction or Error 50 means just that the Fuser Unit Assembly is faulty and requires replacement. As easy way to tell if your Fuser Unit Assembly is indeed faulty is to feel for any warmth emanating from the Fuser Unit Assembly.

A cold Fuser Unit Assembly will generally inform you that something is wrong with the Fuser Unit Assembly. It is always better to replace the entire Fuser Unit Assembly along with the Meshing Gears that it links up with.

AC Power Supply Faulty The AC Power Supply supplies power directly to the Fuser Unit Assembly. Although, you may have power circulating throughout the printer, the circuit responsible in providing voltage to the Fuser Unit Assembly has failed. Unfortunately faulty AC Power Supplies also cause damage to the Fuser Unit Assembly. Sometimes both of these devices require replacement.

DC Controller Faulty The DC Controller is really the heart and soul of control functions within a LaserJet Printer. The DC controller is also the cause of Fuser Malfunctions. Repair or replace the DC controller.

8.24.4 Installing and Configuring Printers in Windows 7

You can install printers in Window 7 using the Add a Printer under Printer Tasks.

Using the Add a Printer Wizard

1. Click the Start button, and then, on the Start menu, click Devices and Printers.
2. Click Add a printer.
3. In the Add Printer wizard, click Add a local printer.
4. On the Choose a printer port page, make sure that the Use an existing port button and the recommended printer port are selected, and then click Next.
5. On the Install the printer driver page, select the printer manufacturer and model, and then click Next. Follow the instructions on the screen to finish adding a printer with the Add Printer Wizard.

☞ *The only difference between installing a network printer and a local printer with the Add Printer Wizard is that you must specify the path to the network printer or browse to find its network location.*

8.25 PLOTTERS

A plotter is an output device that is used to create high-quality graphics, visuals, charts, graphs, tables, or diagrams (See Figure 8.15).

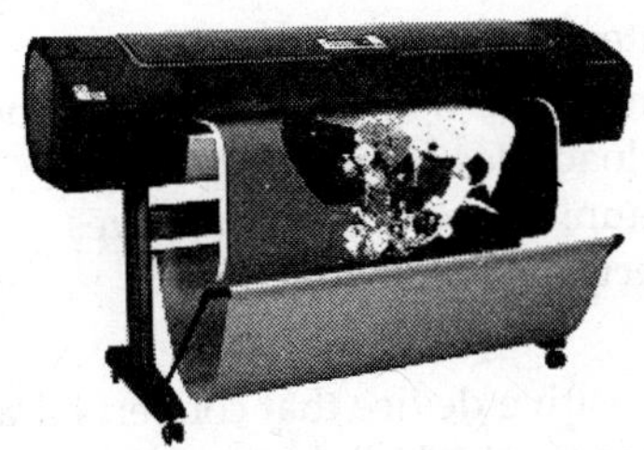

Figure 8.15 Plotter

They use ink pen or inkjet to draw graphics or drawings. Either single colour or multicoloured pens can be used. Drawings can be prepared on paper or polyster film. Colour transparencies can also be prepared. Pen plotters are slow devices. The graphics produced by pen plotters are uniform and are of very good quality. Plotters are used in applications like Computer-Aided Design, (CAD) which require high-quality graphics on paper.

Plotters fall into two basic categories depending on the type of paper and/or pen moving mechanisms involved. The paper for a flatbed plotter, as the first type is known, is mounted on a stationery platform. An arm moves along the bed, while a pen moves back and forth across the arm.

☞ *A flatbed plotter consists of a stationary horizontal flat surface on which paper or any other medium is fixed. The pen is mounted on a carriage that can move along the horizontal and vertical axes.*

The second type of plotter is the roller bed variety. In this, update of the old drum plotter, the paper lies flat instead of being wrapped around a cylinder. Both the pen and the bed of the roller type plotter move. The paper is shifted back and forth along one axis, the pen, suspended from a rail, moves along the other. In the case of roller-bed plotter, various wheels or clamps secure the edge of the paper. To accommodate plotter utilizing the larger size of paper–paper measuring 8 1/2 by 11 inches in designated size 'A', 'B' is 11 by 17 inches, and 'E' the size offering the largest. Others plotters are

- Drum plotter
- Micrographic plotter
- Inkjet plotter
- X-Y plotter

8.25.1 Drum Plotter

A drum plotter contains a long cylinder and a pen carriage. The output paper is placed over the drum. The drum rotates under the control of plotting instructions sent by the computer either in clockwise or anti-clockwise direction. The pen is mounted horizontally on the carriage. The pen moves horizontally along with the carriage left to right or right to left on the paper to produce drawings. Both the drum and the pen moves under the computer's control to produce the desired drawing. Several pens with links of different colours can be mounted on the carriage and multicoloured drawings can be produced.

8.25.2 Micrographic Plotter

These plotters do not use drums. The paper or any other medium is held on both sides at the edges by pinch wheels which give back-and-forth movement of the paper.

8.25.3 Inkjet Plotter

These plotters use inkjets in place of ink pens. The paper is placed on a drum and inkjets with different coloured inks are mounted on a carriage. These are capable of producing multi-coloured large drawings.

8.25.4 X-Y plotter

X-Y plotter is a plotter that operates in two axes of motion ("X" and "Y") in order to draw continuous vector graphics. Plotters differ from Inkjet and Laser printers in that a plotter draws a continuous line, much like a pen on paper, while inkjet and laser printers use a very fine matrix of dots to form images, such that while a line may appear continuous to the naked eye, it in fact is a discrete set of points.

EXERCISE

1. What is BIOS? State the different step through which the system boots?
2. Explain steps for maintenance of printers.
3. Explain working of laser printer.
4. Explain working of Inkjet printer.
5. What is plotter? Explain different types of plotters.
6. Explain various components of laser printer.
7. Only Blank page is printed on laser. Troubleshoot problem and give probable reasons.
8. Explain six different stages of laser printing.
9. Differentiate between line printer and character printer.
10. Write short notes on Printer port
11. What is Thermal printer? Write its advantages and disadvantages.
12. What is POST? Write its function.
13. Explain any three cleaning tools.
14. What precaution you will take while cleaning Monitors.
15. What do you understand by fragmentation?
16. What do you mean by operating System Diagnostics.
17. Explain boot process in WIndows 7.
18. What is Bootstrap loader?
19. What do you mean by Upgrading the BIOS.
20. What are the advantages and disadvantages of Multi-function Printer?

REVIEW QUESTIONS WITH ANSWERS

1. Multiple Choice

1.1 A USB bus is capable of supporting how many devices at one time?

a. 31　　b. 63

c. 3　　d. 127

Ans (d)

1.2 The device which allows you to enter data into the computer
a. Mouse b. Keyboard
c. hard disk d. Scanner

Ans (b)

1.3 The name given to a device that is attached to a computer.
a. Program b. CPU
c. Peripheral d. Registry

Ans (c)

1.4 Where is POST located?
a. DRAM b. Hard drive
c. RAM d. ROM

Ans (d)

1.5 The following is the assembly and disassembly procedure:
a. Case or cover assembly b. Adapter boards
c. Motherboard d. All of the above

Ans (d)

1.6 The ________ printer makes lot of noise.
a. Laser b. Dot matrix
c. Inkjet d. None of the above

Ans (b)

1.7 Special paper is used for ________ printers.
a. Inkjet b. LASER
c. Thermal d. Dot matrix

Ans (c)

1.8 Bar code reader is an example of ________.
a. Network b. Scanner
c. MIDI d. Printer

Ans (b)

1.9 The dot matrix printer available in the market can be classified according to number of pins used in their print head
a. The 9-pin print head b. The 24-pin print head
c. both a and b d. None of the above

Ans (c)

1.10 A disadvantage of the laser printer is:
a. It is quicker b. Print output is of low quality
c. It is very slow d. None of the above

Ans (d)

1.11 To create large-size drawings, architects and engineers often use a device called a:
a. Plotter b. Band Printer
c. Line Printer d. Laser Printer

Ans (a)

1.12 One of the following is Diagnostic Software
a. Windows 7 b. Office-2013
c. Norton Antivirus d. Unix

Ans (c)

1.13 A computer port is used to:
a. Communicate with other computer peripherals
b. Download files from the web
c. Communicate with all hard drives
d. Connect computers together

Ans (a)

1.14 A light-sensitive device that converts drawings, printed text or images into digital form
a. mouse b. scanner
c. keyboard d. laser printer

Ans (b)

1.15 The resolution of a dot matrix printer is measured in
a. Megabits b. Dots per Inch
c. Hertz d. Inches

Ans (b)

1.16 BIOS software is a part of ________
a. CPU b. memory
c. motherboard logic d. HDD

Ans (c)

1.17 Special paper is used for ________ printers.
a. inkjet b. LASER
c. thermal d. dot matrix

Ans (c)

1.18 Printer commonly seen in ATM, Credit card swipe, Restaurant bill counter etc.
a. Multifunction Printer b. Photo Printer
c. Thermal Printer d. Laser Printer

Ans (c)

2. State whether the following statements are True or False

2.1 Plug and Play is a combination of hardware and software feature.

Ans True

2.1 Non-impact printers produce less noises as compared to impact-printers.

Ans True

2.2 Printer drivers controls the operation of the printer.

Ans True

2.3 Drivers for the peripherals of a PC can be a part of the operating system or they can be installed separately.

Ans True

2.4 Cartridge used in a printer contains ink for printing.

Ans True

2.5 Printer device is not used currently with serial port in a PC.

Ans True

2.6 A computer's CD-ROM drive can read data disks, but it cannot play audio CDs.

Ans False

2.7 Dot-matrix printer technology is available in serial and line printers.

Ans False

2.8 The BIOS beep codes can be used to troubleshoot the system.

Ans True

2.9 F1 key is used to exit the BIOS setup utility from the main menu page without saving the changes.

Ans False

2.10 A parallel port allows the transfer of all the bits of a word simultaneously.

Ans True

2.11 An inkjet printer hammers rows of pins against paper to produce words or pictures.

Ans False

2.12 The Recycle Bin is a folder that provides a convenient place to store frequently used documents, graphics and other files.

Ans False

2.13 There are only two types of page orientation - portrait and landscape.

Ans True

2.14 Recycle Bin is an icon on the desktop that holds deleted files temporarily.

Ans True

2.15 Dot matrix printer uses optical technique to print.

Ans False

2.16 Optical disks are used for ________ memory.

Ans External

2.17 Laser printers are appropriate alternatives for plotters.

Ans False

2.18 Disk cleanup utility in Windows enables you to free space on your hard drive.

Ans True

2.19 CMOS memory is used to store configuration information of your computer.

Ans True

2.20 A drum plotter contains a long cylinder and a pen carriage.

Ans True

3. Match the following:

3.1	Jumpers	a.	Nero
3.2	BIOS	b.	Two-or three-hole connectors that connect pins on the motherboard
3.3	CD burning software	c.	CMOS battery
3.4	SMPS	d.	Encoded in the Read Only memory of a PC
3.5	Motherboard	e.	Converts AC voltage into different DC outputs
3.6	RTC	f.	protects the settings stored in the CMOS
3.7	Hyper Threading	g.	calendar and watch of the computer
3.8	Plug and Play	h.	improving performance and system responsiveness
3.9	BIOS password	i.	add additional functions and can fix all the errors and bugs
3.10	Updating BIOS	j.	A standard for auto-detecting connected devices
3.11	Ink jet	k.	Laser printer
3.12	A light-sensitive device that converts drawings, printed text or images into digital form	l.	A type of printer
3.13	Is not an impact printer	m.	Scanner
3.14	OCR	n.	Used to connect the printers
3.15	Parallel port	o.	Scan words

Ans 3.1 b 3.2 d 3.3 a 3.4 e 3.5 c
3.6 g 3.7 h 3.8 j 3.9 f 3.10 i
3.11 l 3.12 m 3.13 k 3.14 o 3.15 n

4. Fill in the blanks

4.1 We can boot computer from ________ disk.

Ans Hard

4.2 A flat circular plate coated with a magnetic material on which data can be stored is called ________.

Ans Disk

4.3 The FDD assembly works on ________ principles.

Ans Magnetic

4.4 The ________ is one of the major components that is required for the personal computer to function.

Ans Motherboard

4.5 Optical storage technique is used in ________.

Ans CD-ROM drive

4.6 CMOS is an abbreviation for ________.

Ans Complementary Metal Oxide Semiconductor.

4.7 The parallel interface of a PC is called as ________.

Ans Printer port

4.8 Inkjet printer is an example of ______ printer.

Ans Non-impact

4.9 To create large size drawing, architects and engineers often use a device called ____.

Ans plotter

4.10 ________ switches are located at the back of the printer.

Ans DIP

4.11 The resolution of a printer is measured in ______.

Ans Dots Per Inch (DPI)

4.12 Line printers and dot-matrix printers are ________ printers.

Ans impact

4.13 The software needed to handle the interface through the controller card is called a ________.

Ans device driver

4.14 ________ is a systems tools in Windows for better working of a hard disk.

Ans disk defragmenter

4.15 The disk defragmenter searches ________ files, rearrange them and place them in a single location of the drive.

Ans fragmented

4.16 The _____ beep codes can be used to troubleshoot the system.

Ans BIOS

Q.5 (a) Write short notes on

(i) Defragmenter Program

(ii) Disk Cleanup

Ans 5(a)(i)

When Windows stores files on your hard disk drive, it often divides them into multiple pieces (or fragments) so they fit into available space on the drive. When you attempt to open a fragmented file, it must be retrieved from more than one place, so the process takes more time. The Disk Defragmenter program groups the fragmented files together on your hard disk drive to improve PC performance. This does not affect the location of files and folders on your PC.

Ans 5(a)(ii)

The Disk Cleanup program frees up space on your hard disk drive by removing temporary and unused files (including Temporary Internet Files and files in the Recycle Bin). You can run Disk Cleanup manually, or you can set it up to run automatically.

Q.6 What are the preventive steps necessary for keeping a monitor in good health and minimizing problems?

Ans 6

The following points are for the preventive maintenance of monitor and to keep it in good condition:

- Operate the monitor away from extreme hot and cold weather.
- Avoid damp or dusty locations.
- Allow good ventilation to cool monitors.
- Do not place anything on top of the monitor that might block the ventilation grill in the rear or top of the cover. This is the most urgent need for the convection to cool internal components.
- Do not place two monitors close to one another. The magnetic fields may cause either or both to suffer from shaking images. Likewise, do not place a monitor next to a TV, if possible.
- Place loudspeakers and other sources of storing magnetic fields away from the monitor. This reduces the possibility of colour purity or geometry problems. The exception is with respect to good quality shielded multimedia which are designed to avoid magnetic interference problems.
- Keep other devices away from the monitor, which may cause interference, such as problem with power transformers including audio equipment, AC or DC wall adapters and laptop power supplies, fluorescent lamps with magnetic ballast and motorized or heavy duty appliances.

Q.7 What is Plug and Play (PnP)?

Ans 7

Plug and Play (PnP) is a capability developed by Microsoft for its Windows operating systems that gives users the ability to plug a device into a computer and have the computer recognize the device. The user does not have to tell the computer. In many earlier computer systems, the user was required to explicitly tell the operating system when a new device had been added.

With Microsoft's participation, Plug and Play has been replaced by an open, industry standard, Universal Plug and Play (UPnP), which uses Internet protocols for seamless device plug-in.

Q.8 Write short notes on Printer Drivers and Printer Port.

Ans 8

A driver is a program that controls the behaviour of device connected to a computer. It provides a connection between peripheral devices and the operating system. All devices, such as monitors, modems and printers require drivers for their functioning. Drivers for certain devices, such as the keyboard form a part of the operating system. Other devices like printers need to have their drivers installed separately.

The parallel port connector has 25 pins to connect devices, such as printer. So parallel port is also called printer port. Newer systems feature on Enhanced Capabilities Port (ECP) able to provide duplex operation and higher data rates.

Q.9 Explain various parts of a laser printer.

Ans 9

The basic parts that a laser printer consists of are a toner hopper, corona wire, discharge lamp, laser scanning unit, fuser, developer roller and a photoreceptor drum assembly. Each of these parts have important role to play in the printing process.

Toner Hopper

The toner of the laser printer is stored in a little compartment that is known as the toner hopper. This toner hopper section is basically a small little container that is built into a removable casing, so that it can be removed filled and put back into the laser printer without any sort of trouble.

Corona Wire

An initial storage of the printing, a light sensitive drum is given a positive charge with the help of a wire and the drum starts revolving. This wire is known as *corona wire.*

Discharge Lamp

The bright light of the lamp exposes the entire surface of the drum, erasing the previous pattern of electric changes.

Laser Scanning Unit

Laser scanning unit is capable of radiating heat generated by a light source.

Fuser

Fuser is a device which basically compromises of two rollers, which are heated. The heat element in the fuser is a very important aspect of finishing the printing job. When the paper goes in between these two rollers that are heated, the toner powder that has remained loose will melt and will combine with the fiber that are present in the paper. After this the fuser simply passes the paper into the output tray.

Photoreceptor

The most important part of the laser printer without which it cannot function is known as the photoreceptor. The photoreceptor basically consists of a cylinder or a drum that revolves, using highly photoconductive material that is dispersed by light photons.

Q.10 What is IRQ (Interrupt Request) ?

Ans 10

An IRQ (Interrupt Request) value is an assigned location where the computer can expect a particular device to interrupt it when the device sends the computer signals about its operation. For example, when a printer has finished printing, it sends an interrupt signal to the computer. The signal momentarily interrupts the computer so that it can decide what processing to do next. Since multiple signals to the computer on the same interrupt line might not be understood by the computer, a unique value must be specified for each device and its path to the computer. Prior to Plug-and Play (PnP) devices, users often had to set IRQ values manually when adding a new device to a computer.

If you add a device that does not support PnP, the manufacturer will provide explicit directions on how to assign IRQ values for it.

Q.11 How will you clean the keyboard?

Ans 11

Cleaning the keyboard

Shutdown your PC and remove the main plug. Unplug the keyboard and hold it upside down to release any debris from in between the keys (pressing the key is a good way to clean it).

Now, take one of the cotton buds and put a couple of drops of the cleaning fluid on it, use the cotton bud to clean the sides of the keys.

After cleaning the sides of the keys take your free cloth and dampen it with cleaning fluid. Do not put the liquid directly on the keyboard. Give the surface of the keyboard a good wipe over using the cloth to trace the contours of the keys. When you have finished, give the keyboard a wipe over with the dry cloth/duster. You should now have a nice clean keyboard.

Q.12 Explain different categories of impact printers.

Ans 12

The impact printers are further classified into the following categories:

(a) Line printers

(b) Character printers

Line printers

A line printer prints one line of the text at a time. Printing speeds may vary from 300–3000 lines per minute. Different types of line printers are–*Drum printer* and *Chain printer*.

Drum Printer

A drum printer consists of a cylindrical drum on which characters are embossed. One complete set of characters is embossed for each and every print position on a line. The drum is rotated at a high speed. There is a magnetically-driven hammer in each character position of the line. A character is printed by striking a hammer against the embossed character on the surface.

The printer receives all characters to be printed in one line of the text from the processor. The hammers hit the ribbon and paper against the desired character on the drum when it comes in the printing position. Its noise level is high and speed varies from 200 to 2000 lines per minute. They are expensive also.

Chain Printer

A chain printer uses a rapidly, rotating chain which is called print chain. Magnetically-driven hammers are located in each print position. To print a line, the characters in the line are transmitted from the memory to printer buffer. The band is rotated at a high speed. With the rotation of the band, a hammer is activated when the desired character comes in front of it. Thus, for a printer with 132 characters per line, 132 hammers will be positioned to strike the ribbon.

The noise level of the printer is high and its speed lies in the range of 400-2400 lines per minute.

Character Printers (Serial Printer)

A character printer prints one character of the text at a time. They are low-speed printers. Their printing speed lies in the range of 30-600 characters per second. Different types of character printers are–*Dot matrix printers* and *Letter quality printers*.

Dot matrix printer

A dot matrix printer is the most popular serial printer. The printhead contains a vertical array of pins. As the printhead moves across the paper, selected pins fire against the ribbon to form a pattern of dots on the paper.

The printhead contains a vertical array of 7,9,14,18 or even 24 pins.

A dot matrix printer is faster than a letter quality printer. These printers operate at two or three speeds. The lower the speed the better is the printing quality. Higher speed is for draft printing and lower speed is for near-letter quality (NLQ) printing, i.e., the printing is as good as that of a letter quality printer. Many dot matrix printers are bidirectional, i.e., they print one line of text from left to right and then the next line from right to left. Dot matrix printers do not have fixed character fonts. They can print special characters and graphics. There are 80 column and 132 column dot matrix printers available in the market. Dot matrix printers are common in accounts department, warehouses and have many administrative purpose, including mailing labels etc.

Letter Quality printers

These printers print full characters, which means that a character is not made up of dots. The most popular printer of this type is daisy-wheel printer. In a daisy-wheel printer, the printhead resembles a daisy flower, with its print arms appearing like the petals of the flower. The character to be printed is sent to the printer buffer. The hub is continuously rotating at high speed and a hammer strikes the appropriate character when it is in position. The daisy-wheel printer has a speed up to 90 characters per second. These are no more in use today.

Q.13 How laser printer is different from inkjet printer?

Ans 13

The laser printer is different from an inkjet printer in a number of ways:

(a) The toner or ink in a laser printer is dry. In an inkjet printer, it is wet.

(b) Inkjet printer is about ten times more expensive to operate than a laser printer, because ink needs replenishing more frequently.

(c) The printed paper from an inkjet printer will smear if wet, but a laser printed document will not.

(d) If your printing needs are minimal, an inkjet printer is sufficient. But if your printing volume is high, consider buying a laser printer.

Q.14 Write short note on laser printer.

Ans 14

Laser printers are non-impact type printers. They print one page at a time. These printers use laser or some other light source to produce an image on a photosensitive drum. Laser printers are quiet and produce high-quality output. These printers are expensive and require periodic maintenance.

Q.15 What is the difference between impact and non impact printer?

Ans 15

	IMPACT PRINTER	NON-IMPACT PRINTER
1.	In these printers, there is a mechanical contact between the printhead and paper. They create impression on paper by striking an ink ribbon.	In these printers, printhead does not have metal pins that come out from the printhead. Instead they use ink spraying mechanism or ink fixing by heating process.
2.	Its printing speed is very slow.	Its printing speed is faster.
3.	Its printing quality is lower.	Its printing quality is higher.
4.	It normally uses continuous paper sheet.	Its uses individual paper sheet.
5.	It generates noise during printing.	It does not generate noise during printing.
6.	It uses inked ribbon for printing.	It uses toner or cartridge for painting.
7.	It is less expensive.	It is more expensive.
8.	Dot matrix, Character, Line and Drum printers are impact printers.	Laser and Inkjet printer are non-impact printers.

Q.16 Explain the basic differences between a Keyboard and Mouse?

Ans 16

Programs and data are entered into a computer through a keyboard which is attached to a computer. A keyboard is similar to the keyboard of a typewriter. It contains letters, digits, special characters, function keys and some control keys. When a key is pressed, an electronic signal is produced, which is detected by an electronic circuit called *keyboard encoder*

A mouse is a pointing device. It is held in one hand and moved across a flat surface. The mouse can also be used to draw sketches, diagrams, etc. on the monitor screen. It is also moved on the graphic tablet for drawing work. The mouse is also used to edit text. For editing a text on the screen, the cursor can be quickly placed close to the desired point of the screen by moving the mouse on the mouse pad.

Q.17 Explain the working of a mouse.

Ans 17

Optical mouse contains a full pattern-recognition hardware/-software in its digital processor IC.

This pattern-recognition capability allows the new optical mouse to be used on any surface without the need to use any special mouse pad.

As the mouse is moved, it compares the image of its current position with the image of the previous position stored in its memory. The difference between two images inform about the direction, the mouse is moved.

This new optical mouse contains three basic parts

- LED to illuminate the surface on which the mouse is used.
- A sensor made of Photo-Detector Array, basically a small video camera to detect the pattern on the surface.
- Digital Signal Processor (DSP) for pattern recognition purpose.

An Optical mouse can sample at a rate of 1500 to about 6000 images per second. This mouse has no moving parts, it does not require frequent maintenance and does not easily wear out. One drawback of this mouse is it may not work on surface which is highly reflective such as glass surface.

Q.18 What is Booting? Explain two types of booting.

Ans 18

Booting is just the process of starting or resetting the computer. There are two types of booting: cold booting and warm booting. Cold booting is the booting process happening when we first turn on computer and warm booting is the processes happening when we reset the computer. During the booting process the computer loads the operating system to its memory and prepares it for use.

Q.19 Explain system boot files used on Windows 7.

Ans 19

The following system boot files are used on Windows 7:

- Boot manager (bootmgr) file. This is a hidden system file located at the root of the system partition.
- Boot configuration data (BCD). The BCD is used instead of the Boot.ini file to identify the location of the operating system. On multiboot systems, it includes information for additional operating systems and a default operating system.
- When the bootmgr completes the initial load, it runs Winload.exe from the \Windows \System32 folder. This starts Windows.

Q.20 What is the use of Label printer?

Ans 20

A label printer is a computer printer that prints on self-adhesive label material and/or card-stock (tags). A label printer with built-in keyboard and display for stand-alone use (not connected to a separate computer) is often called a label maker.

Label printers have a wide variety of applications, including supply chain management, retail price marking, packaging labels, blood and laboratory specimen marking, and fixed assets management.

Q.21 What is Inkjet Plotter?

Ans 21

These plotters use inkjets in place of ink pens. The paper is placed on a drum and inkjets with different coloured inks are mounted on a carriage. These are capable of producing multi-coloured large drawings.

APPENDIX A

ASSEMBLING PARTS OF PC

A.1 PC AND ITS VARIOUS PARTS

A PC (Personal Computer) consists of electronic components connected to various peripherals, accessories that let users send data to the computer (input) or receive information from the computer (output). Although PCs vary in shape, size, capacity, speed and price, they all include elements that enable them to perform the following essential task:

(a) Receive data
(b) Save data
(c) Manipulate data in various ways and
(d) generate a result after processing data

Computers receive most data from either the keyboard or a hard disk. Information is usually saved on hard disk. Data is manipulated and changed (processed) by the microprocessor, and the resulting output is either displayed on a monitor or printed on paper. Although many computers may include additional components, such as scanners, modems, magnetic tape drives, sound cards and so on.

The system unit, monitor, keyboard, mouse, etc. are essential components of a computer and its functions are regulated by software and electronic parts. All the parts of a computer are internally built by using electronic circuits. The electronic components and internal connection within the system unit of computer are discussed below:

(a) **Monitor:** The monitor displays both data entered by the user and information processed by the computer.

(b) **Keyboard:** The keyboard is the principal means of communicating with the computer. It enables users to enter data or to type commands that instruct the computer to perform specific operations.

(c) **Mouse:** A mouse lets users communicate with the computer by moving an onscreen arrow to point at graphical objects, and then clicking a button to execute a command or display information.

(d) **Printer:** The printer lets users create a hard copy of information by transferring the results of their work onto paper.

(e) **Motherboard:** The motherboard is the large printed circuit board inside the computer that carries and connects all of the principal electronic components, such as the microprocessor and memory.

(f) **Power Supply:** The power supply transforms the 220 volt alternating current of electrical outlets into the low-voltage direct current that sensitive electronic components and peripherals require.

(g) **Expansion Cards:** Expansion cards, also called interface cards, connect peripherals (such as monitors, disk drives, and so on) to the PC's motherboard. They are essential for transferring and translating data to and from electronic devices.

(h) **Hard Disk:** The hard disk is the main storage area of a PC. It can hold huge amount of programs and information in magnetic form. It retain that data even when the computer's power is turned off.

(i) **CD Drives:** A CD-ROM (Compact Disk Read Only Memory) is a drive that users disks that store large amount of information. The disk for the CD-ROM drive is known as CD or CD-ROM disk. The data contained on these disks are audio files, software applications and graphics. Combo drives are also fitted that contain DVD(Digital Versatile Disk) and CD drive.

A.2 ASSEMBLING PARTS OF PC

A computer is a system formed by assembling a number of components. Assembling a computer involves connecting internal and external computer components. Internal components include the ones that are installed inside a system case, such as motherboard, RAM (Random Access Memory), disk drives. External computer components are devices that are attached to the system case, such as mouse, keyboard, scanner, printer and modem.

Before, starting, verify that you have all of the necessary components with you. Depending upon the requirements of the user, the components may vary. Components that are required for assembling a personal computer are:

(a) 1 IDE (Integrated Development Environment) Hard Drive
(b) 1 Memory Module(s)
(c) 1 PCI Network Interface Card
(d) 1 Video Card (optional)
(e) 1 IDE CD ROM
(f) 1 Processor
(g) 1 Heat sync and Fan
(h) 2 IDE Cables
(i) 1 Floppy Drive Cable
(j) 1 Power Supply

Tools Required

(a) Slot Screwdriver Set
(b) 1 Chip Puller
(c) 1 Needle-Nose Pliers
(d) 1 Tweezers
(e) 1 Hex-Head Allen-Wrench Set

(f) Philips screwdriver – you will use this the most as all screws are this type.
(g) Screwdriver
(h) Long nose pliers – for picking up those tiny screws you drop
(i) A cup – to hold the small screws
(j) Pen and paper – for diagramming the component connections
(k) Use an air duster to blow the dust from the system case
(l) Make use of plastic ties for loose cabling inside the system case
(m) Use a small torch to see the connections in the system case

Before you start

(a) Clean your work area of dust, debris and anything else that might get in the way.
(b) You must also take precautions against static electricity. A static discharge can damage or ruin your computer. Before opening your computer case and touching or removing any parts inside, you should ground yourself with a grounding strap.
(c) A grounding strap prevents static electricity from building up in your body and discharging into the equipment. Eighty volts are enough to hurt a computer.

General Handling Notes

(a) Touch things as little as possible.
(b) Hold the parts by their edges.
(c) Avoid touching the motherboard components, chips, connectors and leads with bare hands.
(d) Avoid touching memory module contacts and chips with bare hands
(e) Place the parts on a grounded antistatic surface or on the antistatic bag in which it came.

Basic Precautions

Computer assembly requires some basic precautions. These are as follows:

(a) Never force computer parts into place. If you have to force a part into place, it is possible that you are inserting the wrong component or installing it improperly. Stop and check to see what you are doing wrong before you continue to build your computer.
(b) Never open the power supply. The power supply has extremely high voltages inside which can be extremely dangerous.
(c) Never work on your computer with the power on. Doing so can cause electrical surges that can damage your computer parts.
(d) Never try to clean any part of your system with any liquid detergents or wet cloths.

A.2.1 System Case

System case is the box that holds the different components of a computer. PCs can be classified into three general categories according to the design of their cases (See Figure A.1).

- The desktop (horizontal case) PC. These cases come in two heights. Standard (6") and mini, or slimline (4"). Lengths and widths can vary widely from 20" × 16" for the largest (often called "Standard AT cases") because they are the size of the modern PC's ancestor, the IBM AT (International Business Machine Advanced Technology) to 14" × 12" for smaller "mini-ATs".
- The tower (vertical case) PC. These cases are usually 7" wide and 16" deep (mid-tower), but height can vary from 12" (mini-tower) to 24" (full tower). Even large models, commonly used as network servers for many users, also exist.
- Portable computer cases are horizontal and are 3/4" to 1-1/2" thick. The length and width are usually equal to or smaller than the size of a standard 8-1/2" × 11" sheet of paper. The three main types of portables are laptops (13 pounds), notebooks (6 pounds), and sub-notebooks or handbooks (4 pounds or less).

A.2.2 Open The Case

Different types of cases open in different ways.

For some cases you need to:

(a) Remove 4 or 5 screws in the back of the case. Be sure that these screws hold the case and not some other component like the power supply.
(b) Slide the case forward on its slots and remove it.

For other cases

(a) Remove one thumbscrew or one or two Phillips head screws from the back of your case that may hold one or more panels.
(b) Remove the top panel and/or one or more necessary side panels.

A.2.3 Installing Power Supply

Power supply box is the unit that supplies electricity to all the internal components of system that is connected to it.

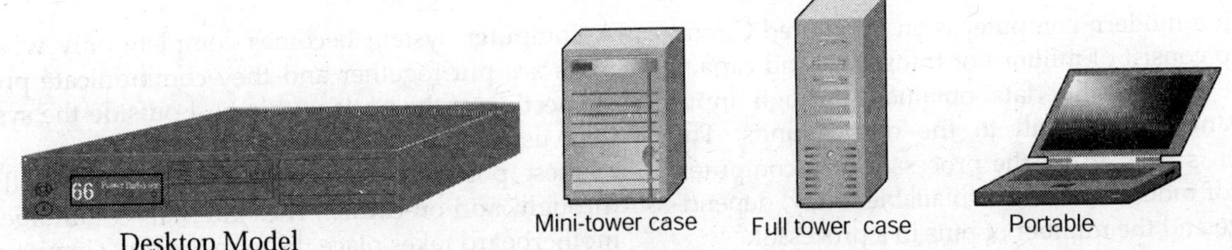

Figure A.1 Different system case design

The power supply provides direct current (5 volts and 12 volts) to the motherboard and disk drives through three types of connectors. Two 6-wire connectors supply power to the motherboard. They plug into the board side by side, with the black wires of each connector next to each other.

☞ *If you ever need to replace a power supply, be careful not to reverse these connectors.*

Each power supply has several 4-wire connectors (the number of connectors available is proportional to the unit's overall power capacity). The smaller 4-wire connectors power floppy disk drives, and the large ones are used for hard disk drives and other peripherals. If you want to install a new drive but have no free connectors, you can use a Y-cable to split a connector into two separate plugs, but doing so may overload the power supply.

The life expectancy and reliability of a computer's electronic components depends on the power supply providing quality, spike-and interference-free current. The generated current, measured in watts, must be sufficient to power all the installed components and peripherals.

Place the system cooling fan below the power supply box. A fan assembly is also provided in the power supply to keep the computer cool by circulating outside air inside the cabinet. If this fan fails, computer may overheat and starts giving problems or it may completely stop.

A.2.4 Motherboard

The main component inside the main system unit is the motherboard. This is the biggest electronic circuit board inside the computer system, on which many other boards are attached. The boards that attach to the motherboard are known as daughter board or expansion board.

The motherboard is a circuit board to which all the electronic components of computer are connected. These include both internal parts of the system unit like processor, display card of the monitor, sound card, memory, etc. and external parts like mouse, keyboard etc. The 'ports' and 'slots' which connect these components. The motherboard helps in data transfer among the components. The important parts of a motherboard are:

(a) Processor socket
(b) Interface slots
(c) Memory slots
(d) Ports

Processor Socket

The processor in a modern computer is an Integrated Circuit (IC) chip. A chip consist of millions of transistors and capacitors which can process the data obtained through input devices and transfer the result to the output units. The processor socket is used to fix the processor in a computer. Different kinds of motherboards are available today, depending upon the size and the number of pins in a processor.

The two main parts of a processor are Arithmetic and Logical Unit (ALU) and Control Unit (CU). The function of the ALU is to do the processing and mathematical calculations of the information obtained through input devices. The control unit sorts of this information and sends it to the different pats of the computer like the manager of an office. The control unit organises and co-ordinates various functions of a computer. The orderly and fast functioning of a computer indicates the efficiency of the control unit.

☞ *A fan is often fixed on the processor to remove the head generated by continuous activity. This fan is known as processor fan.*

Interface Slots

Interface cards are the circuit board which connect the equipment outside the system unit with motherboard. These are connected to the slots of motherboard in such a manner that the ports to which the external equipments are to be connected can be seen externally. The TV tuner card used to watch television programmes in a computer, the sound card is used to hear recorded sounds, the network card is used to interconnect several computers are examples of add-on-cards.

☞ *The slots present in a motherboard that are used to connect add-on-cards to it are called interface slots.*

Memory Slots

Information for the functioning of a computer is temporarily stored in a chip called RAM (Random Access Memory). The slot where the RAM board, which has to interact constantly with motherboard, is fixed to the motherboard is called memory slot. RAM is also an integrated circuit. There are several RAM slots in a motherboard.

☞ *All motherboards include a small block of Read Only Memory (ROM) which is different from the main system memory used for loading and running software.*

The ROM contains the PC's Basic Input/Output System (BIOS). BIOS is fixed on the motherboard. BIOS first checks the working condition of each part of the computer. BIOS checks the hard disk and memory during booting. Activation of BIOS is otherwise called POST (Power on Self Test). Being a ROM, the commands in a BIOS are permanent and will be safe even during a sudden power failure.

Ports

A computer system becomes complete only when different parts are put together and they communicate properly. The connection of the parts within and outside the system unit is done using ports or connectors.

These ports are connected directly to the motherboard or through add-on-cards. The internal communication in a motherboard takes place through the tiny circuit printed on it.

We can connect a computer to another computer to an input/output device to a data storage device. Different kinds of ports are discussed below:

IDE Port

Integrated Device Electronics (IDE) port is used to connect a hard disk, CDROM drive, CD writer or DVD drive to a motherboard. There are two such ports in a motherboard. These are primary and secondary. Two devices can be connected to each port.

FDD Connector

The Floppy Disk Drive (FDD) connector is use to connect a floppy disk drive to the motherboard. The size of the FDD connector and the number of pins in it are smaller than those of an IDE connector.

- **Serial port or communication port**
  Serial port is used to connect the mouse or modem. They are called com 1 and com 2. 'com' is the short form of communication. Usually, in a communication port there are either nine or twenty five pins.
- **Parallel Port**
  In a parallel port, there are holes to connect pins. Printer, scanner etc are connected through the parallel ports.
- **USB Port**
  Universal Serial Bus (USB) port is a kind of port available in modern computers. Many devices can be connected in serial and parallel ports, a large amount of data can be transferred at a very high speed through USB ports. All peripherals like printer, modem and scanner are now available in versions that can be connected to the USB port. Two or more USB ports are normally seen in a motherboard.
- **Power Port**
  The electrical supply for the working of the computer can be provided through the power port. Power port is located at SMPS (Switched Mode Power Supply), the power monitoring unit of the system of a computer. Each port of a computer requires electric current in different quantities. The power unit of the computer namely the SMPS converts the current obtained from a line into small units required for each of the component like motherboard, hard disk, floppy disk, CD drive, etc., For heat radiation a small fan is also attached in an SMPS.

A.3 CONFIGURING MOTHERBOARD

Configuring the motherboard is traditionally done using jumpers. (A jumper is a small metal connector with a plastic cover used to connect two metal pins together) that are used to change how the circuitry on the motherboard functions. Some newer boards today are called jumperless, because they do not use jumpers but rather a special group of BIOS (Basic Input Output System) setting to set most of the configuration options that are set with jumpers on conventional boards.

To configure motherboard do the following:

(a) Physically locate all the jumpers on the motherboard by looking in the manual.

(b) Set the jumpers for CPU voltage. New processors have two voltage specifications for the CPU and for the external (I/O) voltages.

(c) Set the jumper setting for system bus speed and the multiplier. Some CPUs use a multiplier that is interpreted differently by the CPU. A multiplier is a number that when multiplied by the bus speed gives the CPU speed.

(d) Some systems have a flash BIOS jumper setting for enabling the flash BIOS feature. Set this jumper to be disabled. This jumper is usually set to "normal" position except when doing a BIOS update.

(e) Some systems have a CMOS clear jumpers for clearing the contents of the CMOS memory. This feature is required to clear the memory incase of a forgotten password. Ensure that this jumper setting is default, or you will not be able to make any BIOS settings.

(f) A Battery source jumper is available in some system that decides whether the CMOS memory will be powered by the onboard battery or an external battery. Unless you are using an external battery, ensure that this settings is default (on board battery)

(g) Some motherboards have disable jumpers that allow you to enable or disable motherboard parts. Ensure that these jumpers are set properly.

(h) Very rarely seen on new boards, jumpers to set the size of the system memory were common on 486-class boards. Set these if your board requires them.

(i) Double check jumper settings as incorrectly jumpered motherboards are a leading cause of system problems and can be very hard to diagnose.

(j) From the system case, find the different connectors such as the hard drive LED (Light Emitting Diode), speaker, and reset connectors. Follow the instructions on the manual to connect these parts to the connectors on motherboard.

(k) Fix the power connector from the power supply to the motherboard.

(l) Fix the drive tray back into the system case. Ensure that the motherboard does not touch the system case or the drive tray directly. Touch the motherboard gently to ensure that it is rigid and tightly fixed. The motherboard should not bend when touched.

(m) Most of the present day motherboards are provided with additional connector brackets for connecting USB ports, game port etc. To properly connect these additional connectors, you must remove the adapter slot cover and fix the connector bracket onto the PCI (Peripheral Component Interconnect) slot.

(n) Connect the different port connectors to the appropriate connectors or slots on the motherboard.

☞ *Always think about future expension of your PC when selecting a motherboard. Evaluate your present needs, and select the motherboard that is bigger than your present need.*

When building a computer, the motherboard manual has information you must have. When buying a motherboard, do not forget to get the manual.

A.4 MOTHERBOARD INSTALLATION

Always disconnect the power supply from the AC mains before you connect, disconnect, install or remove any motherboard component. Failure to do this could result in damage to the equipment. Some circuitry on the motherboard can continue to operate even when the front panel power switch is off.

To install motherboard, do as follows:

1. **Orient Case or Mounting Panel:** Arrange the case, so that the expansion card slots and keyboard and other connectors are farthest away from you. The edge of the motherboard where the connectors go as the "back" of the motherboard.
2. **Find Motherboard Mounting Hole:** Examine the motherboard and locate its mounting holes. These are usually found as follows:
   - One row of three or four holes along the back of the board, where the expansion slots are.
   - A second row of either two or three holes somewhere in the middle of the board. These may not all be in a straight line.
   - A third row of usually two holes, but may be three, along the front edge of the board.
3. **Find System Case or Mounting Panel Holes:** Examine the system case and see what types of mounting holes it uses. You will generally see the following:
   - **Threaded screw holes:** These are small screw holes that are intended to take screw-in metal standoffs. All cases have at least a couple of these. Some may have more than others.
   - **Eyelet holes:** These are large, along holes about an inch or so in length that take the sliding plastic standoffs. They are narrower at one end than the other. Some cases no longer use these at all.
4. **Orient Motherboard and Match Motherboard Mounting Holes to Case Mounting Holes:** Take the motherboard and physically locate it in space a few inches over the case (or removable case panel). Orient the motherboard so that it is approximately where it will be when installed. Any integrated connectors on the back of the motherboard should line up with the holes in the case designed for them, especially the keyboard connector. Then take note of the following:
   - Determine which motherboard mounting holes line up with threaded screw holes on the case or mounting panel. There must be at least two of these or you cannot properly secure the motherboard to the case. These will usually be found in the back of the case near the expansion slots.
   - Determine which motherboard mounting holes line up with eyelet holes on the case or mounting panel. They should line up with the narrow end of the eyelet hole.
   - Determine which motherboard mounting holes line up with no holes at all on the case or mounting panel. This is quite common and nothing to be concerned about as long as most of the holes do line up. It is most common for the holes along the front of the motherboard do not line up with the holes along the front of the case, because the size of motherboard varies from the nominal standard. The holes along the back and middle will almost always line up.
5. **Install Standoffs:** Attach the mounting hardware, following these specific instructions for each of the different case hole types mentioned above:
   - For those motherboard holes that line up with screw holes, screw a metal standoff into the case (or mounting panel). Use a 3/16" screw driver.
   - For the motherboard holes that line up with eyelet holes, insert a plastic slider standoff into the motherboard. Push the pointed end into the appropriate hole from the bottom, until it pushes through the top of the board.
   - For the motherboard holes that do not have a matching case hole, take one of the plastic slider standoffs mentioned just above. Using a pair of wire snips or a knife, cut off the small plastic disk at the end of the standoff opposite the pointed end. Then push the pointed end into the hole from the bottom as for the eyelet holes. Cutting off the disk at the end will allow this modified space to support the motherbord without having to insert into the case in the location where there is no matching hole.
6. **Slide Motherboard into Place:** Follow the appropriate directions depending again, on the type of holes being used.
   - If there are eyelet holes in the case, then place the motherboard so that the round plastic parts at the end of the plastic standoffs are inserted into the wide part of the eyelet holes. Then slide the board so that the standoffs move toward the narrow part of the hole. Double-check that the alignment is correct. Be careful when sliding the board not to rub the bottom of the board against anything, including any metal standoffs in the case.
   - If there are no eyelet holes, then you can just put the motherboard down directly into the case. Double-check that all of the holes line up with the metal standoffs underneath them.

   When you have completed doing this, the other mounting holes should line up with the metal standoffs they are mated with.
7. **Determine if Washers are Required:** Examine the heads of the screws that you will use to secure the motherboard to the metal standoffs under the screw-in mounting holes.

If the head of the screw is large enough that after tightening the screw the head might make contact with the circuitry on the motherboard, you must use a plastic or paper washer under the screw head to prevent accidentally shorting the motherboard.

8. **Screw Motherboard into Place:** Using washers (if necessary), screw the motherboard into the metal standoffs underneath it. First insert all the screws and hang-tighten them, then tighten them all using a screwdriver.
9. **Replace Removable Panel:** If your case uses a removable motherboard mounting panel, replace it into the case now. This basically means undoing whatever you did to remove the panel in the first place. Most cases either have a pull-down, spring-loaded "handle" that loosens the panel, or they use screws to secure it. Be careful to make sure that the bottom of the panel is in the right place where it fits into the bottom of the case.
10. **Test Motherboard Installation:** An incorrectly installed motherboard results in unpredictable behaviour that can be very hard to diagnose. Check the following after installing the board:
    - **Level:** Check the board to ensure that it is flat in the case. All parts of the motherboard should be intact.
    - **Contact:** Make sure that no part of the motherboard is touching anything that it should not be. Look under the board too, if possible.
    - **Fit:** Check to make sure that the motherboard is in the correct position. The expansion card slots should line up with the expansion slot holes in the case. The keyboard connector should line up as well.
    - **Rigidity:** The motherboard must be adequately supported to ensure that it can take the biggest torture test that any motherboard goes through insertion and removal of expansion cards. Test the installation of a video card. For example, start typing to insert the card into a slot. If the motherboard starts bending more than a tiny amount, stop right way. This means that the board has not been properly supported and you will need to address this before proceeding. The motherboard should not flex under the pressure of inserting or removing the card.
11. From the system case, find the different connectors such as the hard drive LED, speaker, and reset connectors. Follow the instructions on the manual to connect these parts to the connectors on motherboard.
12. Fix the power connector from the power supply to the motherboard.
13. Fix the drive tray back into the system case. Ensure that the motherboard does not touch the system case or the drive tray directly. Touch the motherboard gently to ensure that it is rigid and tightly fixed. The motherboard should not bend when touched.
14. Most of the present-day motherboards are provided with additional connector brackets for connecting USB ports, game port, etc., To properly connect these additional connectors, you must remove the adapter slot cover, and fix the connector bracket onto the PCI slot.
15. Connect the different port connectors to the appropriate connectors or slots on the motherboard.

☞ *Always think about future expension when selecting a motherboard. Evaluate your present needs, and select the motherboard that is bigger.*

When building a computer, the motherboard manual has information you must have when buying a motherboard, do not forget to get the manual.

A.5 INSTALLING MICROPROCESSOR

The motherboard has one or more sockets or slots to hold the microprocessor. The type of socket or slot used dictates the type of processor that can be used by the motherboard.

Locate the processor slot on the main board. Note that the processor only connects to the chamber one way.

For square sockets: Because the CPU is so sensitive, its slot is very intricate. It is flat and generally square. Examine the top of the processor that should have a small dot in one of the corners. This dot indicates where pin one is located on the bottom of the processor. Now look at the socket on the motherboard. This socket should have a missing hole or should have a 1 indicating pin one.

☞ *Position the processor so both pin 1 and hole 1 match and then place the processor down.*

Some newer processors also have another safety measure designed to protect the pins on the processor during insertion. It is called a zif-socket, or a zero-insertion-force socket. The main addition is the presence of a lock to hold the CPU in place.

Insertion is easy. Lift the lever lock. Then, as above, carefully install the CPU by aligning Pin 1 on the CPU with Pin 1 on the socket, making sure the pins actually fit into the socket. Do not force CPU into the socket. Check the pin alignment of the CPU pins to socket holes before pressing down. Lower the lever arm until the CPU is held in place.

For Single Edge Connectors (SECs) Do not force the processor into the slot. Make sure it is oriented correctly. Find the exposed end of the processor and lower it onto the circuit. Using the support arms as a guide. Press down firmly until the processor is securely seated into the chamber. Pull the retaining clips at the top of the chamber away from the processor to lock it down.

☞ *Not all CPUs match all motherboards. Most motherboards will accept more than one type of CPU as model, manufacturer and speed is concerned. But they generally only accept one socket type. The major CPU manufacturers include Intel, Motorola, IBM and Advanced Micro Devices (AMD).*

A.6 INSTALLING HEATSINK AND FAN ON PROCESSOR

A heat sink is a heat conducting metal piece usually made from aluminum with a lot of pins on top, when attached on the top of the CPU, they absorb the heat from the CPU and radiate heat away. Place the fan heat sink on top of the processor so that the fan cable is facing the right edge of the board. A heat sink looks like a three-dimensional comb – rows and columns of metal teeth, each designed to lead heat away from the processor. A fan screws on top of the heat sink.

The heat sink will generally snap right into a notched brace that straddles the CPU socket. It is a good idea to use what is called thermal compound to make sure that there is a snug fit between the chip and the heatsink. Thermal compound can be purchased from any computer parts dealer.

☞ *When attaching the heat sink clip to a socket processor be careful not to scratch the motherboard with the clip. Be gentle when attaching the heat sink bracket. If too much pressure is applied the plastic clip will break.*

A.7 INSTALLING MEMORY (RAM)

Most motherboard today come with between 2 and 8 sockets for the insertion of RAM memory. These are usually either SIMMs (Single Inline Memory Modules) or DIMMs (Dual Inline Memory Modules). These sockets can be of different sizes.

The motherboard usually labels these sockets "SIMM0" through "SIMM7" or "DIMM1" through "DIMM3", etc. The sockets are almost always filled starting with the lowest numbered socket first. Most Pentium class or higher motherboards require SIMMs to be inserted in pairs, but DIMMs may be inserted individually.

To install a RAM, do the following:

(a) Locate the memory banks on the mainboard. Most main boards will have two or three black banks for the memory slots.
(b) Check the notches of the RAM module
(c) Hold the RAM module at an angle of 45 degree.
(d) Make sure that the retention clips are open, or pressed outward from the banks. Slide the memory into the bank, making sure that the slot on the module orients to the slot on the bank. There is only one way the memory can fit properly. Make sure that the short row of pins is lined up with the short gap in the socket, just as the long row of pins should line up with the long gap in the socket.
(e) Using two hands, press down (press and hold – do not rock the module) on both sides of the memory until the retention clips lock into position. The clips will fold to lock in the memory under your pressure.
(f) You should not have to manually fold the retention clips. They are designed to fold into the lock position when the RAM is seated into its bank. If the retention clips do not fold, remove the chip and make sure that it is oriented correctly.

A.8 INSTALLING PCI DEVICES

The most common devices that slide into PCI (Peripheral Component Interconnect) slots are network cards or Network Interface Cards (NIC) and sound cards.

PCIs are usually indicated on a main board as a white slot. They are most commonly anchored on the motherboard near the rare of the case so that external cables can be connected to them.

Most cards will simply slide into place in the way the RAM does. A notch in the bottom of the card matches a break in the PCI slot to make sure the device slides in the right way around.

After the PCI card is in place, its metal backplate should be flush with the rear of the case. Fasten it to the case with a screw through the pre-drilled hole.

A.9 INSTALLING VIDEO CARD

It is not always necessary to install a video card. Some motherboards already have what's called an on-board graphics chip. Video cards go injust the way PCI devices do, but sometimes they fit only into a specially designed slot called and AGP (Accelerated Graphics Port) Slot.

To find out if you motherboard has an on board graphics card, look at the rear of the computer to see if there's a VGA port, often coloured blue. If it does not have one of these already, you will need to install a video card to attach a monitor.

A.10 INSTALLING IDE DEVICES

Three kinds of devices attach to the computer's motherboard via a piece of cable called an IDE cable. The IDE cable is grey, thin and wide, with one hard plastic grid fitting on each end. Sometimes there is one more fitting in the middle. Each fitting has a squared notch on one side called a guide. It makes sure you can not put the IDE cable in upside down.

The three devices that attach with an IDE cable are the hard drive, the CD-ROM and the floppy.

To Install Hard drive do the following:

Configure one hard disk as master and the other as slave if you are installing two hard disks in the system on the same IDE cable. If two dives are on the same cable, you have to specify the priority of one drive in relation to the other.

These priorities are set using a small set of pins at the rear of the drive called jumpers. A movable plastic clip, can be placed between a pair of jumper pins to trigger certain settings. Inside the plastic clip pieces of metal that close a circuit when the jumper is in place are arranged. The state of the circuit (open or closed) determines the jumper setting.

Attaching the cable

When connecting IDE devices to the main board, it is important that you correctly orient the IDE drive and the main board if the IDE cable is not installed properly to the main board, the computer will not recognize any drive on that cable. If it is not correctly installed to the device. The computer will not recognize that device. Also, incorrect orientation of either the drive or the cable can damage the drive itself.

A.11 FITTING CD-ROM

1. In most cases, you should install a CD-ROM drive as the secondary master. That means it is on a separate IDE channel from the hard drive, but that it is the highest priority on that channel.
2. Verify that the drive is set to be a "Master" on a single IDE channel. The jumper settings are indicated on the drive itself.
3. Connect an IDE Ribbon cable to the main board making sure that Pin 1 is oriented correctly (Pin 1 is identified with a red stripe on the ribbon cable and by the number 1 on the secondary master connector on the main board).
4. Attach the CD-ROM drive to the IDE Ribbon Cable on its master position (at the end of the IDE Ribbon Cable). Make sure that the IDE Ribbon Cable is positioned to Pin 1 on the CD-ROM drive (Pin 1 on the CD-ROM drive faces the power connection).

☞ *Place the drive in the 5.25" bay at the top of the computer's chassis and secure the drive down using 4 drive screws.*

A.12 CONNECTING PERIPHERAL DEVICES

After connecting the internal components, you can close the system case and then connect the external components, such as keyboard, mouse, modem and scanner.

A.13 CONNECTING MOUSE

Depending on the type of your mouse, you will connect it to the appropriate port on the back of the computer.

A mouse can be connected to computer system in one of the following ways:

- Using a serial port
- A bus connection
- PS/2 mouse port
- USB port
- Wireless

Let us see these different types of mouse connections in detail.

A.13.1 Serial Mouse

A serial port is the most common method of connecting a mouse. A serial mouse is connected to either COM1 or COM2, i.e., to any one of the available serial port on the computer.

Connecting a serial mouse is very easy as one need to just plug in the connector attached to the mouse wire to the vacant serial port on the computer.

Sometimes, one need to configure the mouse drive to specify the COM port used for the mouse, but most of the new mouse drive software can automatically sense the port to which the mouse is connected and auto-configure themselves.

A.13.2 Bus Mouse

Difference between a bus mouse and a serial mouse is, a serial mouse is connected to a serial port, whereas the bus mouse is connected to a special cord made just for the mouse.

This special mouse adapter board is installed into the PC's expansion slot and then the mouse is connected to the connector provided at the back.

A.13.3 PS/2 Port Mouse

Now a days, many computers come equipped with special mouse port for connecting the mouse. This method is similar to the bus mouse approach except that the mouse control circuitry is directly built into the motherbord of the PC and not connected as a separate card.

This type of mouse is called PS/2 mouse because these connector are common with IBM/s PS/2 range of computers.

A.13.4 USB Mouse

The USB port can be used to connect a mouse. As the mouse is not required during power on/bootup process, no special BIOS is required for handling USB mouse.

Hardware installation of the USB mouse requires just plugging in the mouse to the USB port. Windows XP operating system will automatically install it in the PC.

A.13.5 Wireless Mouse

In this type of mouse, everything is similar to the conventional mouse except that no cable is used to connect the mouse to the computer system.

Basically there are two types of wireless mouse:

- Infrared Wireless Mouse
- Radio-controlled Wireless Mouse

Infrared Wireless Mouse

The infrared mouse communicates with the receiving unit connected to the main system unit using infrared light. As the infrared light can not pass through objects, this requires an infrared mouse to be in direct line of sight with the receiving unit connected to the main system.

Radio-controlled Wireless Mouse

When the radio-controlled wireless mouse is moved, radio signals are transmitted by it to a special receiver unit connected to the main system. The radio signal received by the receiver is sent to the computer as any normal mouse signal received through the cable is sent.

Most of the Infrared Wireless mouse and Radio-controlled Wireless mouse requires the mouse to be within six feet of the receiving unit.

As the radio signal can pass through objects, the radio-controlled mouse need not be in line of sight with the receiving unit.

In case, more than one wireless mouse is being used at one place, they cause different radio frequencies, so one need not worry about signal from one mouse getting disturbed by the signal from another mouse.

☞ *Before connecting the mouse, it is safest to turn the computer off and unplug it. If your mouse is a USB device, your computer may be kept on.*

A.14 CONFIGURING MOUSE

ß **To configure the mouse setting in CMOS do the following:**

(a) If you installed a serial mouse, check the CMOS (Complementary Metal Oxide Semiconductor) settings to ensure that the serial or COM ports are enabled and assigned.

(b) If you installed a USB mouse, check the CMOS settings to ensure that the USB in enabled.

A.15 CONNECTING KEYBOARD

Depending on the type of the keyboard, you can connect it to the appropriate port on the back of the computer.

ß **To connect a PS/2 Keyboard do the following:**

(a) Connect the keyboard cable to the PS/2 port. Be careful to connect to the correct PS/2 port, as the keyboard and mouse PS/2 ports look identical. If the PS/2 ports on your computer are coloured, the keyboard PS/2 port is usually purple in colour.

ß **To connect a USB Keyboard do the following:**

(a) Connect the USB keyboard to the USB port on the PC. If there are other USB devices, connect the keyboard to the USB hub. You will have to install the drives for your keyboard if it has additional advanced features. You will also have to install the software for the keyboard in this case. If need be refer to the keyboard manual.

A.16 INSTALLING MONITOR

Monitor is an output device used to display information on screen. The monitor must be installed by attaching the signal cable to the system and the power cord to the power outlet.

ß **To install the monitor, do the following:**

(a) Connect power cable one end to the power port at the back of the monitor.

(b) Connect the other end of the power cord to the power outlet or the system power supply case.

(c) Check the monitor using the built in Power On Self Test (POST).

(d) Connect one end of the signal cable to the video port at the back of the monitor, if it is not already connected to the monitor.

(e) Connect the other end of the signal cable to the back of the system case, to the video adapter.

(f) Turn the hard screws of the signal cable to lock the signal cable to the system case.

A.17 INSTALLING AN EXTERNAL MODEM

Modem is technically called the modulator–demodulator. It is an electronic device, which helps in transmitting programs and data locally or around the world through telephone lines. The main function of a modem is to transform digital signal into analog signal and vice versa. For installing an external modem you need to connect the modem with a computer and a telephone line.

ß **To install the external modem, do the following:**

(a) Place the external modem on the desk.

(b) Locate the serial cable that comes with the modem. Note that the cable has a 25-pin male connector at one end and 25-pin female connector on the other end.

(c) Plug the female connector of the serial cable into the 25-pin serial port on the back of the system unit.

(d) Now plug the male connector of the serial cable into the modem.

(e) Secure the connectors with the help of screws on both the sides.

(f) Plug the power cord of the external modem into the power outlet.

(g) Locate the two phone jacks labeled phone and line on the back of the external modem.

(h) Plug one end of the phone cable into the line jack and another end of the phone cable into the phone outlet.

(i) Plug one end of another phone cable into the phone jack and the other end of the phone cable into the telephone. This step is optional.

(j) A similar procedure is followed for installing modem for wide band modem.

A.18 INSTALLING A SCANNER

Many scanners use the parallel port connection. This connection provides the means of data transfer between a scanner and the computer.

ß **To install a parallel port scanner, do the following:**

(a) Place the scanner on a flat, smooth surface near the computer. The cable must be long enough to reach the computer.

(b) Attach the 25-pin end of the cable to the parallel port of the computer. Fasten the side screws of the cable end.

(c) Attach the other end of the cable to the appropriate slot on the back of the scanner. Refer to the scanner manual for the location of the slot. Secure the side screws or wire holders on the scanner.

(d) Some scanners have a slot for printers. Such scanners can be used along with printers. In this case, connect the printer cable to the printer slot of the scanner.

(e) Connect one end of the power cord to the scanner and the other end to a power outlet. Some scanners turn on by themselves at this stage. If your scanner has an on/off button, use that button to turn the scanner on.

(f) Turn the computer on. Windows XP Operating System will detect the new device through its plug and play feature.

(g) Follow the instructions on the computer and insert the installation CD or disk when prompted by Widows XP if need be.

(h) Read the manual for instructions on settings for the scanner and also to run a test scan. Many scanners come with additional software. Read the documentation that comes with scanner and install any additional software if it comes with your scanner.

(i) Calibrate the scanner according to instructions in the manual. Calibrating a scanner ensures better results.

A.19 DISASSEMBLING A PC

The process of disassembling a computer is to take out parts of a computer. You may have to disassemble a specific part of the system to replace the defective part or to upgrade some part of the system.

Precautions for disassembling a computer:

(a) Disconnect the PC before opening the system case.

(b) Handle PC peripherals with due care and always employ some method to disperse static electricity, such as anti-static wrist strap.

(c) Never try to clean any part of the system with liquid detergent or cloth.

A.20 REMOVING COVER OF CPU

First step in disassembling the PC involves disconnecting all the peripherals, such as speaker, monitor, mouse, keyboard, printer and scanner from the system. Now remove the case outer cover. Open the screws that may be holding the outer cover of the PC.

A.21 DISCONNECTING THE INTERNAL CABLES

Internal cables consist of power cables and IDE cables. Power cables are the wires that connect the computer power supply box and the various internal components of the computer. The power cables include disk drive connectors and motherboard connector. The disk drives connectors are wires that connect various devices to the power supply. The motherboard connectors connect the motherboard and the power supply box.

☞ *The power cables are a combination of red, green, blue, black, yellow, green, orange, purple and white wires. The motherboard connector is one of the power cables.*

A.22 REMOVING DEVICE CARDS

Devices cards are cards that make the internally components or devices work. These cards have slots that, when fixed to the system case, can be viewed from outside the system case.

The different internal components, such as floppy, CD-ROM, modem, mouse and speakers have device cards. In recent times, motherboard comes equipped with in-built functionalities that do not require external cards. These external cards are also called as non-integrated cards. Some users prefer such non-integrated cards to improve the performance and enhance functionality of the device. For example, there are various graphical cards that improve the display of 3-D images.

A.23 REMOVING DISK DRIVE

After removing the internal cables and the device cards, you can now remove the disk drives.

☞ *The disk drive connectors are small in size.*

A.24 REMOVING RAM CHIP

RAM is the memory chip that is attached to the motherboard. This chip is placed on the memory slots on the motherboard.

A.25 REMOVING PROCESSOR FAN

The processor fan is used for cooling the processor chip. The chip is placed below the cooling fan.

A.26 REMOVING PROCESSOR

Processor is the chip that actually makes the compute work. It is placed exactly below the cooling fan. The processor is also called as microprocessor or CPU.

A.27 REMOVING COOLING FAN

Similar to the processor-cooling fan, the system-cooling fan, cools off the heat generated by the internal components of the system.

A.28 REMOVING MOTHERBOARD

After disconnecting all the wires that are connecting the motherboard you should remove the motherboard from the system case.

A.29 REMOVING SMPS POWER SUPPLY

SMPS power supply is the box that supplies power to the system. All the internal components of the system case require power for proper functioning. Each internal component of the system is connected to the power supply box with the power cables. Remove the connection and open the screws holding the SMPS with the system unit.

Glossary

8-bit, 16-bit, 32-bit

The 8-bit, 16-bit and 32-bit specifications are the computer's internal word size, which is the amount of data the processor can hold in its registers and work on at the same time. Large-scale supercomputers hold 64 bits. All things being equal, a 16-bit computer works twice as fast as an 8-bit computer; however, this specification measures only one aspect of a computer performance.

Access time

The time interval between the instant at which data is called from a storage device and the instant delivery begins.

Access Bus

Access bus is a new standard intended to connect relatively low-speed devices such as keyboards, mice, modems, and printers.

Address Bus

The portion of a system bus used to transfer address. Typically, the address identifies a main memory location or an I/O device.

Address Mode

The address mode is how a machine instruction refers to memory and peripheral devices.

Address Register

A register in a processing unit, that contains the address of the storage location being accessed.

Address Space

The address space is the total amount of memory that can be used by a program. The address space may refer to, if virtual memory is used, the virtual limit of memory, which includes physical memory and disk storage.

Accumulator

A local storage area, called a register, in which the result of an arithmetic or logic operation is formed. It is also a register in which one operand of an operation can be stored and subsequently replaced by the result of that operation.

ALU (Arithmetic Logic Unit)

It is one of the components of the Central Processing Unit (CPU) of the computer which performs all mathematical and logical operations.

Analog transmission

A continuously varying electromagnetic wave that may be propagated over a variety of media.

Architecture

The overall design, construction, organization and interconnecting of the various components of a computer system. It refers particularly to the processor hardware and the size and ordering sequence of its bytes.

Archive

Backup storage. Usually a secondary storage medium, such as magnetic tape or a mass storage device that operates on semi-direct access and sequential principles.

Artificial intelligence (AI)

A branch of computer science that deals with computers that possess reasoning, learning, and thinking capabilities that resemble those of human beings.

ASCII (American Standard Code for Information Interchange)

A standard coding system for computers. ASCII-7 is a 7-bit code and its extended version ASCII-8 is an 8-bit code.

ASCII File

It is a document file in the universally recognized text format called ASCII (American Standard Code for Information Interchange). An ASCII file contains characters, spaces, punctuation, carriage return, and sometimes tabs and an end-of-file marker, but it contains no formatting information.

Auxiliary storage

A storage that supplements the primary internal storage of a computer. Often referred to as secondary storage, this section of the computer's memory is characterized by low cost per bit stored.

Alphanumeric

A combination of letters, digits, and special characters used to form an expression, such as a part number. An example of an alphanumeric expression follows.

PN A-10036-001

Notice that alphabetical, numeric, spaces, and punctuation characters may exist in an alphanumeric expression.

Analog Computer

Analog Computer is a computer that accepts and processes data made up of continuously varying voltages.

Associative memory

A memory whose storage locations are identified by their contents, or by a part of their contents, rather than by their names or positions.

Backup

Alternate facilities of programs, data files, etc., that are used in case the original one is lost, or fails to operate.

Bandwidth

The range of frequencies available for data transmission. The wider the bandwidth of a communications system, the more data it can transmit in a given period of time. It is expressed in Kilobits per seconds. The bandwidth determines the rate at which information can be sent through a communication channel.

Bar Code

A coding structure in which characters are represented by means of a series of parallel bars.

Baud

A unit for measuring data transmission speed. It is used to describe the capacity of a carrier. In general usage, baud is identical to bits per second.

Baud rate

The speed of data transmission, usually in bits per second.

BCD (Binary Coded Decimal)

One of the early coding systems used by computers which is based on the idea of converting each digit of a decimal number into its binary equivalent rather than converting the entire decimal value into a pure binary form.

Benchmark

In the electronic information disciplines, a benchmark is an established performance standard for processing data, against which new equipment and/or software can be evaluated.

BIOS (Basic Input Output System)

BIOS is responsible for handling the details of input/output operations including the task of relating a program's logical records to a peripheral device physical records.

Bit

Stands for binary digit. The values are 1 or 0 (zero).

BLOB

Binary Large OBject. Essentially, a long bit string used for complex data.

Bluetooth

An open specification for short-range wireless transmission of voice and data that is currently under development. Bluetooth provides a simple, low-cost method of linking Personal Digital Assistants (PDAs), cellular phones, laptops, and other information appliances.

Boot disk or boot drive

Disk drive from which Windows loads on startup.

Boot record

The section on a disk that contains the minimum information DOS needs to start the system.

BOOTP

Bootstrap Protocol. Protocol used by a network node to determine the IP address of its interfaces in order to achieve network booting.

Bootstrap

A small program that is usually invoked to draw larger and more comprehensive programs into a computer.

Bootstrapping

When the computer is turned on or is rebooted from the keyboard with Ctrl + Alt + Del keys pressed together, it loads enough of its operating system into memory to get started; it pulls itself up by its bootstraps program.

Base Address

A numeric value that is used as a reference in the calculation of addresses in the execution of a computer program.

Buffer

Storage used to compensate for a difference in rate of flow of data, or time of occurrence of events, when transferring data from one device to another.

Bus

A shared communication path consisting of one or more connection lines. In some computer systems, CPU, memory and I/O devices are connected by a common bus. Since the lines are shared by all components, only one component at a time can successfully transmit.

Cache

Area on disk (usually a folder) for the temporary storage of information. Browsers store recently viewed Web pages in a cache, in case you want to see them again. Windows also maintains caches for CD-ROMs and removable disks.

Cache memory

A small buffer storage, smaller and faster than main storage (often made of Static RAM), that is used to hold a copy of instructions and data in main storage that are likely to be needed next by the processor and that have been obtained automatically from main storage, such as, hard disk. It is used to increase the speed of processing by making current programs and data available to the CPU at a rapid rate.

Cartridge

A device used to contain a prerecorded program.

Central Processing Unit

See CPU

Chip

A chip is a miniaturized electronic circuit. Chips are approximately 1/16th to 1/2 inch square and about 1/30th of an inch. They hold from a few dozen to several million electronic components (transistors, resistors, etc.). *Synonymous with integrated circuits and microelectronic.*

Clear Memory

To clear memory is to reset all RAM memory and hardware registers to their blank or non-value position. Rebooting the computer may or may not clear memory but turning the computer off and on again ensures that all memory is cleared.

Clock Pulse

A clock pulse is a signal that is used to synchronize the operations of an electronic system. Clock Pulses are continuous, precisely spaced changes in voltage.

Clock rate

Inverse of clock cycle time, usually measured in Mhz.

Computer Instruction

An instruction that can be recognised by the processing unit of the computer for which it is designed. *Synonymous with machine instruction.*

Computer Instruction Set

A complete set of the operators of the instructions of a computer together with a description of the types of meanings that can be attributed to their operands. *Synonymous with machine instruction set.*

Control Registers

CPU registers employed to control CPU operation. Most of these registers are not user-visible.

COM1, COM2, COM3, COM4 or comm port

Serial ports used for connecting peripherals, such as, mouse, joystick etc.

Configuration

An initial set of system values, such as the number of buffers DOS will use, the number of simultaneously open files it will allow, and specific devices that will be supported.

Cycle time

The time interval between the instant at which a read/write command is given to a memory and the instant when the next such instruction can be issued to the memory (also known as memory cycle time).

Cylinder

In a disk pack, a set of corresponding tracks in all the surfaces is called a cylinder. All tracks of a cylinder are accessible by a single movement of the access mechanism.

Daisy wheel printer

A letter-quality printer that uses a printing head with the appearance of daisy and/or a wheel. Each petal of the daisy wheel has a character embossed on it.

DDR SDRAM

Double Data Rate Synchronous Dynamic RAM (Random Access Memory) ? can theoretically improve memory clock speed to at least 200 MHz. It activates output on both the rising and falling edge of the system clock, rather than on only the rising edge. This potentially doubles output.

DIMM

Dual In-line Memory Module - a double SIMM (single in-line memory module); a module that contains one or several Random Access Memory (RAM) chips on a small circuit board with pins that connect it to the computer motherboard.

Display adapter

An add-in hardware board that sends video output signals to your monitor corresponding to the current contents of video memory.

DMA

Direct Memory Access, a system board facility used by a few medium-speed devices to communicate with the CPU.

Disk

A flat, circular plate coated with a magnetic material on which data can be stored by magnetization of portions of the flat surface.

Disk Cleanup

Windows utility that deletes unneeded temporary files to free up space on your disk.

Disk Operating System (DOS)

An operating system which contains the disk-oriented commands and uses disk devices for permanent storage.

Disk optimizer

A program (such as DEFAG.EXE in DOS 6) that rearranges the location of files stored on a disk in order to make the data in those files quickly retrievable.

Diskette

A low-cost, thin, flexible magnetic disk storage device used on small computer systems. Also called a floppy disk.

Display adapter

An add-in hardware board that sends video output signals to your monitor corresponding to the current contents of video memory.

DMA

Direct Memory Access, a system board facility used by a few medium-speed devices to communicate with the CPU.

Drum printer

A line printer that uses a solid, rotating, cylindrical drum on which the characters to be printed are embossed.

Dumb terminal

A terminal that has no local processing capability.

Dump

A process whereby the contents of all or a part of primary storage are copied onto some secondary storage device or displayed on a printer or screen.

DVD

An optical disk technology with a 4.7 gigabyte storage capacity on a single-sided, one-layered disk, which is enough for a 133-minute movie. DVDs can be single- or double-sided, and can have two layers on each side; a double-sided, two layered DVD will hold up to 17 gigabytes of video, audio, or other information.

Electronic mail

A general term to describe the transmission of messages by the use of computing systems and telecommunications facilities.

Electronic Mail/Message System (EMMS)

A system that can store and deliver, by electronic means, text and messages that would otherwise be forwarded through the postal service or sent verbally over telephone lines.

Electrostatic printer

A high-speed printer that uses charged pins to form character matrices on chemically treated paper.

Electrothermal printer

A high-speed printer that uses heated elements to create characters as matrices of small dots on heat-sensitive paper.

Emulator

A program that permits one computer to execute the machine-language instructions of another computer of a different make.

EPROM (Erasable Programmable Read Only Memory)

A semiconductor memory which allows the eraser of the information stored in it by exposure to ultraviolet light. Later new information can be stored in it.

Ergonomics

The science that focuses on how machines and other things should be designed and arranged so that people can interact with them in a comfortable and efficient way.

Error Message

A statement that appears on your screen when your computer is unable to continue processing. The message tells you what the problem is and how to solve it.

Encryption

Converting stored or transmitted data to a coded form in order to prevent it from being read by unauthorized persons. Also application of a specific algorithm to alter the appearance of data, making it incomprehensible to those who are not authorized to see the information.

Executable file

Any "runnable" application program with a file extension of . COM, .EXE, or .BAT. The term is sometimes extended to include files that don't run by themselves but do contain program code, such as .OVL and .PIF files.

Execution time

The total time required to execute a program on a particular system is called its execution time for that computer system.

Executive routine

A master program in an operating system that controls the execution of other programs. It is also known as the executive, monitor, or supervisor.

Executive Workstation Expert System

Special desktop computer-based units designed for busy people who do not like to type. They have special function keys, and may accept input through the use of a mouse or a touch screen. They have the ability to perform word/data processing, manage data bases, produce graphics, and support many other activities.

Extended ASCII

Extended ASCII provides added capability by allowing for 128 additional characters, such as accented letters, graphics characters, and special symbols.

Extranet

An extranet is the part of a corporate intranet that allows companies to communicate with the intranets of their customers and suppliers, facilitating electronic transactions.

Executable file

Any "runnable" application program with a file extension of . COM, .EXE, or .BAT. The term is sometimes extended to include files that do not run by themselves but do contain program code, such as .OVL and .PIF files.

Execution time

The total time required to execute a program on a particular system is called its execution time for that computer system.

Expansion slots

The expansion slots are long thin connectors on the motherboard, near the backside of the computer.

External cache

External cache is a separate high speed memory in between the processor and the main memory which is controlled by a cache controller.

Extended (XMS) memory: Extended Memory is the memory beyond the 1 MB limit, or any memory available after the 1 MB memory is called extended memory.

Faceplate

A connecting point in a cable system that permits a network cable from a movable computer to connect with a permanently installed cable system. This is generally a plate installed in the wall.

Facsimile (FAX)

Transmission of pictures, texts, maps, graphs, etc., over transmission lines, phone lines, and other carriers between geographically separated points. An image is scanned at a transmitting point and duplicated at a receiving point.

Firewall

Router or remote-access server (or several routers or access servers) designated as a buffer between connected networks. A firewall uses access lists and other methods to ensure the security of a network. Also a system or combination of systems that enforces a boundary between two or more networks.

FireWire

Like Access.bus, FireWire is a new high-speed desktop serial bus, also called P1394. It is based on the ANSI draft standard P1394. This bus is jointly developed by Apple and Texas Instruments. It offers many of the same advantages as Access.bus, namely you can daisy-chaining peripherals on a FireWire bus, hanging up to 63 devices off a single port.

Fixed-head magnetic disk

A magnetic disk system that eliminates the use of an access mechanism by distributing all the read/write heads over the disk surfaces.

Flat network design

A network design that has little or no hierarchy or modularity and is generally only appropriate for small shared or switched LANs.

Flash Memory

It is electrically erasable and programmable permanent type memory. Its entire contents can be erased in one operation. It is not byte by byte alterable like EEPROM. Flash memory modules upto 4 GB capacity are available. The modules are available as flash cards and flash drives. Flash drives can replace hard disk drives in some applications. They are static and faster but they are costlier.

Flash BIOS

"Flash BIOS" is a particular type of EEPROM (Electrically Erasable Programmable Read Only Memory) chip that can be erased and programmed in the system itself.

Floating-point numbers

Signed numbers held in a fraction-exponent format. For example, 3216 would be represented as 0.3216×10^4 in floating-point notation.

Folder

Special kind of file that contains a list of other files. Folders can contain other folders.

Format

The arrangement of input data, stored data, or output information.

Formatting

For documents, the elements of style and presentation that are added through the use of margins, indents, and different sizes, and styles of type. Formatting, especially in word processing, is intrinsic to a document in the sense that a certain appearance is, by default, built into the margins, spacing, and typeface of every document.

Forwarding

Process of sending a frame toward its ultimate destination by way of an internetworking device.

Fragmentation

Process of breaking a packet into smaller units when transmitting over a network medium that cannot support the original size of the packet.

Front-end processor

A CPU designed specifically to handle the communications processing task. Its main purpose is to off-load communications processing task from the host computer, so that the host computer can be dedicated for applications and data processing jobs.

General purpose computer

A computer capable of performing a variety of business and scientific applications.

Handshake

A trade term that refers to what takes place when two computers or a computer and a terminal device are interconnected in such a way that they can exchange information.

Handshaking

Process whereby two protocol entities synchronize during connection establishment

Hardware

The physical components of a computer system such as electronic, magnetic, and mechanical devices.

HDD

Hard Disk Drive - the mechanism that controls the positioning, reading, and writing of the hard disk, which furnishes the largest amount of data storage for the PC. Although the hard disk drive (often shortened to "hard drive") and the hard disk are not the same thing, they are packaged as a unit and so either term is sometimes used to refer to the whole unit.

Head slider

The arm on which the read/write head of the disk drive is located is called the head slider.

Heatsink

It is a device that is attached to a microprocessor chip to keep it from overheating by absorbing its heat and dissipating it into the air.

IDE (Intelligent Device Electronics)

Most of an IDE drive's intelligence is built into the drive itself. IDE refers to any drive with an integrated controller.

Interface

The point at which independent systems or diverse groups interact. It consists of the devices, rules or conventions by which one component of a system communicates with another. It is also the point of communication between a person and a computer.

Incremental backup

Backup of only those files that are new or have change since the last backup.

Installation file

File required for a program to run, along with an installation program.

Integrated Services Digital Network (ISDN)

A special phone line that supports modem speeds up to 64 Kbps. However, these phone line can be quite expensive to acquire. Many ISDN adapters support two-channel access.

Intelligent terminal

A terminal having local processing capability. It has a built-in CPU and can perform specific functions, such as editing data, controlling other terminals, etc.

Inter process communication

The topology provided by an operating system to allow concurrent processes to communicate with each other.

Interactive Mode

Used to enter commands directly from the keyboard.

I/O (Input/Output)

Pertaining to the techniques, media, and devices used for man-machine interaction

Interface

The point at which independent systems or diverse groups interact. It consists of the devices, rules or conventions by which one component of a system communication with another. It is also the point of communication between a person and a computer.

Input

The data entered into a data processing system.

Input/Output

Input refers to any information coming into the computer. Output refers to processed information going out of a computer.

Input device

A device used to enter information into a computer or other data processing devices; for example, the keyboard.

Internet Protocol (IP)

A low-level protocol that routes packets of data across separate networks tied together by routers to form the Internet or an intranet. Data travels in packets called IP datagrams.

Internet telephony

Generic term used to describe various approaches to running voice traffic over IP networks, in particular, the Internet.

Internet work packet exchange (IPX)

Novell's NetWare network layer protocol that specifies addressing, routing, and switching packets between a server and workstations and across interconnected LANs. Encapsulated IPX packets can be carried by Ethernet packets and Token ring frames.

Internetworking

General term used to refer to the industry and technologies devoted to connecting networks together. Also collection of networks interconnected by routers.

Intrusion Detection

Detection of break-ins or break-in attempts either manually or via software expert systems that operate on logs or other information available on the network.

K (Kilo)

Used to represent $2^{10} = 1024$ in computers only.

Key-to-disk

A device used to enter data onto a disk device.

Key-to-tape

A device used to enter data onto a magnetic tape.

Kiosk

A booth or display area where an on-screen computer presentation may be set up for use by those visiting the area. An example of a kiosk would be an information counter in a shopping small or booth at a trade show.

Laser printer

A very high-speed printer that uses a combination of laser-beam and electro-photographic techniques to create printed outputs at speeds in excess of 13,000 line per minute.

Latency

1. Delay between the time a device requests access to a network and the time it is granted permission to transmit. 2. Delay between the time a device receives a frame and the time that frame is forwarded out the destination port.

Latency time

In case of disk storage, the time taken for the desired record to come under the read/write head positioned over that track. Maximum latency time equals the time taken by disk to rotate once.

Landscape orientation

A printer mode that causes text and graphs to be printed sideways on the page, across the long dimension.

LCD

(Liquid Crystal Display) is the technology used for displays in notebook and other smaller computers.

Light pen

A pen shaped device that is used as an input device to computers by writing or sketching on the screen of a cathode ray tube.

Line printer

A printer that prints one line at a time.

Local Area Network (LAN)

Network that connects computers that are in the same building or campus, usually with cables.

Logging

The process of storing information about events that occurred on the firewall or network.

Magnetic bubble memory

An electronic secondary storage device constituted of solid-state electronic chips and having no moving parts. It uses the properties of certain materials, under applied magnetic fields, to represent binary 1s and 0s.

Magnetic storage

Storage devices, such as disks, drums, tapes, cores, etc., that utilize the magnetic properties of materials to store data.

Magnetic tape

A secondary storage device that uses a long plastic strip coated with a magnetic material as a recording medium.

Magnetic-Ink Character Recognition (MICR)

An input device that can read cards and paper documents printed with a special magnetic ink.

Magneto-optical Drives

An erasable or semi-erasable storage disc, similar to a CD-ROM disc and of very high capacity, in which a laser beam is used to heat the recording surface to point at which tiny region on the surface can be magnetically aligned to store bits of data. MO drives come in two formats: 3.5-inch, with capacities to 230MB: and 5.25-inch, which can now write 2.6GB cartridge. Because of their excellent performance (20- to 50-ms access times and a 2-MBps transfer rate) and nearly indestructible media, MO drives are ideal for storing large amounts of frequently used data near-line.

Mass storage

Storage systems that provide access to hundreds of billions of bytes of stored data. They are often referred to as archieve storage because of the very large volumes of historical or backup data that they can store.

Microprocessor

A LSI chip which contains the entire CPU of a computer, except main memory.

Millisecond

One-thousandth of a second.

Minicomputer

A relatively fast but small and inexpensive computer with somewhat limited input/output capabilities.

Modem (Modulator-Demodulator)

Devices used to convert digital signals (to be communicated over an analog channel such as telephone line) to sine waves at the sending end and back to digital signals at the receiving end.

Modulation

Conversion of digital information from your computer into analog "sound" information for transmission over the phone.

Mouse

Device for moving the mouse pointer on the screen and selecting the item the pointer points to.

Mouse keys

Accessibility option that enables you to use the numeric keypad to control the pointer.

Mouse pointer

The screen symbol representing the symbolic location of the mouse. When in graphic mode, the mouse pointer is generally an arrow. When in text mode, it appears as a solid movable rectangle.

Multitasking

Running multiple tasks at the same time. Windows 7 is a multitasking operating system, because it can run many tasks (programs) simultaneously.

Nanosecond

One-billionth (10^{-9}) of a second.

NetBIOS

Network Basic Input/Output System. API used by applications on a LAN to request services from lower-level network processes. These services include session establishment and termination, and information transfer NetBIOS is used by network operating systems, such as LAN Manager, LAN Server, Windows for Work-groups, and Window NT.

NetWare

Popular distributed network operating system developed by Novell. Provides transparent remote file access and numerous other distributed network services.

Network

An inter-connection of computer systems and/or peripheral devices with carriers and data communications devices for the purpose of exchanging data and information.

Network File System (NFS)

Network file system is an open operating system designed by Sun Microsystems that allows all network users to access shared files stored on computers of different types. NFS provides access to shared files through and interface called the Virtual File System (VFS) that runs on top of TCP/IP. Users can manipulate shared files as if they were stored locally on the user's own hard disk. With NFS, computers connected to a network operate as clients while accessing remote files, and as servers while providing remote users access to local shared files.

Network interface card

A chip-based circuit board used to connect the PC to a network or server. The card is activated by loading software on the PC. Network Interface Card is a printed circuit board that is installed in a vacant slot in a computer I/O bus. The back of the card contains a physical interface for connectivity between a computer's internal resources and external resources connected to the network.

NIC

Network Interface Card. Board that provides network-communication capabilities for a computer system.

Orientation

For printer paper, indicates whether the document is to be printed normally (for example, in Portrait mode) or sideways (in Landscape mode).

Output

The finished result of processing by a system.

Output unit

The unit of a computer system that supplies information and results of computation to the outside world.

Parallel operation

A system changeover method whereby data is processed by both the old and the new system until the performance of the new system is verified satisfactorily.

Parity bit

An extra bit added to a string of bits that enables the computer to detect internal errors in the transmission of binary data.

Password

A code by which a user gains access to a computer system. It is used for security purposes.

PCI

Personal Computer Interface, a standard type of expansion slot or card that fits into a PCI slot.

Peripherals devices

Since the input and the output devices are on the periphery (edge) of the main processing unit, they are sometimes referred to as peripheral devices. There are many kinds of I/O devices, some of which are more suitable to given applications than others.

Persistence

After being struck by the electron beam, when the beam moves to next dot the illumination of the dot stays for a few milliseconds this is called persistence.

Picosecond

One trillionth of a second.

Pinging

It is a technique to identify network problems. A LAN message is sent to a remote LAN node. The node, in turn, formulates an echo-reply and returns it to the original sender. Successful receipt of echo reply implies that the major components of transport systems are functioning.

Pixel

A picture element. It is used to represent one point in a raster scan display device.

Plotter

An output device that converts computer output into a graphic, hardcopy form.

Plug-in

Program that "plugs in" to your browser program, adding new features to the browser.

Plug and Play

Type of device that can communicate with Windows to provide its own configuration information.

Portability

The capability of a program to run on different types of machines with minimum modification.

Power-on-Self Test

When power is turned on, POST (Power-On Self Test) is diagnostic testing sequence that a computer?s basic Input/Output system runs to determine if the computer keyboard, random access memory, disk driver and other hardware are working properly.

Program counter (PC)

A register in CPU which is used to store the address of the next instruction to be executed.

PROM (Programming Read-Only Memory)

Similar to read only memory with the exception that these chips can be re-programmed by using special external equipments.

RAID

Redundant Array of Inexpensive Disk (RAID), a system where multiple hard drives are connected together to form a single large drive for storage that provides either redundancy performance or both.

Real Time Clock Circuit

Real Time Clock (RTC) circuit keeps the computer time/date upt-to-date. With the help of a battery and CMOS memory, this circuit maintains correct date and time even when the mains AC supply to the computer is switched off.

Random Access Memory (RAM)

Semiconductor-based memory that can be read and written by the microprocessor or other hardware devices. The storage locations can be accessed in any order. The term RAM is generally understood to refer to volatile memory, which can be written as well as read.

ROM (Read Only Memory)

Special memory chips containing instructions which can be read only, therefore preventing accidental destruction of the instructions. ROM is used to store firmware.

Serial ATA (Drive Interface)

Serial ATA (Serial Advanced Technology Attachment or SATA) is a new standard for connecting hard drives into computer systems.

Serial mouse

A serial mouse is a mouse that connects to one of serial ports, such as COM1 or COM2 on your computer.

Serial port

A port through which data are passed serially, i.e., 1-bit at a time, and that requires only one input channel to handle a set of bits, e.g. all the bits of a byte.

Shadow memory

In 80386 and later processor copying the content of the slow BIOS ROM into faster system RAM is known as shadow memory..

Spindle motor

Spindle motor is the main motor which rotates the hard disk drive's platters.

ScanDisk

Windows utility that diagnoses and repairs disk errors.

Scanner

Device that digitizes pictures (or anything on paper) for use by your computer.

Security

The issues of protecting data from unauthorized use, tampering, or destruction are collectively referred to as security issues.

Semiconductor storage

A storage device whose elements are formed as solid-state electronic components on an integrated circuit chip.

Sequential File Organization

A file organization technique in which RECORDS are organized in order of the value of some FIELD.

Sequential processing

A technique in which a number of similar items or transactions to be processed are grouped together and processed in a designated sequence.

Serial access

A storage device or medium where the access time is dependent upon the location of the data. Magnetic tape is a typical serial access medium.

Segmentation

A method of providing virtual memory. A multidimensional linear address space implementation differentiates this from paging.

Serial port

Connector on your computer that is used for connecting Modem for serial communication. You can also connect joystick, mouse and serial printers to a serial port.

Server

Node or software program that provides services to clients. Also the main high-capacity computer where all the information is stored. Also a system that shares resources with one or more workstations on a network.

Service programs

Commonly used in all computer centers for providing better service to users. They include programs to prepare object programs for execution, to store programs on a magnetic disk, sort data stored on secondary storage devices, etc. They are a part of the operating system.

Socket (Slot)

These are holders, which have been soldered to the motherboard, to connect number of component directly to the motherboard.

USB

Universal Serial Bus is an external bus standard that supports data transfer rates of 12 Mbps. A single USB port can be used to connect up to 127 peripheral devices.

Wireless mouse

In this type of mouse, everything is similar to the conventional mouse except that no cable is used to connect the mouse to the computer system.

Word length

A measure of the size of a word, usually specified in units such as characters or bits. Each location of a computer system can store a fixed number of characters or bits called its word length.

WORM (Write Once Read Many)

A disk that is more easily written than CD-ROM, making single copy disks commercially feasible.

Zip disk

Removable disk that stores about 100MB.

Zip file

File that contains compresses versions of one or more files, compressed by WinZip, PKZIP, ZipMagic, or a compatible compression program .ZIP files have the extension `.zip`.

Specimen Answersheet for Writing Answers to Objective Questions

PAPER CODE DATE

Q 1. Fill in the Blanks **(1 mark × 10)**

I.	________	II.	________
III.	________	IV.	________
V.	________	VI.	________
VII.	________	VIII.	________
IX.	________	X.	________

Q 2. State True or False **(1 mark × 10)**

I.	T	F	II.	T	F
III.	T	F	IV.	T	F
V.	T	F	VI.	T	F
VII.	T	F	VIII.	T	F
IX.	T	F	X.	T	F

Q 3. Match the followings: **(1 mark × 10)**

a) b) c)

d) e) f)

g) h) i)

j)

Q 4. Multiple Choice Questions: Tick the best answer **(1 mark × 10)**

I.	A	B	C	D	II.	A	B	C	D
III.	A	B	C	D	IV.	A	B	C	D
V.	A	B	C	D	VI.	A	B	C	D
VII.	A	B	C	D	VIII.	A	B	C	D
IX.	A	B	C	D	X.	A	B	C	D

Q 5. Multiple Choice Questions: Tick the best answer **(1 mark × 10)**

I.	A	B	C	D	II.	A	B	C	D
III.	A	B	C	D	IV.	A	B	C	D
V.	A	B	C	D	VI.	A	B	C	D
VII.	A	B	C	D	VIII.	A	B	C	D
IX.	A	B	C	D	X.	A	B	C	D